NINE LIVES

DEATH AND LIFE
IN
NEW ORLEANS

DAN BAUM

SPIEGEL AND GRAU
New York
2009

Copyright © 2009 by Dan Baum

Published in the United States by Spiegel & Grau, an imprint of The Doubleday
Publishing Group, a division of Random House, Inc., New York.
www.spiegelandgrau.com

SPIEGEL & GRAU is a trademark of Random House, Inc.

The names of certain individuals in *Nine Lives* have been changed in order to protect
their privacy.

"The Negro Speaks of Rivers," from THE COLLECTED POEMS OF LANGSTON
HUGHES by Langston Hughes, edited by Arnold Rampersad with David Roessel,
Associate Editor, copyright © 1994 by The Estate of Langston Hughes. Used by
permission of Alfred A. Knopf, a division of Random House, Inc.

Book design by Lee Fukui and Mauna Eichner

LIBRARY OF CONGRESS CATALOGING-IN-PUBLICATION DATA
Baum, Dan.
    Nine lives : death and life in New Orleans / Dan Baum.
        p. cm.
    1. New Orleans (La.)—Biography. 2. New Orleans (La.)—Social conditions—
Anecdotes. 3. New Orleans (La.)—Social life and customs—Anecdotes. 4. City and
town life—Louisiana—New Orleans—Anecdotes. 5. Interviews—Louisiana—New
Orleans. I. Title.
F379.N553A212 2009
976.3'350640922—dc22
[B]
                              2008031483

ISBN 978-0-385-52319-6

PRINTED IN THE UNITED STATES OF AMERICA

10 9 8 7 6 5 4 3 2 1

FIRST EDITION

For the people of New Orleans

Oy! You ask someone in New Orleans a question,
and they have to start so far back that they never
get to telling you what you want to know!

—MARGARET L. KNOX,
FEBRUARY 24, 2007

New Orleans is still full of brigands,
freebooters, mercenaries, and slaves.

—JACQUES MORIAL,
FEBRUARY 23, 2006

NINE
LIVES

ABOUT THIS BOOK

Most visitors to New Orleans sooner or later start asking impolite questions: Why has the rebuilding since Katrina gone so slowly? Why do you put up with such corrupt and incompetent politicians? How can you waste so much money on Mardi Gras when you're still living in trailers? Doesn't anybody in this city ever show up on time?

New Orleanians are hard to offend. Stop thinking of New Orleans as the worst-organized city in the United States, they often say. Start thinking of it as the best-organized city in the Caribbean.

New Orleans is so strange in the American context that it turns even the most casual visitor into an anthropologist, seeking to unlock the peculiar characteristics of the city's inhabitants. This leads to lots of on-the-fly generalizations that, upon further examination, turn out to be true. That New Orleans is like no place else in America goes way beyond the food, music, and architecture. New Orleanians don't even understand such fundamentals as time and money the way other Americans do. The future, for example: while the rest of Americans famously dream and scheme and chase the horizon, New Orleanians are masters at the lost art of living in the moment. If we're doing okay this minute, goes the logic—enjoying one another's company, keeping cool, and maybe having something good to eat—of what earthly importance is tomorrow or next week? Given the fragility of life, why even count on getting there? New Orleanians are notoriously late showing up, if they show up at all, because by and large they don't keep calendars. Calendars are tools for managing the future, and in New Orleans the future doesn't exist.

As for money, New Orleanians like it well enough, but not so they'd bend their lives out of shape to get some. They have more time than money, and that's how they like it. Ambition isn't a virtue in the low-lands between Lake Pontchartrain and the Mississippi River. New Or-leanians tend to identify more with the welfare of their families, neighborhoods, wards, bands, krewes, second-line clubs, and Mardi Gras Indian tribes than with their own personal achievement, and so are largely free from the insatiable desire for individual aggrandizement that afflicts the rest of us. To the extent Americans strive to make their to-morrows brighter than today, New Orleanians really want nothing more than for everything to stay the same.

Long before the storm, New Orleans was by almost any metric the worst city in the United States—the deepest poverty, the most murders, the worst schools, the sickest economy, the most corrupt and brutal cops. Yet a poll conducted a few weeks before the storm found that more New Orleanians—regardless of age, race, or wealth—were "extremely satisfied" with their lives than residents of any other American city. When Katrina made a "blank slate" of the city, several high-level commissions promoted plans to make New Orleans "bigger and better" than it was before. All of them failed completely. Some people rejected "bigger and better" as code for "whiter," but even more, I suspect, heard "bigger and better" as a recipe for a city driven by the dollar and the clock. Who needs that?

While covering Katrina and its aftermath for the *New Yorker*, I no-ticed that most of the coverage, my own included, was so focused on the disaster that it missed the essentially weird nature of the place where it happened. The nine intertwined life stories offered here are an attempt to convey what is unique and worth saving in New Orleans. Only one of these people is a public official, and he but a minor one. The rest toil pretty much in obscurity. Their lives, though, would be unimaginable anyplace else, and it's New Orleans itself—perpetually whistling past the graveyard—that is the real protagonist here.

These nine people do not all end up sitting on the same flooded rooftop. Nothing in New Orleans is ever that tidy. Besides, no single rooftop would have harbored both a millionaire king of carnival from the Garden District and a retired streetcar-track repairman from the Lower Ninth Ward, a transsexual bar owner from St. Claude Avenue and the jazz-playing parish coroner, a white cop from Lakeview and a black jailbird from the Goose. But that's not to say these lives don't touch one another. New Orleans is a small city. Some of these stories do intersect.

And even the ones that don't come in physical contact share a common problem: how to live in a place that by the rules of modern America has no right to exist. In the context of the techno-driven, profit-crazy, hyperefficient self-image of the United States, New Orleans is a city-sized act of civil disobedience.

These stories come to the reader through two filters. The sensibilities, emotions, and memories of the nine principal characters color them most of all. They all sat for many hours of interviews, unpacking their innermost moments for a stranger, with nothing to gain but the very New Orleanian pleasure of storytelling. Although I supplemented those interviews by talking to many of my characters' friends, relatives, and associates, I chose to recount these nine people's lives from their own points of view. They invited me into their heads and hearts, so that seemed the best place from which to tell their stories.

It is certain that other people will remember the events described herein differently. And memory is a funny thing. Frank Minyard, for example, described to me in detail the epiphany that launched him in the direction of becoming Orleans Parish coroner. While he was sure it happened in 1967, he was equally sure the song that set it off was Peggy Lee's "Is That All There Is?" which wasn't recorded until 1969. But this was how Frank's own story explained Frank's world to Frank. So I left it as he told it.

The second filter is my own. I have re-created scenes and dialogue based upon what my sources told me. I put words to thoughts and feelings that, during the months I spent working on this, were laid bare by these remarkably candid people. I changed the names of three peripheral characters to avoid hurting their feelings. Yet nothing here is invented out of whole cloth. No composite characters haunt these pages. My aim from the start has been to tell the true stories of real New Orleanians as faithfully as possible. I doubtless got some things wrong, and for errors I apologize.

PART I

WHERE DADDY GETS HIS GROOVE

REP. F. EDWARD HÉBERT
OF LOUISIANA:
"So assuming that we would have
another Hurricane Betsy tomorrow,
next week, or next year, the sixteen-foot
levee would protect that area?"

COL. THOMAS J. BOWEN,
U.S. ARMY CORPS OF ENGINEERS:
"Right."

—Discussion of Hurricane Betsy's flooding of
the Lower Ninth Ward, during the hearing of the
Committee on Public Works, U.S. House of
Representatives, September 15, 1965

RONALD LEWIS

DESLONDE STREET
1965

Ronald Lewis walked past one ruined cottage after another. Miss Hattie Guste's yellow bungalow with the gingerbread trim wore mildew like a three-day stubble on a drunk man's chin. The Moseses' place seemed to have been dredged in slime like a piece of useless garbage. Miss Odette's immaculate cottage had become a spooky old hollowed-out skull. Miss Pie's swaybacked shotgun was knocked clean off its bricks so that the porch seemed to be kneeling in the mud. These were Ronald's sacred places, he now realized; he'd been in and out of these houses his whole life. Desecrated they were. Thoughtlessly trashed.

Ronald had seen bad luck before. Houses caught fire, men lost their jobs, children drowned in the canal. Each time, neighbors had given the stricken a bed for the night or a few dollars' help, offering strong backs and consolation. This time, though, bad luck had carried its bucket of bitterness through every house on every block, ladling an equal dose to all. How was anybody to rise out of it, with nobody left unhurt to lend a hand?

Ronald Lewis was fourteen years old, and he'd finally encountered a force of nature more powerful than his mom.

REBECCA WRIGHT was born on the Abbey Sugar Plantation in Thibodaux half a century after emancipation, but not so you'd know the difference. She came up in one of dozens of identical unpainted shacks alongside a cane field, carrying water on her head from a communal pump and listening to her uncles being beaten for the crime of being too sick to work. She had her first baby, Walter, at thirteen, put him on her hip, and lit out for New Orleans. There, she married a quiet man named Irvin Dickerson and had four more children.

When Ronald was born to Rebecca's troubled niece Stella Mae in 1951, Rebecca took him, swaddled in a Charity Hospital blanket, and folded him in with her own-born five, becoming the only mama he would ever know. She took him down to the tidy house Irvin had built her, across the canal in the Lower Ninth Ward.

Life across the canal was heaven for newcomers from the country. The lots were jungly—big enough for chickens, pigs, and even horses. The streets were made of rolled pea gravel and crushed oyster shell: easy on bare feet. Neighbors understood each other. You took care of your family, sat on your porch in the evening, and went to church. No need for all that parading in the street like the city people and the Creoles on the other side of the canal. None of that fancy dressing up and drinking until all hours. It was the best of both worlds for Rebecca—a quiet country life right there by the good waterfront jobs. Irvin worked close by in the sugar factory. When a banana boat was in, the whole neighborhood smelled sweet, and it was bananas in the bread pudding, banana cream pies, and fried bananas for breakfast all week long.

By the time Ronald came, big brother Walter was off at sea with the merchant marine, but the compact house on Deslonde Street was still plenty crowded. Ronald shared a room with Irvin Junior and Larry; Dorothy and Stella shared one down the hall. When they got around the kitchen table every evening, it was all shoulders and elbows. They ate eggplants, corn, and tomatoes from the garden, and eggs from their chickens. Mama bought flour, rice, and grits by the twenty-five-pound bag and, for breakfast, baked biscuits this high before everybody got up; they'd sop them in cane syrup poured from big cans. Dorothy, thirteen years older than Ronald, had a good job by Lopinto's Restaurant and brought home sacks of fishbacks that still had plenty meat on them. The family would crowd into the kitchen late at night, rolling the fishbacks in cornmeal, frying them crisp, and sucking off the flaky white meat, while Mahalia Jackson sang from the radio.

Cousins showed up often from Thibodaux, looking for a better life in the city. Ronald knew times when five or ten might be packed into the house, covering the living room floor at night like dead soldiers, standing around the table at mealtimes, spooning up Mama's rice and gravy, and talking in plantation accents that struck his ear like music. They'd tell of hog killings, alligators long as Cadillacs, and hot pones sticky with molasses. Everybody would be shouting and laughing until

Rebecca, standing over the stove with her spatula, hushed them all by snapping, "When I die, do not bring me back to that place."

She created for Ronald a tiny, exquisitely textured world, like one of the snow globes that Walter brought home from sea. Ronald didn't cross a street on his own until first grade, and even then the known universe extended but a few blocks. She would send him as far as the dago's on Claiborne Avenue with a nickel for a stick of butter, but she'd spit on the floor and say, "That better not be dry when you get back." There was laundry to stomp in the bathtub and run through the wringer, a garden to hoe, chickens to feed, and always plenty of dishes—Lord help Ronald if he left them in the draining board. If word came up the street that he'd failed to say good morning to Mr. Butler or Miss Pie, Mama would send him out back to cut her an alder switch "as long as you are" and wear him out with it.

Dadá passed when Ronald was eleven, and it was left to Mama to see to it he come up a man. She watched from the screen door the day husky Euliss Campbell came round to bully, and called Ronald inside. "Either you beat that boy," she said, "or I'll beat you." From that day on, Ronald was more likely to get a whipping for not fighting than for fighting; she'd rather have him bruised than fearful. As for the white world, she'd come home from doing day work for the white ladies a block away on Tennessee Street and tell him: Look how I do. I do their work, but I don't sing and dance for them.

MAMA WAS ONLY five feet tall but solid as brick, and she strode his world like a colossus. But on the night of September 9, 1965, Hurricane Betsy whipped in across the Lower Ninth Ward, and Ronald watched her confront something bigger than she was. They all huddled together on the couch, screaming to drown out the wind, feeling the shudder and crack of their wooden bungalow in their bones, keeping their eyes on the TV till the room went black and the picture shrank to a glowing pinpoint. Then came the pop and hiss of the oil lamp and its pale yellow halo. Larry banged through the front door, voice cracking, "Water in the street!" and a dark parabola emerged under the door and stretched across the living room—Ronald would remember that as long as he lived. They crossed Deslonde Street, shoulder deep in inky black water, faces bent low to the stinging wind, and clawed their way up the steps to the

Alexanders' second-floor apartment. When Ronald awakened in the sunshiny calm of the morning and looked out the window, there was the roof of their home poking through a shimmering floor of green water and a family of mallards swimming calmly around it. Mama, sobbing on the Alexanders' sofa, looked to Ronald half her normal size.

The weeks after Betsy were a miasma of heat, discomfort, and irritating little injuries from exposed nail heads and sharp linoleum edges as the family struggled to set the house right—gobbling cold suppers on the porch, sitting hunched up on nail barrels. Mama never stopped moving, as though standing still would allow despair to reach up through the floorboards and drag her under. It was usually well past dark when she'd turn off the hissing oil lamp and they'd retreat across the canal to rented rooms at the Crescent Arms on Poland Avenue.

Lawless Junior High had flooded with the rest of the neighborhood, so Ronald spent most days riding around the ruins on the back of a city-owned flatbed, loading up sodden furniture, fallen oak boughs, and floppy sheets of lath coated in wet plaster. The city paid him ten dollars a day, but he'd have done the work for free; it was better than hanging around the wrecked house, mining mulched clothes from the bottom of a closet, or pulling up wet carpet under Mama's grim stare. With no radio, the silence in the house was awful.

Ronald knew the people across the canal looked down on the Lower Ninth Ward, with its hogs and unpaved streets and its hodgepodge of square bungalows and skinny shotguns on brick stilts. It was as far downriver—as far down the social ladder—as you could go in New Orleans. That Betsy had broken only the levee into the Lower Ninth Ward had only confirmed the rest of the city's sense of superiority. Well, he told himself, we just got to live with that.

IT WAS THE RUINED two-story house across from Ronald's that opened the biggest hollow in Ronald's chest. The Alexanders hadn't yet shown up since leaving the storm, and Ronald didn't know when, if ever, he'd see his buddy Pete.

The Alexanders had moved in to that upstairs apartment when Ronald and Pete were in first grade, and the two boys had always had their best adventures together—stringing tin-can telephones between their houses, tying towels around their necks to become superheroes, digging machine-gun nests up under Mrs. Butler's star jasmine, and, lately, trying to get up next to that girl Janice who whooped and hollered in the Morning Star Baptist choir like Aretha Franklin herself.

The Alexanders were different—city people, Sixth Ward Creole Catholics a little lost among the vegetable gardens and chicken coops of the Lower Ninth Ward. Pete's mother, Miss Jerry-Dean, didn't linger on the sidewalk talking to Mrs. Payton or Mrs. Williams the way Ronald's mom did. She kept to herself, upstairs. At first, she didn't much like dark-skinned Ronald bulldogging up her front stairs to bang on the door, and she'd unhitch the screen with a reluctant sigh to let him in. As for Pete's dad, he worked at Godchaux's Department Store on Canal Street and came home every night with two quarts of beer—not Dixie or Falstaff, but Miller in those dazzling clear bottles, like a white man in a commercial. Every now and then a two-door Ford would pull up to the Alexanders', and a white man wearing a porkpie hat and sunglasses would climb out and walk right up the front steps and inside—Miss Jerry-Dean's uncle. To Pete it was the most normal thing in the world to call a white man kin.

Pete himself had copper-colored skin, wavy hair lying in oiled squiggles along his scalp, and the long straight nose of his Cherokee grandmother. There was none of the sugar plantation in Pete Alexander, none of the earnest country ways of the Lower Nine. He was sly and crafty, with a jazzy way of moving and veiled street smarts. He liked to play with hair, of all things. One day Ronald had let Pete straighten his, and when it was done, it lay across his skull like a Rampart Street gigolo; Mama had about died from laughing. Hair was a way to a girl's heart, Pete always said. Let me do Janice's, and I'll be halfway there.

Ronald couldn't remember a day without Pete Alexander in it. By third grade, Miss Jerry-Dean was as good as Ronald's second mother, and if Ronald went home crying from one of Miss Jerry-Dean's whippings, Mama sent him out back for a switch to give him another. The hole they left in his life was bigger than the gap in the levee. Every day since the storm, Ronald checked the Alexanders' house for signs of life a dozen times. But since the morning of the flood, the two-story house loomed over Deslonde Street as silent as a tombstone. The Alexanders were gone, maybe back forever to the Sixth Ward.

No cars moved along Deslonde Street. Easy chairs and sofas that Ronald recognized from paying calls with Mama lay sodden on the curbs. Flower gardens had been flattened, and the air was a heavy green musk, not healthy and alive like pond slime but dank and mildewed, foul with gasoline. Deslonde Street smelled like death.

Before Betsy, life had rolled by on a great, slow-moving wheel—every pebble, every live oak, every fiddling cricket as familiar to Ronald as his own hands and feet. Now that world was gone. He'd been sleep-walking before. He was awake now, but it was too late.

JOHN GUIDOS

COR JESU HIGH SCHOOL
1965

John Guidos Jr. wanted nothing more at fifteen than to be invisible. Un-fortunately, he was big—with a heavy square head and blocky across the chest. So he compensated by staying quiet, speaking only when spoken to. And he prayed a lot.

His was an all-Catholic world, and Hurricane Betsy had given his parents, his priest, and the brothers at Cor Jesu High School a lot to talk about. Was the storm divine retribution against the sin and squalor of New Orleans? And if so, why had God chosen to wipe out the homes of those poor colored people in the Lower Ninth Ward and leave stand-ing those dens of iniquity in the French Quarter? The consensus was to accept the storm as evidence of God's infinite grace and mercy, which was fine by John. He didn't like thinking too much about sin. He won-dered constantly about his own.

He was built for football, and he enjoyed it. Football let him hit peo-ple, a much more comfortable means of communication than speaking. It was the locker room that made football hard. He never knew where to put his eyes. And the talk—tits and pussy and wet dreams—kept his burning face turned into his open locker.

"Faggot" was another word that got thrown around the locker room a lot. He had a pretty good idea what it meant, between the locker room talk, paragraph 2357 of the catechism with its talk of homosexuality be-ing "contrary to natural law," and Leviticus 18:22 calling it an "abomina-tion." If he was a faggot, he was going to hell. But as he walked up

Elysian Fields Avenue toward his father's store after school, John wondered if it was really true. No matter how many times he ran all the
pieces over in his head—which was constantly—he couldn't make them
fit. Sometimes he wondered if he wasn't some third thing, something
neither the catechism nor Leviticus knew about, something maybe even
unknown to God. A memory forced itself up: one of the wicked nuns
from St. Louis King of France Elementary School gliding among the
desks like an iceberg, tapping a wooden yardstick on her open palm.
She'd caught a couple of the boys fighting at recess and as punishment
had dressed them in the plaid skirts and hair bows of their female classmates. The other children had laughed and taunted as the boys sobbed
in shame, but John had felt an unexpected rush of envy. He'd slammed
the door on the monstrous feeling, and had brayed like a donkey along
with everyone else.

A BELL TINKLED above the door of his father's store as he entered. Dad,
thin and colorless but absolutely erect, was helping a customer, turning a
glass poodle upside down to look for the price. John threaded his wide
body between shelves of porcelain figurines and delicate three-legged
picture frames, and moved behind the counter. Instead of a cash register, Dad used an old-fashioned wooden drawer cut with depressions for
pennies, nickels, dimes, and quarters. John sorted through them, looking
for rare coins. He turned over a Kennedy half-dollar, peering at the edge;
it was one of the all-silver originals—1964—the last silver coin minted
to the U.S. government. He took two quarters out of his pocket, looked
them over to make sure they were ordinary copper-alloy coins, and
dropped them into the proper bowl. The smell of scented candles made
him queasy; he couldn't imagine breathing it all day.

Dad drove them home in silence, from the run-down streets of Gentilly to the immaculate lawns and ranch houses of Metairie, concentrat-
ing on the road as though it was the only thing he'd ever thought about.
"School okay?" he said finally.

"Yes, sir." Dad liked the "sir"; he'd retired not long before as a lieutenant commander in the Navy.

"Got any weekend plans?"

"No, sir," John said, and caught a flicker of disappointment on Dad's
face. John's solitude, and his lack of interest in girls, worried him. They

pulled into the driveway at 1921 Poplar, and Dad walked straight into the open garage and took his gardening apron off a peg.

John went inside, where Mom was setting the kitchen table. On the wall, a full-color, foot-tall Jesus writhed upon his cross. Through the window over the sink, John could see Dad pacing a row of zucchini like an admiral inspecting his seamen. The garden stretched behind him— hummocks, mounds, and ditches laced with green hose, alive with green leaves and yellow blossoms, covering an entire lot, as orderly and weed-free as a photograph in *House & Garden*.

The garden kept Dad sane. He'd been captured by the Japanese in the Philippines four days after Pearl Harbor and had spent four years in one of their camps. All that had kept him alive was a patch of squash and tomatoes he'd hidden in the underbrush; he'd weighed eighty-eight pounds at the end of the war.

"We have parent-teacher conferences with Jim tonight, so you'll be on your own after dinner," Mom said. John's racing heart drove blood to his face. Dad and Jim came in, and they sat, bowing their heads and folding their hands in the same motion.

"Bless us, O Lord, and these thy gifts which we are about to receive from thy bounty through Christ our Lord, Amen," they mumbled, and without another word worked their way through the roast and potatoes. Jim scattered his Brussels sprouts around on the plate, but Dad noticed and with the point of his knife silently indicated that he'd better eat those up. John gave his father no such trouble, but dutifully ate every-thing on his plate and then went to work on the dishes while his parents and Jim got ready to leave.

As soon as the car disappeared down Poplar, John pulled his hands from the sink and hurried back to his parents' room, unbuttoning his shirt as he went. His mother kept her bras in the top drawer; his favorite was the light blue one with the cotton rose between the cups. Size 38C; he could barely get it around his broad chest. He kicked out of his pants and punched his thick legs into a pair of panties. He opened the closet door and, seeing himself in the mirror, closed it quickly. He walked up and down the hall, trying to relax into it, trailing a fingertip along the wainscoting, pivoting sharply, like a model. He ran his hands over his muscles, under the bra, down his legs. Then he took the jar of Vaseline from the bathroom and walked back to his bedroom, shutting off the light as he went. By the time his parents and Jim came home, he was sitting at the kitchen table with his math book open and a glass of milk at his elbow, thoroughly engrossed in geometric proofs.

"Bless me, Father, for I have sinned," John said to the priest behind the screen next morning before school began. The blurry profile nodded. "I, uh, took a coin from my father's cash drawer."

"Yes."

"I took the Lord's name in vain."

"Uh-huh."

"I had impure thoughts."

"Is that all?"

"Yes."

"Very well, my son. Put something in the poor box. Say three Hail Marys and three Our Fathers."

The poor box was made of sheet metal and painted light green. It hung on the wall, to which it was attached by a short chain. "Hail Mary, full of grace," John began, running through the two prayers, three times each, as easily and thoughtlessly as exhaling. He put his hand in his pocket. Out came the silver half-dollar, a quarter, and two dimes. He put the half-dollar back in his pocket and slotted the other coins into the poor box, examining the edges of each to make sure that they were the new, copper-filled kind, the kind that weren't very interesting.

ANTHONY WELLS

There was something different about my family; I knew it when I was just a little bitty boy. I could see it in my daddy, the way he moved, you feel me? He had an easy way of moving, like he didn't take being colored too serious. We were living up in the San Fernando Valley, and it wasn't all that long that Negroes could buy houses up there. Black man had to be careful because that door was opening just a crack and you didn't know when it was going to slam shut on your ass. We had the nice house and new Buick and all that. Daddy had him a good job by Lockheed, airplane mechanic—what brought my parents out during the war. They raised us nice. Had a big house, TV, nice clothes. Got us all roller skates one year; I remember that.

Same time, though, across the freeway over by Van Nuys Boulevard, they weren't having any of that shit. They were hanging on their porches drinking malt liquor and just being niggers, you know what I'm saying? Their houses were all shackety, trash all up in the street. It kind of looked good to me, being just a little boy and everything. Just hang out on the street. Be a man. I used to lie in bed and hear the sirens from over that way and think, ooh, that's the cops-and-robbers life.

What tripped me out was that Daddy wasn't all one thing or the other. He'd go off in the morning to work and come home at night, like Rock Hudson and Doris Day or some shit, but he also could be just as cool as the niggers on Van Nuys Avenue, you know what I'm saying? He liked going to this nasty two-chair shop on Van Nuys that had a sawed-off up under the cash register. I saw that with my own eyes, first real gun I ever saw. Daddy'd sit in that chair like a king on his throne, talk to everybody.

Of course, Daddy's daddy was a white man, but he wasn't raised among them. His daddy's family didn't want nothing to do with him. Come up in New Orleans—in Pigeontown, part of the Seventeenth Ward. "They'd kill you on those streets as soon as look at you," is what Daddy used to say. He was tough, but he was smart-tough. He had them hands, man. Big hands. But I never saw him use them on another man. I don't know how he did it. That was Pigeontown, he'd say, Pigeontown, New Orleans. You didn't have to go all in with one type or another in Pigeontown; you didn't have to choose between Uncle Tom and a sawed-off.

You hear about Compton and East L.A., but the Valley got plenty nasty. It's all spread out out there, there's lots of places you can get caught in the middle of nowhere, all by yourself, without your people around. Too far over that way you had to mess with the low-riders; too far over that way and it was cracker mother-fuckers. I'm coming home from my girlfriend one night and these four big white dudes jump out and try to jack me up. I'm fast. I can go, and I went. Tell you what I did, though. We had these cap guns my dad used to buy us. They were heavy in those days, made of metal. I had this one, the Fanner 50. Cowboy gun. I drilled out the barrel and packed it with match heads. Then I filled it up with screws and glass and shit and stuffed a wad of paper in the end to keep every-thing from falling out. Make sure you wrap your hand in a towel so you don't get all fucked-up and then load in a cap and let it go. FOOM! Man, that thing went like thunder, big old flame jumped out the barrel like this big, and little bits of shit flew everywhere. I kept that bad boy with me, and next time some mother-fuckers tried to jack me up, I let them have it, like FOOM! Man, they screamed like girls, all four of them cut to shit ran off crying to their mamas. Tell you what, though. Nobody ever fucked with me again. You put a zip gun up in someone's face you're a bad motherfucker in the Valley.

I never saw my daddy with a gun in his hand. Never even saw him use his fists. He knew how to ease through and get what he wanted without pissing any-body off and without putting his own ass in danger, you know what I'm saying? You go at something from one angle, and then another, and then another until you find the way in, till you find a way that works. That's the New Orleans way. You get what you want without sweating yourself or anybody else. You make it your due.

Tell you what happened one time. There was a five-and-dime up in San Fer-nando and I'm in there one day looking at the Timex watches, thinking about getting one up under my jacket. White man who owned the place comes over and says, "What you doing there, boy?" I was so pissed I slammed that watch down on the counter and walked out. But I used reverse psychology on the motherfucker. I got my little sister's friends to go in there with their little backpacks after school. Then I go in, making myself the shiftless nigger, and damned if that white man didn't take the bait and follow two steps behind me everywhere I went. Mean-while, the girls are stuffing everything they could get their hands on into their lit-tle backpacks, stealing that white man's ass off. Teach him a lesson for stereotyping us. That's the New Orleans way.

RONALD LEWIS

LAWLESS SCHOOL
1965

Lawless Junior High had never looked so good, its halls and classrooms freshly coated in pale green paint, the desks new since the flood. Ronald sat in the front row, chin on his fists, gazing at Miss Rosetta Marchand. Nobody in Ronald's world spoke the way Miss Marchand spoke; she sounded like a white lady on TV, with none of the "ain'ts," "gwines," and "gonna's" of Deslonde Street. She'd gone to Howard University, she'd told the class. She told them that often.

"This is called 'The Negro Speaks of Rivers,' " she said. "You should know that Langston Hughes wrote this when he wasn't much older than you."

Ronald closed his eyes.

"I've known rivers," Miss Marchand read. "I've known rivers ancient as the world and older than the flow of human blood in human veins. My soul has grown deep like the rivers."

Ronald let Miss Marchand's voice pour over him, thinking, I'll talk like that one day. There won't be anybody in the world I can't talk to.

"I bathed in the Euphrates when dawns were young," Miss Marchand read. "I built my hut near the Congo and it lulled me to sleep. I looked upon the Nile and raised the pyramids above it. I heard the singing of the Mississippi when Abe Lincoln went down to New Orleans, and I've seen its muddy bosom turn all golden in the sunset."

Ronald felt a shot of excitement. He'd seen the Mississippi just that way, all golden in the sunset. Abraham Lincoln, the pyramids, the motherland beside the Congo, and, right up with them, the Lower Ninth Ward. It was all one, a Negro life beside the rivers. And he was part of that.

"I've known rivers," Miss Marchand read, lowering her voice to a whisper. "Ancient, dusky rivers. My soul has grown deep like the rivers." The bell jangled, and Ronald was carried outside by the crush of bodies, his mind following Miss Marchand's ancient dusky rivers from the pyramids to Abraham Lincoln to Deslonde Street. I've known rivers, he thought. I've known rivers come and cover my house.

He cut across the back of the school yard to Dorgenois Street and walked toward the canal. A din of hammers, table saws, and generators rose around him. Men were swarming over houses, stringing wires, tacking roof tiles, rolling paint. What a difference two months made. By the look of it, everybody was coming back. People had even found time to replant flowers. The sweet olive and four-o'clocks were fading, and the angel's trumpets and moonflower were coming on strong. Their fragrance riffled Ronald's nose, pages turning in a catalog. The neighborhood was feeling like home again, and it was good to be home.

Only one street in the neighborhood was still largely deserted: Tennessee Street, where the white folks lived. Some had sold out to Negro physicians and lawyers when the schools started integrating in 1960, but most had stuck it out, because they couldn't afford to live anyplace else. Since Betsy, though, few of the whites seemed willing to make the Herculean effort to rebuild here, when they could start over in St. Bernard or Jefferson Parish and not have to send their kids to school with Negroes. This street alone still carried whiffs of that malevolent post-Betsy rot that was gone from the rest of the Lower Nine. It made Ronald shiver, as when a cloud crosses in front of the sun.

Miss Duckie, though, she'd come back quick as anybody. She was the damnedest white lady in the world. Tall, skinny, and grim, with brass-colored hair and glasses, she lived with her husband and son in the house on Tennessee Street whose backyard joined Ronald's. Ronald's mama did day work over there, though it seemed that every time Ronald went over, Mama and Miss Duckie would be drinking Dixie beer and talking together at the kitchen table, switching the radio between the spirituals Mom liked and the Fats Domino tunes Miss Duckie preferred. Miss Duckie ran the city park on Forstall Street, handing out the bats and balls, managing the lifeguards at the pool. Colored kids were supposed to use the park back of town by Florida Avenue, and every now and then the white boys would think to run Ronald and Pete out, but Miss Duckie had none of that. At the first sign of trouble, she'd put her hands on her hips and stare at those white boys until they got their minds right. She didn't have to say a word; that park was hers. Sometimes she even let Ronald switch off the park lights at the end of the evening, throwing the big wall switch like sending a man to the electric chair.

Miss Duckie was full of funny ideas. The city was just starting to expand out into a big swamp northeast of town, by the lake, and she was always asking Ronald and Pete to give her their pennies so she could buy land out there in their names. Someday that swamp will be a neighborhood called New Orleans East, she'd tell them, and they'll be glad they got in early. Pete and Ronald used to laugh, never quite sure if Miss Duckie was joking, because she never, ever smiled. They saved their little bit of money for potato chips and pig lips from Irene's bar.

One afternoon in the November after Betsy, a truck wheel lay on its side in Miss Duckie's driveway, with a round wooden sign rising out of the middle: "Voting Poll, Ward 9, Pcnt 8A." Ronald had always liked watching the white folks filing in and out of her garage on election days, signing their names, and then stepping behind that mysterious blue curtain. Every time, Miss Duckie would take Ronald by the hand and carefully show him the rows of gray levers, even when he had to stand on a cold-drink case to see. Her head bent low beside his and smelling of cigarettes, she always said the same thing: Pay attention, Ronald. Someday you're going to have to know how to do this.

He looked left and right before walking up her path, an old habit. Miss Duckie didn't mind him using her front door and setting on her porch, but her neighbors had never liked it. When she didn't answer, he walked around back and found her in the garage. She straightened and peered at him through her smoke. "You know what happened this summer, right?" she asked.

Ronald stared at her. Betsy had washed the whole world away this summer. But that wasn't what she meant at all. President Johnson, she said, had signed a law guaranteeing the Negro the right to vote. She was about to have Negro registrars in her garage for the first time. Once again, she waved him over to look at the levers on the voting machine, and they went through the whole drill again. He asked her once why she cared so much about colored folk.

"Like I told you," she said. "We're Jews."

Jews? Ronald wasn't sure what that meant. He knew that Miss Duckie and Mr. Louis went to St. Peter Lutheran Church across the canal—maybe it had something to do with that.

The world seemed changed after Betsy, and not all in bad ways. Ronald felt an energy that was new to the sleepy Lower Nine. All the hammering and sawing seemed to vibrate in his veins. Mr. Payton replanting azaleas by his porch. Mr. Butler hanging new gutters. Mr. Williams banging siding into place. Dr. King and the civil rights marchers were a long way from the Lower Ninth Ward, but this was what they were talking about: the strength of the colored man. Self-reliance. Negroes waiting on nobody, taking command of their own lives. And now they would walk into Miss Duckie's garage and vote.

Ronald had an after-school job at the Superette on Claiborne, and, borne forward on a symphony of hammers and handsaws, he banged through the door one afternoon to find old Mr. Earl, jowly and white haired, leaning on the counter as usual with the *States-Item*.

"Hey, Pluto," he grunted at Ronald. "Canned goods in. Start with that."

"Yes, sir," Ronald panted, heading down a narrow aisle of Hubig's Pies and red-and-white Zatarain's boxes. Ronald loved the smell of the Superette, a combination of old wood floors, bacon, onions, and Mr. Earl's cigarettes. His friend Michael stood in front of the walk-in cooler, tying on a white apron. He was handsome, more filled out than Ronald, and his hair stood out a good inch and a half off the skull, whereas Mom kept Ronald's scraped down to the scalp.

"Hey, man," Michael said as Ronald reached for an apron. "Why you let him call you Pluto?"

"He's always called me Pluto, like I call Walter 'Blook.' "

"He oughtn't to do that."

"Why not?" Ronald said, pulling the straps of his apron around front.

"Don't you know who Pluto is?" Michael bent to a case of Blue Runners and wrenched it open. "Pluto's the damn dog on Mickey Mouse."

Ronald froze, a chill spreading over him as though he'd stepped into the walk-in. A dog's name. He saw himself with the broom, the mop, the Windex. He saw Mr. Earl chuckling like a friend one minute, barking orders the next. A bubble rose in his chest, full of Langston Hughes, Miss Duckie, President Johnson, and old Mr. Butler bringing his house back after Betsy. I got to do the work for Mr. Earl, but I don't have to give him no song and dance. I am a man and I live by the river. Ronald hung his apron carefully on its nail and walked to the front of the store. He took a position square in front of Mr. Earl, who glanced up and sat back, laying down the paper.

"Mr. Earl, I don't want you to call me Pluto no more," Ronald said. "My mama named me Ronald, not Pluto, and you can call me Ronald."

Mr. Earl didn't say anything. He cocked his head to one side, and a flush spread from his open collar up his fleshy neck, like a thermometer rising. He snatched off his glasses and glowered.

"Hell, Ronald," Mr. Earl said finally. "You don't have to be so goddamn sarcastic."

Ronald opened his mouth to respond, but nothing came out. Sarcastic? What did that mean? He closed his mouth and marched back to the cooler. He sat on the wooden floor and folded his hands over his skull. Never again, he said to himself, am I ever going to let anybody say anything to me that I don't know what it means.

JOYCE MONTANA

VILLERE STREET
1966

Joyce Montana opened the front door of her apartment and stepped onto the balcony in the chilly dawn. The crowd, gathered among the potholes of Villere Street, let out an expectant gasp.

"It's only me," she called, wishing her voice didn't squeak so, laughing and patting her unruly hair into place. She'd been up all night with Tootie, putting the finishing touches on the suit, and hadn't had a moment even to change out of the old smock she wore while sewing. But what did it matter among friends? She climbed down the long wooden staircase, past the sign for the auto body and fender shop that occupied the space below, waving to Jerome Smith, Bertrand Butler, cousin Sylvester Francis, and young Maurice Martinez.

Maurice met her at the bottom of the stairs, his camera dangling around his neck like a tourist off a cruise ship. Tootie had let Maurice hang around taking pictures on the condition he revealed to nobody the color of the suit. They could trust Maurice. It was true he'd left the Seventh Ward—left all of New Orleans—to work as a college professor in New York City. But he was a Seventh Ward Creole from way back; his grandmother had started the first kindergarten for colored children in Louisiana, on Roman Street between Annette and Allen, and many of Joyce's friends had gone there. Maurice had returned from New York with the crazy idea that the Mardi Gras Indians were worth studying. Only a handful of people in New Orleans masked, most of them neighborhood colored folk without any money or position. Why would anyone in New York City care? Joyce wondered.

"Ohhhh!" The crowd exhaled, and Joyce turned. Tootie stood at the top of the stairs holding out his arms, radiant in turquoise feathers. Sequins flashed from the cuffs of his shirt. Hillocks of intricate beadwork protruded from the apron covering his chest and belly. Joyce had concentrated hard all year, helping to bead those pieces. To see Tootie finally wearing it, out in the early sunshine, made her heart full.

Tootie stepped slowly down the stairs, a royal peacock descending to his flock. Ricky Gettridge and Paul Honoré, young acolytes who'd spent hours helping build the suit, backed out the door above him, holding the crown. "Ohhhh!" the crowd gasped again. Taller than a man and at least as wide, of the same turquoise feathers as the suit, the crown was Tootie's biggest yet.

Tootie stationed himself below the balcony, a black wig of Indian braids framing his angular face. Paul and Ricky lowered the crown onto his head. Tootie had used the guts of an old football helmet—built it right into the crown so the giant headpiece would stay centered. The crowd cheered, and Tootie, twice as big as life, stepped forward, blazing turquoise. "Kuwaa!" he shouted. "Kuwaa!" He pirouetted, every bead and sequin twinkling.

"Big Chief!" the crowd yelled. "Biiig Chief!"

Eleven-year-old Darryl—Mutt-Mutt—ran down the stairs in a lumpy suit of white feathers. Poor little fellow had saved his allowance, washed cars in the body and fender shop, bought his own beads and feathers, and taught himself to sew simply by watching Tootie. That was Tootie's rule; Mutt-Mutt could learn by watching, but Tootie wouldn't teach him, because Tootie's own daddy had taught him *anyé*—nothing. An Indian makes his own suit.

Tootie's spy boy, dressed in a blazing-orange suit of his own, was already dancing up Villere Street toward St. Bernard Avenue, looking for a tribe for Tootie to challenge. The equally resplendent flag boy, carrying a big turquoise banner announcing the Yellow Pocahontas, nodded at Tootie and started off, and Tootie lumbered after him, followed by half a dozen men with drums and tambourines, filling the narrow street with the racketing and chant—"Two-way pocky way! Two-way pocky way!" Neighbors danced and cheered on their porches. Maurice, ever the professor, was lecturing a white photographer. "You hear that 'two-way pocky way'? It's from the French, the Creole. *T'ouwais, bas q'ouwais.* You are not to be believed. You are full of shit. They're taunting the other tribe."

Mutt-Mutt ran after Tootie with an eager, panicked step that just about broke Joyce's heart. Tootie might walk fifteen miles, and Mutt-Mutt would tag along, witnessing one wild encounter after another. But how far would he get? After all his work, would he end the day crushed and disappointed, Tootie's disapproving growl ordering him home?

————

JOYCE HAULED HERSELF back up the stairs, and the longest day of the year began. The apartment felt quiet after the rush to finish—pulling on the gauntlets, adjusting the moccasins—the big men shouldering around, getting the chanting going. After working on the suit night and day for a whole year, after living with it sprawled over the kitchen table and every other surface of the house, seeing it go out the door felt almost like a death in the family. In about six weeks, after one more appearance on St. Joseph's Night, they'd be taking it apart, carefully returning each bead and sequin to its proper can, each feather to a labeled paper sack. The cycle of the suits was their whole life.

Of all people to be so involved with the Indians, she often thought. Growing up at the corner of New Orleans and Allen streets in the heart of the Seventh Ward, she'd been as frightened of the Indians as everybody else. Everyone on Allen Street would run inside and watch through the blinds as the Indians came whooping and hollering up the street. They'd taunt each other until someone lay dead on the banquette—the hard sidewalks of New Orleans—with a knife or a bullet in his belly. If Joyce had met Tootie when he was in feathers, instead of in a respectful gray suit at a dance at the Monogram, she'd never have given him two seconds. What had worried her, that first night, was only how suddenly the slender, courtly Creole boy had taken his leave after they'd danced. I have to go home and sew, he'd said. Sew? What kind of excuse was that? She was sure he was brushing her off.

One night early in their courtship, Tootie had shown up at the home Joyce shared with her toddler girls and baby boy—she'd divorced her no-count husband—carrying a mass of feathers and beaded cloth. Blood soaked through the shoulder of his jacket. It was his teenage son, he said, as she peeled the jacket off to reveal a long gash. They'd gotten into a humbug, his son had cut him, and his wife, drunk again, had gathered up the half-finished Indian suit, wadded it into a ball, and stuffed it through the window into the street. The way he talked, the woman might as well have discarded his immortal soul. Tootie had stayed the night with Joyce, and never left. He went to work every morning as a lath-and-plaster man and came home every evening. On Friday, he cashed his paycheck at the Circle Food Store and put the money up under the bedroom rug for her to take, as needed. He'd drink a can of Schlitz once in a while, but that was all. He didn't run wild with his men friends, and he didn't chase women. All he wanted to do was sit up late at the kitchen table with her, sewing. This piece here, like that, he'd say, drawing a row of blue against a row of black, a swirl of red inside a disk of orange. Sew that. I have the whole picture here, he'd say, touching his skull above those glittering brown eyes: you just worry about that little piece—you'll see.

She'd asked him early on how it came to be that black men dressed up as Indians on Mardi Gras day. She'd heard the standard explanations, of course—that it started as a way to honor the Indians who'd taken in escaped slaves during the bad days, that it started as a way for blacks to evade the prohibition against their participating in Mardi Gras. But she wanted to hear it from him; he'd really know. His answer made her love him all the more. I don't know, he'd said simply. They were doing it before I got here. I only know I love it.

On their living room mantel was a forest of framed photos. In the oldest, a fifteen-year-old Tootie and his uncle Becate wore beaded tunics, baggy suede trousers, and, for headdresses, sadly drooping strings of turkey feathers. They looked like Indians in an old black-and-white western. Tootie hated those suits. They wouldn't do what he wanted them to do, he'd told Joyce early in their courtship. And what was that? she asked him.

He only shook his head. For a long time, he didn't answer that question. Then one day, he told her: he wanted to stop the fighting.

Joyce had snorted and flapped a hand. To her, it seemed the whole point of being an Indian was the fighting. For years, it was the same after every Mardi Gras and St. Joseph's Night; Tootie would walk in with his suit cut up and bruises all over his face. The battlefield always seemed to be the little pontoon bridge over the canal at Fourth and Rocheblave, the one they called the Magnolia. Someone would start with the *"humba, humba"*—the Creole bow-down challenge—and it was on. Joyce had often asked why they had to cross that bridge, and Tootie's explanation was always infuriatingly the same: Indians go where they like. It made her crazy.

Tootie always blamed the suits. If a man put more of himself into his suit, he said, he wouldn't need to fight. Every year, he went down to the Circle Food Store to see the man who slaughtered the fowl, got his turkey feathers, and made another suit. And every year he'd come home from Mardi Gras bloody.

Then came the year he didn't go by the Circle for feathers. Instead, he'd taken three buses out to a costume-and-hobby shop in Metairie and come home with shopping bags full of garish feathers in a bright crazy orange God never intended a bird to be. Another bag held beads and sparkly sequins in a mind-boggling array of colors and sizes. Joyce had peeked under the rug when he wasn't looking; all the money was gone.

Tootie had set to work right then, with a bruise from the Mardi Gras humbug still fresh on his cheekbone. He'd used half egg cartons, lifting a flap in the apron of the costume, wedging an egg carton under, so that it pushed out a dazzling grid of beads: a three-dimensional suit, he called it. His father had dreamed of such a suit. This suit, he'd told her, was going to make them stop fighting with the gun and the knife and start fighting with the needle and thread.

Tootie had always been careful to put his suit in progress away when people came to call, but with the three-dimensional orange suit he became obsessed with secrecy. Nobody could pass through the door until he had every piece of the suit packed away. He'd go over every rug and sofa cushion, so that not a trace of bright orange feathers showed anywhere. The suit was so bright it was painful to look at under the harsh kitchen lightbulb. The headdress—Tootie called it a crown—radiated in every direction, with a snake rising from its middle. Pirouetting in the kitchen, Tootie had become a man of beaded flame. No vestige of that Hollywood Indian remained.

It had worked just as Tootie had hoped. He'd come home unbruised that year. His suit had struck the others blind. And they started taking after him; nobody made those tired old blanket-and-turkey-feather suits anymore. Everybody came out in colors. It took beaucoup work to make a suit that could stand up to Tootie's, and nobody wanted to work all year and take a chance of having a suit cut up and bloodied by some knucklehead with a broken beer bottle. For his part, Tootie made it his mission to stay ahead of everybody else. The green suit, the white suit, the pink suit—year after year, each was more beautiful, more elaborate, more extreme than the last.

JOYCE SPENT THE AFTERNOON dropping in on Mardi Gras parties up and down the block, running into her children from her first marriage— Gwendolyn, Phyllis, and Charles—who were looking after her youngest, little Denise. A little after five, Joyce was in the kitchen, rolling catfish fillets in fish fry, when she heard a hubbub out in the street. She opened the door and there stood Tootie, his face contorted, Mutt-Mutt behind him, clutching his pant leg. Tootie's crown was missing. His beautiful turquoise suit was torn and matted. Across his cheekbone spread a green-ish bruise. Mutt-Mutt was crying. She ran to them, put a hand on Tootie's feather-covered arm, and felt water squish up between her fingers.

"Fire hoses!" Tootie said, pulling himself out of the ruined suit. "We were at Orleans and Claiborne, like always, peaceful. The police showed up with dogs and a fire engine and bullhorns. 'Mardi Gras's over!' Like they're not still parading up on St. Charles. Like they're not all up in the bars on Bourbon Street. No, but we got to clear the streets, because *our* Mardi Gras's over!"

Mutt-Mutt shivered in his wet feathers. Joyce pulled his apron and shirt over his head and sent him to take a hot bath. "Let me see that bruise," she said, but Tootie shrugged her off and took from the fridge a bottle of water with garlic cloves swirling around in it—his Creole cure-all.

"No permit, they said, like Indians ever had to have a permit to come out on Mardi Gras day!" He drank a glass of garlic water. "They came in swinging before anybody had a chance to get out the way." Tootie was fighting back tears. "Knocking women and kids over, just running them down. They turned the fire hoses on us like we was riot-ing."

Tootie sat down heavily on the couch.

"The police don't know," he said. "They see Indians, they think we've got knives and guns up under our suits. They treat us like animals." His brow lowered, and his jaw muscles worked. "Look at my suit," he said. "I don't even know that I'll be able to use these feathers again."

Joyce could do nothing to help.

"The police don't know," Tootie said. "They just don't know."

fRANK MINYARD

BOURBON STREET
1967

Dr. Frank Minyard took off his white sport jacket and hung it on a parking meter. "Shoes or barefoot?" he shouted. Across the street, Paul Hornung was taking off his jacket and rolling up the sleeves of his shirt.

"Shoes!" Paul shouted back. "I'm too drunk to find my laces."

A small crowd had followed them outside and stood on the sidewalk, some with Old Absinthe House napkins still stuck in their collars. It wasn't every day you got to watch a Heisman Trophy winner in a footrace up the middle of Bourbon Street—especially Paul Hornung, the star halfback who'd left the Green Bay Packers to help get New Orleans's new football team off the ground. And everybody on Bourbon Street knew Frank.

Frank flexed his chest and arms, feeling every bit as fit as Paul Hornung. He took his time getting ready, letting the crowd build and taking a deep breath to clear the martinis from his head. He loved the French Quarter perfume: Creole cooking, tourist-buggy horses, coffee, and the rich green undertone of the Mississippi River. As word spread to the bars and restaurants along Bourbon, people came out onto the sidewalk, clutching their drinks. Pete Fountain came out of his club to watch, still holding his clarinet. Jim Garrison, the district attorney, emerged behind him. "Frank! You break him, you bought him!" yelled John Mecom, the boyish owner of the Saints. Laughter rolled up and down the block.

Emelie staggered out into the middle of Bourbon in her high heels, waving her arms to stop traffic, her black hair wild. Frank laughed as the cabbies meekly obeyed. His wife might be tiny, but she was ferocious. She waved her long silk scarf, and Frank and Paul took off. Frank had him for about fifty feet, but Paul began to pull away, and Frank had no choice but to bodycheck him. They both went sprawling into a heap of garbage on the curb, laughing so hard Frank thought he'd choke.

"Everybody back inside!" Frank yelled. "I'm buying!"

———

IT WAS A GREAT LIFE. Frank was a baron of the city, welcomed like a son in all the best places of the Quarter, known to everybody, loved by all. He couldn't walk into La Louisiane, the Napoleon House, or even the New Orleans Athletic Club without spending half an hour greeting friends. At thirty-eight years old, Frank was New Orleans's premier gynecologist; no other doc put women so at ease as they lay back in the stirrups. Nobody else had that soft purring manner, that delicate touch, that way of gazing deeply into a patient's eyes. No other gynecologist knew so well how to touch women, how to speak to them, knew so well how to ask delicate questions. None other had that Charles Atlas physique and those ice-blue eyes, either. Women loved Dr. Minyard, and Dr. Minyard loved them back—their fragrance, the way they moved, the funny little workings of their minds, the emotions they kept so delectably near the surface. He loved them one way in the examination room, another way after hours. They saturated his life. Emelie had walked out on him ten times in ten years for his philandering, but she'd come back every time because, of all the women Frank loved, he loved Emelie most and she knew it.

Frank maintained two offices: one in the new and growing section of the city up by the lake called New Orleans East, the other in the city's most fashionable address, the soaring International Trade Mart that had just opened at the river end of Canal Street. He was earning fifteen thousand dollars a month, more than his father had ever earned in a year, and not just because women loved him. Frank worked constantly, feverishly, never turning away a referral, never failing to step in for fellow docs who overbooked or went on vacation. He offered himself to the city's hotels as the house doc on call, showing up at all hours to earn a ten-dollar bill. And, in a stroke of real moneymaking genius, he was now making Thursday rounds at Flint-Goodridge Hospital, the only white ob-gyn in New Orleans treating colored women. He took heat for that from the white doctors in the Orleans Parish Medical Society, but they were tying one moneymaking hand behind their backs out of something as trifling as prejudice.

He couldn't get enough. He had a racehorse stabled at the track, a thirty-foot sailboat moored at the marina, a Cadillac, a Mercedes, and a Porsche. His mother had been a dance-hall pianist when she'd met Frank Minyard Sr., who bounced from job to job as a printer. When Frank junior was ten, Ma bought him a secondhand trumpet at Werlein's for Music on Canal Street for sixteen dollars. No lessons, of course; the Minyards couldn't afford that. Ma stood him beside the cigarette-scarred upright in their little Myrtle Street house and taught him herself, starting out on "That Old Rugged Cross" and "What a Friend We Have in Jesus." She raised him on a diet of hymns and grievance: against the wealthy Dallas family that had disowned her husband for marrying a Catholic, against her lifelong priest who wouldn't baptize baby Frank because her husband was a Baptist, and most of all against the wealthy swells uptown, who, she never stopped reminding little Frank, "don't like us poor downtown whites." He begged, during the hot summers of his childhood, to go to the pool at Audubon Park, but his mother wouldn't hear of it. Our kind stays below Canal Street, she told him. From the time he was a teenager, he had the run of the French Quarter and everything downriver, but uptown was off-limits.

The only thing he didn't like about being a rich doctor was finding himself too often in the company of the uptown swells his mother had taught him to despise. He did all he could to avoid them—eschewing membership in the country club, avoiding the restaurants of the Garden District and slumming instead at the jazz clubs on Bourbon Street, keeping out of the clubhouse at the track and drinking beer from paper cups in the free grandstands. The best way he'd found to avoid feeling inferior was to pile up more wealth than the white-shoe snobs of the Garden District and Audubon Place—newer and fancier cars, the finest clothes, and, of course, the palace in Lakeview. Carved out of swampland after the Second World War, it was a kind of Los Angeles suburb within the city, designed for people who'd had enough of the quaint cheek-by-jowl life of New Orleans, who were sick of termites eating their antebellum houses, fed up with pedestrians. It spread out on such a scale that one didn't have to greet one's neighbors; one could come and go in the privacy of the family car, pushing a button on the remote garage door opener. Lakeview meant exclusivity, quiet. But more important to Frank, it meant a place to enjoy wealth without having to rub elbows with uptown swells. No matter how much Frank earned, he'd never be accepted on St. Charles Avenue. In Lakeview, you didn't have to have a pedigree. All you needed was cash.

Still, from time to time a darkness would get the better of him. He'd find himself berating Emelie to tears because her high heels clacked too loud on the floor, or because she'd changed her hairstyle. More than once he'd flown into a rage for no reason at all, accusing her of affairs he knew she hadn't had, storming out of parties, embarrassing everybody. Lately, his mood plunges were taking him straight to the bottom. He'd shouted one night at Emelie that he was going to drive all the way down Canal Street and into the Mississippi River, and until he got as close as Baronne Street, he'd really thought he might do it. Just last Christmas he'd given her a real scare; they'd been on their way to buy a tree when he'd suddenly announced that he was going to make her watch him jump off the Mississippi River bridge. She hopped out of the car at a light and walked until she found a policeman. By that time the blackness had lifted, and he'd sheepishly come around the corner to pick her up.

He wondered sometimes where his old trumpet was. He hadn't played it in years.

One night in 1967 he came in late from a night of carousing. Emelie, the children, and the maid were all asleep. Peter, Frank's Great Dane, lumbered up to rub his head against Frank's hand. Ciebe, Emelie's poodle, came as close as the hallway door to take a look at him and retreated without a greeting. Even the dogs seemed to know that Peter was Frank's and Ciebe was Emelie's, and neither Emelie nor Frank would feed or pet the other's. Frank crossed the living room, poured himself a bullshot—vodka and beef bullion—and stacked some jazz records on the turntable. He turned the patio speakers to low, slid open the glass doors, and stepped outside.

It was like standing on the grounds of a fine hotel. The vast rectangular pool glittered in the moonlight; the impeccable, flowered landscaping extended all the way back to the grassy slope of the Seventeenth Street Canal levee. He settled himself into a poolside chaise longue, took a pull of his bullshot, laid his head back, and looked up into the stars and the scraps of white cloud scudding along in the moonlight as the intricate melodies of Lee Konitz enveloped him. He had ideas perhaps to buy an airplane, or maybe a chauffeured limo with a phone in it. A long one. Black.

Inside the house, the Konitz album ended, the automatic changer dropped a fresh album onto the turntable, and Peggy Lee's smoky voice came up, singing her new hit song, "Is That All There Is?"

Frank felt another of his moods coming upon him. He set down the bullshot and gripped the arms of the chaise. "I had the feeling that some-thing was missing," Peggy Lee whispered. "I don't know what, but when it was over, I said to myself, 'is that all there is to a circus?' " She seemed to be speaking straight into his soul. The cars, the house, the clothes—is that all there is?

Watch yourself, he told himself. Wait it out. The mood will pass; it always does.

But this was the worst one yet, like being in an elevator with a cut cable. His vision went black, and he couldn't draw breath. What is this crap I've surrounded myself with? he asked himself. What have I done with my life? The silly women with whom he'd betrayed Emelie paraded before his eyes. His sailboat sank into a murky sea. He put a hand on his sweaty forehead. He was worse than those seersuckered, self-centered, pompous uptown swells Ma couldn't stand. He was a poseur, a fake, a gilded bauble with a vacuum at its center. He curled into a ball on the chaise, his hands clasped over his head, until he finally blacked out.

FRANK OPENED ONE EYE. He lay still, testing his limbs as though he'd been hit by a car. Slowly, he raised himself to his elbows. Something was different; something was changed. He'd never failed to sleep off one of his moods before. This morning, though, his luxurious backyard looked like the backdrop of someone else's life. Frank could catalog the morn-ing's beauty, but he couldn't feel it.

Emelie looked up, startled, from her cup of coffee as he hustled through the kitchen. "Got an emergency," he said, and pushed through the door to the carport.

Nobody ever stirred on the early morning streets of Lakeview but maybe a couple of colored women trundling through the chilly dawn from the bus stop to their housekeeping jobs. It was a neighborhood of things, not people—picture windows and Buicks, lantern-holding iron jockeys and hundred-dollar boxwood shrubs. It wasn't New Orleans at all.

Halfway down Canal Street, around Mandina's Restaurant and the old streetcar barn, the city began to look like itself. He stopped for a light at Claiborne Avenue. The sidewalks bustled with Negro men in narrow-lapelled suits and short-brimmed hats. Downtown. He breathed a little easier.

He parked on the riverfront at the foot of Canal Street, where the modernist, cruciform International Trade Mart building rose like a ziggurat. In his office, the big black telephone was ringing on his desk. The receptionist wasn't in yet. Frank picked up.

"Frank? Barbara Poche. You went to Holy Cross with my husband, Carl."

"Oh, sure."

"Sister Mary David asked me to find out if you know Pete Fountain."

"Sister Mary who?"

"Sister Mary David, from the Bethlehem House of Bread. She wants to ask Pete Fountain to play a benefit."

The Bethlehem House of Bread? It sounded like a Jewish delicatessen. Frank looked at his watch. "Listen, ah, I have patients waiting . . ."

"Sister Mary David has a little breakfast program on Dryades. She was hoping you'd ask Mr. Fountain to come visit, and maybe play a benefit. Can you do that?"

Frank had known Pete for as long as he could remember; they used to push toy cars around in the sawdust at Bozo's bar while Pete's dad opened oysters for Frank's. They'd done a lot of drinking together over the years, and Frank marched every year in Pete's irreverent Half-Fast parade through the Quarter. Pete was a wild man. The thought of dragging him to meet some nun made Frank squirm. But this was a strange morning. "How about this?" he heard himself ask. "How about I come up myself and see if it's right for Pete?"

Ten minutes later, Frank was cruising slowly up Dryades Street, past the Jewish-owned groceries and tailor shops that catered to colored New Orleans. He trembled slightly, still shaky. He parked in front of Handelman's department store, found the address, and pushed open a plain plywood door. In a vast barn of a room, colored women and children sat at long folding tables, spooning up breakfast out of white crockery bowls. The room smelled of coffee and steam-table oatmeal. Black men in combat fatigues and berets—looking like soldiers of Patrice Lumumba—carried trays of dishes to and fro. A mix of religious and revolutionary propaganda covered the walls: quotations from Matthew, mawkish renderings of Jesus on the cross, posters of Malcolm X, drawings of raised fists in stark reds, greens, and blacks.

A short, fat white nun bustled toward him in a black habit and stiff white wimple. One eye was milky blind, the other stared bizarrely to the side. "Are you Dr. Minyard? I'm Sister Mary David."

"Who are they?" Frank said, gesturing at the young black men dressed for combat, hustling about with pots of coffee or mops or holding crying children on their laps.

"Why, the Black Panthers," she said, as though any fool would know. "They look scary, but this is what they do—feed breakfast to poor children all over the country. I'd been trying to start a breakfast program and having no success until they showed up. The archbishop gives me a little money, they provide eager hands, and we get by." The women at the tables were of every age and shape, some in obvious castoffs, none too clean, others with stiff, straightened hair and skimpy dresses of exaggerated sexiness. A few looked as though they'd slept in the street. Most had babies or young children. They went about their breakfast with businesslike determination. "They're prostitutes, mostly," Sister Mary David said. "Look at their arms and thighs; you can see the bruising. Most of them are addicted to heroin—or alcoholic. This is the one square meal they'll get all day. If Pete Fountain would play a benefit for us, it would mean the world."

FRANK SPENT the rest of the day examining one pampered uptown matron after another, smiling, bringing all his charm and professional calm to bear. But as the afternoon wore on, he felt the malevolent coldness gathering in his feet, rising up his legs. His breath grew short, and at three o'clock he had to buzz the receptionist and ask her to hold an appointment. He sat at his desk with his head in his hands, staring at the floor.

He lifted the phone and dialed Pete Fountain's club on Bourbon Street. "It's Frank; let me speak to him," he told the bartender. "It's an emergency."

BILLY GRACE

OCTAVIA STREET
1969

Billy Grace emerged slowly from the extravagant sleep of a teenager. Above his head, on the creamy plaster wall, hung a black-and-orange pennant—WOODBERRY FOREST—and another, in green and white, anticipating freshman year at Tulane. On the wall beside the bed hung a print of red-jacketed riders jumping a hedge and, dangling from a purple, green, and yellow ribbon, a medallion of the Rex Mardi Gras krewe. He could hear Lorena, the family cook, making breakfast downstairs. His open closet revealed a row of blue blazers, seersucker suits, a camel's hair jacket, and crisp button-down shirts in white-and-blue pinstripe. On a chair lay a new pair of jeans and a folded blue work shirt.

Billy's father stood in the doorway. "Hey," he said with a gruff laugh. "You're not a Eustis or a McCall. Get up and go to work."

BILLY, TALL AND HUSKY, walked toward the St. Charles Avenue streetcar stop in his stiff work shirt and jeans, the boughs of grand oaks forming a ceiling that bathed Octavia Street in a cool green light. Nothing moved, save a middle-aged colored lady walking, eyes down, from the streetcar stop to her day job. Behind lush hedges of oleander and forsythia, big wooden houses rose, stolid, to either side, as though watching him with their arms folded.

Billy had never known anything other than the uptown life, but his father never let him forget they were relatively recent arrivals. Bill Grace Sr. had been raised on Esplanade Avenue by a mother who took in boarders. No Tulane for him; he'd gone straight to work after high school as a teller for Whitney Bank, which unexpectedly turned out to be the portal to uptown society. Whitney was more than uptown's bank; it was almost a cult—clubby, intimate, and discreet to the point of secretive. From his lowly perch, young Bill Grace quickly figured out why. A surprising number of the elegantly mannered clients who appeared on the other side of his teller's cage had little or no money, and Whitney existed largely to help them maintain appearances. Their grand mansions had been in the family for a century or more, long enough for generations of sluggards and playboys to whittle away the filial wealth. Some of the oldest names in New Orleans clocked in at law firms or brokerages owned by their fathers' friends, yet spent most of their time at their lunch clubs, at the racetrack, or sashaying about the Quarter. Others simply couldn't bring themselves actually to work; they managed by slowly and quietly selling off the family antiques. And when the going got too tough—when the blushing daughter of a fine old family was selected, say, queen of Comus, and tradition required the family to host a ten-thousand-dollar luncheon—the young teller watched the white-haired men of Whitney step in with a quiet loan. These may not have been the most advisable loans for a bank to make, especially in the late 1930s, but those who might have objected—the bank's depositors and shareholders, say—were themselves uptown New Orleanians, none of whom would be served by an embarrassment in the community. Theirs was a village with little in the way of achievement to recommend it, but possessed of charm and taste that it prized above all things. Against the seamless maintenance of appearances and pleasantry, what were a few percentage points here or there? It didn't take Bill Grace long to realize that, poor as he was, he had all he needed to be someone in uptown New Orleans.

Handsome, witty, blessed with a gift for remembering names, he moved quickly from behind the teller's cage to the more delicate task of repossessing automobiles. He therefore knew who among Whitney's august clientele could and could not afford their Packard. Uptown New Orleans knew he knew, and uptown New Orleans could see that he was a young man who could keep his mouth shut. What's more, Bill Grace was an awful lot of good fun—big, jovial, never said "when" and never got drunk, excellent at the small talk that keeps parties going. People liked having him around, which, ultimately, is all that really mattered. He was in high demand as a walker—escorting unattached ladies at parties—especially during the war, when he was 4-F and all the other young men were away. A hand shaken here, a back slapped there, and by the end of the war Bill had talked himself firmly under the wing of Leon Irwin, who had a massive contract to represent the John Hancock insurance company all across the South. Selling insurance came naturally to Bill; all a man had to do was make himself liked. By the time Billy—the third child and first son—was in kindergarten, Bill was Mr. Irwin's full partner, and the family was ensconced here on Octavia Street between Prytania and St. Charles—about as good an address as they come.

But Dad never let Billy mistake himself for a member of the leisure class. The summer Billy turned twelve, Dad had secretly paid a nearby gas station twenty-five dollars a week to hire Billy—for twenty-five dollars a week. No son of Bill Grace was going to while away his summer at the Audubon Park swimming pool. Dad was willing to pay Billy's tuition at Tulane, but Billy had to earn his own spending money.

The streetcar came swaying and clanging up the grassy neutral ground of St. Charles Avenue, and Billy climbed aboard, taking a seat halfway back, noticing, as always, the brackets on the backs of the seats for the "screen"—the movable sign that once announced, FOR COLORED PATRONS ONLY. Streetcar segregation had ended by the time Billy was eight, but he remembered his maternal grandmother, taking him to lunch at the D. H. Holmes department store, sitting erect in her floral hat and white gloves, studiously ignoring the Negroes crowding behind the sign. And he remembered the half-page ad that Dad and his friends had run in the *Times-Picayune* around the time formal segregation was falling apart in New Orleans: a news photograph from Mississippi of Negroes being pinned against a building by the stream of water from a fire hose and another of a Negro in a porkpie hat cringing from a vicious-looking police dog. "Let's not let this happen here," the ad exhorted. "Let's respect the laws of the United States." Billy had been only ten or eleven then, but he recalled the phone ringing off the hook the night the ad ran, and Dad saying into the receiver again and again, "Well, I'm sorry you feel that way."

Billy was away at school, at Woodberry Forest in Virginia, when Martin Luther King was murdered. They'd gathered all the boys into the chapel for eulogies praising the standard-bearer of Negro freedom, without so much as acknowledging the irony that Woodberry Forest was segregated. Billy was managing editor of the weekly *Oracle*, and he'd stayed up late that night, orange-and-black tie loosened, scowling at the typewriter, writing what he hoped would be a ringing call for integration. "There are many boys from the South, including myself, who have never had the opportunity to converse with an educated Negro," he'd written. "When someone mentions Negroes to me, I immediately think of the maids, laborers, etc., at home." He'd spilled three thousand words into that editorial, but when it had come time for the call to action, all he'd been able to muster was that Woodberry "does not necessarily have to accept the Negro, but it should let its admissions policy be open to all." A year later and he was still embarrassed.

The streetcar wound its way around Lee Circle and up Carondelet to Canal Street, where Billy jumped off. He crossed Canal and walked up to South Rampart to catch the number 84 bus downtown. As it crossed Esplanade Avenue, the downriver border of the French Quarter, Billy realized this was the first time he'd ever been this far downtown. Rampart bent slightly and became St. Claude Avenue. The businesses here were shabbier, their windows covered with burglar bars. When the bus bumped over the railroad tracks, Billy said to himself, the Ninth Ward. Now I can tell people I know the Ninth Ward.

He changed buses at Louisa Street, heading toward the Desire housing project. By the time he pulled the stop cord at Humanity Street, he was the only white person on the bus. Electricity and telephone lines crisscrossed the sky, jury-rigged and jarringly naked, with no trees to hide them. He passed shabby bungalows, drooping in the muggy heat, their old paint flaking. It was hard to find a truly straight line on them. Negroes lounged on their stoops, talking, laughing, listening to music on transistor radios, watching kids bounce balls on uneven sidewalks. Some were drinking beer at nine in the morning. They shouted from porch to porch in torrents of argot, and when they laughed, gold flashed in their mouths. "Good morning!" Billy called as he strode along. Mostly the people on the porches stared in silence. Every now and then one of them called, "All right." *Ahhite.*

He arrived at a gravel lot full of giant steel Dumpsters. The job, arranged by a friend of his dad's, was to wash, scrape, and repaint all of them. This won't be so bad, Billy thought: the hose will keep me cool. He turned on the faucet, hoisted himself onto the lip of a Dumpster, and aimed the nozzle at the filth covering the bottom. Orange rinds, crawfish heads, and coffee grounds crawled around under the stream of water. Grimy droplets spattered his face. He lowered himself into the foul-smelling cavern and went to work on the floor with a wooden-handled wire brush.

The sun crossed overhead and dropped toward the Garden District as he worked his way through the Dumpsters. He heard laughter, close at hand, and he stood to peer over the lip of a Dumpster. Four colored men were setting a huge aluminum pot atop a propane burner across the street. They wore straw hats with tiny brims, pushed back carelessly on their heads, and loud shirts with square bottoms that hung loose outside their pants. They walked to and from the house, shouting to one another, carrying metal folding chairs, a table, a cooler. Billy felt like an explorer in a pith helmet, spying through palm fronds at an exotic tribe. Something in their manner struck him as—what?—the words "insolent" and "disrespectful" flashed across his mind, but he knew that was wrong. He realized that he'd never been ignored by a Negro before. Usually, they were either focused on him   like Lorena, or the waiters at Galatoire's— or studiously making themselves invisible, like the gardeners who came once a week to mow the lawn and trim the hedges. The poor things, he'd said to himself more than once, squirming under the forced cheerfulness of a porter's greeting or noting the cringing, averted eyes of a busboy. Yet these four men, waiting for their pot to boil, were unembarrassed. Undiminished. "Broke in a new guy last night," a man in a blue shirt was saying. "Little bitty fella. Light skinned. Man, he jumpin' up and down in the hirin' hall, wavin' his Social Security card like it's the first day of school and he know the answer." The man laughed, a deep, rumbling smoker's laugh. "He gets out on the dock and he's grabbing sacks and wrestling them all by hisself. I watched him for a while until I been had enough of that. I said, 'Whoa there. Stop. We gots to do this all night.' "

"Hear that," an old man in a yellow shirt said.

"It's like a dance, little fella. It's like a dance," continued the blue-shirted man. He held his fists down by his hips, as though holding one end of a sack. He swayed. "*Bup bup bup* BAM!" He swung his arms and popped his hands open. "Easy like. No back in it."

"Man's got to learn," said the yellow-shirted man, cutting lemons with a pearl-handled knife, dropping wedges into the pot.

"Man's got to be taught," said the blue-shirted man.

Billy heaved himself out of the Dumpster.

"Hey there, son," called the old man in the yellow shirt, holding up a dripping bottle of beer. "Come have one. You working hard enough for all of us."

Billy smiled and crossed the street. Each man held out a hand to shake, but didn't get up. The man in the blue pulled a milk crate close. "Sit," he said.

"How much they paying you to clean them Dumpsters?" the old man said.

"Eighty a week."

"Eighty a week!"

"I'm saving for a car."

"A car!" said the man in the blue shirt. "What kind of car you going to buy on eighty dollars a week?"

"I got my eye on a Volkswagen Beetle. Eleven hundred dollars, brand-new."

"Shit," the old man said. "That's no kinda car." They launched into a complex argument about the relative merits of the Lincoln Continental Mark IV and the Cadillac Fleetwood Brougham.

"Which do you drive?" Billy asked, and the old man laughed.

"Number 80 bus is my car," he said, and his friends rocked in their chairs with raspy laughter. "You married?"

"No, sir. I'm only nineteen."

"That don't mean nothing. I was married at nineteen. Still married, too."

"That's great."

"Course I got something on the side. You know what I mean."

Billy blushed. "How does that work?"

"Oh, I make it work."

Billy looked at the ground, embarrassed. The man leaned in close. "Son," he said, "what's your favorite thing to eat?"

"Steak, mashed potatoes, and green peas."

The old man's eyes were rimmed with red and he smelled of the day's beers. "Now, young fella, how'd you like to eat that three meals a day every day for the rest of your life?"

Billy blushed again and took a long pull from his beer. Man, he thought. This city is a lot bigger than the Garden District and the French Quarter. He looked around at the ramshackle houses with a warm feeling of belonging. Ninth Ward. Eighth Ward. Seventh Ward. The East. Algiers. The Irish Channel. Christ, I love New Orleans.

FRANK MINYARD

ST. AUGUSTINE CHURCH,
ST. CLAUDE AVENUE
1969

The unair-conditioned utility hall of St. Augustine Church smelled of old perspiration and cigarette smoke. A long table ran down one side, holding paper cups of Tang. A line of sad-looking Negro women shuffled beside it, some with babies in their arms or toddlers pulling at their hands, or both. Long-haired volunteers in jeans handed over the Tang, watched the women carefully as they drank, and made notes on clipboards. At the end of the table, a Negro man worked a big coffee urn. Another handed out doughnuts.

Father Therriot, hulking and bearded like a mountain man, was a Josephite priest from Boston who had been dragged by the archbishop into running the methadone mission—and had come to love it as much as Frank did.

Frank looked at the women filing along the table. "We've got to do something about the jail," he said to Therriot. "That one over there? In the gold lamé? She was starting to get cleaned up when she got picked up for something. Shoplifting. I don't know. She came out of the jail hooked all over again."

"The cell block is about the easiest place in the city to score heroin," Therriot said. "They all say that."

Frank called Louis Heyd, the Orleans Parish criminal sheriff, who ran the jail. They'd been friends for years. Frank told him about his problem. "I can keep them off the hard stuff with methadone, but every time they go through your jail, they come out hooked again." He asked if he could bring methadone into the jail itself.

Heyd was in no mood. He'd just been sued by the ACLU over the conditions in his jail. And the health of the inmates wasn't his purview anyway. The parish coroner, he said, ran sick call in the jail. That struck Frank as odd—the man responsible for the dead was also the jailhouse doc?

Frank drove his Porsche up Broad Avenue to the hulking sandstone criminal courts building. The coroner's office had its own, rather grand entrance around the side. A stone staircase climbed a full story to the door, above which was carved CORONER—PARISH OF ORLEANS. The secretary let him into an office whose ceiling must have been eighteen feet tall.

"Come in, come in," said Carl Rabin. He was balding and gray haired, like a country doc.

Frank explained the methadone program, and why he wanted to extend it into the parish jail.

Rabin flapped a hand. "Junkies," he said. "Can't do anything with them."

Frank paused. "You know, I work with them every day," Frank said evenly. "Methadone is starting to make some of them productive."

Rabin cut him off. "Once a dope fiend, always a dope fiend."

Frank stood. "So you won't let me bring methadone into the jail."

"No, sir." They looked at each other.

"Who's your boss?" Frank asked.

Rabin smiled. "I don't have a boss. I'm elected."

Frank leaned across Rabin's desk. "You motherfucker," Frank heard himself saying. "I'm going to run against you and take your job."

ANTHONY WELLS

When my grandfather died in 1959, Daddy went out and bought a brand-new Chevrolet station wagon with air-conditioning and power windows, and we set out for New Orleans, all nine of us, because by then we had Roger and Sharon. My dad was showing us something. "Things is different out here," he said as we lit out across that desert. "We're not in Los Angeles no more. You watch me and learn." We ate baloney sandwiches all the way across. A couple of times my mom wanted cooked food and we'd stop but not go in and sit at a table like I was use to by the Chinaman's in Los Angeles. My dad would go around back of the restaurant and come back with a paper bag. It's different out there, man. It would make my dad walk different, too, not easy like he was here in Los Angeles, but all stiff and nervous-like. All that thing that I liked so much, that New Orleans thing I wanted to soak up—all that left him out there. We couldn't even go to the bathrooms; had to pee out there in the tall grass. Saw my first colored bathroom out somewhere in Arizona or some shit. And it was like days and days before we saw another black face; the whole middle of the country is nothing but white folks and Mexicans.

Then one day I woke up from a nap in the backseat and everything was green. I mean like green. Water everywhere. It looked like we were driving over water that had this thin skin of grass on top, like if you scraped up a spoonful of grass you'd find water underneath. And that spooky Spanish moss shit hanging from the trees—you ever seen that? Like you're in a horror movie. Green. And my dad's music came on the radio. You should have seen my parents, man. Like they got their groove back. "Here we are. We're in New Orleans," my dad says, and I'm seeing it, this place I been dreaming about. It's all jam-packety, pretty old houses lined up one beside the other, each one a different color, with curlicues and flowers, and, man, streets just full of people. White people, black people, mixed-race people, all jumbled up together and walking. Music right on the sidewalk, and I don't mean like one nigger with a guitar, but a whole band and drum set and everything, like the whole city is a big party. I'm looking out the window, eyes big as saucers—eight years old—and I'm thinking, this is a whole different way to be a Negro; I'm thinking, this is where Daddy gets his groove.

We pull up to a light, and a cop car pulls right next to us. The cops are white, of course, but not like the storm troopers they got out in California; they're kind of fat and rumpled up, like a couple of plumbers or something, you know what I'm saying? They kind of nod and smile, and Daddy smiles back. Smiling at a couple of white cops!

My grandmother lived out on the edge of town in the place they call the Goose, which wasn't jam-packety like downtown but more normal: little lawns, little driveways. We pull up to this tiny brick house, and, man, people start pouring out of it like clowns out of a car in the circus. You wouldn't think you could get so many people into one house. Everybody knows my name, and aunts and uncles I never heard of are crying and whooping and handing us around like sacks of corn. Googlobs of kids, man. These kids, they're all over me, like, "You in the Ninth Ward." Like it was a privilege. Like I might not measure up.

Running around, we kids didn't go but about six, seven blocks, but it felt like the whole world. What tripped me out, man, was every place we'd go, no matter how far, everybody knew me. I was Ant'ny Wells, Edward and Deloris's boy. People I never seen before would come up and say I looked just like my grandma Ceola. I could be all the way across the Goose and some lady would invite me for some bread pudding, some red beans. Kick my ass, too, if she'd a mind to, a lady I never seen before, like I was her own kid. I was connected, you feel me? It was *like being in the Bible with the begats: "My auntee was married to your mother's auntee's second husband."*

Then I get home to San Fernando, and I'm a stranger. Nobody knows my name. Life is all cut up. Home, school. Grown-ups, children. Van Nuys Boulevard, Brownell Street. White, black, Asian, Mexican. New Orleans ain't like that. It got me thinking.

BILLY GRACE

2525 ST. CHARLES AVENUE
1969

Billy looked at the slip of paper in his hand. Sure enough, it said 2525. He looked up. The Rex mansion.

Billy had admired it all his life, a classic Queen Anne masterpiece of the Garden District, among the loveliest houses on St. Charles Avenue. It was here that the entire Mardi Gras parade crossed the neutral ground every year so that Rex, king of carnival on his throne atop the lead float, could receive the annual toast. The flags of Comus and Rex hung on stanchions above the balcony, announcing former kings and queens of carnival, going back generations, who had resided in this house. How like Anne not to clue him in that this house was in her family. She'd merely invited him to dinner "at Aunt Virginia's."

Billy walked up the wide steps and pressed the bell beside the imposing front door. Anne's father, George, answered. He had longish graying hair that fell in a wave over one eye, big plastic-framed glasses, and a manner that took nothing seriously. He owned the Muzak franchise in Louisiana and was among the warmest and most empathetic men Billy had ever met. As they waited for dinner, he took Billy on a tour. "All right now, this is Robert Henry Downman, Anne's great-grandfather, who bought this house in 1907," he said, stopping in front of a gloomy dim portrait. "He founded the Louisiana Lottery and was one of the first presidents of the Levee Board—for what it's worth."

Anne's mother, "Big Anne," strode across the living room, chin high, pumps clicking on the intricately inlaid wooden floor. Though she was not particularly tall, her posture made Billy feel as though he were standing in a hole. In each hand Big Anne held what Billy took to be straw-berry milkshakes. Ojens, she called them. The pink was Peychaud's bit-ters. "Can't use any other kind," she pointed out. It was sweet, rich, and flavored like Good & Plenty.

George continued his tour of the wall portraits. First George's own father in a gold-framed portrait. Lawyer to Sam Zemurray, who started out selling bananas on the streets of Mobile and ended up owning United Fruit.

"Got himself thrown into a Honduran prison," George said.

And that's where the next portrait came in. Senator Joe Ransdell, perhaps Huey Long's greatest enemy and George's great-uncle. He sent a fleet of Navy gunboats to blockade the port of Tegucigalpa until they freed George's father.

George was as deeply rooted in the soil of uptown as anybody, and at the same time seemed to relish challenging it. The time he invited that Jewish friend of his to the Atlanteans' ball came to mind; everybody up-town knew about that. In 1972, George had been a driving force behind the Rex krewe's decision to knuckle under to Mayor Moon Landrieu's threats and invite a few black couples to its ball for the first time. (The photograph in the *Times-Picayune* the next morning just about blew up-town's gasket and cemented Landrieu's reputation as "Moon the Coon." But then, that was the year the homosexual krewe Apollo held its ball in the sacred Municipal Auditorium and the police shut down parading in the Quarter, so the whole season had an end-of-the-world quality to it.) Just in the last couple of years, though, George had really called down the wrath of uptown upon himself. As board chairman of the Audubon Zoo, which used to be so decrepit the federal government had threat-ened to shut it down, George had pushed a radical, multimillion-dollar renovation. It had taken Billy a while to figure out why anybody would object to such tireless agitation to improve a civic asset. Turned out, the people who for generations had lived in the grand stone mansions sur-rounding Audubon Park had come to think of it as their private play-ground. Black people who visited the zoo understood they were to stay riverside of Magazine Street and not be seen on the golf course or along the lovely shaded paths of the park's vast interior. George's plans to ex-pand the zoo and turn it into a destination for the entire city were tan-tamount, among many uptown, to racial treason. Some couched their objections in terms of traffic and congestion, others were ringing his home phone and calling him a nigger lover. Billy was proud to stand beside him.

But he'd come for Anne—whom the Montgomerys called "Little Anne"—that figure, those eyes, that gravelly laugh. She didn't care about her famous uncle, any more than she cared whether Billy drove a Bug or a Bentley.

They ate red beans and rice in a dining room fit for a Bourbon king, the walls rich frescoes done in red, black, and gold. The Montgomerys asked how Billy liked Tulane, and he said it was fine. He'd wanted to go to Dartmouth, he said, and get a taste of the wider world outside New Orleans, but his father had come up with diabetes and wanted Billy closer. At Anne's urging, he finally got around to telling about his summer job cleaning garbage Dumpsters in the Ninth Ward.

George threw back his head and laughed. He reached over and clapped Billy on the shoulder. "Good for you!"

FRANK MINYARD

WASO STUDIO
1972

"We're back with Dr. Frank Minyard"—Keith Rush leaned into the microphone—"who joins us each week to answer your questions about medicine and health. Let's take a call."

Radio took Frank away from his practice and volunteering, but if he wanted to run for coroner again, he had to raise his profile. Fifty thousand dollars he'd spent on the last campaign, and Carl Rabin had creamed him.

"Frankie?" said a familiar voice in Frank's earphones.

"Ma?" Frank leaned into the microphone, laughing. "Everybody, I'd like you to meet my mother, Mrs. Norma Minyard. Hello, Ma."

"Frankie, I found your old trumpet in the attic. What should I do with it?"

Keith's face lit up.

"Give it to Goodwill, Ma," Frank said.

"I can't do that. I paid sixteen dollars for it."

"I'll give you the sixteen dollars," Frank said.

"You should play it! Instead of running for coroner again, which is the craziest idea I ever heard."

"Mrs. Minyard, you don't like the idea of your son running again for coroner?" Keith asked.

"It's crazy. After he worked so hard to become a doctor? After all our prayers?"

"Okay, Ma," Frank said.

"Listeners, what do you think?" Keith said. "What should Dr. Minyard do with his trumpet?"

"Come on, Ma, ask me something about medicine." Frank laughed.

"Goodbye, Frankie."

"Hello, you're on the air," Keith said.

"Dr. Minyard?" The caller sounded like a very old lady. "Why don't you play your trumpet for us on the radio?"

"Yeah!" Keith laughed.

Frank shook his head. "I haven't played in twenty years."

"Go home and practice," the lady said.

"Come on, Frank." Keith leaned into the microphone, tilting his head at Frank. "Listeners, let us know. Should Dr. Minyard play for us next week?"

FRANK TURNED THE BIG Mercedes over to the Negro teenager at the grand entrance to the Metairie Country Club and tucked his arm through Emelie's. She liked being the wife of Dr. Frank Minyard and worried where his foray into moralistic unpaid do-goodism would take them. The more time Frank spent at the House of Bread, the methadone clinic at St. Augustine, and the civil rights marches downtown, the less money rolled into the Lakeview setup on Bellaire Drive. She wanted them to join the country club, and this evening was a chance for the membership to look them over. He agreed to make the effort. It was the least he could do.

As soon as he got inside, though, Frank felt his necktie tightening around his throat. The place was lousy with the kind of uptown swells his mother had taught him to revile. Emelie excused herself to the powder room, and Frank lurched for the bar. A Negro barman, whose white jacket hugged his muscular frame, leaned in close to hear Frank's order.

"You look familiar," Frank said as the man came back and set a bull-shot on the bar.

"Give it a minute; you'll get it," the Negro said. He rubbed at the bar top with a damp towel. "The coffeepot at St. Augustine."

"I'll be damned." Frank extended his hand. The barman hesitated, twitched his eyes around the room, then put out a hand so big and rough it felt like he was wearing a catcher's mitt.

"One of the ones drinking that medicine is my old lady," the barman said. "You got her straightened out more in two months than I'd been able to in two years." He put a fresh drink in front of Frank. "These are on me, by the way."

Frank flushed with happiness, glad he'd come out to the country club after all. "Hey, that's a hell of a grip you got."

"Oh, I try to stay in shape."

"Me too. I bench two fifty-five. You?"

"I do all right."

"Let's see," Frank said, putting his elbow on the bar, hand straight up. The barman chuckled.

"That's not a good idea," he said, looking left and right.

"Come on. One time." Frank looked over his shoulder. The bar was empty; people were drifting toward the dining room. "I don't think you can take me."

The barman gave his head a little shake, chuckled, and bent in over the bar. He planted his elbow next to Frank's, slapped his fingers around Frank's wrist, and the next thing Frank knew he was flying backward off the stool, his forearm mashed flat onto the damp surface of the bar. He threw out his other hand to catch the bar but missed, and landed heavily on his butt between two stools. The barroom door swung open and Emelie walked in on the arm of the country club president. They froze, and Emelie's eyes went dead.

JOHN GUIDOS

HATTIESBURG, MISSISSIPPI
1973

It was nice living with a woman. John couldn't very well paint his own toenails, but he could paint Kathy's. He lay on the floor at her feet in the master bedroom on Green Street, tucking tufts of cotton between her toes.

Kathy said it made her feel like a queen, sprawling backward on the bed for her pedicure, her left hand adorned with a swirling diamond ring and gold wedding band. The rings had been a stretch on the salary of a college student working swing shifts in a galvanizing shop. But it was what a man does: get a girl pregnant, buy her the engagement ring she wants, and marry her. John was a husband and a father now. An ordinary man. He was doing it.

He looked up at Kathy, whose breasts rose like two perfect cinder cones. He'd always liked busty girls, enjoying the soft firmness of their breasts and the lacy brassieres that held them so alluringly in place. To have beautiful soft curves on one's own body—the thought made him gasp with envy.

It was like being in a play. The character he portrayed was a guy named John Guidos—football player, husband, happy father. He had breakfast with Kathy every morning and kissed her on the cheek. He went off to class, the manly rigors of football, and then the galvanizing shop. He came home evenings, gave Kathy another kiss, and played with the baby. They had dinner together and many nights went bowling. Since the baby, he and Kathy had stopped making love because Kathy was sore and Sandy needed to feed every couple of hours. John was delighted; one scene of the drama he no longer had to perform. It was good. Kathy was great. He loved her.

But whenever he was alone in the house—when Kathy went to have her hair done or shop for groceries—John found himself in her underwear drawer, having a furtive little party.

He finished the second foot, massaging the arch lightly while he blew on the nails to dry them. "Sandy's six months old already," Kathy said, slapping her hands on her stomach. "I got to take off some of this weight." John looked up in alarm. If she went down a size or two in underwear, he wouldn't be able to fit.

"You are just perfect to me, sweetheart," he said.

RONALD LEWIS

ST. CHARLES AVENUE
1974

The track jacks gathered in the shade of an oak on the St. Charles Avenue neutral ground, in front of a large white Garden District mansion with Mardi Gras flags hanging off the front. Ronald barely glanced at the house; it existed in another dimension. He picked up a pickax and jounced it in his hand, enjoying the heft. He handed a shovel to the new D helper. "We ain't going to have but about ten minutes to get this done. You ready?"

It was only ten in the morning, and the man was wheezing with exhaustion, sweating like a bar of chocolate. His eyes swam, and his mouth hung slack. He had a long way to go to make it to A helper, let alone a full track repairman.

"Moses, right?" Ronald said.

"That's right," the man panted.

"Where you from, Moses?" Ronald said.

"Bayou Goula." Deep country, upriver.

"Been in New Orleans long?"

" 'Bout three weeks."

"Well, good luck to you."

The track hummed under Ronald's foot; two blocks away an olive green streetcar loaded passengers. A hand tapped him on the shoulder and he turned. "What are you getting ready to do?" said Freddy the foreman, a short, red-faced white man in coveralls.

"Got some rotten ties up under here, Freddy," Ronald said.

Freddy frowned and puffed up like he was about to burst. "Tie's fine," he said. The ties were invisible under the dirt and grass. Only the thin rails showed.

"No, it ain't," Ronald said. "You watch. Streetcar's going to roll like it's on the ocean."

The streetcar came clattering up the tracks. They stood back to let it pass, and sure enough, it listed toward the riverside like it was about to tip over. Ronald heard someone inside give a frightened little yip.

"Needs some fresh slag is all," Freddy said.

"How many tracks you fixed with your own hands?" Ronald smiled, giving Freddy a full shot of the grille—the full mouth of gold teeth that never failed to freak out white folks. Freddy winced. "Leave it to the experts," Ronald said. "If we're going to dig up the track to put fresh slag under, we might as well replace those rotten ties."

"Ties are fine," Freddy said, growing red in the face. "Just replace the slag." He glared around at the track jacks listening in. Moses, the skinny kid from Bayou Goula, jumped and said, "Yes, Mr. Freddy."

Country boy, Ronald thought. Minstrel man. Mr. Freddy this and Mr. Freddy that. He calls you Moses and you call him Mr. Freddy. "Well, Freddy," Ronald said. "Let's get the dirt off'n the track and we'll see what we got."

Charlie Harper passed behind Ronald and whispered, "Easy. You want your raises, you got to swing it a bit."

Ronald turned to face him. "Man, I do their work," he said loudly. "I'm due my raise and I'll get it." Charlie shook his head and slunk away. A good man. Hard worker. But another minstrel man. These Mississippi boys from the cotton fields, these sugar-cutting boys from the bayou country, they'd missed out on the liberation movement. Ronald had spent his teenage years eating bean pies with the Black Panthers and handing out their literature on Canal Street. His boyhood friend Pete Alexander from across Deslonde Street had dropped all that talk of being Creole and accepted the beauty of his blackness, and together they'd formed a club called the Black Crusaders. They taught children black poetry and the rudiments of self-defense in an abandoned house in the Lower Nine. Unlike these minstrel men from the bayou and the cane fields, they'd beaten their souls against the anvil of repression to make themselves strong; it's what coming up in the city did for a man. They quoted H. Rap Brown and Brother Malcolm to one another, but for Ronald it really all went back to Mama: you got to do their work, but you don't have to give them a song and dance.

Ronald had a wife now—a small, fiery girl from the Desire Project named Minnie, who wore her hair in a proper Angela Davis natural. She was tough and liked to have her way, but it was up to Ronald to be a man and take charge of the household. That was a tenet of the liberation movement, too: a man is a man at all hours. When their son was born, Ronald wouldn't hear of saddling the boy with the name Ronald junior. He might be a baby now, Ronald said, but he'll be a black man someday and he needs his own name, a freedom name. Ronald named him Reynaldo.

The streetcar approached, white faces peering out with curiosity. Ronald pumped his hand, palm down, to let the motorman know the section was settling into the soupy earth. He glanced at Freddy, who watched from the shade of a spreading oak, his arms folded. The streetcar eased by, and Ronald immediately bent to shovel dirt from between the ties. The others fell in beside him, working fast. His muscles bunched and stretched pleasantly under his rough cotton shirt. He liked the feeling; with every shovelful of soil, he grew a little stronger.

Within minutes, they'd laid bare fifty-two feet of rails and ties. Sure enough, three of the ties were rotten, crushed in the middle, the slag displaced from beneath them. The men dropped their shovels with a clatter and picked up long nipping bars to pry out the spikes. The sun poured like lava over Ronald's back.

"Man." Moses wheezed. "Why don't they have us do this after the sun goes down?"

"You don't want to be up here at night," grunted Oscar Crandell, as he heaved dirt into a wheelbarrow. "White folks see you on St. Charles Avenue after dark's likely to call the police."

"Stand up here in the middle of the day without a white foreman, see what they do," Ronald said, and he and Oscar laughed. The join plates came unbolted with a loud groan. The men leaned into their nipping bars and pried a long section of rail free.

A light blue Lincoln rolled to a stop, and Bob James, the general manager of New Orleans Public Service Incorporated, stepped out, along with three other white men Ronald didn't recognize. Out-of-towners. Shareholders maybe, or vendors. It always seemed to Ronald that James liked bringing white men out to watch his darkies sweat in the sun. Ronald paid no mind. When Charlie Harper saw them, though, he began singing chain-gang blues. Ronald snorted. He liked Charlie's deep baritone but hated when Charlie poured it on for the bosses.

The track jacks rolled the two rails atop the new ties, and using chin-high nipping bars as levers and Charlie's singing to set the timing, they massaged them into place. Oscar re-bolted the join plates. A streetcar stopped two blocks away, taking on passengers. Ronald grabbed his sledgehammer and beat a spike into place with four quick, heavy blows. The streetcar was rolling now, barely a block away. Charlie and Oscar put on a show for Bob James, each grabbing his hammer halfway up the shaft and twirling it once before bringing it down on the spike head: Charlie then Oscar, Charlie then Oscar, a neat, precise dance, synchronized to Charlie's baritone. They finished seconds before the streetcar rolled by, clanging and clacking merrily. Bob James and his guests piled into the Lincoln and rolled away. All that remained was to shovel the dirt back into place, smooth it, and throw on a little grass seed. Ronald wiped the sweat from his face on an upper sleeve. His muscles burned pleasantly.

"Hey, look there, where's little Moses going?" Oscar said. The man from Bayou Goula was throwing his hammer into the back of the work truck. He headed on down the neutral ground, without looking back. "Couldn't take it," Charlie said. "Didn't last a day." They laughed, and Ronald felt a warm glow in his belly. This was men.

ONE MORNING a money green Cadillac pulled up to the corner of Third Street, and Pete Alexander got out, dazzling in a wide-lapelled, ankle-length powder blue coat and matching wide-brimmed fedora—the full Superfly getup. Ronald had to laugh. Not six months ago, Pete had been done up like Shaft, in a black leather coat and pointed boots. Six months before that, it was a dashiki. Before that, the combs and the 'fro. Or did the dashiki come first? No matter, with that Cherokee nose and copper red skin, Pete looked good in all of it. He'd gone his own way when the days of revolutionary poetry and bean pies ended. Pete Alexander wasn't one to take up the sledgehammer and the pickax. But he never questioned Ronald's choice, and Ronald never questioned his. From time to time Ronald needed a little help, and Pete would whip out a big roll and peel off three hundred dollars like it was nothing, with no talk of Ronald ever paying it back. And when Pete needed a break from the fast life, he could take off that powder blue coat and sit up at Ronald's table for a dish of Minnie's bread pudding like they were both still ten years old.

Pete held open his Cadillac door with an elegant flourish, like a chauffeur. In back, Ronald saw a passel of Pete's girls. He was delivering them someplace, along with packages of whatnot that Ronald didn't care to know nothing about.

"Freddy," he said, throwing down his nipping bar. "I'm taking me an early lunch."

fRANK MINYARD

ORLEANS PARISH CORONER'S OFFICE
1974

Frank pushed through the "No Admittance" door and stepped down the dimly lit stairs. He spent as little time among the autopsy rooms as possible. It was his little secret: he didn't like being around the dead. He was glad to have his pathologists and their assistants—the deaners—do the cutting and examining. Ever since medical school, cadavers gave him the willies.

His eyes adjusted to the dark as he descended, and the temperature dropped ten degrees. A narrow hall led to the examination rooms. He shivered.

A young black man with haunted eyes sat on a milk crate outside one of the autopsy rooms, head bent to a little transistor radio, right hand pantomiming the valves on some sort of horn. He wore tan coveralls— the new trustee sent over by Orleans Parish Prison.

"Hey," Frank said. The man jumped to his feet. "Sit, please," Frank said. "Nothing going on?"

"Quiet today."

"What's your name?"

"Edgar Smith."

"Mind if I ask what you're in for?"

"Charge was armed robbery, but all I did was try to collect money I was owed."

"Spare me," Frank said. "You bothered by working with the dead?"

"I was with the Marines at Pleiku," he said. "I'm used to the dead."

The music issued softly from his radio, and his fingers unconsciously pushed imaginary valves.

"What do you play?" Frank asked.

"Sousaphone."

"You any good?"

"Grew up in the bucket of blood," Smith said in a deep, gravelly voice. "Gravier and Rocheblave. Third Ward. And I started the first brass band there, the Bulldog Brass Band."

"I play in a little band that could use a sousaphone."

"Well, I'm in jail right now, as you know." He gave a short, mirthless bark.

"Oh, that's nothing. Foti? The new sheriff? He and I were elected on the same day. The DA—Connick? Him too. We go way back. If you want to play with us on Saturday, I'll fix it."

BELINDA CARR

ALABO STREET
1974

Belinda lay on her narrow bed, reading *Nancy's Mysterious Letter.* It was Friday, and a weekend's worth of third-grade homework from Lawless Elementary School had taken her all of about two minutes to complete. Her little brother Alvin was watching cartoons in the living room. He'd asked for a snack, but all the fridge held was a half-eaten package of baloney. Belinda was free to lose herself in Nancy Drew's world, where children came home to freshly baked cookies, the chief of police was your pal, and nobody's dad ever walked out.

Mom came in the front door singing tiredly "Just a Closer Walk with Thee." She worked by the hospital all day as a nurse's aide, but on Sundays, at Greater Harvest Baptist Church on North Rocheblave, she was the powerhouse of the choir. She could have been a professional, they said: another Mahalia Jackson. But something had gotten in the way. Something had stuck Mom with a career of changing bedpans and the tedium of raising three kids on her own in a raggedy rented house on Alabo Street.

Calvin came running in on his thick two-year-old legs; Mom had retrieved him from Grandma's on the way home. Belinda picked him up and walked into the kitchen. Alvin turned off the TV and followed. Mom sat at the chrome kitchen table with her shoes kicked off, rubbing her feet. She was broad shouldered and thick limbed, with short straight hair and a square jaw. Belinda's willowy height came from Lord knew where; her dad, gone two years ago to a trucker's life in Texas, was stocky. "We going to eat?" Belinda asked.

"I thought we'd go by Aunt Polly," Mom said.

"Dy-no-mite!" Alvin shouted, an expression he'd picked up from *Good Times.* Belinda hated that show; she saw enough unruly shiftless behavior in her own life. She preferred *Happy Days* and *The Waltons*, shows about normal people living normal family lives.

They walked together through the twilight, Belinda carrying Calvin. The evening was warm, and people were out on their porches; it took Belinda and her family half an hour to walk five blocks because they had to say hey to everybody. The air was spicy with the fragrance of vegetable gardens—onions, cabbages—and it was getting dark as they turned onto Egania Street, where Uncle Sammy owned a row of cottages that housed most of Belinda's relatives. Yellow light and laughter spilled through the oleander hedge in front of Aunt Polly's, a lilac-colored shotgun. It was a card-game night.

Alvin ran ahead, up the steps to the crowded porch, where neighbors were taking a break from the games, fanning themselves and smoking cigarettes. The front room was tiny; the walls seemed to squeeze around Aunt Polly's big furniture. Four men, faces sweaty, sat at a folding table playing a boisterous game of tonk as another half dozen stood around, watching and shouting encouragement. The air was thick and hot, rich with cigars and garlic. Fats Domino was singing on the record player; people in the Lower Nine loved their local boy.

Belinda snaked her way among the hot, tobacco-and-whiskey-smelling bodies to the kitchen, where Aunt Polly stood at the old stove with a glass of cold drink in one hand and a cigarette in the other, laughing with Mrs. Jenkins and Aunt Florie. "Hey, girl!" With two soft hands, Aunt Polly pulled Belinda's face into her yielding, apron-covered belly. Belinda could feel the crinkle of bills under her cheek, in an apron pocket. Aunt Polly took a cut of every pot, in return for hosting the games and serving massive quantities of smothered pork chops, baked macaroni, chicken, red beans, broccoli and cheese, and jambalaya. By dawn, she might have two hundred dollars in her pocket, and she'd move on to cooking eggs, grits, biscuits, and bacon for the cardplayers. Cousin Faye, a slim eighth grader with shiny, shoulder-length curls, handed Belinda a plate heaped with food and said, "Let's go out back."

They sat on the stoop, watching a yard full of boys cut up. Lionus Jenkins and Kermit Ruffins, both from Belinda's class, were sword fighting with alder switches. Cousin Stevie and Belinda's brother Alvin lay down to leg wrestle in the weedy dirt just as Grandma came around the corner holding baby Katina, Belinda's newest cousin. "You boys acting like satmallie fools!" Grandma shrieked, raising a palm to smack them. "Stop that ruining them clothes!"

Belinda finished her pork chop and licked her fingers. "You ever been whipped?" she asked Faye.

"Nope."

"Me neither," Belinda said, setting down her plate. "Miss Wheaton says I'm going to college someday."

"College?" Faye screwed up her pretty face. "You dreaming, girl."

Belinda shrugged. In truth, she didn't really know what college was, other than something for shirt-and-tie people on television. That was good enough for her. Eight years old, and she wanted out of this life so bad she could taste it.

RONALD LEWIS

NEW ORLEANS
PUBLIC SERVICE INCORPORATED,
BARONNE STREET
1976

Jimmy Zansler put out a big calloused hand as Ronald came up the front steps of the blocky brown downtown office building where NOPSI kept its offices. Jimmy was a bear of a man, with a beard and stylishly long hair, the damndest white man Ronald had ever met. He worked in the body shop of the Carrollton streetcar barn and was trying harder to end discrimination on the job than most blacks. He and Ronald were struggling to organize all three of NOPSI's departments—power, gas, and transit—into the International Brotherhood of Electrical Workers, to end NOPSI's system of separate unions for black and white employees. Both were company controlled, and both were useless. To Ronald, politics had always been about black pride and black power. To join up with a white man to do politics—that was new. He'd have liked to set up on Miss Duckie's porch again and tell her about it. She'd be proud, he knew. But she'd finally sold her house on Tennessee Street and moved with her family out to New Orleans East; it had become popular, just like she'd predicted.

Ronald and Jimmy entered the break room and took seats side by side at a Formica-topped table next to the vending machines. Frank Nettles, a big, studious white man who rebuilt streetcar motors at the Arabella barn, sat beside them. A few minutes later, NOPSI's three big guns walked in: Bob James, his shoulders hunched and a pipe in his mouth; tough little Hero Evans, strutting like he was ready to peel off his jacket and throw down; and big, elegant Clarence Eckelmann—professorial, smiling slightly, in tiny wire-rimmed glasses and a beautifully cut suit. Behind the three big guns, a line of sallow and sullen lawyers seated themselves along the wall in a row of plastic chairs.

Ronald smiled widely, giving them a big view of his grille to knock them off balance. "We got to talk first about pay on the roadway," he said. "Right now, we're second-class workers."

Bob James took the pipe from his mouth and banged it on the tabletop. He snatched off his glasses and leaned forward. "Roadway," he growled, "is nothing more than digging dirt."

"Bullshit," Ronald said, and the three white executives sat back in their chairs. "You were out there just the other day. You take a man from maintenance and put him on the tracks. See if he can get ties, tampers, and slag replaced in the time it takes two streetcars to pass. You got to be roadway to do that."

"There's no way we're going to pay . . . ," Hero Evans began.

"Hey," Ronald said softly. "Don't make me tell OSHA you got us riding on the back of a dump truck, with no seats, and covering us with a tarpaulin. And that general manager you got using roadway men to build his house; who should I tell about that?"

"Can I say something?" said Jimmy in his meaty Irish Channel accent. "I'm old NOPSI. My father worked in the power department. I love this company. But let's admit it; roadway is South Africa."

"What's mechanical and body shop going to say if we start paying roadway the same as them?" Hero barked. Ronald knew what he was saying: How are white men going to feel about being paid the same as blacks?

"You let me worry about them," Jimmy said.

"Well, then," Hero said. "How you going to feel when everything's"—he smiled—"equalized?"

"Let me tell you something," Jimmy said. "When I joined the Army and realized I was going to be taking orders from a black sergeant, I thought it was the end of the world. That guy, the guy I was, is the guy you're trying to talk to now. But let me tell you, it didn't take me long to realize there were only two colors in Vietnam: dark green and light green. And red. We all bled the same color. So let me worry about the guys in maintenance and body shop."

Hero turned his reptilian eyes on big, gentle Frank Nettles. "What about you, Frank? You ready to go back and tell the rest of the guys in mechanical that they're going to earn the same as the bo's digging dirt on the roadway?"

"Some of them won't like it," Frank said softly. The three executives had to lean forward to hear him. "But I'm sitting here remembering something. I was working the night we got rid of the screens." Ronald turned in his chair to listen. The screens—wooden slats printed, "For Colored Patrons Only"—occupied a special place in New Orleans mythology, as one of the city's few explicit Jim Crow rules from the bad old days. Everybody over a certain age remembered their delicate dance, moving up and down the seats as the streetcar filled with white or Negro riders. One day they'd mysteriously disappeared.

"They called me in that night, late. Told me to be at the Canal barn," Frank said, looking down at the tabletop. "They'd set up a band saw right there. They told me and another man to take all the screens and cut them in half, all of them. They had a supervisor there, and a watchman with a gun, in case there was trouble." Frank lifted his eyes from the tabletop. "Something changed that night. Or, perhaps I should say, started changing. Would any of us really like to go back to the way it was?"

Bob and Hero sat back in their chairs, scowling. Clarence took off his little round glasses, laid them on the table, and leaned across, smiling. "Ronald," he said. "Maybe you've had enough of roadway. Maybe you'd prefer to put some distance between yourself and the pickax. Could we find you a position, in, say, the storeroom?"

"We done tried that, Clarence," Ronald said. "They sent me over the storeroom one time, but, sir, it didn't suit me. Couple weeks of that, I asked to go back out to the wilderness. To my people."

Eckelmann spread his hands. "This is for your benefit."

Ronald felt a wave of electric heat rise up his backbone, out his shoulders and arms. He tapped a fingertip on the table. "You're not doing nothing for my benefit," he said, his jaw clenched. "Unless you're doing something for my people on roadway, you're doing nothing."

fRANK MINYARD

ORLEANS PARISH CRIMINAL COURT
1976

The bailiff called Frank's case, the doors to the courtroom flew open, and the French Market Jazz Band marched in, playing "When the Saints Go Marching In." Frank, wearing the second-line band's traditional bus driver's cap, led the way, waving his trumpet and grinning at the TV cameras. Edgar Smith, cheeks as big as apples and dressed in a beige jail suit, brought up the rear on sousaphone. Judge Andrew Bucaro sat at his elevated bench, laughing and beating time with a gavel. Spectators filled the benches.

"Do you have a lawyer present?" Bucaro asked, when the band stopped playing.

"No, Your Honor," Frank said, panting from exertion. "I am acting as my own lawyer."

"Then you have a fool for a client," Bucaro said, and the crowd roared. Frank winked at the eye of a television camera.

"You and your band were cited for performing on Royal Street without a permit," Bucaro said. "You are charged with disturbing the peace and begging. How do you plead?"

"Guilty as hell," Frank said.

"Well, I know you're not a beggar, so we'll drop that one. But you sure as hell disturbed the peace. So here's your sentence: community service. You're to take that trumpet of yours and go do some good with it."

"Yes sir, your honor."

Frank and Edgar walked out the courthouse into bright sunlight. "You should practice more, Dr. Minyard," Edgar said, "and you shouldn't play the fool. Music is serious." He handed Frank the sousaphone. "If you'll excuse me, I have to go back to jail."

FRANK DROVE HOME to the antebellum French Quarter town house he'd bought after Emelie divorced him. The front of the house had two apartments; he rented those out and lived in the old slave quarters, which were across a small courtyard in back. He mixed himself a bullshot and called all the musicians he could think of: Milton Batiste, Harold Dejan, and old Danny Barker, who'd been playing banjo around the Quarter since the 1950s. The idea, he explained, was to hold a benefit concert for local charities, but with a twist. Instead of charging high ticket prices and donating the proceeds, Frank would hand out tickets to the charities and let them sell them. And here's the twist, he said. We set a price limit of five dollars, so that the same people the charities served could come and enjoy the music. Within an hour, he'd lined up horns, guitars, and, once Al Hirt agreed to play, a big-name trumpet.

"We need a piano player, Jumbo," Frank told Hirt.

"Well, how about your ma?"

Frank was about to call her, when the phone rang.

"Frank, it's Harry Connick." The district attorney.

"Am I in trouble?" Frank asked. "No, let me guess. You want to perform at my benefit."

"Close," Connick said. "How about you let Harry junior sing?"

Frank laughed. "What is he, eight?"

"Nine."

Well, sure, Frank thought. We're only charging five dollars. No one's expecting Louis Armstrong.

WILBERT RAWLINS JR.

3035 BURGUNDY STREET
1980

Wilbert Rawlins Jr. was never allowed to forget he was Wilbert Rawlins Junior. At ten years old, he was the biggest kid at Thomas Alva Edison Elementary—a head taller and fifty pounds heavier than even the biggest sixth grader—but Da towered over his world like the sun and moon rolled together. Da worked all day on the waterfront, hauling hundred-pound sacks of coffee, and when the muscles moved under his shirt, it looked like he had cats fighting under there. Four, five nights a week Da would come home, change into his tuxedo, and go right back out to play drums for Miss Irma Thomas. But even so, it seemed to Wil like Da was always around—fixing the bikes of every kid in the Marigny, cooking meals in the family's cramped kitchen, taking everybody out to eat, hovering over him at school. Wil knew kids without fathers, but it was hard for him to imagine what that must be like. The whole world came to Wil filtered through Da. This is how you fix a radio, Da might say as he snapped the thing apart and together without a moment's hesitation. This is how the toaster works. And this is what I expect of you. "Do you understand?" Da would say, putting the eye thing on Wil like his gaze could nail Wil's head to the wall. "If you don't understand, I'll break it down for you. But if you tell me yes, and then you break the rules, that's blatant disrespect."

The family was living that year at 3035 Burgundy, renting half a tall duplex whose front steps went up a full story to the porch. Ma taught math at Helen S. Edwards Elementary, and though she was already shorter than Wil, her authority was no less ferocious than Da's. Let Wil come home with disappointing grades. Let one of his teachers call her in. He wasn't too big yet for her to put him over her knee. Chubby little Lawrence, two years younger than Wil, was like a little ball of sunshine in that house, always smiling, always laughing. And why not? He didn't have to hear Da growling down at him, "I did not give you my name to play with it in the streets that way."

Ma and Da both left the house at five o'clock every morning. Miss Camille would pick up the boys in her big station wagon and carry them across the canal to their grandmother's house on Deslonde Street. The air those mornings was warm, wet, and fragrant: a hedge of star jasmine in the churchyard across Burgundy, coffee roasting on Congress Street, fish coming into the Spain Street wharf, the big old sweet olive hanging over the corner of Louisa. But what lit Wil up inside was the music—a ship on the river sounding its horn across the Marigny, the clickety-clack of the trains along the Press Street tracks accompanied by the eighth-note ding-ding-ding of the signal lights at Dauphine. The music was all around and inside him.

JOYCE MONTANA

VILLERE STREET
1981

"Tootie, we're going to be late to Gallier Hall!" Joyce stood at the stove in her nightgown and robe, making a pot of strong coffee. Her head ached. It was eight o'clock, and the mayor wanted Tootie at Gallier Hall for nine. They'd been up almost all night, along with Ricky Gettridge and Paul Honoré, feverishly sewing beads and sequins into a brilliant pink suit.

"I can't help that," Tootie said calmly, hunched over the kitchen table in his pajamas, sewing sequins into a moccasin. "The suit's not done."

The mayor had invited Tootie and Joyce to receive an award and sit with him on the reviewing stand in front of Gallier Hall to salute Rex, king of carnival. Who'd ever have thought the city of New Orleans would honor a Mardi Gras Indian? And to greet Rex—the mayor was essentially inviting black Mardi Gras into white Mardi Gras, an unheard-of thing.

"The mayor," Tootie snorted, "ain't nothing but a Seventh Ward boy like me."

Dutch Morial had been a fixture of Joyce's childhood, a respectful, light-skinned, wavy-haired youth, standing with his foot up on a porch step, chatting with an elder, always a book tucked under his arm. He'd gone as far as they'd all expected: first black graduate of LSU Law School, first black to serve in the Louisiana legislature since Reconstruc-

tion, first black juvenile court judge, first black justice of the Louisiana
Fourth Circuit Court of Appeal.

"I'll get there when I'm done," Tootie said, without looking up. "It's
Mardi Gras day, and the suit's not finished."

The doorbell rang, and Joyce padded to the front door in her bare
feet. Tootie's spy boy and flag boy, no doubt, come to get him into his
suit and fill the house with their drumming and chanting. She pulled the
door open.

Dutch Morial stood on the porch—short, broad chested, arms
cocked at his side as though ready to throw a punch—wearing a crisp
double-breasted suit. Behind him, impeccably dressed in a pale green
suit, was his beautiful wife, Sybil—a doctor's daughter—and three of
their children, scrubbed to shining. A hot wave of embarrassment
washed over Joyce. She pressed her bathrobe closed over the old nightgown.

"If everything I've heard about Tootie Montana is true, he's not
budging from this house until his suit is ready," Dutch said, his dark eyes
sparkling. He held up a fancy-looking framed document. "Muhammad
won't go to the mountain, so the mountain came to Muhammad. May
we see him?"

ANTHONY WELLS

*Cali is cold, man. Cold. Got into a little thing, so I was on probation, and once
you on probation, man, they got you. Get a parking ticket, don't see your parole
officer, not working, any of that gets you picked up again. They want you to report
what you're making, where you working, like under communism or something.
You're not working, you're violating your parole. You move without telling them,
that's absconding, and that's automatic violation. It don't stop. They finally sent
me to this fire-suppression camp, and I finished high school there. They were like,
"Ant'ny Wells, you got to find another way to deal with your anger," and I
thought, they're right. I never saw my daddy use his fists. Never saw him use a
gun on another man. So one day, me and a dude get into it, and I walk away.
I'm thinking, what's the New Orleans way? Use your head. Go around instead
of through.*

My job was in the scullery, washing pots and shit. Tile floor. Other dude don't have no rubber boots, so I put safflower oil and water on the floor, and then I talked some shit and he come charging through, slip on that oil, and bust his head on the tile. Blood everywhere. They charged him with being unauthorized in the scullery and didn't do shit to me. The New Orleans way, man; it works.

Vietnam come along and I get drafted. Did my service, but I don't get no benefits on account I got a discharge. They drafted me into the fucking Seabees. We was three black dudes, two or three Mexicans, but the lieutenants and captains, they were all white. They told us as soon as we finished our basic training we were going to Nam to build highways and shit in the jungle. So we smoked weed, got drunk, started fucking up on purpose. I got in a fight with a lieutenant at the PX and tore that place up. Three of us got put out.

Only thing is, I should have gotten more peacoats and shit out of it.

Got introduced to freebase in 1979. It wasn't no big deal; nobody could afford it. I'm out on Van Nuys Boulevard in my turquoise pants and French cuffs, doing my thing—some F40s, Tuinals, nothing big, you dig?—and this crazy motherfucker, Cecil, comes up and he got one of them old service revolver .38s. I could see the bullets in the chamber. So I go running across Van Nuys Boulevard, the busiest motherfucker in L.A., like eight lanes of traffic, and he's like Pow! Pow! Pow! I had on this cold-blooded leather coat and I can feel them bullets hitting it. When I stop running, my friend says, "Ant'ny, look at your coat." And I'm like, motherfucker: my brand-new Orbach's leather coat. Six holes in it and not a scratch on me. Some kind of voodoo. That's when I'm thinking I had to get back to New Orleans.

WILBERT RAWLINS JR.

ST. ROCH PARK
1981

Wil stood on first base, daydreaming. Our Lady Star of the Sea Catholic Church loomed over one shoulder, the creepy mausoleums of St. Roch's Campo Santo Cemetery loomed over the other. Heat rippled from the bare dirt of the baselines. His team, St. Roch Park, was up six to five in the top of the ninth. One more out and he could dive for the shade and some ice cream.

"Wilbert!"

Wil snapped awake and looked around. Parents were laughing and talking, Lawrence and his friends were hunting for treasure in the litter under the bleachers, but Da sat erect as a statue, glaring through aviator sunglasses with an intensity that burned a hole in Wil's ribs. "Wake up and look sharp!"

Wil waved his glove.

With a loud, flat crack, the ball rocketed up the first-base line. I can end the game, Wil thought, stepping toward it. The ball smacked the ground and hopped crazily. Wil's hands tangled, meeting the ball, and two bright yellow bolts of pain shot up his arms. "Aaah!" The ball skittered into the outfield. The base runner brushed past. Wil flipped off his mitt and stared at his hands. Both pinkies jutted at odd, terrifying angles. The pain rolled up his forearms in waves.

He was instantly surrounded—ump, coaches, teammates—as he sobbed over his searing, broken fingers. Da shouldered through everybody, carrying his drumstick bag and snatching off his shades. He took Wil's wrists in his enormous hands. "You stop that," he hissed. He lowered his head to drill his gaze clean through to the back of Wil's skull. "Don't be doing this with my name out here."

Wil clamped his mouth shut, pinkies bright with pain.

Da opened his drumstick bag and came up with a roll of white tape. Wil had never seen Da look in that bag without finding the thing he needed. Da turned and trotted over to an old man with a pushcart of ice cream, rooted in the cart—and trotted back. He tore open two Popsicles at once, knocking the ice off the sticks on the side of his shoe. "Give me your hands." In one motion, he pressed both pinkies straight. Shafts of pain shot up Wil's arms and it felt like his eyeballs would blow out the front of his head, but he bottled it up. Da laid the sticky-cold Popsicle splints against Wil's pinkies and wrapped them with the tape, reassembling Wil's hands as competently as he would a toaster. "You are the only first baseman they've got," he said, through heavy breaths. He wiggled Wil's mitt back on, tucking the splinted pinkie carefully into place. His eyes drilled into Wil's. "It's all about the game," he said. "You've got to suck up the pain." With a shout to the umpire, he trotted off the field.

Wil's pinkies throbbed. He was dizzy from the shock. Next to his foot lay two lumps of sandy, melting ice. The pitcher hurled the ball, and with a dull crack the ball appeared to hang harmlessly in the air above Wil's head. He reached up, and it thumped into his glove.

fRANK MINYARD

KENNER
1982

Frank stood beside his car in the fading light looking down a swath of destruction—six houses burst open and smoldering, trees singed, the crumpled wreckage of a big white 727 jet strewn across what had once been a neighborhood. Edgar Smith, the sousaphone-playing former jail-bird and now a full-time deaner, handed him a handkerchief, and he pressed it to his nose and mouth. He could feel the heat of the fires on his face, and the air was caustic with jet fuel, char, and the sickly sweet odor of burned flesh.

Pan Am 759 had taken off from New Orleans International a little after 4:00 p.m., risen about a hundred feet, and fallen back to earth. Frank had heard the crash—all of New Orleans had heard it—and almost simultaneously the Jefferson Parish coroner's office had called, begging for help.

Young Joe Maumus was heading back into the smoking fuselage for—what?—the fifth time? Joe had been the coroner's driver when Frank took over the office, a big jolly fellow so loyal to Frank that it was like having a son in the office. Frank had pushed him to become a New Orleans policeman and then arranged to have him returned to the coroner's office as an investigator. Moving bodies wasn't really his job, but there was no stopping him. He'd spread a tarp at Frank's feet, and as Frank watched in wonder and admiration, Joe was retrieving corpses—blackened, twisted, horribly disfigured. His face was blank, his uniform was smeared with gore and carbon, and his shoes were thickly crusted. He laid the bodies on the tarp—some no more than limbs—waved away a drink of water, and went jogging back for more.

JOHN GUIDOS

EILEEN'S HALLMARK, CATON STREET
July 1982

Dad's old wooden coin organizer, heavy mahogany worn smooth by decades of pawing fingertips, moved the numismatist in him. When he circled his finger idly in the dimes, the clinking was loud in the empty store. He'd keep his eyes down, because he couldn't bear to look up at what he'd done to his father's heritage.

What on earth had he been thinking, to borrow so much money? How could a guy working so hard to be normal—to do the plain, ordinary things everybody else did—get into such a mess? Dad had run Eileen's Hallmark out of a nine-hundred-square-foot niche for decades and earned enough, with his Navy pension, to support the family and send John and his brother, Jim, to Catholic schools and college. John had foolishly expanded Eileen's to the size of a small supermarket—a vast barn of trinkets and doodads that nobody needed. John's thinking had been: Why sell a little glass kitten for eight dollars when a porcelain ballerina, pirouetting on a filigreed music box, went for a hundred and twenty? Why sell a twenty-nine-dollar pen-and-pencil desk set when one made of titanium—and containing clock, barometer, and four-function calculator—went for two hundred dollars? Ronald Reagan's election had inspired John to stock full-color, foot-tall soldiers and sailors with giant angels standing over them, their translucent glass wings spread wide. Beautiful things. Eighty dollars. A bunch of them went out the door in a patriotic fever when Reagan was first inaugurated, so John had ordered a boatload more. Meanwhile, the headlines had melted from euphoric patriotism to jobless recession. The few people milling around the vast, inadequately lit store seemed unable to afford more than greeting cards and the occasional scented candle.

As for the marriage, John and Kathy were going through the motions. He needed her for the masquerade. His compulsion to dress as a woman and pleasure himself was only growing stronger. After closing, he'd drive down Elysian Fields and go for a walk in the French Quarter, finding himself, inevitably, outside the Roundup, Gregory's, the Wild

Side, or the Double Play, watching beautiful, laughing men go in and out, loud and free and playful. Every time, he turned away.

As for Kathy, she needed him for the status and big house in Metairie with the stained-glass front door, the all-black bathroom with gold fixtures, the swimming pool. She'd interpreted the expansion of Gentilly as evidence that she was a wealthy woman. No matter how many times John explained that the growth was built on borrowed money—that they could lose everything—she saw only her broad-shouldered husband at the helm of a glittering empire. She'd insisted on a new car, replied to every credit card offer that came in the mail, and maxed out on all of them. She left the kids—Sandy and Paul—with a nanny to go shopping in her Cadillac most days. She was lost in a fantasy role of her own—the nouveau riche Metairie matron. If something didn't change soon, he'd end up losing the business Dad spent a lifetime building.

If that happens, he told himself, I'll keep the old change drawer.

BILLY GRACE

2525 ST. CHARLES AVENUE
Christmas 1982

Billy Grace was nervous. Hosting the annual Christmas party at 2525—the Rex mansion—was a solemn responsibility. For seventy-five years, the doors had swung open at precisely noon on Christmas Day—usually with a crowd huddled on the porch and spilling down the broad stairs. Silver bowls of potent eggnog adorned the grand table beneath the dining room chandelier, and tiny sandwiches of sliced duck were passed around by servants. But not too much of either, because at precisely two o'clock everybody was ushered out and the grand doors locked. The 120-minute Christmas party at 2525 was an event that nobody who mattered uptown would dream of missing. At age thirty-two and playing host for the first time, Billy was vigilant.

It was a long tumble down the chain of inevitability, he now realized, that had him and Anne finally living in the Rex mansion. After Tulane and Tulane Law School, he and Anne, newly married, had finally gotten the taste of the wider world for which Billy had longed. They'd moved to New York City so Billy could earn a one-year master's in tax law at New York University. Their apartment on Bleecker Street was small and dismal but ineffably romantic, and once Billy was finished, he had an invitation to clerk at the U.S. Tax Court in Washington, D.C. It seemed that finally the big world was busting open to greet him.

But then Anne had gotten pregnant, and after many long talks he agreed to move back to New Orleans so she could have her mother nearby. They moved to a house at Sixth and Prytania so dilapidated that when Anne first saw it, she burst into tears. When their daughter was born, they gave her the rather grand name Anne Ransdell to honor the great anti-Long, gunboat-wielding senator. (With Big Anne and Little Anne already in the family, they called the baby Ransdell to avoid having to call her Littler Anne.)

Upon his unexpected return from New York, his father's friend Harry McCall had made a place for Billy at his law firm, Chaffe McCall. But Billy's was an odd specialty—state and local tax—and his salary barely paid the bills. When Liam was born, they bought a larger house, at Eighth and St. Charles. It was hard living the Garden District life, caring for the daughter of George and Anne Montgomery and two babies, on the salary of a junior associate—especially now that oil was booming, New Orleans was suddenly flooded with wealthy Texans, and prices in stores and restaurants were rising accordingly.

The disconnect was going to be even greater now that he was responsible for this gigantic and historic house. Grandmother Kock had died in 1978, and Aunt Virginia, who suffered from polio, wasn't able to manage such a behemoth of a house alone. For years she'd been talking about either selling it or breaking the house up into apartments. Then, earlier this year, as Anne was getting ready to give birth to their third child and Billy was looking for yet a larger house, Aunt Virginia asked if they wouldn't all like to come live in 2525. If Billy still harbored dreams of making it in the big world outside New Orleans, those were now well and truly over. The Rex mansion's gravitational pull had drawn him inside from as far away as Bleecker Street. It wasn't just a nice address; this was going to be like residing inside the beating heart of uptown New Orleans.

So Billy Grace—son of a onetime bank teller—found himself hosting New Orleans's most important Christmas party. The Rex mansion never looked prettier than at Christmas, encrusted inside and out with generations of gilded baubles, upholstered ornaments, wreaths of live holly, twinkling lights, candles. Everybody was dressed in elegant holiday finery—the women in long velvet dresses with their hair piled up and their jewels out, and the men in dark suits with gay red and plaid waistcoats. Billy had known most of these people his entire life, and most of them he loved like family: the McCalls—whose ancestor wrote the city charter; the Walmsleys—descended from the former mayor who was one of Huey Long's greatest antagonists; the Reilys—owners of the giant processed-food company that bore their name; the Eustises—masters of the city's insurance and mortgage industries. They were like the great oaks out front: their roots in New Orleans's shifty soil unimaginably deep, their wealth and influence spreading over the city like mighty crowns and casting everything around them into deep shade. They may not have bank accounts to match the oilmen from Texas who were then overrunning New Orleans, but they had history here, and manners. They'd do anything for Billy, and he'd do anything for them. I could have practiced law in Washington, D.C., or New York my whole life and not had friends like these, Billy thought.

At the same time, though, a sliver of shadow had fallen between him and some of the others he spotted in the crowd quaffing his eggnog and duck sandwiches. The same ones who'd given George such a hard time over the zoo, who'd grown frosty when George had brought his Jewish friends to the Atlanteans' ball, were noticeably colder to Billy now. It was hard for Billy to define; nothing overt was ever said. But a coolness had descended between Billy and some of the people he'd known since his childhood. It sometimes felt like a draft from a leaky window, a faint chill whose source he couldn't place, and which seemed to pass before he could analyze it.

That chill crawled around his neck now as he reflected that 1982 had ended without his being invited to join the Louisiana Club. On one level, it didn't bother him. He was a member of the Boston Club on Canal Street, after all; how many lunch clubs did he really need to belong to? And it wasn't as though Billy had made the mistake of asking to join the Louisiana Club. He knew full well that even to indicate one would welcome membership was a disqualifying social felony. A man was put up secretly for membership by a member, and then was subject, without his knowledge, to the tyranny of the blackball. Any member could veto another's prospects simply by saying no and organizing four friends to do likewise. Nobody was ever asked to explain his veto, so nobody ever had to be so uncouth as to say out loud he found the fellow too liberal, too pushy. In theory, the poor guy would never even know he'd been considered, but in practice, of course, one of the great unmentioned pleasures of being a member of the Boston or the Louisiana was making sure everybody knew exactly who had been found wanting. None of the swaggering oilmen from Houston, for example, would ever set foot inside, and everybody made damned sure they knew it. That Billy had been pointedly excluded as well stung him. The Louisiana Club, tucked away a few blocks off Canal on a short street called Union, was one notch above the Boston Club; it meant a higher level of acceptance into uptown society. It meant automatic membership in Momus, one of the really old, truly blue-blooded Mardi Gras krewes. Billy's father belonged, and that usually was enough to assure a son's membership. But Billy had been passed over.

George appeared out of nowhere, clapping Billy on the shoulder. He had a smashing red-and-green holiday vest on under his suit jacket. His face was flushed and damp with excitement and exertion, his longish white hair falling over one eye. He pointed out Leon Irwin III, the forty-three-year-old son of the benefactor of Billy's dad. Leon was a much-beloved and flamboyant uptown character. Everybody knew he was homosexual, but nobody ever mentioned it, and certainly nobody held it against him. Just this past February, WDSU had aired a fifteen-part series on male prostitution and had caught poor Leon soliciting sex in a flower shop on North Rampart Street. Leon, to his good-natured credit, didn't deny it—he even talked openly about the experience. But he hadn't been the same since; he was drinking more, and a trembly, tragic pall had settled over his former cheer. The whole affair had uptown simply furious with WDSU. "See to him, Billy," George instructed. "And Helen over there? Her mother's quite ill; don't forget to ask after her, and remind me tomorrow to send something. Oh, and look at *her*," George said with a flick of his eyes at another lady. "She shouldn't be wearing Armani. It drapes on her all wrong." Billy laughed. It was one of George's private party games, to be the sotto voce critic of the women's fashions. Whether he genuinely knew anything about women's clothes, Billy had no idea. But he fancied himself an exquisite eye. Billy had never known anyone quite like his father-in-law. The energy the man had for his friends—for making everybody around him feel good, and for arranging social events—was mind-boggling even by the standards of uptown men. Billy remembered being struck, during his and Anne's brief sojourn in New York, how it was always the women who seemed to invite them places and organize get-togethers. Their husbands just seemed to go along. He realized then how different was New Orleans from the "real" world. With all the events on a Mardi Gras krewe's calendar, it was the men of uptown New Orleans who piloted their families' social calendars—the balls, the coming-outs, the luncheons—not the women. Nobody put more into it than George.

Billy had no doubt that his being excluded from the Louisiana Club had something to do with his being George Montgomery's son-in-law. Billy had joined George and Big Anne in their very public support of Dutch Morial when he ran for mayor in 1978. Few uptown New Orleanians ever came right out and said they wouldn't abide having a nigger mayor, but the division between those willing to accept the reality of a changing New Orleans and those who weren't was plain. New Orleans was no longer ruled from the card rooms of the Louisiana and Boston clubs, that was for sure, and Billy knew plenty of people—some of them right here in this room—who couldn't quite get their minds around it.

This frostiness Billy was feeling, though, might not have been about race at all. It may be he was just too hungry for the leisurely gentlemen of the Louisiana Club. Billy knew he'd been pretty open about his eagerness to earn more money to supplement his associate's salary at Chaffe McCall. He'd wanted a second automobile. He'd wanted to become a member of the New Orleans Country Club and play golf. He'd wanted a second home in Destin, Florida, where he and Anne had vacationed. So he'd started letting on around town that he was looking for businesses to buy into, for investment opportunities, for a little action on the side. He'd advertised himself as a young man on the make, without a lot of money but with plenty of entrepreneurial drive and a boundless appetite for hard work. He'd identified himself with this new money-oriented turn the city had taken since the oil boom had started. Looking around his bedecked and swirling living room now, he realized that among certain of his guests, entrepreneurial drive and an appetite for hard work were as off-putting as support for a black mayor—if not more so. A certain breed of coupon-clipping uptown New Orleanian didn't need that kind of energy stirring the unruffled air inside the Louisiana Club.

Billy was a striver; he couldn't help it. He'd been raised by one and had gotten a sharp early lesson in the price of uptown lassitude. When he'd arrived at Woodberry Forest in Virginia, he'd found that the easygoing gentleman's C education of Metairie Country Day hadn't prepared him at all to compete with equally privileged boys from elsewhere. Unlike his classmates, he didn't understand quadratic equations, hadn't read *My Ántonia*, couldn't name the first ten amendments to the Constitution, had no grasp of the periodic table of the elements. While all his friends went on to tenth grade, he alone had been sentenced to the burning humiliation of repeating ninth.

That was never going to happen to him again. Billy had torn into his studies during his second ninth-grade go-around as though trying to outrun a forest fire, and discovered that there was a deeper pleasure in achievement than in the boozy backslapping of uptown poolside pleasantries. As his dad liked to say, he wasn't a Eustis or a McCall. Working suited him.

So it was fitting, perhaps, that he wasn't going to be part of Momus. Instead, he'd been invited to join Rex. Rex wasn't as old as Momus, Comus, or the Atlanteans—it was founded after the Civil War, a crucial distinction—but it was built around the most important person on Mardi Gras day: Rex himself, the king of carnival. Rex was neither crassly overdemocratic like the new superkrewes that accepted anybody who could pay the dues—Bacchus and Endymion—nor stuffily exclusive like Proteus, Momus, or Comus. It was the perfect happy medium; one still had to be invited, but it was much bigger in membership than the old-line krewes, and its motto, *"Pro bono publico,"* perfectly captured its civic mission to serve and entertain the entire city, not just the bluest of the blue bloods. It was a big, vigorous organization, much more the kind of place a comer like Billy Grace belonged than the rarefied atmosphere of Momus or the Atlanteans. Billy was proud to be a part of it.

Rex: Its infatuation with a storybook idea of royalty was so over the top that Billy could tell himself it was all a goof, a laugh, a joke. The thirty-foot gold-lamé-and-ermine trains that the king and queen wore! The ten-year-old pages in brocaded uniforms and stockings, the bejeweled crowns. The fake beard the king always had to stick on with spirit gum. The wildly overdone pomp, the men in white ties and tails bowing . . . It was all a little boy's idea of royalty. Nobody could really take it seriously, could they?

But Billy couldn't look around his Christmas party without noticing how many of the men he loved were members of Rex. It wasn't a hoot or a goof at all, really. It was important. It was historic. Planning for the balls, choosing a queen, selecting the maids and dukes, conceiving a theme for the parade, and, of course, anointing Rex himself—these rituals gave shape to uptown life, and had done so for more than a hundred years. They set New Orleans apart from other cities. They bestowed a specialness upon the deeply rooted elite of New Orleans, who, Billy understood all too well, couldn't compete with their counterparts elsewhere in either wealth or enterprise or genius. The rituals of Rex weren't ridiculous at all; they were beautiful—elegant, regal, and worthy precisely because they consumed so much of uptown's time, money, and mental energy.

Rex is not Momus or the Atlanteans, Billy told himself. It doesn't exist entirely in the service of privilege and exclusion. It exists, really, to put on for New Orleans—rich and poor, black and white—the greatest free show on earth.

They will show me the way, Billy thought. They will illuminate the path that winds between the highest reaches of uptown New Orleans and an enlightened attitude toward the city's black citizens that would make my father proud. Above his head elaborate molding crawled around the ceiling, the crystal chandeliers that had once swung over the heads of the likes of Robert Downman and Senator Ransdell. I, Billy thought, am the next generation of Rex.

BELINDA CARR

EGANIA STREET
1982

Life in the Lower Ninth Ward never got easier for Belinda Carr. As she grew into a teenager, she increasingly felt like the duckling whose egg had rolled into the wrong nest. Everybody around her was all about Lower Nine this and Lower Nine that, how the Lower Nine was the most wonderful place on earth. Didn't they see what a dead end it was? Didn't they see the pea-gravel streets and the rusted old cars? Was she the only person who wanted something better than dreary day work and a broken-down rented house? Belinda loved her mother and her brothers, Aunt Polly and Aunt Doll, cousins Faye and Greg and Stevie—but she yearned for conversation about something other than whose azaleas were coming in nicely and who's having another baby. She didn't even eat the same food as everybody else. Crawfish, oysters—all those spicy, creepy-crawling things everybody made such a fuss over—made her ill. She stuck to fried catfish, plain chicken, and other normal-people food. There were times when she grew so restless—and so lonely in her restlessness—that she could barely leave her room. She'd hole up in there for hours, feverishly consuming one romance novel after another, aloft in an immaculate dreamworld of fine-speaking people.

Lawless High School made her feel like a car racing with its engine stuck in low gear. What passed for honors classes slipped past effortlessly, with little to engage the hungry sprockets of her brain. The kids in her class were nice enough, but they were all about sports and dances and who-likes-whom. Walking home alone day after day, Belinda struggled to make herself want to join in, to be the kind of teenager she liked watching on *Happy Days*. She knew that she'd grown into an attractive young woman, with long legs and high, regal cheekbones. If she'd wanted to play the game, the game would have her in a heartbeat. That Lionus Jenkins, a distant cousin by marriage she'd known all her life, was suddenly the big man around Lawless—the star of both the football and the basketball teams. By being the only girl who didn't swoon before him, she'd inadvertently caught his eye; even somebody as socially clueless as she could see that. But she put him off, like she put off all the boys, by failing to laugh at his silliness, by standing with her arms folded when she should be wiggling her butt, by looking down her nose when she should be gazing up. The whole boy-girl thing made her shudder.

I'm going to get out of here, she'd tell herself. I'm going to have the white-picket-fence life like on *Family Ties*. I'm going to live a normal life. The way out, she knew, was college, but nobody she'd ever known had taken that route; nobody in her world even understood what it meant. She was about to start applying, and she wasn't going to tell a soul. Until it came time to go, up-and-out would be her secret.

fRANK MINYARD

MAINE
1982

Frank walked up from the dock, along the path between the dunes, wind ruffling his thick, graying hair, the sand warm on his feet. He breathed heavily from a long swim. At fifty-three, he needed firm routines to stay in shape.

The phone in the cottage was ringing. He sprinted onto the porch, pushed through the screen door, and picked up the receiver—a heavy black Bakelite artifact from the 1950s.

"Sorry to call, Dr. Minyard." It was Gloria Boutté, from the coroner's office. "You're not going to believe what happened to Joe Maumus."

Frank sank into a wicker rocker. He had to ask Gloria to repeat the story three times. Joe had been arrested at the Fairmont Hotel by Internal Affairs while naked, in bed with a woman, with a gram of cocaine in his wallet. He'd walked off his shift, leaving his police horse tethered to a garbage truck in an alley.

"Damn." Frank laughed, despite himself. Joe was a good cop—that night at the plane crash still filled Frank with admiration—but he was something of a wild man. It's why Frank loved him. He dialed Joe's house, the old rotary clicking loudly. "It's me," he said. "What were you thinking?"

"It's entrapment. They set the whole thing up, paid the woman . . ."

"Joe," Frank said. "I believe you." To come to the defense of a cop found naked in bed with a woman while on duty—with cocaine in his pocket, no less—would be politically risky. On the other hand, if a guy like Joe couldn't make a little mistake in New Orleans, where could he? Joe was Joe, as good as a son to Frank. There was no cutting him adrift. It's times like these Frank was glad he had the city wired. "I'm on my way," he told Joe. "I'm going to save your ass."

RONALD LEWIS

TUPELO STREET
1982

Ronald loved the view from his front porch. Tupelo Street was wide, with a fat, grassy neutral ground—less intimate but much grander than Deslonde. The homes were small and simple, with none of the fussy curlicues of the ones across the canal, but every one of them between Claiborne and St. Claude was owned by its occupant. Miss Catherine always had some candy in her apron pocket for little Reynaldo and Rashad. Miss Crystal, Miss Hall, and Miss Beulah were usually out on their porches to greet Ronald when he came home from work. He couldn't quite walk to Deslonde Street to set on his mama's porch, the way his legs were acting up, but it was only fifteen blocks away.

It was a fine thing to own one's home. Soon as the NOPSI guys had voted in the IBEW and he'd gotten his raise, Ronald and Minnie had bought this place for $26,500. They put down $1,500 and took a bank loan like anybody else.

Buying this house had shown Minnie's dad. Still, the old man had tried to make Ronald feel small. When Ronald and Minnie had had no choice but to ask him to co-sign the loan to buy themselves a stove and fridge, he'd said, right in front of everybody, "You'd better be a man because if you don't pay for this I'm going to take it." Ronald still tensed when he remembered it. As though Ronald W. Lewis might fail to be a man!

No matter how important Ronald grew on the job—he was shop steward now—he could never quite gain the respect of Minnie's side, the Hills. It burned him, made him feel less than whole. It reminded him he'd been born a bastard child who didn't know his own blood parents. One day during a Hill gathering Ronald had come upon the old man lecturing little Reynaldo and Rashad about how lucky they were to be Hills, and Ronald had ruined the whole party by taking the old man on. "These are Lewis children," he'd said. "I am their daddy, Ronald W. Lewis. You are just their grandpa." It made Minnie and her sisters furious, and it had made Ronald feel both big and small at the same time. It was good to take on old man Hill, but a man shouldn't have to explain such things.

The screen door opened, and out walked Minnie's cousin James Brown with a glass of iced tea in his hand. James, a quiet man who liked to twist his beard into a little braid, sat down next to Ronald without saying anything. There was no need, and it was one of the things Ronald loved most about life across the canal. If you didn't have something to say, it was enough just to set together on the porch.

Ronald liked James; he had been married to the same woman since he was seventeen. James had a serenity about him that Ronald admired. He'd been born with a veil—the doctors at Charity had to snip a flap of skin off his face—and it had left him with the ability to see spirits. Minnie had told Ronald about how James, when they were little kids, would suddenly walk out onto the front porch and start talking to the air. The spirits didn't frighten James, but they were a nuisance—popping up when least expected. He worked from time to time for the big funeral home across the canal, fixing dead bodies for burial. He said the only place the spirits didn't visit him was when he was in the presence of the dead.

"Dead bodies," Ronald once said to him, wrinkling his nose. "That's not for me."

"I like it," James said. He turned and leveled his even gaze at Ronald. "They don't move."

PETE'S MONEY GREEN Cadillac swept around the corner of Urquhart Street and stopped in front of the house. The car was getting old, which did Ronald's heart good. Pete was out of the game, finally had himself his own hair shop over on Caffin and Galvez. The long coat and fedora were gone, but nobody ever looked as sharp as Pete, with his long, wavy oiled hair and, always, the finest shoes in the Lower Ninth Ward.

"Smile again!" Pete called from the sidewalk, lifting his big wrap-around sunglasses. "Damn, Ronald, you lost your grille!"

"You know I joined the Masons, right?" Ronald said as Pete sat himself on the stoop. "Nutusken Lodge no. 5, Prince Hall order."

"And what, you can't have a grille to be a Mason?" Pete asked.

"Well, it's like this: My Wishful Master, Big Joe Long—you know him, works by the phone company—he put his arm round me and said, 'Brother Lewis, I likes you. But I'd like you better if you didn't have all that gold in your mouth.' I had a hunch he was right. So I went to the dentist and got unslugged. And I'll tell you what. They treat me different down at NOPSI. Hero Evans himself said, 'Ron, you look different.' "

"You gave up your grille to get a smile out of Hero Evans?" James asked.

Ronald smiled. "The grille was good. But I got my people to think about. If I can get a little more for them without the grille, then I'll do without it. Of course, I couldn't divest myself of all my history." Ronald smiled wider and pointed to a single gold incisor. "I kept one."

They fell into the usual Lower Nine conversation, a rundown of the welfare of everybody they knew. This one was out of work, that one was out of work. It was the containers, they all agreed. Containerized shipping was doing away with all the good jobs on the waterfront. Pete told them he was looking to buy his first house, but not in the neighborhood. He was looking out in New Orleans East, he said. "We should have given Miss Duckie our pennies."

James mentioned a man they all knew who'd been shot and paralyzed in a drug deal right there on Galvez. "He's stuck on stupid," Pete said. The trick of being in the game, he said, is knowing when to get out. "Joseph Kennedy, the biggest bootlegger during Prohibition, became a captain of industry and totally legit," Pete said. "When the game gets tough, you legitimize your hustle. I'm getting old. I want to sleep with both eyes closed."

A killing on the streets of the Lower Nine was a bad omen. As the jobs disappeared, more men were spending their days sitting on their porches. They weren't the role models they once were; without the paycheck, they didn't swing authority in the families. Youngsters took advantage, brought their own way of doing things into the neighborhood, and now they were shooting each other up on Galvez.

A shadow was falling across the Lower Ninth Ward, no question about it.

PART II

WALKING
ON
GLASS

"With every contract you complete,
you increase the level of protection.
If a levee is two feet below its
required level, it can protect
against most hurricanes, but not
the worst hurricanes."

—Robert Guizerix,
Lake Pontchartrain project engineer for
the U.S. Army Corps of Engineers, to the
Times-Picayune, September 9, 1983

WILBERT RAWLINS JR.

COLTON JUNIOR HIGH SCHOOL
1983

The band room, deep in the redbrick schoolhouse on St. Claude Avenue, was a windowless bunker. The walls needed paint, the floor was crusted with years of tracked mud and spilled Coke, and the stale air smelled of sweaty polyester. But it was fast becoming Wil's favorite place on earth.

He sat on a folding chair in the second row, wrapped in the heavy brass arms of a sousaphone, rocking gently as he played, feeling weightlessly top-heavy. Around him, the other junior-high schoolers were blowing like crazy, girls leaning into their trumpets, boys frowning as they struggled for the right embouchure.

Wil was finally making music. After years of his listening to Da play for Miss Irma, the music he'd carried around inside him was making its way out through his fingers. He'd turned away offers to use his height on the basketball court, his bulk on the football field. He could see that while everybody at Colton went to games, they wandered around the stands during the ball-playing, talking and playing grab-ass. But they stopped moving and listened up close when the bands started playing. Band was the thing. Junior-high and high-school bands were the musical backdrop of the Mardi Gras parades. They were the heartbeat of the festivals. All the jazz musicians in New Orleans talked about the band teachers from their school days. Band meant something in New Orleans. It's where the music was born.

"You've got to look at this score as a snake," Mr. Jones said. "Every piece of music we pull out is different. You might have dealt with a cobra before, but this is an anaconda. You take your eyes off that snake, he'll bite you." He raised his arms and twitched them, and the band started in again on "When Doves Cry."

Colton's band was coming on strong. Last time they'd played against Gregory at the football halftime, they'd gotten beat, fair and square;

Gregory was tighter, fuller, more intense. But last week against Lawless, the Colton band had come right off the chain.

Now Wil was troubled. Mr. Jones had the mellophones playing on the C and the baritones playing on the G. Everybody knew the G was right for the mellophone and the C was right for the baritone. Mr. Jones had them playing outside their register. He was sacrificing intensity. Wil's hand shot up. "Mr. Jones!"

Mr. Jones reared back. Students did not speak unless spoken to. Wil stood. "Why don't you give the G to the mellophones and the C to the baritones? They need to play in their . . ."

"Wilbert! This is my damned band!"

"But it would be more powerful. You got 'em playing outside their registers."

Mr. Jones stomped over to the back wall and snatched up a framed diploma. He sidestepped his way into the sousaphones and shoved it under Wil's face.

"You have one of these? No? Then you be quiet. Children are on a need-to-know basis. You don't need to know why you're playing. You just play."

Wil stepped back. Even Da didn't talk to him this way. Even Da explained himself. Mr. Jones had the mellophones and baritones crossways and was trying to bully Wilbert Rawlins Jr. into accepting it. Wil yanked the mouthpiece out of the sousaphone, untangled himself from its coil, and leaned over Mr. Jones. "You know what? I'm going to get that degree—I'm going to have a band that will blow your band *out!*" For emphasis, he raised his fist high over his head and slammed the mouthpiece onto the floor.

The room was silent.

Wil walked out the door, letting it slam behind him.

He was instantly sorry. He'd probably bent his mouthpiece, and Mr. Jones would put him out of band for sure. He crouched by the door, opened it a crack.

"I'll tell you what," Mr. Jones was saying. "Wilbert is right. Reversing the mellophone and the baritone would be more powerful. But I don't want all that power. Music has to start softly and grow. That's how it lifts the soul." Wil felt himself shrivel; he hadn't thought of that.

JOHN GUIDOS

EILEEN'S HALLMARK, METAIRIE
1983

John leaned on the counter. On the shelf beside him, a regiment of foot-tall Christs, identically beseeching, provided a kind of silent, agonized cheering section to his failure. It was amazing, really, that he'd kept the stores going this long. The bank should have stopped him. They never should have lent him the money in the first place. Somebody should have said something.

The mailman came in and handed him a thick bundle of envelopes. John shuffled through them—mostly bills—and then in the middle a compact manila envelope the size of a paperback book, from Curtis Circulation in Hackensack, New Jersey. Bingo. "I'll be in back," he announced to his salesclerks idling by the window, and headed for his office at the back, a cluttered, windowless room, fluorescent lit and bleak: his refuge. He opened the envelope from Hackensack and pulled out the November edition of *Penthouse Variations*: "For Liberated Lovers." He'd never been much of a reader, but he consumed *Variations* every month. It was a window on a hidden world where quirks like his were not only normal but celebrated. It had taught him a useful word: "fetish." A fetish wasn't something dirty or abnormal or wrong—it was creative and liberating. The magazine's credo, printed on the back cover of every issue, summed it up: "Tapping the exciting heartbeat of contemporary American eroticism with provocative sexstyle exposés." *Variations* made John feel like a member of a secret, worldwide confederation of sexual sophisticates. Anyone without a fetish was square, uptight, pitiable. The cover of this issue promised "My Phantom Leather Lover," "Licking Secrets in Glossy Color," and "Sex Games People Play." At the bottom of page 126, though, was a little box so dry and mundane that it drew John's eye. No racy photo or exclamation points, just a postbox and: "Like to dress? Write the Sorority."

A NOTE ON the gleaming granite kitchen counter said Kathy and the kids would be home at nine. Plenty of time. John fixed himself a South-

ern Comfort and went out to the garage for his "tools." Twenty minutes
later he was in a familiar personal heaven, painted and dressed, alone with
an intoxicating cylinder of beige plastic whose vibrations, placed just so,
radiated through him in a way that dissolved the tension, loneliness, and
shame that built up in his muscles day to day. The longer he pressed it to
himself, the deeper he sank into a blessed refuge. He pushed it a little farther, and a little farther still. Delicious spasms overtook him, and for a
moment he blacked out. Enough. His fingers felt for the vibrator, but it
was gone. The sensations continued, stronger than ever—was it after-
effects? He groped around on the mattress, but the vibrator wasn't there.
The sensations still boiled up through his body.

He'd lost it inside.

He tightened his stomach muscles to push against it and reached
with his fingers. It wouldn't budge. The sensations were becoming less
pleasurable, becoming painful even. Frightening. He started to panic. The
clock. Kathy would be home in forty-five minutes. The buzzing went
on deep inside. His desperate grunting and poking yielded nothing. It
wouldn't move. He needed help. He stripped off his lacy lingerie and
pulled on mannish jeans and a sweatshirt. He stopped in the bathroom
and scrubbed off the makeup, peeling off the eyelashes roughly and jam-
ming them deep in his jeans pocket. He hid his clothes and makeup in
the garage and climbed into the car, buzzing.

The emergency room was quiet. "I need to see a doctor," he told the
nurse behind the counter. Could she hear the thing? She handed him a
clipboard with a pen and lifted the phone. "What's the problem?" she
said. John hesitated. She was middle-aged and hard faced, with a whiff
of the Catholic-school nun about her, but the ethic of *Variations* buoyed
him.

"I have a vibrator stuck," he said, with a sheepish grin.

She didn't blink. "Take a seat," she said, and John, over the edge,
made an uncharacteristic joke.

"I think I'll stand."

It was a bigger deal than he'd expected. He had to be admitted and
sedated. He came to in a hospital bed with no idea of how much time
had elapsed. A curtain surrounded his bed, covered with orange-and-
blue geometric shapes, lit by sunshine. Morning. Officious hospital
sounds leaked through the curtain. At the foot of the bed stood Kathy,
looking stricken.

"What is it?" she asked, when he opened his eyes. "Nobody would tell me anything. They said I should ask you. Is it bad?"

She looked quite beautiful, voluptuous and blue eyed, as alluring as when they'd first dated in Hattiesburg. She should, he thought ruefully, given how much she spends preserving herself. But through the layers of makeup and jewelry and fur, she really looked worried. "I had a little dizzy spell, that's all," he said. "Probably too much worrying about the store. They ran a bunch of tests. I'm fine."

Kathy wiped away a tear with a long aquamarine nail. "When nobody would tell me anything, I thought it was really bad."

"I'm sorry I scared you."

A nurse pulled back the curtain. "Good morning." Over her arm, she held John's sweatshirt and jeans. In her hand was a plastic bag, and in the plastic bag, the vibrator. "Here's your things!" she called cheerily, dumping them on the chair beside the bed. She took John's wrist in her cool fingers and looked at her watch. John used his eyes like barbecue tongs, clasping Kathy's face toward his. But her gaze drifted off toward the pile on the chair. He watched her face with the detached, slow-motion wonderment of someone skidding a car into a telephone pole. Her eyes were blank, the worry starting to slough itself off. Then they focused. Still no visible reaction, just focused eyes, looking down at the chair.

"How are the kids?" John said. Kathy kept looking at the chair. "They with your mom?" John asked.

Kathy's head tilted slightly. One eyebrow ticked upward a millimeter. John was pulling on the wheel to no effect, the brake was useless, the pole headed straight for him, and wasn't it interesting? Kathy's eyes changed, as though the sun had gone behind a cloud, and hardened slightly at the edges. The corners of her mouth twitched downward. She detached herself from the foot of the bed and, without so much as a glance at John, walked to the chair.

"You're fine," the nurse chirped. "They're working on your paperwork, and then you can go. Bye-bye, now, have a nice day."

John could have put his arm out and snatched the plastic bag, but he didn't. He was far away, watching with detached curiosity. Kathy picked up the bag and studied it, then pivoted her whole body and looked into his eyes. Her face was hard, cold, furious. He knew it immediately: she'd known all along. It wasn't his fetish that enraged her, he realized. It was being forced, finally, to confront it. Until now, she'd been able to spend his money and gad about in her Cadillac, with beauty parlor appointments and shopping dates in old Metairie, the coddled suburban matron—respectable, normal, married to a couple of big flashy stores. She might have found his dresses and makeup years ago, but she'd never have said a word. She was angry all right, because now she had to hush up and live a lie or face having a pervert for a husband.

She closed her exquisitely made-up eyes, opened them slowly, rolled them, and tossed the vibrator back on the chair. Then she shook her head, pushed through the geometrically patterned curtain, and was gone.

WILBERT RAWLINS JR.

DAUPHINE STREET
1983

Chicken took the miniature pies from the oven and laid them tenderly, one by one, on a rickety folding table—sweet potato, lemon, pecan, cherry. He tapped his booted heel to the beat of "Billie Jean," which was blasting from tall speakers mounted beside the kitchen cabinets.

If Da knew Wil was hanging in Chicken's place, he'd kill him. Chicken, wiry and light skinned, had never had a dad, and his mom had run off. He lived on his own around the corner on Dauphine Street. The boy was trouble; Wil knew that.

As the pies cooled, Chicken tucked plastic pouches of white powder into the gooey filling of each one. "You want a nickel bag, that's the pecan," he said giggling. "You want a dime, that's the sweet potato." What blew Wil's mind was that even though the pies were just for cover, Chicken made them from scratch, rolling out dough he mixed himself, cutting up fresh fruit from Frady's market. "It's how my mama taught me," he explained. Chicken knew that Wil, who could never get enough to eat, would be willing to help in return for a couple of warm pies. He liked having Wil along. "Ain't nobody mess with a nigger boy your size."

Even though his parents were clear on one point—"Ain't nothing in the Quarter for a black boy but trouble"—Wil sometimes carried Chicken's cooler to the corner of Dumaine and Chartres, a block off

Jackson Square on the downriver side of the Quarter, where tourists didn't go much but where Chicken's regulars knew to find him. Wil would sit on the cooler in front of Harry's Corner bar, dreamily fingering imaginary sousaphone valves. Ta-da ta-da ta-daaa. Quarter notes: Coca-Cola, Coca-Cola. One evening when Wil was deep in a sousaphone reverie, Chicken said, "Hey."

Wil opened his eyes. Chicken was holding up the front of his shirt, showing the handle of a silver pistol tucked into the top of his pants. Before Wil could say anything, Chicken had the pistol out of his pants and was holding it behind his butt, walking up Dumaine to Royal and turning right, shoulders hunched, bouncing on the balls of his feet. Wil followed nervously.

Chicken flicked his jaw at a skinny bald-headed white man leaving the Golden Lantern. Weaving slightly, the man noticed Wil and Chicken walking toward him and crossed the street, which filled Wil with a strange combination of anger and sadness. It was typical of a white man to think two young black men were trouble. On the other hand, Wil and Chicken were proving him right.

Chicken brought the gun up. The man cowered pathetically, trying to cover himself up and raise his hands at the same time. Then suddenly his pale face started flashing blue.

Wil looked over his shoulder. A police car had rolled up right behind him. Chicken ran up Governor Nicholls toward Rampart; Wil darted the other way. Someone shouted. Wil pumped his arms and picked up speed; he heard hard leather soles smacking the pavement behind him. He zipped into an alley, popped out on Barracks, turned right, found another alley, and rocketed in. Dead end. He crouched behind a Dumpster, his heart going like a bass drum, his wheezing so loud it echoed. A siren whooped. Had they caught Chicken?

Wil crouched there a long time, shivering. As his heart slowed, he could hear Da's voice: I didn't give you my name so you could play with it like this in the streets.

BELINDA CARR

EGANIA STREET
1984

Belinda jumped out of the car and ran inside ahead of her mother. She stormed across the living room to her bedroom, slammed the door, flopped on the narrow bed, and punched herself in the stomach. "Die," she said. "Die." Mom was putting on a kettle in the kitchen. Alvin was shooting baskets in the driveway. Calvin was shouting to a friend in the backyard. Belinda ached from her toes to her temples, a vague, nauseating throb, and the bed spun slowly, auguring into the earth.

"Belinda, honey?" Mom tapped gently on the door. The light in the window was soft; she must have slept. "We all make mistakes, baby," Mom said, sitting on the bed and rubbing Belinda's leg. Belinda didn't answer. Mom rose and shuffled away up the hall. She had repeated that line all the way home from the doctor: we all make mistakes, we all make mistakes.

I know, Mom, Belinda thought, rolling over and sitting up: I was yours. You dropped your dreams of singing professionally because I came along. It seemed to make some kind of terrible, comforting sense to Mom that Belinda should make the age-old, almighty, inevitable mistake in the never-ending circle of mistakes.

If she'd prided herself on anything, it had been control. And now look. All honors classes, and she hadn't even been aware what was happening to her. It had taken Aunt Florie to suggest a visit to the doctor.

Everybody had pushed Belinda to break out of her "unhealthy" bookworm's cocoon and enjoy the last year of high school. She'd joined the basketball team and the pep squad. She'd dated, tried a few dances. She'd even gone to see those wild Mardi Gras Indians and the even sillier masked white men of the big parades. She'd kept studying, though, and escaping through books to a place where boys knew how to make conversation, men had grace and manners, and endings were happy. It was only after Lionus Jenkins got his basketball scholarship to Southern University at Baton Rouge that she'd let him talk her into the prom. He was going to college, after all, just like her. What happened in the back of the limousine after the prom—the alcohol, the pawing, the whole shameful business—she had quickly buried under the soothing routines of her dwindling senior year. Lionus had murmured an apology, she'd forgiven him, and they'd gone their separate ways. She'd hardly thought about him since.

Pinned to the wall above Belinda's desk was a typed letter congratulating her on her acceptance to Southern University at New Orleans. Even now, her family didn't really understand what it meant to go to college. Cousin Faye, who loved books as much as Belinda did, had tried to talk her into secretarial school, which in itself would have been a stretch for a girl from the Lower Ninth Ward. But Belinda had her sights on a real college.

What she wanted, she realized, was an abortion. But if she said it, Mom would swoon, and the pastor at Greater Harvest Baptist Church would fill her ear with hellfire. She lay back on the bed in the darkening room, wiping her eyes. "Time to go," Mom whispered through the door.

The stars were coming out as they scuffed through the pea gravel and shells of Egania Street. The porch light was on at Lionus's. Belinda followed Mom up the neatly swept front steps, like a steer up a ramp to the slaughterhouse.

Mrs. Jenkins opened the door, wearing a pink housedress and smiling timidly. Mr. Jenkins sat in an armchair, a king on a throne. "Lionus," he called. "They're here!" Lionus slouched in like he'd punctured and all his bluster had leaked out. He nodded to Mom. "Ma'am."

This can't be happening, Belinda thought. Her bones ached, and her stomach fluttered. Mr. and Mrs. Jenkins swiveled their heads toward Lionus, who looked at the floor. "Son," Mr. Jenkins said, "you got to step up."

"I know," Lionus said.

The room tilted. Instead of Southern University, Belinda realized, Lionus was headed for a laborer's job. Instead of SUNO, Belinda was headed for long days changing diapers in a shackety house—another Lower Nine teen with a baby on her hip. That was the payback for ten minutes in the back of a limousine after the prom.

"Lionus." Belinda struggled to control her voice. "You got your scholarships. You go to your college, and I'll go to mine. I can manage. Let's not drag each other down."

"No," Lionus said, squaring his shoulders and looking at his father. "I'm going to step up. I want to take care of my child."

WILBERT RAWLINS JR.

722 ST. ROCH AVENUE
1984

Evening was Wil's favorite time of day, especially when Da wasn't gigging with Miss Irma. Often Da would cook barbecued shrimp for the family—one of Wil's favorites—and then sit on the porch with his arms folded, watching St. Roch Avenue with the imperious concentration of a theater critic. The landlord on Burgundy had raised the rent, so the family had moved to 701 St. Roch. Just as they were getting comfortable there, the landlord threw them out; he needed the apartment. Luckily, they found a place a few doors down. It was smaller, but it sat right across from Schiro's Grocery, where a trio of regulars often sat on folding chairs out front, hats on the backs of their heads, noodling up and down the scales of their clarinets and guitars.

Moving, always moving. The Rawlins family always stayed right in the neighborhood, so it wasn't like he and Lawrence had to make new friends or get used to a new school. But Wil wondered sometimes why they couldn't own their own house. Da worked so hard at Dupree moving those coffee sacks. Mom taught math in the schools. How come they couldn't own their home like other people and stop being chased all over the neighborhood?

Someday, he told himself again and again, I'm going to own my own house.

The kids in the neighborhood always brought their broken bikes and instruments around by Da because they knew he could fix anything. He'd reach in his drumstick bag and come up with wire, duct tape, tools—that bag was magic. As Da worked, he'd purr in this Mr. Cool Jazz voice—"Hey, little bro, how's it shakin' "—that Wil hated because it sounded so fake. Sure Da played jazz with Miss Irma, but as far as Wil was concerned, the real Da was all business: What did you learn in school today? Where are your sneakers? Get in the car.

Wil and Da were sitting on the porch after dinner one night, enjoying the music from across the street and the cool breeze off the river, when Wil felt his gut drop. Pimp-rolling up from Dauphine Street came Chicken. Wil got up to intercept him, lest Da overhear.

"Hey, bra," Chicken said. "Come help me sell some pies."

Wil glanced up at Da, who was looking down at them with no expression at all. Da knew Chicken.

"No, I'm not doing that no more," Wil told Chicken softly, hoping he'd vaporize before Da started asking questions. "I told you that."

"Bitch," Chicken said loudly, and little as he was, he stepped inside Wil's hands and gave him a hard shove. His eyes were shiny, his jaw tight. He'd been into his own cocaine.

"What, you scared of me?" Chicken said, giving Wil another rough push. He pulled up his shirt and showed his tight tan belly. "I ain't got nothing! I ain't scared of you."

"Wil!" Da said, his voice rumbling down from the porch like thunder. "What is this?"

"Nothing."

"Son, don't you give me that. I see something's happening here." Da was standing now, putting the eye thing on Wil, so there was nothing to do but offer up the most honest answer Wil could summon without pushing Da into taking action on his own with them hands.

"This boy wants me to do something that I don't want to do."

"Are you scared?" Da asked.

"Yeah, I'm scared."

Chicken had heard enough. "Go back in your house, you old nigger!" he shouted at Da.

Wil froze. He half expected Da to turn into a pillar of fire and come roaring down the front steps of the house to annihilate little Chicken on the spot. But Da didn't move; he might not even have heard Chicken.

"You heard me, you useless old nigger!" Chicken said again. "Get your ass in your house and leave me kick the ass of this punk-ass motherfucker my own self!"

The guys in front of Schiro's were watching now, the clarinets silent. Everybody on the street knew Da, knew you didn't fuck with Wilbert Rawlins. Even the mockingbirds seemed to be holding their breath, the ships on the river frozen in place. Da stood with his arms folded, his chest and shoulders massive under his tight-fitting black sport shirt; the man was a slab of solid muscle from moving those hundred-pound sacks of coffee around the Dupree warehouse all day. Da didn't move or change his blank expression.

"What!" Chicken yelled up at Da, the cords in his neck standing out.

The little guy was winding himself up to a frenzy in the deep shade of Da's imposing silence. "What I tell you! Git!"

"Wil," Da finally rumbled. "What do I tell you about fighting?"

"What?" Wil asked. Da's calm had him thrown off balance.

"What do I tell you about fighting?" Da asked again.

"Don't fight," Wil said, numb with confusion.

"That's right," Da said calmly. "You never have to fight. You can always walk away."

"Walk away!" Chicken shouted. "Walk your narrow nigger ass in the house and let me finish this punk-ass!"

"Wil," Da said, in that same flat, eerie calm. "You need to whip his ass."

Chicken and Wil both froze, and as they looked into each other's eyes, they were, for a brief second, the childhood friends they used to be, allied against the parents. Had Da just told Wil to fight? Chicken recovered first, and smacked Wil in the chest. Wil looked up at Da, who hadn't moved. Wil grabbed Chicken's flailing arm and, having a good hundred pounds on him, spun him around like a doll. He started banging Chicken on the head and neck with his big open hand, and only now he started feeling himself get angry. Call my da a punk-ass nigger! Mouth off to my da! He had Chicken by the shirt with one hand, and his other arm was working like a piston on Chicken's head. Get me mixed up with the police! Turn me into a thug! Chicken stopped fighting back; he had his hands up and was yelling, "Leggo!" like a ten-year-old. But Wil was just getting started. Chicken went down and Wil started kicking him with his big right leg, really hammering Chicken's skinny little ribs. Chicken was scrabbling across the pavement like a crawfish, trying to get away. Wil grabbed him by the back of the shirt and threw him forward into a parked car. The bang of Chicken's head against the fender reverberated up the street, and one of the guys in front of Schiro's keened, "Oooo-ooo!" Wil looked up at Da, who hadn't moved. Wil took Chicken by the shoulders and slammed his head into the car again. I'm a bandleader. I'm the best bandleader. I am Wilbert Rawlins Jr.

Chicken stopped struggling, though whether he was knocked out or faking, Wil didn't know. Wil's anger was starting to leave him, and beating up on Chicken was starting to feel like work. Da hadn't moved. Wil looked up at Da with what he hoped was a visible question: Can I stop now? He's stopped moving; is this enough? Da, though, seemed to have fallen into a kind of sleepy trance watching his son kick the shit out of a street punk, and he didn't answer. Wil was feeling a little sorry for Chicken now. He looked up at Da, hoping Da would say, "That's enough," and then Ma appeared at the screen door and came flying down the porch yelling, "What you doing! What you doing?" and pulling Wil off Chicken by his ear. Mom reached way up over her head to slap Wil's dumbfounded face, and Da finally broke his silence, laughing like a man at the circus.

ANTHONY WELLS

I finally got to New Orleans in 1982, and it was a breath of fresh air. We didn't have to deal with the white world at all. My uncles were plasterers. I had people, you feel me? Peanut: he was the Mescals' grandson. Spoonie and Poochie: them's my cousin Jerry's sons. They had my back, you hear what I'm saying? People. Had me a car, too; the bee I called her, on account she was yellow and black. If trouble came, we dealt with it.

I did maintenance at the Municipal Auditorium, got it ready for their Mardi Gras balls and shit, which was like fucking Gone With the Wind. Then I fell off a scaffold and broke my arm, and the city terminated me. I'd a been all right if I could have gotten the right kind of assistance, but all I got was like two thousand dollars workmen's comp. Then I was all set up to be a security officer, investigator, some kind of shit. They had this place on Canal Street, the Lawton School, where you learn investigations, latent fingerprints, all that, and they give you a certificate. I thought it would be good; I could work for insurance companies and lawyers. The first day, they helped us fill out the form to get a federal education grant of four thousand dollars. They gave us books—Louisiana law and all that. I went there four weeks. They were about to take us for target practice, give us our little badge and gun, when one day I go down there and all the doors are open and the management people are gone. The computers and everything. They took that federal money and vamoosed.

After that, I took care of my parents; they died in 1986. I did labor work in construction all over the city; couldn't go to no Seventh Ward, though. I could work with my uncles a little bit, but what I loved about it, man, was if I said, "Fuck the world," and got pissy drunk, there would be someone in the Goose to pick me up, give me something to eat.

WILBERT RAWLINS JR.

701 ST. ROCH AVENUE
1986

Da climbed from the passenger seat of Ma's car, holding up a hand wrapped in white gauze, like a bowling pin. He looked gray and weak; Wil had never seen him like that. The guys at Schiro's set down their clarinets and got to their feet; Wilbert Rawlins was hurt.

"Hush," Ma told Wil. "Hold the door." She helped Da up the front steps, into the living room, and settled him in his chair. "All right now," Da said. "You know that big grinder we got in the middle of the warehouse? I was pouring in beans and the bag got caught. I reached in to pull it out. I got these two fingers caught." He held up his good left hand, wiggling the middle and ring fingers. "Ground them down to here." He hooked the tip of his thumb onto the first knuckle of the middle finger.

"Will they grow back?" Lawrence asked. Wil belted him on the arm with the back of his hand.

"No, son, they won't." Da smiled kindly, propping up the bowling pin with his other hand. "It could have been worse, right? Could have taken my whole arm."

During dinner, a smoky spot of red appeared on Da's gauze bandage. By the time Ma had cleared away the bread pudding, it was big as a rose, blooming over the top. Ma took Da to the bathroom to rewrap the bandage, then to their bedroom. She laid Da's tuxedo out on the bed.

"You gonna play?" Wil asked from the doorway. Da pulled off a shoe, one-handed.

"I am Miss Irma's drummer," Da said. "I am it. I don't show, she can't go on."

Ma's jaw muscles bunched, the way they did when she wanted to say something but didn't let herself.

"I'll tell you what," Da said, standing up and shuffling gingerly into his jacket. "You all come tonight. We're playing a festival on Bayou St. John. You'll see. I'll be all right."

The night was hot, and the crowd a little drunk. Men with sweaty faces stood in the backs of pickups, moving slabs of pork and split-open sausages around on big iron barbecues, the sweet-smelling smoke drifting over the crowd. Wil looked down at Ma as they made their way toward the bandstand. Her jaw was set. Da's whole world was his music, but there wasn't a bit of jazz in Ma. She was all math teacher.

They settled on the grass beside the low stage, next to Da's drum set. Miss Irma came over, long fringes swaying on her sparkly silver dress. She gave Wil's hand a squeeze, stepped up onto the stage, and sashayed over to the microphone. Da counted off, and the band launched into "Suffering with the Blues." Wil leaned back on his elbows. Da had been playing with Miss Irma for as long as he could remember, and every time it washed over him fresh and mysterious how every member of the band did his own thing but it all clicked together like a puzzle to become one thing. Miss Irma slid up and down to her notes, bending and stretching the words. Da's white bulb bounced up and down in perfect rhythm; if he was hurting, his face didn't show it. Miss Irma sang "He's My Guy," "Safe with Me," and "I Haven't Got Time to Cry." Lawrence fell asleep with his head on Ma's outstretched leg and Wil felt his own eyes drifting shut. Miss Irma sang "It's Starting to Get to Me Now" and "It's Raining." Wil lay back on the grass, floating on her voice and Da's even, muscular drumming.

When Wil woke up, Miss Irma was drinking a glass of water, the guitar player was lifting his guitar over his head, and Da was turning from the drum set, grimacing up at Ma with a helpless look. The bulb of gauze had gone entirely red. Ma fished in a grocery bag, came up with a fresh roll of gauze, tape, and scissors, and moved in front of Da, blocking Wil's view.

Da stood, his right hand in a fresh white bulb, his left hand holding a bottle of beer. He stood laughing and talking with the guitar player until it was time to sit back down and begin the second set. He counted off once again, and the bouncing white bulb went back to work. Wil lay quietly on the grass, throughout the second set, thinking about what he'd seen.

JOYCE MONTANA

EMPIRE STATE BUILDING
1987

The spires of the monstrous city rose around Joyce like trees in a forest. It was hard enough looking through them, at distant rivers and bridges; a glance straight down, at the cars and buses scurrying around like palmetto bugs, set her stomach to heaving. Joyce's equilibrium was so sensitive that she could barely ride a New Orleans streetcar. Tootie was just as bad. He got carsick riding in a taxicab. Yet here they were, a thousand feet up in the wind, looking down on New York City. She felt like she'd just taken a slug of liquor.

Tootie, though, was enchanted. He wouldn't fly in an airplane— they'd traveled all the way from New Orleans on an overnight train that made both of them motion sick—yet the observation deck of the Empire State Building suited him. "It's that one I love," Tootie shouted over the wind, pointing to a silvery building that looked close enough to touch. The top was an echelon of arcs, like an old-fashioned table radio.

"You have good taste," shouted Maurice Martinez. "That's the Chrysler Building, the most beautiful building in New York."

After years of pushing a camera into their faces, Maurice had done them a favor; he'd put Tootie up for a Heritage Award from the National Endowment for the Arts. It had seemed crazy to Joyce that anybody outside New Orleans would care about the Indians, but Tootie had won. The first thing the lady from the NEA had said was, please don't take apart any more of your suits. The award came with a big check so they would be able to buy new feathers and beads every year and not have to spend weeks disassembling old suits.

But things at home were worrisome. Darryl—sweet little Mutt-Mutt—was coming to no good. He hadn't masked Indian in years; he was hanging with Tootie's son from his first marriage, Boobie, who was out of Angola for the first time in years. Next time back, Boobie would probably take Darryl in with him. Darryl had been smoking that marijuana and then, she was sure, selling it. It wasn't a far piece, in the Seventh Ward, from using and selling marijuana to using and selling cocaine. Darryl was jumpy and irritable lately, his eyes shining in a way she didn't like. Some new kind of cocaine was showing up, changing hands right there at the corner of Villere and Annette streets. It looked like handfuls of teeth; people smoked it.

Maurice, Tootie, and Joyce walked out onto Sixth Avenue and into a blur of people. Everyone seemed so rich in New York, dressed in fine jewelry, suits, and ties. Joyce felt like a lost soul from some remote bayou. The past ten years had been hard on New Orleans, seemed it got real poor real fast. Nobody talked about the waterfront anymore, and too many men were spending their days on the street corner. Welfare didn't do any good; there were too many people having fifteen children just to get the checks, huddling up in them projects in a big pile.

And, of course, the drugs.

Maurice, Joyce, and Tootie climbed into a big yellow taxi, and after a very fast ride up a canyon of windows and concrete the taxi stopped in front of a giant building as fancy as Gallier Hall. Joyce was queasy; Tootie, too. "This is the Museum of Natural History," Maurice said as he paid the cabbie. "There's something in here I want you to see."

Joyce felt like a wide-eyed ten-year-old as Maurice led them through a fantasyland of animals, frozen in natural settings: wolves, lions, buffalo. Tootie was transfixed by the bison's great, woolly collar; the tiger's black-slashed orange coat; the spreading ears of an angry elephant. "Come," Maurice said, urging them down a broad, high-ceilinged hallway. They rounded a corner, and there stood a Mardi Gras Indian made of solid stone, fifteen feet tall.

Tootie stopped, his mouth open. The statue looked very old, maybe hundreds of years, but it also looked like Tootie on Mardi Gras day—the way the crown spread out from the head, the way the stone feathers stood up from the shoulders.

"Lord, Tootie," Joyce heard herself squeak. Her voice echoed off the marble walls. She pointed to the star-shaped pattern on the figure's breastplate. "Look! You had that, one year!"

"I'll be doggone," Tootie said, walking slowly around the statue. It was uncanny how similar the garb was to Tootie's suits. There might have been egg cartons under the statue's suit.

"It's Mayan," Maurice said, "about three thousand years old."

"I never been to New York before," Tootie said, "let alone to this museum. You know that." He looked bewildered, standing in the vast hallway, a skinny, brown-skinned man whose hair was going white, gaping up at the mighty chief of stone.

"I know," Maurice said. "Tootie, I think you are a reincarnation of that man."

BILLY GRACE

ANTOINE'S
1988

Billy Grace entered Antoine's from Rue St. Louis through the Mystery Room and was struck immediately by how empty it was. He recalled from his childhood this red-walled room packed with people, the din of laughter and clinking china racketing between the rust-colored floor tiles and low-slung ceiling so intensely he used to get headaches waiting for the grown-ups to finish. And it seemed like just a couple of months ago every table was full of big loud men in powder blue suits who kept their three-hundred-dollar Stetsons on as they washed down their chateaubriand with Lone Star. None of the Mystery Room's beautiful round tables was occupied now; fresh bouquets waited patiently in the center of each creamy white tablecloth. The oilmen were gone, and the oil boom with them.

The waiter led him down a long hallway and opened the door to the Rex Room, and Billy's momentary gloom vanished. It was like stepping into the private dining room of the Wizard of Oz—the carpet a rich purple, emblazoned with large oval Rex emblems; the walls kelly green, trimmed in gold leaf; the ceiling a riot of golden orb lights, recalling the gaudiness of the floats. Purple, gold, and green had been the colors of Rex, and by extension of Mardi Gras, since 1872.

As the executive committee of the Rex krewe filtered in, greeted each other, and took cocktails, Billy made his tributary rounds of the walls. Framed black-and-white eight-by-tens of former Rexes hung between display cases, in which mannequins dressed in royal finery presided among scepters, diadems, medallions, Rex-ball invitations from a century back, and elegantly penned greetings from the crowned heads of Europe. It was a museum, a sanctuary, a refuge from the quotidian troubles of crime, corruption, collapse. To step inside was to pass through the looking glass into a bubble where all that mattered was the theme of next year's floats, whose daughter would be queen, and who might be invited to the ball. In the Rex Room, even strivers like Billy could experience—however briefly—the frivolity of the idle rich. The space itself wasn't exclusive. Other people could dine in the Rex Room if Rex didn't need it—*"Pro bono publico!"*—but on a moment's notice, Antoine's would make it available to Rex's officers, to the point of moving people mid-meal, their napkins dangling from their collars.

Billy seated himself next to John Charbonnet, the Rex captain. John, owlish in big horn-rimmed glasses, was old uptown, but like Billy he worked for a living—as the owner and manager of a successful construction company. As white-jacketed waiters set platters of oysters Rockefeller along the tables, Billy leaned over and asked John softly if they should discuss "the Giarrusso ordinance." City councilman Joe Giarrusso, avenging generations of excluded Italians, was circulating an ordinance that might, if read a certain way, forbid any Mardi Gras krewe that discriminated against blacks to parade on city streets. The majority of New Orleans's *publico*, after all, was black. Bacchus and Endymion, the new superkrewes made up largely of out-of-towners, had included blacks from the start. None of the old-line krewes had any in their membership, though, and Billy knew that John shared his view that of all the old-line krewes, Rex should have integrated long ago.

"Perhaps we should," John said thoughtfully. "I'll bring it up if we have time."

John ran them through a long list of logistics. Floats: Who would liaise with the float builder Blaine Kern in his complex of Quonset huts across the river? Throws: Gold doubloons or purple and green, as well; and how many colors of beads? Flambeau carriers: Continue the tradition of having black men carry oil lanterns to illuminate the floats, even though improved streetlights obviated them? The ball: Which limos, what orchestra, gardenias again? Like Eisenhower assigning beachheads for D-day, John compelled volunteers, elicited agreement, nudged the conversation toward conclusions that boosted morale.

As Billy pushed through the doors onto Rue St. Louis, blinking in the bright sunshine, John caught up to him.

"Hey," he said softly, taking Billy's elbow as they walked. "I didn't want to tell you this inside. Amoco's packing up."

Billy stopped abruptly and stared at him. John was chairman of the Chamber of Commerce; he'd know. "Packing up?" Billy asked.

"Leaving New Orleans."

Billy felt the sidewalk heave under his feet. Amoco was a Poydras Street anchor; more than four thousand people worked in the company's gleaming tower.

"I just got back from Chicago," John said. "We took everybody up there: the governor, Bennett Johnston, the mayor. Everybody. We offered the moon. Larry Fuller was polite. But when we were through, he said, 'I'm not going to mislead you. The decision's been made.' "

"They didn't ask for anything? A tax break? Nothing? Nobody hinted this was coming?"

"I'm not socially acquainted with oil executives," John said. "Are you?"

"I see them at the country club."

"I know, but they're not part of the lunch clubs. They're not part of our krewes. They never were exactly included, if you know what I mean."

"You saying we drove Amoco out through snobbery?"

John rested a hand on Billy's shoulder. "In other cities, the guys who run a major corporation with thousands of downtown white-collar workers are social leaders, fixtures. Here they had to have their separate Mardi Gras krewes."

Billy opened his mouth, but John went on.

"I'm sure it's not just that. Mostly, it's the glut. And computers. But the oil business and New Orleans were never the best fit."

Billy nodded. The oil business was all about growth and money, and New Orleans, at heart, was about neither.

They walked in silence for a minute.

"Hey," Billy said, stopping. "We never got around to Giarrusso's ordinance."

"You're right," John said. "Maybe next time."

fRANK MINYARD

ORLEANS PARISH CORONER'S OFFICE
1989

Frank and Edgar stood a few feet back from the autopsy table, watching the new deaner reach his arm up to the shoulder into the bowels of the man on the table.

"He's got stones," Frank muttered to Edgar. "I forget where you found him."

"He walked in, looking for a job," Edgar said, weighing a liver on a dangling scale. "Told me right up front he had a record. I told him, 'Join the club.' Thing is, he's a little odd."

"Odd?"

The new man pulled out the bladder and laid it on the stainless steel counter. Frank and Edgar watched as he weighed the organs, took samples for chemical testing, tossed the organs into a big plastic bag, and eased the bag into the chest cavity. When he was done sewing up the chest, he removed his surgical gloves and walked over to Frank and Edgar.

"Dr. Minyard, this is James Brown," said Edgar.

"You're good," Frank said. James seemed to be in his forties, his beard twisted into a snappy little inch-long braid beneath his chin.

"I worked by Glapion for years," he said. "Dead don't bother me a bit. It's the one place the spirits don't get to me."

Edgar nudged Frank with his elbow.

"Well, we're glad to have you," Frank said.

Half the people working for him were jailbirds, and the other half are jazz musicians, Frank thought. And the new guy, he talks to spirits.

THE TWIN GASLIGHTS twinkled merrily in front of Frank's house on Barracks Street. He parked the Porsche in the courtyard and started for the slave-quarters apartment in back. A shadow stepped out from behind a sapling growing in a planter. Frank jumped.

"It's just me, Joe Maumus."

"Joe! What are you doing here at this hour?"

Joe had a big hound on a leash. He turned and said over his shoulder, "Come here, son. It's okay." Joe junior stepped forward, his eyes wide and sad.

"She threw me out," Joe said. His dark hair was longer than his usual cop crew cut, he had a stubble beard, and his big meaty cheeks were pale. After getting caught in the Fairmont Hotel sting, Joe had fought his dismissal from the police force for two years, all the way to the Fourth Circuit Court of Appeal, claiming entrapment. He'd won, and had been reinstated with back pay. But the Fourth Circuit couldn't reverse his romp in the sheets with the police informant, and his marriage had been rocky ever since.

"I'm sorry," Frank said.

Joe looked at his feet. "I'd have gone to Earl Hauck's, but he's got the girls this week. Could I bunk with you for a couple nights?"

Nobody knew better than Frank Minyard how hard it was when a marriage dissolved. Joe had his faults, but nobody was more loyal to Frank. In many ways, Joe Maumus was a younger version of Frank Minyard, and having risked his career defending Joe before the Civil Service Commission, Frank felt a kind of paternal responsibility for him. If for nothing else, Joe would always be a hero to Frank for his amazing work the night of the Pan Am crash. One of the front apartments of Frank's Barracks Street town house had just come vacant, and he offered it to Joe. It would be nice having Joe under his own roof.

JOHN GUIDOS

KENNER
1989

John pulled in to the hotel parking lot and switched off the engine, but didn't open the door. He sat staring through the windshield at Veterans Highway, the speeding red smears of taillights. Two words ricocheted around the inside of his skull: rock bottom.

The stores were gone. Kathy was gone. His secret life was gone; Kathy had outed him to his parents in an evening of yelling and crying that made his stomach freeze to recall. He sat alone in his Mustang, a thirty-nine-year-old manager of a Domino's Pizza outlet, a pervert without a penny to his name. Rock bottom.

On the seat next to him sat a Dorignac's grocery bag, a wisp of auburn hair rising above the rim. He pushed the wig down, folded the top over, and cradled it in his lap. He'd never worn his wig, makeup, and clothes out in public, and he wasn't sure he could go through with it. But the ad had kept showing up in *Penthouse Variations*, month after month: "Like to dress? Write the Sorority." Finally, he'd typed out a one-line letter saying, "Yes, I like to dress." Two weeks later, a manila envelope had arrived from someone named Lee. "You are not alone." John had shaken out two photographs, one of a nice-looking older man with gray hair and a warm smile, wearing a houndstooth jacket and an open-necked dress shirt, another of an aging showgirl with wild black hair and dramatic makeup, wearing a high-necked red satin gown stretched over a provocative bust. They were both, of course, Lee. New Orleans was full of men who enjoyed dressing as women, Lee wrote. Their reasons were as varied as the men. From time to time they'd meet to share grooming tips and swap clothing, but mostly to be themselves for a few hours. John would be most welcome to join the sorority, Lee wrote. An event was coming up.

This night. This place. John sat in the darkened Mustang, watching people park and walk inside the hotel. Were they the men? Some of them had women with them; they couldn't be going to the sorority, could they?

If he opened the door of the Mustang and walked inside, would people find out? Would he lose his job, become unemployable? Did he want to begin a life as a public freak? On the other hand, how much longer could he carry his secret around inside him? How much longer could he get by on solitary sex in the locked office of a pizza outlet after hours? When could he share sex in a way that made sense to him? What would it look like? Twenty years into adulthood, he still didn't know what he was. Lee had seemed so calm in the letter, so sure of himself, no tortured wondering. This is the way I am, he seemed to say, and it isn't a problem. I am not alone, and neither are you.

A car door slammed and a man with a suit bag over his shoulder walked toward the entrance. What was in the bag? A blue blazer for to-morrow's business or a silver lamé gown and a pair of stilettos? The man looked like any other—middle-aged, chunky. He wore no pain in his face, no tension, no shame. If he was on his way into the sorority, John wanted a little of what he had.

He opened the door of the Mustang on the whooshing of Veterans Highway. Shouts and laughter burst from the front of the hotel, people greeting each other. Was that them? Or a couple of sales reps rendezvousing for tomorrow's presentation? He locked the Mustang, walked toward the entryway, and entered the bright lobby. The young woman behind the counter watched him cross to the elevator. Did she know what was going on up there in suite 300? Did she know that's where he was going? He stepped into the elevator with a short, plump man carrying a gym bag. "Three please," the man said pleasantly. John touched the three button and kept his eyes on the changing numbers. The man said nothing. When the doors opened, both turned in the same direction, but the man stopped at room 318. "Have a good night," the man said.

John stood in front of the door to suite 300, clutching his Dorignac's bag, listening to the muffled sounds of conversation, laughter, music, glasses tinkling. He looked hard at the spot on the white painted door, at the spot where he would knock if he could summon the strength to lift a hand. He forced himself to breathe.

The door popped open. A garish woman stood before him. No. The blockiness of the jawline and the sandpaper skin under pancake makeup made it clear it was a man. "Whoops!" she shouted. She grabbed his arm and pulled him inside. "Come in, honey, come in. Don't just stand there."

The suite was full of women, or people who looked like women, waving drinks, touching each other's hair, pivoting for inspection. "I'm just running down the hall for some ice," the woman who'd opened the door said. John must have looked terrified, because the woman's face softened and she said, "Oh, no. I guess I won't." She gazed into John's eyes with tender concern and took him by the arm. "This is your first time, isn't it?" she whispered.

John nodded.

"Okay," she said, positioning herself squarely in front of him, taking his upper arms in her hands, gazing into his eyes from her own heavily mascaraed orbs. "Breathe. You're among friends. Nod if you can hear me."

John nodded and, in spite of himself, smiled.

The woman smiled. "Okay. What's your name?" She had a high, thin voice.

"John."

"Got another?"

"Another?"

"Another name. You know, a girl's name."

"No."

"I'm Beth," she said. She let her face relax under the paint and eyelashes into a mask unmistakably male. A deep, froggy voice came out. "And Bob." The muscles of her face swept upward into a wide smile, and she tittered gaily. "Just freaking you out!" she said in her high girl's voice. "Those your clothes there?"

"Yeah."

"Good." She swiveled, lifted her chin, and, to John's infinite horror, shouted above the din. "Hey, everybody! Quiet a minute! I want you all to meet John. He's a little nervous because this is his first time."

The women surged toward him, arms outstretched. It was a funhouse tableau: big, heavily painted creatures with glittering eyelashes and bright red mouths. A figure he recognized loomed up, the black hair, the red satin gown: Lee leaned in close. "I'm glad you made it," she said, her voice high and breathy.

Hands with flaming nails tugged at John's shirt. Someone took the bag from his hand and rummaged through it as they led him toward the bedroom. "Hey, hon," said a woman next to him. "I'm the real thing. That's my husband over there." She gestured toward a short fat man done up in a yellow sundress and blond wig. "Want to get dressed on your own?"

John nodded.

"All right, ladies. Back off. Our new friend here would like a moment. Let him dress and then you can start in." She herded everybody out of the room, winked, and closed the door.

John looked at himself in the mirror above the dresser, the same old John, short hair, broad face, big in the shoulders and chest. A football player. A laborer. Not a sexual sophisticate. He took off his shirt, found his makeup in the bottom of the bag, and went to work on his face the way he always did: base, eyeliner, lashes, lips, rouge. He'd shaved close but still had to put the base on thick to cover a ghost of stubble. He'd brought the short wig, a fine copper helmet with a widow's peak that suited the shape of his face. He finished undressing, put on bra, panties, and stock-ings, and topped them with a metallic blue dress and matching shoes. He straightened and looked in the mirror, and his insides unknotted a little. This was who he really was. His shoulders came up, his back arched. He felt weightless, the terror gone. He could fill his lungs with air for the first time all evening. He ran his hands down his front, smoothing his clothes, smoothing his body, ready to share the woman in him for the first time. He blew himself a kiss, blinked twice, and pulled open the door.

They were incredibly kind. They handed him around, professing to love the dress, the shoes, the wig. Some of the men looked a fright, mak-ing no effort to move, speak, or behave like women. They clumped around the room with their shoulders rounded, speaking in gruff voices. Okay, I get it, John thought; they like the makeup and clothes. Others, though, were transformed by their getup, and a few were knockouts. They not only had the clothes, hair, and makeup; they had the figures and the moves. Someone put a glass of white wine in John's hand. Lee appeared beside him. He was good. The red gown flattered his olive complexion.

"So what's with them?" John asked, gesturing toward a group of real women who were standing in a corner, laughing and talking.

"Wives," Lee said, in his breathy voice.

"They put up with it?"

"They like it," Lee said, and John felt the world tilt under his feet.

"For some of us, it's all about the clothes and makeup," Lee said. "We're men—straight men, not gay—but we get off on the clothes. For some of us, though, this is the real thing. The act we play all day is fake."

"Are some of these guys fagg— gay?"

Lee frowned, thinking hard. "Not the way you mean, I don't think," he said. "Gays sometimes crash this sorority, thinking it will be fun, but most of the guys don't have any patience for that. You'll find some of the biggest gay haters right here in this room."

"So they like doing women? They just like the clothes?"

"Some of them." Lee looked at John with new interest. "What about you?"

"What do you mean?"

"What's your scene?"

"My scene?"

"You like the clothes. Is that all?"

"I don't know."

"Do you, as you say, 'do' women?"

"I was married."

"Was."

"When she found out about this"—John gestured at his dress—"she split."

"I'm sorry."

"It was a while ago."

"And since? Which is it? Men or women?"

John laughed. "Neither. Me alone, to tell you the truth."

Lee brightened. "The safest sex there is!" He leaned in close and asked softly, "And when it's just you, who's there in your mind? A man or a woman?"

John blushed. "Ah, let's wait until we know each other a little better."

Lee raised his hands in mock surrender. "I withdraw the question," he said, with an elegant dip of the shoulder. "Now"—he frowned at John's wig and eyes—"there are some people here you should meet. You could use a little coaching."

He took John by the arm and introduced him to a real woman, one of the wives—the naked swell of her breasts, above the plunging neckline, gave her away—and a man-woman so perfectly done up that only her Adam's apple and slightly lumpy falsies gave her away. They fell on him like bridesmaids, pushing him into a chair before a big lit mirror and going to work on his face. They showed him how to apply the pancake with upward strokes, to better fill in the trace of beard. They dialed back the intensity of his eyeliner and suggested a gauzy scarf to complement the dress and hide the Adam's apple. Little by little, his reflection in the mirror became more naturally feminine. They worked with his size instead of against it, changing his look from that of a husky guy trying to look like a flouncy sexpot to that of a big thirty-nine-year-old woman. They were taking him more seriously as a woman than he'd ever taken himself. He'd been forcing himself into a cartoon caricature. They were applying a woman's finesse.

They twittered above him, trying this and that. "I'm up to a 34B now," said the real woman, "but I think I can get myself to a C."

"Just by increasing the dosage?" the man-woman said.

"Can't hurt to try."

"I gotta hand it to you," the man–woman said, "you've got balls."

"Not for long, honey." A high girlish laugh skittered out of the real woman. John twisted in his seat and stared. The breasts were real, no mistake; but above them, unmistakably, was an Adam's apple.

"You're not a woman?" John asked.

"Oh, I'm a woman, honey. I just wasn't born in a woman's body."

John's mouth dropped open. "What do you mean?"

She looked at him curiously. "What I said. I'm a woman living in a man's body."

John's head tingled, as though she'd rung a brass bell next to his ear. A woman in a man's body! "So, you're . . . you're not, uh, gay?"

"Well, let's see." She pantomimed thinking, index finger on lower lip. "I like men. In fact, I like men a lot." She giggled and swatted playfully at him. "But then, so do most women."

"But you're a man," John said. "I mean, you were born a man."

"I was born with a man's body. I was born with a man's parts. But I'm fixing that." She laughed and took his hand, pressed it against her right breast. It yielded like a freshly baked cake. "These, for example, are the real thing."

"How?" John stammered.

"Oh, honey," she said. "You've just got to see the good doctor."

BELINDA JENKINS

EGANIA STREET
1989

Lionus Jenkins turned out to be a good husband. He let go of all his basketball-star swagger and turned away from the Southern University scholarship with so little regret that Belinda had to wonder if he'd ever really wanted to leave the Lower Nine in the first place. With the help of his parents, he bought a house on Delery Street and got himself a job on the waterfront. When he was laid off, he went to work at Shoney's. He brought home his pay every week and didn't spend all his evenings out with the fellas. When the baby was born, Belinda named her Lionesha, to honor him.

Lionus's willingness to work long and dispiriting hours let Belinda nibble at her dreams of getting an education. She took a course in word processing at Audubon College. She earned a degree in medical transcription at Sidney Collier Vo-Tech, which got her a good-paying job in a doctor's office. Many evenings, she and Lionus would walk over to Aunt Polly's. It was easier than cooking, and Aunt Polly needed bucking up. Her daughter, Belinda's cousin Faye—who had first turned Belinda on to reading—was slipping away into drugs. Faye's sons, Ditty and Skeeter, were increasingly dependent on Aunt Polly, and Skeeter was a handful; he didn't make eye contact or talk. For Aunt Polly to have her high-achieving niece Belinda at her table, along with her hardworking husband, did her good.

Belinda had never loved the Lower Ninth Ward, and lately she liked it less. Faye didn't have to go far to get her dope; lots of young men hung on the corners of St. Claude Avenue, in front of the old Jewish stores long boarded up, watching over this shoulder and that. Sometimes late at night, Belinda heard gunshots. She kept dreaming of that white-picket-fence life.

The doctor for whom she worked didn't have half the sense she did, so finally, in 1987, she began taking classes at a real college—Southern University at New Orleans, where she'd been accepted three years before. She sat in classes with young people who thought of themselves as future professionals, who would work because it meant something to them, not just because it paid the bills. She loved the heft of a textbook in her lap; she could practically feel knowledge course through her, from her eyes on the page, down through her arm, and into the fingers that took careful notes on clean lined paper. Math. History. Accounting. It seemed to Belinda that her brain was changing color, from a dry and starved gray to a flushed pink, full and juicy, for the first time.

Then, out of nowhere, she missed a period. Soon she felt ill; the baby was in trouble. The doctor ordered her to bed, and there went her college education, again. She spent seven months lying flat in the hot little house on Delery Street, imagining where she'd be in her studies. Latisha, whom everybody called Mookey, was born in 1988.

Now she was a mother of two, trapped in the Lower Nine and living on one meager salary. The white-picket-fence life that had loomed so close receded again beyond a screen of snowy static, like an episode of

Happy Days during a lightning storm. If Lionus knew she was unhappy, he didn't let on. He got up every morning to work, came home every evening to play with the girls. He was a good man. She couldn't complain about him. But somewhere along the way, he'd moved in to his bedroom, and she'd moved in to hers.

fRANK MINYARD

ORLEANS PARISH CORONER'S OFFICE
March 1990

Everybody was misunderstanding him. That was the problem. And even Pete Fountain was fed up. His voice on the phone was fading from commiseration to petulance.

"What can I tell you, Frank?" he said. "We took a shot."

"You're sure they got the tape to the right person? You asked Doc?" Frank asked. Doc Severinsen knew Frank. They'd played together on the Endymion float. They'd had a lot of laughs. And Doc and Pete—they were genuine pals. Surely Pete explained it to Doc.

"For the hundredth time," Pete said. "It's not up to Doc. It's up to the producer, and the producer's call was no. Way he put it was, 'Pretty good for local TV.'"

"But that's my whole point!" Frank said. "I know I'm not good enough on the trumpet to be on the Carson show. For Christ's sake, Pete, I'm not that dumb. Like we talked about; I'd be funny! The big-city coroner. Dr. Jazz. If they let me play something, the fact that I'm so bad would be part of the joke. Johnny would have had a ball with it."

"It didn't fly, brother," Pete said tiredly. "Take it from me; that's showbiz."

Frank thanked him, said goodbye, and hung up. Damn. Pete and Al Hirt had really got him believing they might get him onto *The Tonight Show.* He'd have been terrific, too. Could have talked about his friendship with Jim Garrison, and being medical adviser to Oliver Stone's upcoming movie, *JFK.* Could have told the story of getting arrested for playing jazz in the French Quarter. Could have talked about his eighty-year-old mother playing honky-tonk piano at his annual Jazz Roots concert. In that context, his inept trumpet playing would have been funny.

THE SHOUTING in the reception area was getting louder. Frank walked over and opened the door. Gloria Boutté was crying. Two Orleans Parish sheriff's deputies stood beside her, red faced and agitated. "What's going on?"

"Earl Hauck's been shot."

"No!" Earl was Joe Maumus's pal, a hell of a guy—a New Orleans cop on his own with two adorable little girls. "How bad?" Frank asked.

"We don't know," one of the deputies said. "We heard it on the radio. And listen to this." He held out a police radio, pinned to his shoulder like a corsage. Angry voices competed. "Somebody kill him." "Somebody shoot that motherfucker."

"Jesus," Frank whispered. "They got the guy?"

"Apparently." They all bent to listen.

"They ought to start killing these assholes or we all going to die," a cop shouted. He sounded like he was crying.

"Hey," a cop hissed. "This is all being taped at headquarters."

"Fuck the tape!" someone shouted. "Where is he? I'll shoot him myself!"

"In the balls!"

"Execute the fucker!"

It was sickening. Frank had never heard anything like it. Louder and clearer, a voice Frank knew well said, "Listen, ah, we're pulling up to Charity with him, but I don't know." It was Joe Maumus—he had the suspect. That was Joe, always in the right place at the right time.

But, Jesus. Earl was Joe's best friend in the department.

"There's a pretty big crowd of cops here on the Charity ramp," Joe was saying. "I don't know it's safe to bring him in here." Frank shook his head in admiration. The bastard shoots Joe's best friend, and Joe's thinking about his safety.

"He hurt bad?" a cop said.

"Gunshot to the arm," Joe said.

There was a pause, filled with cries of "Kill him!" "Shoot him!" They'd tear the guy apart. Joe was thinking straight, to get him out of there.

"Joe," someone said. "Why don't you take him to First District until this quiets down." The First District police station was on North Rampart Street, a short drive from Charity.

The deputy holding the radio made a face. "Why aren't they taking him to another hospital?"

"I wish they'd say something about Earl," Frank said. "I want to go see him." Earl had more than twenty years on the force, and he had those terrific little children.

A voice broke through the shouting on the radio: "Earl's dead."

AT FIVE O'CLOCK the next morning, Frank's phone rang. It was James Brown.

"I'm bringing Adolph Archie in from Charity," James said.

"You mean Earl Hauck," Frank said sleepily.

"I got Hauck, too," Brown said. "But, no, I mean Adolph Archie, the guy that killed Hauck."

"He's dead, too?"

"That's right."

"All right," Frank said, swinging his feet to the floor. "I'll be right in." It would be a long day. Deaths in police custody were a headache.

Frank arrived at the office as the coroner's wagon was pulling in. James and the driver wheeled the draped bodies of Hauck and Archie into two separate examination rooms. Frank couldn't bear to look at Earl, but he followed James, who was pushing Archie.

James switched on the garish overhead light and heaved the body onto the stainless steel examination table. Frank pulled back a corner of the sheet. "Christ almighty."

The bruises, the swelling, the split skin—Archie had been beaten very badly. He dropped the corner of the sheet.

James nodded at him, expressionless.

"Let me know, as soon as you know."

"Mmhmm. McGarry's on his way." The pathologist.

Frank walked back upstairs and pushed open the door to his office. Joe sat in the visitor's chair, in uniform. Frank closed the door.

"You should see Earl's kids," Joe said.

"I can't even imagine," Frank said, giving Joe's shoulder a squeeze as he crossed to his desk. "I'll go over there this afternoon."

"Twenty-one years on the force," Joe said. "He had his gun in his holster. He was all by himself, trying to cuff Archie."

"Terrible," Frank said. They fell silent. Joe rubbed his hands on his thighs and looked out the window.

"Why'd you take Archie to First District?" Frank asked. "I mean, I heard the radio traffic, the mob at Charity. But why not University Hospital?"

"I don't know. First District was close, and we didn't think we'd have him there long, till they cleared Charity." Joe looked at his hands, then up at Frank. "Archie was fighting like a bastard. Maxie and I got him inside, which wasn't easy, and stuck him in a chair with his hands cuffed behind him. Next thing we know, he's stepped through the cuffs and he's going for Maxie's gun. Actually had his hands on it. We got to fighting him all over again. I had to hit him a bunch to get him to let go. He may have slipped and fallen a couple of times, too."

Frank nodded, thinking of Archie's face.

"Then the chief showed up, and we got Archie over to Charity. He was fucked-up, but he was okay. He was conscious. Wasn't till this morning I heard he'd died."

A CLUTCH OF REPORTERS gathered in Frank's office around closing time. They looked about sixteen years old, hollering questions all at once, like a cheering section at a high-school football game. The lights on their cameras were hot.

"Adolph Archie died from a basal skull fracture," Frank said. "That's what the pathologist, Dr. Paul McGarry, found."

"Police baton?" someone called.

"Gun butt?"

McGarry wouldn't say what did it, and neither would Frank. All he could say—all he had to say—was the cause of death: basal skull fracture. He said it over and over.

"And the man Archie killed," Frank called above the din, "a police officer with two little girls, died from four bullets fired at close range into his chest, because he was trying to take Archie alive. I don't know if that interests you."

The reporters kept braying for a guess about what had killed Archie.

"Adolph Archie murdered one police officer, shot at another, and

tried to shoot more, but his gun was out of bullets," Frank said. "He resisted arrest the entire time. Several officers had to subdue him. He continued fighting at the First District station. But he was alive when he
reached Charity Hospital, so it does not appear that he was 'beaten to
death,' as you say, at the police station."

"But if he was beaten badly at First District and died later at Charity,
wouldn't that constitute being beaten to death?"

"He could have slipped on the floor," Frank said.

Every head bobbed in unison, every pen flickered, and Frank knew
he'd blown it.

JOYCE MONTANA

WASHINGTON CORRECTIONAL INSTITUTE,
ANGIE, LOUISIANA
1991

Darryl walked into the visitation hall in white trousers and a white
pullover shirt. The older he got, the more he looked like Tootie, the same
high cheekbones, pointed chin, and caramel-colored skin. He smiled the
sweet, wise smile from his childhood, the smile that had disappeared during the years he was mixed up with them drugs. Joyce's heart grew full as
he crossed the hall. Rain beat hard on the tin roof with the sound of a
grinder. Joyce and Mutt-Mutt sat on hard plastic chairs, facing each
other, their knees almost touching. "I am sorry to make you come all
these ninety miles, Joyce," Darryl said quietly, looking at the floor. He
and the other children had always called her Joyce instead of Mama.

"You my son." Joyce longed to fold him into her arms, but the rules
were no touching.

"I'm Tootie's son, too," Darryl said.

"Oh, don't fret about that. He just been had enough of visiting the
jailhouse with Boobie." Boobie was back in Angola, this time for good.

Darryl looked at Joyce intently, drinking in her face, her glasses, her
whitening hair, as though to store them for the coming days of drought.
"You tell him I have a tribe of three hundred guys, singing Indian songs

every day in the fields," he said. "Even the guards on horses, with their shotguns, say, 'Montana, you going to sing today?' "

Joyce smiled. "You won't believe this. I have Tootie going to church." Darryl reared back in disbelief. Joyce nodded. "St. Augustine has a new priest from Lake Charles named Father LeDoux, and I'll tell you, he's something else. He meet you one time, he remember your name, just like that. He speak German, he speak Creole, he speak every language."

"St. Augustine is Sixth Ward," Darryl said.

"I guess so," Joyce said.

"But you go to Corpus Christi."

"I can go to St. Augustine, and Tootie likes it!"

"Tootie?" Darryl shook his head, the wise smile making Joyce giggle.

"He a Catholic just like me!" Joyce said. "He went to Holy Redeemer before Betsy tore it up. Lots of people from Holy Redeemer moved to St. Augustine."

"He go every Sunday?"

Joyce laughed. "No. He mostly go when there's a funeral. The way Father LeDoux does a funeral touch his heart."

Darryl took her hands in his. A guard blew a whistle and pointed with his nightstick, and Darryl recoiled in a way that made Joyce think he'd felt that nightstick before. He clasped his hands to his chest. "Before they sent me up here, Tootie told me, 'Boy, you need to get some feathers on,' and I wish I'd listened. I might not be here if I had. So you tell him, I'm changed. You tell him, when I get out, I want to be his son. I want to be his son for real."

BILLY GRACE

2525 ST. CHARLES AVENUE
December 19, 1991

Billy's study, on the second floor, was his favorite room anywhere. Its ceiling was high, the built-in bookshelves stuffed with volumes from his boyhood. On the walls hung heads of kudu, white-tailed deer, and a Cape buffalo, each redolent of fabulous hunting trips around the United

States and in Africa. Above the fireplace hung a yard-long tarpon that Billy's grandmother had landed in the 1930s, the long brass lure still in its mouth.

Billy sat in one of the two giant oxblood-leather chairs that dominated the center of the room, taking no joy, for once, in his surroundings. The images on the television were too awful. John Charbonnet, the owlish captain of Rex and one of the most decent men in New Orleans, sat at a table in front of a microphone under harsh lights that made him look a hundred years old. He hunched behind the mic in a defensive crouch, head pulled deep between the lapels of a fine suit, speaking in clipped, nervous monosyllables. Beside him, broad-backed Beau Bassich, co-chair of the mayor's Mardi Gras Advisory Committee, sat crumpled in on himself like a schoolboy being scolded. Billy's mentor and boss, Harry McCall, a legal giant and the fairest of men, was struggling for the right tone.

"The essential character of any voluntary organization is the privilege of its members to choose those with whom they will associate," McCall said.

Billy winced. White men had been defending segregation with the "freedom of association" line as long as he could remember.

"It is implicit in any organization that new members will be congenial with existing members," Harry said, and Billy groaned. In the run-up to the gubernatorial election, Harry had made a stink by urging the Chamber of Commerce to reject the reelection bid of the legendarily corrupt governor Edwin Edwards. The problem was, the other candidate was the Klansman David Duke. Harry wasn't the best person to be arguing against the forced integration of the Mardi Gras krewes to a majority-black city council.

The camera switched to council members, sitting at a raised dais. "What is before us is discrimination! Discrimination; that is what is before us," said Dorothy Mae Taylor, her eyes wide behind severe, square glasses. With her hair pulled back in a bun, she looked like the school librarian from hell. Taylor had picked up the baton from Joe Giarrusso, who'd first proposed an antidiscrimination ordinance three years earlier in order to get Italians into the krewes, and she was sprinting for the finish line. This whole hearing was a charade. The ordinance to refuse parade permits to Mardi Gras krewes that excluded blacks was sure to pass. She was roasting John, Beau, and Harry for the sheer pleasure of it. "You get upset by the word 'dis-crim-i-na-tion,' " she said, articulating every syllable. "Then stop discriminating."

Billy put his face in his hands. The world of the Mardi Gras krewes was full of genteel bigots, but these guys weren't. Rex wasn't Momus, Comus, or the Atlanteans. They'd had Jews at the Rex ball since George started bringing his friends back in the 1960s. Mayor Dutch Morial had always come. The current mayor—Sidney Barthelemy, another Creole—regularly put in appearances. "What krewes do you belong to?" Dorothy Mae asked Beau Bassich.

The camera switched back to John, Beau, and Harry, cowering behind their microphones like a trio of Watergate villains. The angles worked against them, shooting up at Dorothy Mae and imbuing her with grandeur, and down at the Rex officers, shrinking them to bugs under a microscope. "It's secret," Beau said with a mirthless laugh. "That's part of the tradition. It's part of the fun. We don't discuss what krewes we belong to. That's why the riders on the floats are masked."

"No," Billy whispered. This was no time to be justifying masks and hoods.

Beau finally relented, listing his krewes and throwing in a short primer on the selection of members. "There's no set system," he said. "A member proposes someone. If people know him and like him, he might be invited to join. The blackball system is to prevent people joining whom the members don't like, who don't have the right character profile. But membership isn't exclusive by design." Billy knew what he meant. It no more made sense to throw membership open than it did to invite strangers to a party at your house. But that line, "right character profile," was sure to come back and haunt the krewes.

It was all so unnecessary. Rex could have invited Norman Francis, the president of Xavier University, or Hank Braden, a well-known physician, years ago. The same names have been coming up for a decade. But it would have taken someone actually to put them up for membership. That would have meant putting other Rex members in the position of saying no and explaining why. There was always a reason to put off such an uncomfortable conversation, and the years had simply slipped past.

Councilman Jim Singleton took the microphone. "I think you gentlemen are here only to stonewall," he said.

Mike Smith, captain of the krewe Hermes, had already announced that if the choice was being forced to admit black members, his krewe wouldn't parade. The Louisiana Club had said it would no longer request a city permit to erect grandstands outside its house on Union Street, lest the city use the permit as a cudgel to force integration. Moreover, the Louisiana Club announced that its parading krewe, Momus, which had paraded annually since 1872, would not parade. Ditto Comus, founded in 1857. Mardi Gras was going to be a disaster.

BILLY EASED THE Mercedes out onto Third Street, turning left onto St. Charles and lowering the window. The air was cool on his face, and the avenue looked beautiful, the mansions and hotels decked out for Christmas. The opulence faded, though, by about Jackson Avenue. Solid Victorians gave way to vacant display windows, abandoned cars, and boutiques converted to discount stores. The rot was creeping uptown. He turned left on Poydras Street and cruised past the gleaming highrise, now half-empty, that had once housed Amoco. What's wrong with us? he thought. Are we proud of being backward and insular? When New Orleans was awash in oil money, it had refused to invest in the harbor, which was now being superseded by such pikers as Mobile. It had failed, when it had the chance, to correct a school system that produced students who could barely speak English or do sums. When northern companies fled unions and taxes for the Sunbelt, and cities like Memphis and Dallas were doing all they could to attract them, New Orleans turned a cold shoulder. No tax breaks, no city-built industrial parks, no incentives at all. Worse, Billy's face heated as he recalled the times he'd had to explain to newcomer executives that, no, you had to wait to be invited onto a Mardi Gras krewe. No, you can't just walk into the Boston Club. No, it's not simply a matter of fees.

Enough of that, he thought as he pulled in to the courthouse parking lot and switched off the engine: enterprise, imagination, and new friends will cure what ails you. Dutch Morial's oldest son, Marc, was starting his campaign for mayor, and he had said an interesting thing: if elected, he might privatize the collection of property taxes. One of New Orleans's most embarrassing open secrets was that residents owed millions and millions of dollars in unpaid taxes that the bureaucracy was too inept, underfunded, and listless to collect. Officials took payoffs and protected their friends. Even those found delinquent only paid an absurd 1 percent penalty; you could make money on the arbitrage, investing what you owed and paying the penalty out of the profits. The result: wretched schools and infrastructure.

Billy crossed the courthouse lobby and descended the narrow stairway to the tax records room. He was a tax attorney. He knew what he was looking for. He spent hours, that day and many days after, leafing with Talmudic reverence through big, dusty pages of property-tax records, making marks in a leather-backed notebook. He was trying to get a sense of how many millions in uncollected taxes were out there. If he could form a company to do the collecting, and the commission was high enough, it might be a tidy little side business.

"It's a little early to tell," he told his brother-in-law Westy, "but I'm guessing there's about seventy-five million dollars out there in unpaid taxes."

They agreed they'd never get all of it. The big taxpayers were protected by powerful friends; it was simply a fact of New Orleans life. Even so, Billy figured this sideline might make him twenty, twenty-five thousand dollars a year. He had three children to educate. Every little bit helped.

It wasn't just the money. Billy needed something to look forward to, something constructive and optimistic to wash away the taste of watching his city willfully decline, of watching his beloved Rex krewe pilloried for failing to do something it should have done years earlier. This tax-collection business might help the city move forward a little bit. Business, not that sorry racial business on television, was the future.

RONALD LEWIS

VIBRATIONS HAIR SALON,
CAFFIN AND GALVEZ STREETS
1992

Ronald Lewis sat back in one of Pete's plastic waiting chairs and folded his hands happily across his belly. Not only was Vibrations successful; it was important, a place where conversations took place and things got done. People came from all over New Orleans to have Pete do their hair. Uptowners crossed the canal. Crips and Bloods flew in from L.A. on al-

ternating weekends. Pete's shop was giving the neighborhood the respect it deserved. Ronald leaned over to reach himself another beer from
the cooler. His forty-one-year-old legs ached like old driftwood, but
that's what happened to a man who did a man's work.

Pete's handsome Cherokee face caught the pink late-afternoon light
from big picture windows. His long, delicate hands fluttered around
Edgar Jacobs's elegant graying hair, smoothing it in oiled waves down
the back of his neck. Pete's eyes were half-closed, and he kept up a
soothing, musical patter. "That was my heart, my grandmother, that was
my heart," he said mournfully. Pete had lost his grandma, and Ronald
knew how he felt. His own mom was gone three years. To this day, when
the shadows got long, Ronald would say to himself, time to go set on
Mom's porch. And every day he'd experience her loss anew, a poke in
the heart.

A brutish voice burst in. "Yo! I'm next, right?" Derrick Jenkins, a
husky, gold-toothed man in his twenties, sprawled in Pete's other barber
chair. Ronald had known him since he was in diapers. His mama lived
over by Egania Street, good people, but Derrick had gone his own way.
His posse, all younger boys, sat in a circle of Pete's plastic waiting chairs
with their knees touching, pulling wads of money from a pile of brown
paper bags and making neat stacks of currency. Ronald knew all of them,
all their mamas, too. It particularly pained him to see Michael, a little
red-skinned fella, sitting among them, talking trash with his cap on sideways. Michael wasn't more than about seventeen. He'd come up in the
Mount Carmel Church with Ronald's children. What Michael and the
others were doing was a pity and a shame, but there was no use in scold-
ing them. They got enough of that.

At least they'd stayed in the Nine. Other people's children went off
to college, which for years Ronald had interpreted as a positive thing.
Lately, though, he wasn't so sure. The children who went off to college
hardly ever came back. It was as though the hard work of getting that
college degree bent them out of shape, focused them too much on their
own personal achievement. Once you got that degree, it was all about
getting ahead in the monetized struggle, and they forgot the community that raised them. Ooh, live in the Lower Nine; not me. Ooh, do a
day's work with your hands; I won't touch that. The neighborhood
gained something when one of its children went off to become a doctor
or an engineer, but it lost something, too. Ronald was glad that every-

body in his clan still lived within fifteen blocks of one another. That's how they stayed strong.

Derrick stepped up into Pete's chair. "Put all the ones in that bag there, and we'll hand them out," he said to his posse. "I don't fuck with no ones."

The bell above the door tinkled, and the boys in Derrick's posse jumped to their feet. The sickening click-click of guns being cocked filled the room, and they all held big pistols. Even Pete held one—an elegant little one—sideways at the end of his long bronze arm, looking as stylish and cool as he did with a comb and shears; Ronald hadn't known he kept a gun up under his smock. A skinny young man stood in the doorway, eyes wide, holding a long bundle wrapped in a blanket. "Whoa!" he said. "Cool! Cool!"

"Who the fuck?" little Michael yelled.

"Got something for Derrick!" the kid yelled, holding out the bundle.

Derrick laughed, low and loose. "Put 'em down," he said, flapping a hand. "It's all right. Put 'em down. Go ahead." Pete's gun disappeared under his smock. Derrick's posse put theirs up under their sweatshirts, reluctantly, eye-fucking the kid with the blanket and rolling their shoulders. The kid stepped forward, put the bundle in Derrick's hands, and fled out the door. Ronald found he was breathing. Pete resumed clipping Derrick's ear hairs as though nothing had happened, murmuring of the old days.

Derrick's voice cut across Pete's. "That's what I'm talkin' about!" The blanket on his lap was thrown open, and on it lay the kind of gun Ronald had only seen in the movies. It was short and nasty looking, with a brown wooden stock. Derrick fitted a long, curved magazine into it. He held it up like a torch, turning it to catch the light.

"Damn," Pete said. "That shit's an AK-47. I seen them in Vietnam."

"Later, man," Derrick said in a dreamy air of bliss, rising to his feet. His posse rose with him. Derrick held the rifle down near his leg. In a tight little group, he and his posse squeezed through the door, looking nervously this way and that, and slithered on down Caffin Street. They had a lot to be looking out for, between the police and their rival gangs. Ronald couldn't imagine how it must be to feel unsafe on Caffin Street.

———

RONALD'S LEGS ACHED all the time, mostly around the knees. He'd been twenty-something years on the tracks, swinging those big hammers, leaning into the nipping bars. He loved the tracks, but they were wearing him out.

He spent a lot of time now at Vibrations. It was like their clubhouse, with Pete presiding at the center chair, his comb and scissors in his hands. Edgar Jacobs often stopped by. Ricky Gettridge from the Desire Project was often there, too, sewing on a piece of his Mardi Gras Indian suit. Ricky masked with the great Tootie Montana and tried to get Ronald to make a suit of his own. "You don't master the needle," Ricky told him when Ronald's big fingers were failing to make the needle dance, "the needle masters you." Ronald had tried it for a year or two before discovering that what he liked more than actually masking was all the folklore that surrounded it—the chanting and drumming, the stories of the old-timers masking back when.

One day Ricky was telling them about a practice of the Ninth Ward Hunters, one of the Lower Nine's tribes, over by the Ponderosa Ballroom. It had been off the chain, Ricky said. They'd drummed and chanted until all hours. "That reminds me," Pete said. He'd heard that Celestine, who owned the Ponderosa, was interested in hosting a second-line club. Ronald, Ricky, and Edgar went silent at the news.

"A second-line club?" Ronald asked. "In the Lower Nine?"

Second-liners saved all year for their annual parade. They spent a fortune on matching suits, shoes, and hats, hired brass bands, paid the police thousands of dollars for parading permits. Then they'd take to the streets with their bands, dancing across the city for hours with hundreds of people falling in behind. It was the quintessential New Orleans art form—a jazz funeral without the body—but the Lower Ninth Ward had never gone in for it. Second-lining was a city thing, and the people here cross the canal had always remained, at heart, country people.

Sure enough, the first thing Edgar Jacobs said was, "You know what people going to say about a club in the Lower Nine." All that zoot-suit flashiness, that wasn't the Lower Nine's way.

But maybe times had changed, Ronald thought. Maybe a second-line club was just what the neighborhood needed. It would bring a little pride back, bring a little life and hope to these streets. Right now, he thought, the only men who look like they're having any fun, the only ones wearing fine clothes and jewelry, are the drug dealers. And what kind of role model is that for children? Put a club of workingmen out there in colorful suits and five-hundred-dollar shoes. Take over the street, from banquette to banquette, and fill it up with a brass band or two. Make the police work for us for a change. Pete put the "Closed" sign on the door, and the men talked late into the evening. Parading permit cost this much, a band that much. No point in coming out at all if you couldn't put a three-hundred-dollar hat on your head. It would take sacrifice. The Ponderosa might host the coming-out, but who'd host stops along the way? Who'd host the party at the end? What's the role for the wives? They chewed it all over, the pros and the cons, before letting themselves address the really important question. "What do we call ourselves?"

JOYCE MONTANA

ST. AUGUSTINE CHURCH
1992

Joyce sat two-thirds of the way back on the left side of St. Augustine Church, smiling at the pink-and-white walls, the gold-leafed columns, and the little green banner above her head that read, in Swahili, *"Imani."* According to the corresponding green banner across the aisle, *imani* meant "faith."

She'd had faith—faith that Darryl would set himself right, faith that Tootie would soften toward him just a little. Tootie now sat to her left, a black-and-white-check porkpie hat on his lap. Darryl sat to her right, looking more like Tootie every day, his skin glowing healthy over those high Montana cheekbones. Joyce's heart was so full it kept overflowing. She dabbed at her eyes with a lilac-colored handkerchief. Darryl had his head back and his eyes closed, smiling like he'd been lost in the desert and it was starting to rain. She squeezed his hand; he opened his eyes and smiled down at her with a depth of joy and sadness that took her breath away.

Prison had changed Darryl. He moved slowly now, and spoke carefully, but most of all he appreciated everything and everybody around him. He looked up at Tootie, and nodded solemnly as the Mass began.

Father LeDoux, in a tie-dyed dashiki, spread his arms wide. "It is

New Year's Eve, what we Catholics call the Hour of Watching. Happy New Year to you all!"

"Happy New Year, Father!" In front of and behind Joyce sat lots of Sixth Ward friends—Cecilia Galle in her wheelchair; stately, stolid Sandra Gordon, the president of the parish council; and Marion Colbert, so refined and elegant, thirty years the powder-room attendant at Brennan's.

The band on the raised altar jumped to life, Carol Dolliole on piano, her sister Cynthia on saxophone, the mysterious Esquizito on guitar, and on trumpet a white man with white hair and a wide, handsome smile. "I especially want to thank our friend Dr. Frank Minyard, who does us the service of playing his trumpet here every New Year's Eve," Father LeDoux said. The congregation clapped, and Dr. Minyard raised his instrument with a grin. "This is the only place you want to see him, though," Father LeDoux went on. He cupped his hand around his mouth and stage-whispered, "Because he's the coroner." Laughter from the congregation, a rim shot from the drummer.

Dr. Minyard stepped forward. "I'd like to play for you the first piece my mother taught me."

"What's that?" Father LeDoux walked over to the altar and stood, smiling up at him.

" 'That Old Rugged Cross.' "

"Very good," Father LeDoux said, turning back to his pulpit. "While he does that, let us offer one another a sign of peace."

The congregation dissolved into its customary pre-Communion half hour of wandering the pews—hugging friends, shaking hands with strangers, and murmuring, "Peace be with you." Father LeDoux darted toward Joyce, Tootie, and Darryl, holding out both hands to Darryl. "I am so happy to have you with us!"

"He's going to get some feathers on," Tootie volunteered.

"That's right," Darryl said. "I'm trying to regain my way."

Darryl told Father LeDoux he was working at Great Expectations, a program for pregnant women hooked on drugs. Just this week, he'd been handing out flyers to get pregnant women to come in for help, when he ran into some of his old drug-dealing friends. "I went down there and talked to them and gave them flyers," Darryl said, "and they said if any pregnant bitch—'scuse me—came looking for crack, they wouldn't sell to her but would give her the flyer."

Father LeDoux threw back his head and laughed. "That's marvelous." He took Joyce's hands in his. "You must be very happy."

"Life is good, Father," she said, "you wouldn't believe how good."

ƒRANK MINYARD

ORLEANS PARISH CORONER'S OFFICE
1993

James Brown opened Frank's door a crack and pushed his face in, his beard braid leading. "Got something you should see," he said.

Frank followed him down the stairs to the dank basement and into an examination room. Edgar Smith stood waiting. A fully autopsied young man lay on the table, his chest cavity open and empty as the trunk of a car, the ribs and spinal column shockingly white under the harsh overhead light. The scalp was peeled down over the face. The top of the skull was missing. On a second table lay the brain and all of the kid's organs, lined up like choices in a cafeteria. James was orderly.

"Look here," James said, pointing with his rubber-gloved finger to a slit in the boy's side. "Entrance wound." He turned to the second table and pointed to a hole in the liver. "Went through there." He turned back to the hollowed-out cadaver. "Then it hit here." He pointed to a small gouge in the spinal column. "From there, it goes straight up." He touched the body under the chin. "Comes out of the lungs and goes back in here. I think it's up in the sinuses somewhere. Won't know till we get him x-rayed."

"Good God," Frank said.

"Then there's this bullet," James said, and described another tortured route, from the shoulder, through the chest cavity, and into the meat of one thigh. "And this one: ricocheted off this rib, here, and ended up in the bladder."

Edgar pointed to the bladder. "Now, a fourth bullet . . ."

"Wait a minute," Frank said. "How many times was he shot?"

"Near as we can tell, eleven."

"Eleven!"

"It's going to take us most of the night, because of the way these bullets tumble. Hit you here and come out here," he said, touching his shoulder and his kidney.

"It's the AK-47, man," Edgar whispered. "We knew those mother-fuckers in Nam. Tear you up."

"This is my fourth this week shot up with an AK," James said. "It ain't nine-millimeters anymore."

Edgar nodded. "This shit's a whole new thing."

RONALD LEWIS

THE PONDEROSA BALLROOM, NORTH ROBERTSON STREET

1993

Ronald was scurrying about the Ponderosa as fast as his aching legs would carry him, lining people up. Like everybody else in the parading club, he wore a black tailcoat and tuxedo trousers, a top hat, and black snakeskin shoes. He looked like a black version of the capitalist character from a Monopoly set. Out front, the Little Rascals were tuning up. In a moment, the Double Nine High Steppers Social Aid and Pleasure Club would break out the door and hit the streets for the first time.

A long black Cadillac limo, worn and dusty, pulled up in front—the Poo Cab. At the wheel sat Minnie's cousin Jessie Hill, his skin an un-healthy gray, his forehead sweating. Jessie's R&B song "Ooh Poo Pah Doo" had been a huge crossover hit in 1960, but Jessie never had really caught on again. He had debts, and liked the liquor. He was a sweet man and, as far as Ronald was concerned, a Lower Nine hero. Nowadays, he was trying to get by hiring out rides in the Cadillac limo he'd bought during his glory days. He called it the Poo Cab. It pained Ronald to see Jessie down. His decline seemed to mirror that of the neighborhood.

But his heart lifted when his big sister Dorothy stepped from the back, dressed like to meet the queen. "I think this may be the first Sun-day I ever missed church!" she hollered, thrusting out her arms to hug him. "You knew I couldn't resist a ride in no limo!"

Ronald kissed her and told her to wait right there. He signaled to the Little Rascals, then hustled back inside the door. The Little Rascals broke into "Do Whatcha Wanna," Ronald pushed open the Ponderosa's front door, and the Double Nine was on the streets. Ronald danced out first, swinging his hips and waving two enormous fans festooned with black-and-white ostrich plumes. His knees ached, but he pushed through the pain. Pete danced out right behind him, waving his own fans, and then came Edgar, Ricky, and the rest, bobbing and spinning and mugging for the crowd as the Little Rascals blared.

Oh, those plumbers and laborers and dishwashers in their thousand-dollar finery, Ronald thought as he whirled and danced on up to Claiborne Avenue with half the Lower Nine falling in behind. We don't need any guns up under our clothes to be somebody on the streets of New Orleans! Men! Using money we earned by working to light up these streets—celebrating our community no matter how whipped, underpaid, or neglected! This is a day when no policeman is going to demand you turn out your pockets, no gangbanger is going to stick a gun in your face and take your wallet, no ten-year-old boy is going to be told, "Here, run this up the street a ways and I'll give you five dollars." This is a day to remind the world that that man you usually look straight through—that sanitation man, that busboy, that gardener, that truck driver, that man you never see—that that man is a king! That that man is somebody!

FRANK MINYARD

718 BARRACKS STREET
October 30, 1994

The main part of Frank's house—the part whose salmon-colored stucco facade faced the street—was divided into two small apartments. Joe Maumus and his boy were still living in one of them. Frank had stuck by Joe all through the Adolph Archie mess because that's what friends do. He and Joe had too much history together for him to turn his back when Joe was in trouble. The second front apartment Frank had converted into a cozy club for entertaining. One wall had a great mirrored bar running along it. Another was made of broad, dark rough-wood planks pulled from a barge that had floated down the Mississippi in the

nineteenth century. There was plenty of comfortable seating and a terrific sound system. Photos of Frank's musician friends—Harold Dejan,
Al Hirt, Pete Fountain, Milton Batiste, and more—smiled down from
frames. Some legendary parties had taken place in this room, parties that
could have cost a dozen or more public officials their jobs had details
ever leaked out. Frank smiled at the memory of those parties as he sat
on his leather sofa, sipping a bullshot and waiting through the commer-
cials. Then a big ticking stopwatch appeared on the screen. Frank's big
moment of fame was at hand.

The talk of New Orleans for the past six months was that *60 Minutes*
was preparing a big story on the brutality, corruption, and ineptitude of
the New Orleans Police Department. That it was finally airing now
seemed a pity to Frank, since a new chief had just taken over two weeks
ago and the poor guy hadn't been given a chance. On the other hand,
some cops had just shot a woman dead on the street for having the
temerity to report police brutality, and the feds had uncovered a big cocaine ring operating right inside the department.

For months, Mike Wallace's people had called Frank, asking him to
be interviewed on camera about the Adolph Archie case, and for months
Frank had refused. The whole topic was painful. It was Charity that
messed up, he believed, by failing to notice on Archie's medical chart that
he was allergic to iodine. Charity had injected Archie with an iodine dye
before running him through a CAT scan, and Archie, seizing up, had
slammed the back of his head against a bed rail. That was the cause of
death. Frank was sure of it.

But he had to admit he'd made a mess of the whole thing by running his mouth early on. The *Times-Picayune* cartoonist had printed a
caricature of Frank standing over a shrouded body labeled "Truth" and
saying, "She accidentally slipped at the First District Police Station."
Then had come a lawsuit against the city, and a Justice Department in-
vestigation, and autopsy after autopsy. At the end of all that, who knew
what to think? Frank ultimately had stepped in the shit all over again by
ruling Archie's death "homicide by police intervention." Even his old
and dear buddy Charles Foti, the criminal sheriff, had called him up and
scolded him. "For Christ's sake, Frank," Foti had said. "Just do cause of
death; leave the blaming to the goddamn grand jury."

But despite all the rallies demanding Frank's head, he'd hung on as coroner. And no charges were ever pressed against Joe or any other cop. He and Joe had both kept their jobs.

Any other city, both Joe and I would have been canned, Frank thought as he waited for the show to start. I love New Orleans.

The *60 Minutes* people had been very persistent. Finally, Frank had thought of a way to get them off his back. He agreed to be interviewed on the condition that they let him play his trumpet on camera for a full minute. Through his intermediaries, Mike Wallace had agreed. Frank had rented the bar at the Fairmont Hotel for three hours, paid for an open bar, and had gotten a half-dozen members of his band together. Mike Wallace and his crew had shown up and kept their big camera trained on Frank the whole time. Frank had played a few numbers, everybody had some drinks—a great time. Frank had recently made some hilarious posters of himself, bedecked in a gleaming white suit and playing his trumpet on the Ninth Ward levee. "Dr. Jazz," they said. It was very vain, sure, but perfect for an occasion like the taping at the Fairmont. He'd presented a copy of the poster to Mike Wallace, who'd asked him to autograph it.

Then had come the interview, which took a lot longer than Frank had expected. It went on and on. Wallace didn't seem to know anything; his aides kept whispering questions in his ear. But the long interview meant Frank had been able to make his whole case, which felt good. At the end, he'd looked straight into the camera and said, "This is my palace of truth." It was a perfect conclusion. When people see that, they'll finally have to believe me, Frank thought as he watched the stopwatch ticking. And what a hoot to play trumpet on *60 Minutes*!

The segment started with an interview with Joe Orticke, who'd only been chief for a year and now was gone. Then came an NOPD cop talking from federal prison about the money he'd taken and the people he'd beaten up. Finally, Wallace got to the Archie case. Suddenly Frank was watching video of himself on national television. Wallace was saying: "Dr. Frank Minyard is New Orleans's coroner. At a news conference, Minyard said that Archie had fallen backward and hit his head on the floor after being punched by an officer and that, according to the coroner, caused Archie to go into a coma and die."

Well, it figures Wallace would home in on that, Frank thought.

"But the U.S. Department of Justice," Wallace went on, "suspecting a civil rights violation, sent their own pathologists to check the cause of death and they disputed the coroner's version."

Now the screen was full of Wallace as Frank remembered him, sitting in Frank's high-ceilinged office.

"He had massive skull injuries, broken facial bones," Wallace was saying. "His teeth had been knocked up into his head. He had a fractured rib. His larynx was crushed. His testicles had hemorrhaged."

Frank remembered this moment. Wallace had ambushed him with an autopsy Frank's own people hadn't conducted. It had been the very start of the interview, and Frank remembered stumbling along but recovering nicely later. We sat there for hours, Frank thought, and this is what they're using? His own face filled the screen, looking confused. "Now, hold on, hold on. What you're reading . . ."

Cut to Wallace, peering cruelly. "Yeah?"

Back to Frank. "Is the third autopsy."

"Right," Wallace said.

"My pathologist didn't find any of that," Frank said.

"And he didn't come across the skull injuries, the facial bones that were broken . . ."

"He came across the sk—— No, he came across . . ."

"The teeth knocked up into his head, the fractured rib, the crushed larynx, and the hemorrhaging testicles?" Wallace pressed. "He somehow missed that?"

"He didn't miss it," Frank heard himself saying. "He didn't miss it, because it wasn't there, is what I'm telling you. It was not there."

"Well," Wallace said, drawing out the syllable in exasperation. "Who did all this damage to the corpse?"

"I don't know," Frank's image on the television said, and the camera instantly cut away to Mary Howell, the incredibly persistent attorney that Archie's family had hired, saying that no cop had ever been arrested for killing Archie.

Frank felt himself go cold all over. The only thirty seconds he'd flubbed out of a two-hour interview were the thirty seconds they'd used.

It'll be okay, he told himself, when they get back to him and he makes eye contact with the audience delivering that "palace of truth" line into the camera. And his promised one minute of playing the trumpet will be a knockout.

The segment went on. Lots of Mary Howell, lots of the cop in prison, more Orticke, and good old Antoine Saacks, a couple of chiefs back until he got fired for corruption and retired as a millionaire, telling Mike Wallace he didn't take a vow of poverty when he became police chief. Oh, brother, Frank thought. Then Mike Wallace appeared on camera again. "Two weeks ago the mayor of New Orleans appointed a new chief, Richard Pennington of Washington, D.C.," Wallace said. "His mandate: to reform and rebuild the New Orleans Police Department." And then the stopwatch filled the screen again.

Frank's mouth fell open.

The show never returned to him. They didn't use his "palace of truth" line. And where was the one full minute of him playing the trumpet that they promised him?

Frank went straight to his desk and pulled out a piece of stationery. "You're not an honest person," he wrote to Mike Wallace. "I want my poster back."

WILBERT RAWLINS JR.

SARAH T. REED HIGH SCHOOL
1995

Wil pulled in to the parking lot of Sarah T. Reed High School, a cinderblock box at the far end of New Orleans East. When his eighth-grade shop teacher, Theodore Jackson, had called to say he'd become Reed's vice principal and needed a band director, Wil had driven right down from Baton Rouge. He was about to get his music education degree from Southern University and was ready to come home.

The entry hall looked like the reception room of a county jail—stark, unadorned, overseen by a fat police officer wearing a gun. Reed was the Orleans Parish School Board dumping ground—the last stop before a kid was expelled. Lord knew if they had uniforms, or even instruments. But that was fine with Wil. It's schools like Reed, he knew, that most need a good band. He wasn't afraid to work. Watching Da play a gig with two bloody stumps for fingers had set the bar. He was Wilbert Rawlins Jr. There was no job too hard for him.

The fat cop pointed Wil to the office, where Mr. Jackson stood amid a swirl of students and secretaries like a rock in a river. Wil's heart lifted. Mr. Jackson's thick beard was graying, but his suit was still as precisely creased as ever, his posture like an upright piano.

"We don't have bad children here," Mr. Jackson said as he ushered Wil into his office. "We have bad parents." Wil sank onto a stained gray couch. Mr. Jackson tilted back in his swivel chair, facing the door. "They want to be their children's friends because they're children themselves." He leaned forward, brown eyes intense in his big, square face. "I don't need anybody here who is going to like the children. I need someone who is going to love them." He leaned back, tapping the tip of a pencil on his desk. "So let me ask you something, Wil. What do you see as your work hours?"

Wil shrugged. "I figure I'll always be working, what with band practice, writing scores, and such."

Mr. Jackson nodded, and his beard cracked open in a smile. "That's the right answer. Teachers who say, 'Eight to three thirty,' I don't hire."

"Yes, sir."

"You married?"

"Yes, sir."

"What's her name?"

"Michelle." Wil smiled. "We call her Luscious."

"Children?"

"She has one, a little boy."

"This can be hard on wives, Wil. A lot of hours."

"That's okay. We're saving to buy us a house."

Mr. Jackson launched into a long, grim discourse on the state of New Orleans's schools. Desegregating the schools in the 1960s had one distinct downside: it did away with corporal punishment. No white parent would stand for a black teacher whipping his kid, and no black parent would stand for a white teacher whipping his—it would have been too stark a reminder of slave times. Teachers had become afraid to discipline, Mr. Jackson said, so the kids run riot. No teacher wants a disruptive or inattentive student back in his classroom, so they promote unqualified children to the next grade or have them expelled. The result, he said, was a whole generation of children graduating high school without being able to read, and the really troubled kids—the ones who need the most attention—wandering around the streets.

"You can see where this is taking us," he concluded.

"Yes, sir."

"Wil, let me tell you why we have an opening," Mr. Jackson said, lowering his voice. "This school had a band teacher last year. Nice man. Good musician. Led the band in the Mardi Gras parades. But something happened; we don't know what. A bunch of kids set on him and his wife with a baseball bat after a parade: band kids. Beat them so bad I don't know if he'll ever return to work. So we have an opening. We need a band teacher, and we're having trouble finding one. You hear what I'm telling you?"

JOHN GUIDOS

SOUTH RAMPART STREET
1995

The diabetes syringe was pencil thin. John stuck its needle through the rubber cap of the estrogen bottle, filled it, and twisted to reach his buttocks. He injected himself deftly and started to toss the syringe in the trash, but on second thought he plunged the needle into the estrogen bottle again and, his butt still stinging, injected himself a second time. Then he pulled up his jeans and closed them with a big death's-head belt buckle. He reached into the medicine chest for a bottle of Premarin. "Once daily," read the label, but what the fuck did that nellie doc know? John was in a hurry. He shook three tablets into his big palm, tossed them onto the back of his tongue, and swallowed them with a slug of Southern Comfort. He closed the medicine chest and looked in the mirror at a new man. Sort of. He had a ponytail, and a beard that gave him the look of a pirate, but leaning forward he could see the reflection of his growing breasts. He ran his hands over them, soft under his palms. His mother and grandmother had been big busted; maybe he'd get lucky.

A wave of nausea overtook him, and he leaned on the chipped sink. Whenever he pushed the hormones too far, his liver acted up. Sometimes it got so bad he had to lie low for a couple of days, backing off the pills and shots. But as long as the doc was willing to keep writing scrips, John was willing to chance getting sick. The doc's whole practice seemed to be people like John, chemically adjusting their sexual identities. He was a godsend, really. John was lucky to live in a place like New Orleans, with a French Quarter full of experimenters. As the queasiness spiraled through him, his eyes roamed over the peeling paint on the bathroom wall behind him. His warped and splintery old house here on South Rampart Street, the edge of the Quarter, was a million miles from the Green Street palace he'd shared with Kathy in Metairie. By a lot of standards, he'd come down in the world. His job didn't pay much and kept him on the road all week. But it was all worth it. Sharing his femininity on weekends was like being released from solitary confinement into the French Quarter's community of sexual sophisticates—people like the delicate, kindly, and elegant Donnie Jay, who was thoroughly male as Chef Don at Jaeger's House of Seafood on Conti by day and convincingly female in a lip-synching act at Travis's by night. Down at the Roundup, Gregory's, the Double Play, the Wild Side, John was finding that he was attractive to men. He was playful in the way of newcomers. The old-timers liked that. He was more of a social success than he'd ever been among football players and bowlers. The Knights of New Orleans, a leather club, had elected him vice president and insisted that he play Mrs. Claus at their holiday ball. He had Deaf Fuck, a boyfriend of sorts, with whom he could be a woman all the way and who, Lord knows, didn't gum up a nice evening with a lot of conversation. On weekends, John was starting to call himself JoAnn.

As the queasiness subsided, John took a sip of Southern Comfort and reached for the sports bra that pressed his breasts flat. Then came a work shirt, and over that a heavy black leather vest with breast pockets. Now his growing breasts were invisible. On his head he cocked a flat-topped, black-leather cap so that the visor shaded one eye. Now he was fully John, the barrel-chested, biker-leather type known to hospital administrators all over the South as the guy who maintained the MRI and CAT scan machines. He looked a little weird for the Baptists in Oxford, Shreveport, and Little Rock, but that was okay; they expected a little weirdness from New Orleans. He was competent and painstakingly respectful—lots of "sir's" and "ma'am's."

He grabbed his overnight bag, locked the front door, and climbed into the company truck for the long drive to Hot Springs, Arkansas. As he glided over the I-10 causeway toward I-55, he listened to a tape he'd ordered from the back of *Variations: How to Speak Like a Woman*. "Modulate," the voice on the tape told him. "Men speak in monotone. Women let their voices rise and fall." All across Mississippi, John practiced: "I'll have the *sea bass*, please!"

RONALD LEWIS

SANDPIPER LOUNGE,
LOUISIANA AVENUE
1995

Rebirth fell in behind the dancers, the trumpeter Derrick Shezbie pressing a hand to a ballooning cheek as though afraid it might pop. The Pigeontown Steppers bopped and twirled and shook with the music in their baby blue and yellow getups, making their way down Louisiana Avenue, the crowd parting for them and then falling in behind in the timeless manner of the second line.

"They're off the chain!" Pete yelled. From a man dragging a cooler the size of a coffin, Pete bought two icy Budweisers for two dollars and handed one to Ronald.

Ronald nodded and, raising his beer to his lips, noticed a young white woman following the parade with a pad in her hand. Second lines were never announced in the *Times-Picayune* or on the radio, so tourists almost never found them. Local white folks rarely had the nerve to climb out of their cars and join in. A few did show up occasionally—hippies with tattoos and piercings, or photographers weighed down with camera gear, like they were on safari, shooting the wildlife. This woman, though, wasn't either type. She was correct and proper, with glasses, short dark hair, and a trim, shin-length skirt. She'd watch the dancers for a minute, and write on her pad. She'd watch the crowd, or the band, or the police on horseback, and write some more. If she hadn't been so young and innocent looking, he might have figured her for a cop.

Nobody in the crowd spoke to her; even in the mid-1990s, there was no easy way to strike up a conversation with a white lady. But Ronald had grown up with Miss Duckie. He'd faced down Bob James and Hero Evans over the lunch-break table at NOPSI. He was proud of his ability to talk to white people; it's part of what set him apart from other men. He planted himself before the white lady and said, "How do you do?"

"I am just fine!" she said. She put out a hand to shake: big, bony, and strong.

"My name is Ronald W. Lewis."

"Helen Regis."

"I notice you are interested in the second line," Ronald said.

"I'm a doctoral student at Tulane. I'm writing a paper about it."

Rebirth passed; there was no talking with a brass band walking by in full blow. The towering horses clopped past, mouths foamy and smelling strong. The crowd advanced, carrying Pete with it. Ronald stood with Helen, grateful for a chance to rest his aching knees.

She launched into an explanation of what she was about that set Ronald's head to swimming—something about "contested urban space" and "the commodification of culture." Ronald settled back and took it in; he liked hearing white people talk. It was like learning another language. Then she said she was contrasting second lines with "minstrelsy," and Ronald perked up. He'd had enough of minstrel men.

"What you mean by that?" he asked.

"Minstrelsy being exaggerated blackness, cartoon blackness, for the entertainment of whites," she said. "The second line strikes me as the exact opposite."

She got it. Ronald put his big hand out again. "I think what you're saying is you want to know about our tradition," he said. "If so, I'm your man." He read her his phone number. "Give me a call and I'll tell you all I know about the culture. But listen: when you go over the top—when you get famous—don't forget me."

"Deal," she said.

WILBERT RAWLINS JR.

SARAH T. REED HIGH SCHOOL
1995

Wil paced the gridiron in his braided uniform, sizing up the opposition. They looked sharp: McDonogh 35, one of the best high-school bands in New Orleans. Their leader was the best. The little man in the plumed hat over there, he'd surely forgotten Wil. But there had been times at Southern when the work was so hard that the promise Wil had made to Herman Jones was all that had kept him going: I'm going to get that degree! I'm going to have a band that will blow your band out!

Wil turned to watch his bandsmen filing to their seats. They looked surly and detached, in stained, ill-fitting uniforms. Hard-luck kids, all of them—with dads and brothers in prison, moms on drugs. They were kids who went weeks without a hug. Many were hungry and sleep deprived, on the verge of flunking out. That they showed up for band at all was a miracle.

Their horns, too, were dented rejects. If it weren't for Da, coming by after work with his drumstick bag full of wire and tape, half the kids wouldn't have instruments at all. Da could nigger-rig anything. He sat now in the stands behind the band, straight as a board, hands planted on thighs, chin raised in expectation. Wil waved, and he nodded. Da had never missed a performance of Wil's—not in junior high or high school, not even when it meant driving to Baton Rouge to watch the Southern band, the Human Jukebox, perform. Whenever Wil took a stage or a field, Da was there to clap.

A blare of horns spun Wil around. Mr. Jones had him a big old band—maybe seventy-five kids. He stood on a step stool, one hand jerking up and down, the other rising slowly from hip level. His mellophones were playing on the C and the baritones on the G, just like twelve years ago. He was building the mood. His band sounded good.

"Listen up," Wil shouted. "Soon as they finish up over there, we start playing "Love Don't Live Here," "Do Whatcha Wanna," and "Listen to Me," back-to-back, just like in band room. Got that?" They stared at him sullenly. Most had never held a horn before the start of the school year. Teaching kids to play horn, though, was the easy part. Teaching them to arrive on time, to practice, to join something bigger than they were—that was the challenge.

Mr. Jones's right arm slashed down, ending a great tune, "Purple Carnival," with a blast. The McDonogh stands erupted in cheering. Wil raised his arms, ran his eyes over each child's face, counted off, jerked his arms, and was practically knocked backward.

Sound boomed out of the Reed band in waves he could feel against his tunic. The kids weren't only blowing with their mouths, they were bobbing back and forth, pushing the music through their horns with their whole bodies. And tight! Every rest was crisp, every beat precise. Some of them had their eyes closed. All of them were lost, utterly lost, in the music.

They slid sharply from "Love Don't Live Here" to "Do Whatcha Wanna" to "Listen to Me" and finished with an explosion of sound. The stands went wild. People jumped to their feet, waving their arms. The kids wiped sweat from their faces and gave each other weary high fives. Proud smiles dawned across their faces. Da clapped, laughing. Wil raised both fists.

He pivoted like a soldier on a parade ground and walked onto the gridiron. He hadn't seen Mr. Jones in a decade, but the man loping toward him in a tall, cylindrical hat had hardly aged. His eyes shone. "Your band is awesome," he said, grasping Wil on the upper arms, slamming him on the back. He leaned in close. "You blew my band out, just like you said in eighth grade!" He reared back, laughing, holding on to Wil.

Wil's throat constricted and his eyes sprang wet. "You remember that?"

"I never forgot." Mr. Jones's eyes streamed tears. "I've been looking forward to this day as much as you have."

BELINDA JENKINS

THE DREAMERS BAR
1996

Belinda took a sip of her drink, made a face, and yelled over the thumping music, "What?"

"He's cute!" Robin leaned across the table.

Belinda shrugged and glanced at the man at the bar, who was looking their way. Her cousin Stevie was trying to keep Belinda from slipping back into her bookish solitude now that she no longer had a husband. He was constantly urging his wife, Robin, to take Belinda out and fix her up. It was a nuisance for Belinda. Between work, school, and the girls, she didn't have much free time, or much energy. And the last thing she wanted, really, was another man. But she loved Robin, and Robin said thirty was too young to retire from the scene. If God had wanted her to be a nun, he would have birthed her into a Creole family from across the canal.

"We been through this," Belinda shouted. "Every guy you find is either married or has a girlfriend."

"How do you know?"

"When they give you a phone number and it's one of those cell phones, you know. You find me a guy that gives me his home number, I'll listen."

Belinda glanced at the man by the bar. He raised his glass and smiled at her. Robin nudged her.

Belinda looked up at the man and smiled. He slinked over and held out his hand.

"They call me Snooker," he purred. This, Belinda thought as she rose to dance, is so silly.

JOYCE MONTANA

VILLERE STREET
1997

The sun was sinking over St. Bernard Avenue, casting a salmon-colored light across the small, raised houses of North Villere Street and the crowd in front of number 1633. "When Tootie Montana started masking fifty years ago, the Indians was killing each other!" Fred Johnson cried in a high, clear voice. "Tootie taught us a new way to battle: with pretty. He said to the world, 'I'm going to bust your ass with this suit!' " The crowd laughed and applauded. "But pretty is about more than a masterful piece. It's about escaping the sense that's been bred into us that we're ugly niggers." Fred was light skinned and sturdy, with a way of talking about tradition that raised bumps on Joyce's arms. He was one of the best of the young men coming up, not only spy boy for Tootie's tribe, the Yellow Pocahontas, but also a founder of the Black Men of Labor Social Aid and Pleasure Club.

Tootie sat next to Fred on a straight-backed dining room chair, still in the pants, moccasins, and braids of his white suit, but without the enormous apron and crown in which he'd walked ten miles. Tootie's suit had been perhaps his most beautiful ever, but at seventy-five years old, walking all the way to Washington and La Salle and back had taken it out of him. A banner hung from the porch roof, declaring this to be Tootie's fiftieth year masking. "Appreciate this man! What Tootie Montana did was a labor of love!" Fred cried. "There have always been two carnivals in New Orleans; white people have theirs up on St. Charles Avenue, and they forced black people to have our own! But when that crown got lowered onto Tootie Montana's head here on Villere Street, Rex wasn't even part of the conversation!"

Joyce spotted Bertrand Butler, an old friend from uptown who was following Tootie's lead in reducing the traditional hostility between uptown and downtown tribes with something called the New Orleans Mardi Gras Indian Council. Bertrand, a small-boned man with a neatly trimmed white beard, ear stud, and hajji cap, had worked for the Housing Authority for thirty-something years and been married to the same woman for about as long. Joyce was glad to see him here; it was another sign of peace.

Drumming and chanting swelled from the direction of St. Bernard Avenue, and people turned, squinting. Here came Darryl in a huge white suit with half a dozen friends behind him, banging their tambourines. Darryl had done something nobody had ever seen; he'd built his suit around a theme—King Tut. A gold-and-blue head of the Egyptian boy-king rose from Darryl's crown, another from the long-plumed staff he carried, and little King Tuts repeated in the beadwork all over his crown, down the front of his apron, and on his shins. Mouths had dropped open all day as Darryl passed. He'd taken Tootie's craftsmanship to a whole new level.

Fred Johnson stretched out an arm. "Here comes the new chief of the Yellow Pocahontas! Tootie Montana is handing it off to a new generation, to his son! Appreciate this man!"

Darryl came through the crowd, smiling tiredly, letting friends inspect the tiny beadwork Tuts. His chanters helped him out of the crown and heavy apron; Joyce came down and handed him a bottle of water. He walked tiredly up the stoop and squatted next to Tootie, who looked at him sideways. "I had a lot of other people in line to be chief over you."

"I know that." Darryl nodded.

"I took a chance of people getting angry with me."

"I appreciate that." Darryl took a sip of water but kept his eyes on Tootie.

"They're not my son."

"I know."

After a while, Tootie stood stiffly and walked inside, the glass storm door banging shut behind him.

Joyce touched Darryl's hand. "He loves you."

"He loves me as a son," Darryl said, "but as an Indian, I don't know."

"Your suit was beautiful; everybody says that."

"Thank you." Darryl smiled his wise, sad smile. "But it doesn't matter what they all say. I've never heard Daddy say, 'You're pretty.' "

"He made you chief."

"He didn't say I was pretty." Joyce shook her head and frowned. We can't quite get over, she thought. That Tootie made Darryl chief of the Yellow Pocahontas made her heart full, but they couldn't quite get over. She found Tootie hunched over a glass of garlic water in the darkening kitchen.

"Why don't you tell Darryl how pretty his suit look?" she asked.

"That King Tut suit come out of a book," Tootie said, driving a knobby forefinger into the tabletop. "It come out of someone else's head. He didn't draw that book, so I can't give him no credit."

ANTHONY WELLS

My brother Roger, he's a hustler. Had him a house on Dell Street, in the Goose. Guy come to the house, want some girl, want some drugs, Roger, he know where the drugs is, where the girl is, so the dude give Roger the money to go get it, then he smoke it up, do it up, at Roger's house. Roger would provide that service. Roger, man, he's smart. He's like a giant squid with eight tentacles.

Crazy-looking dude, too, Roger. One time a roof jack jumped back on him and knocked out his four front teeth. They give him new ones, but then he put a piece of pizza in a microwave and got it real hot. He took one bite and them four teeth came right out. After that he said, "Fuck it," and let them be.

Tell you what happened one time, though. Roger got it going on in his house with the girls. Came a knock on the door, Roger opens, and this dude Peanut shoots him, BAM, BAM, BAM, with a .38. Roger's in the hospital and he's like, "Why the fuck he do that?" Little dude Peanut came right there to the hospital and apologized. Said he was trying to get someone else. Roger let it go, but I'll tell you, man, if he hadn't apologized, Roger would have apologized for him. You feel me?

One Valentine's Day we were at my cousin Mae's having us a card party. Lights go off, and these guys come in shooting. Seventh Ward dudes; got hoods and masks on. Two guys died—Edward and Butch, Mae's boyfriend. I got hit twice in the upper right chest. Twice in the back. Here, man. Look.

Didn't want to go to Charity, because that's where the police look for you. A lot of people get killed in Charity. I went to Methodist on Read Boulevard. My uncle come in and say, "The paper said you can identify the perpetrators." Well, that's a death sentence. I snatch the IVs out my arm and I'm gone. Got me a .38, and I'm hanging on my porch, cousin Jerry changing the bandage on my back, putting gauze in there. Sunday or Monday, I'm walking down the street, the police see me, and I can't move fast enough 'cause I'm all fucked-up. They got me with the gun in my pocket. Some guy had been shot with it. I shoulda knowed better, but I'd rather get caught with it than without it.

Charge was aggravated battery and possession with intent to distribute, and they sent me to Angola. Nothing but killers in there, man. Nothing but alligators and sharks. Dude say, "I got your back," he wants something. Don't ask nothing from nobody. Don't do nothing for nobody. That's how you get by. I was planting fucking carrots for seventeen cents an hour. That deals up to about thirty dollars a month. Got a little store there. If you got money on the books, they look it up. Coffee, sugar. Bugler is low, so you're better rolling your own. Potato chips are twenty-five cents a bag. You can get a box of Little Debbies. Honey buns. Mayonnaise, mustard, squeeze cheese. Envelopes. Got to be careful, though. If you go to the doctor and you got money on the books, they take it out your money. You're supposed to get twenty dollars at Christmas, and if you owe money at Christmas, you don't get shit.

What you don't want to be doing is eye-fucking the guards. It'll be like, "What's wrong with your face, boy? What's wrong with your eyes?" They'll put you in the Hole for looking—for thinking—like you might kill him. You got to be all, "I'm just waiting to get started on my day, sir!"

The Hole is a little tiny cell, like a damn closet. No TV, no reading materials except the Bible, no smokes, no candy. After breakfast chow, you got to throw your mattress out; the only time you get it back is when they cut the lights off at night.

No shoes—they give you fucking thongs. And a black-and-white jumpsuit, like a zebra. It's hot—no fans, no air-conditioning. What it is? It's like Cool Hand Luke. "I got my mind right, boss!" It's like an invisible whip; you can't see it but you feel it.

WILBERT RAWLINS JR.

BATON ROUGE
1998

Theodore Jackson exited Interstate 10 and wended his pickup through the unfamiliar streets of Baton Rouge. His gray beard was neatly trimmed. He wore a pink shirt, a blue diagonally striped tie, and a pin-striped suit with wide lapels that emphasized his rock-solid shoulders. Wil had never seen Mr. Jackson dressed so fine.

Mr. Jackson had just saved his career. Wil had put the pine across the ass of one of his band kids at Reed, and the girl's parents had tried to get him fired. Wil still couldn't believe it. Everybody knew a certain kind of child needed a lick or two with the board to restore focus. Wil had never been cruel about it. The kids themselves didn't mind. A couple of good licks was quicker, kinder, and more effective than suspension or putting a child out of band. All that did was leave an already troubled soul with even less supervision. Lots of parents had called Wil to thank him for whipping their child. Some had called to beg him to do it, especially the single moms intimidated by their teenage sons.

Officially, striking a child was against the rules, and this one parent had screamed to the school board. Mr. Jackson had stepped in with an artful compromise: Wil would leave Reed at Christmas break to finish his certification. During that semester Wil was off—studying for the test and working at Home Depot—Mr. Jackson was appointed principal at George Washington Carver, a combined junior and senior high at the edge of the Desire Project. Come the fall, Wil had been one of his first hires.

Carver, if anything, was rougher than Reed. Most of the Reed kids had had at least one sane parent. Carver kids, most of them growing up in the Desire, were right out of *Lord of the Flies*. If they had parents at all, the mothers might be turning five-dollar tricks on the living room sofa, the fathers selling off the family TVs, PlayStations, and microwaves to buy drugs. The Carver kids couldn't play in the project courtyard, because that's where the knuckleheads peddled their crack. They didn't have a quiet place to sleep, much less study. Most of the kids were messed up with that welfare mentality, that bullshit about the world owing them a living and the white man standing on their necks. On Wil's first day, maybe seven kids had shown up for band—listless, bored, and sulky. Da had come in with his drumstick bag full of wire and tape, and they'd cobbled up the usual cast-off instruments. As for uniforms, it was khaki pants and T-shirts; Carver's colors were green and orange, but it was a long way from being able to field a band in uniform. He didn't have but a dozen bandsmen now.

Most of his kids seemed to have been born with crack in their blood and couldn't calm down enough to pay attention. Wil often had to stop practice and take them outside for a touch-football game to let them blow off energy and regain concentration. And always, the pine. The board of education. Indispensable, and Mr. Jackson quietly supported him. Most days he never had to touch it. During an unruly practice he'd send a kid to the office to "get that wood," lay it across his knees, and ignore it—usually, that's all it took to bring the band into focus. But occasionally, he'd send a kid to his office to grab the top of the desk, and he'd close the door. Never in anger. Never as revenge. Pain was like Ritalin. A measured dose could bring a child back to himself. A child was happier focused.

Many days, Wil had had Da around school during practice, endlessly rummaging through his magic drumstick bag for whatever a kid needed to fix an instrument. Lately, though, Da hadn't been coming around, and Wil had just found out why. He'd gone to have dinner with his parents on Dwyer Road, and without any preamble Da had sat him and Lawrence down at the kitchen table and said, "I got something to tell y'all. I got cancer, and there's nothing they can do for me." Da wasn't one to say something in thirty minutes that he could say in one.

Mr. Jackson turned in to an alley and parked behind a sooty warehouse. A small sign beside the door read, "Louisiana Schoolbook Depository."

"This will be a relief," he said. "I've been embarrassed—really, embarrassed, to hand out the books we got at Carver. They're not just tore up; they're egregiously outdated." He frowned, his square face bunching. "What's the use of a civics book from the 1950s?"

"I'm impressed you got this done," Wil said as they walked inside. Mr. Jackson had been fighting the school board for months to get funds for new textbooks.

"We're a poor school." Mr. Jackson stopped and straightened his tie.

A young, pretty clerk sat at a window. "I have your order right here," she said, pulling out some yellow papers. "It's for the middle school and the high school, is that right?"

"That's right." They ran down the list: new science, math, social studies, and English textbooks for everybody.

"You brought the check?" she asked.

"Right here," Mr. Jackson said, opening his briefcase and taking out a checkbook the size of a photo album. He bent to write the check. "Eighty. Three. Thousand," he said, fluidly filling in the number. He signed it with a flourish. She clipped the check to a sheaf of yellow papers and lifted the phone.

It took Wil, Mr. Jackson, and a couple of workmen from the warehouse an hour to fill the pickup bed with cartons of new textbooks. Wil tarped and tied it carefully.

Mr. Jackson was unusually quiet as they made their way back to the interstate. He didn't talk at all until they had crossed the causeway through the swamps west of New Orleans, passed the airport, skirted the flossy commercial section of Metairie, and entered Orleans Parish.

"Well, Wilbert," he said. "I hope you're ready to go to prison."

"I beg your pardon?"

"Jail! Prison! Fraud!" Mr. Jackson sang. He looked over at Wil with a wide smile. "I don't think there's more than about three hundred dollars in the Carver account."

"You wrote a bogus check?"

"I couldn't do it anymore." Mr. Jackson squeezed the wheel, and his smile faded. "I couldn't face the kids another day with those raggedy-ass books."

BELINDA SMALLS

UNIVERSITY OF NEW ORLEANS
1998

Belinda touched the tender spot on her cheekbone. The other women in
the office never said anything about her bruises. Maybe they couldn't
recognize discoloration on dark skin, or maybe they figured it was normal in Belinda's world. But men on Egania Street didn't hit their
women. Dad may have run out, but he'd never struck Mom, and Lionus
would never have raised a hand.

She wondered, for the thousandth time, why she'd let herself get
mixed up with Snooker. She'd been doing fine on her own, Lionus paying his share and seeing the girls every few days. Belinda had been working, taking care of her girls, living a quiet life with her books. Snooker
didn't do a thing for her but drink her pay and beat her up—and give
her one more child, a baby boy named Curtis.

She had to get Snooker out of her life before he killed her.

That white-picket-fence life seemed to move further away the
closer she tried to get to it. Even getting a bachelor's degree at SUNO
hadn't changed her life. The best job she could find was here in the per-
sonnel department at the University of New Orleans—the white coun-
terpart to SUNO. And as she watched the others in the office, she
realized she'd made a terrible mistake. SUNO degrees weren't respected.
Of course not; SUNO was a black college. The other clerks in the office would look at a résumé, notice that the applicant had graduated
from SUNO, and put the application in the wastebasket. The end of the
twentieth century, Belinda thought, and not only are there still white
and black colleges, but the black colleges aren't respected.

Her older daughter, Lionesha—whom everybody called Niecy—
was fourteen now. Latisha—Mookey—was ten. It was time to start being
a better role model, Belinda thought.

One afternoon she heard two of the women talking about a class
they were taking. It turned out anybody working for the University of
New Orleans could take classes for free. Belinda rolled the thought
around in her head for a few days before coming to her decision: she was
going to start college all over again. It hadn't been enough to claw her

way through to vocational schools and an accredited four-year college. If she really wanted to get ahead—if she really wanted that white-picket-fence life outside the Lower Ninth Ward—she was going to need a white lady's education.

That fall, while caring for three children, working full-time, and divorcing her husband, Belinda started in on her second bachelor's degree.

TIM BRUNEAU

FORT POLK, LOUISIANA
1998

Tim Bruneau screeched his jeep to a halt, stepped out, and cocked his fists on his hips. He wore mirrored sunglasses and a white helmet. An automatic pistol and a nightstick gleamed from the white web belt encircling his waist, and a black armband emblazoned "MP" wrapped his upper arm. His jump boots were polished to a high shiny black. In the shower, Tim Bruneau was a pale, skinny twenty-three-year-old E-4, but on the parade ground he was the Man.

A captain stood with his back to him, addressing a company of soldiers. Tim walked up and shouted over the captain the name of an unlucky private.

The captain wheeled. "What the hell are you doing?"

"Sir!" Tim said, thrusting an out-turned palm. "Do not confuse your rank with my authority!" Tim kept his eyes on the soldiers. A soldier in the back broke ranks and walked forward sheepishly. Tim turned to the captain. "Dirty urine, sir," he said. "This soldier will be coming with me." The captain rolled his eyes.

Tim cuffed the private, helped him into a jeep, and ignored his wheedling protests all the way to the stockade.

All Tim had ever wanted, from the time he was eight years old in Boerne, Texas, was to be a cop. Until then, his mother had been the most powerful authority in his universe. Even Tim's stepdad, a kindly soft-spoken fellow named Gary, hadn't wielded the imperial command of the great and powerful Mom. Then one day a Texas state trooper pulled Mom over as they were driving up Highway 46. She'd started to argue;

nobody kept her from getting home after work and getting out her shoes. The trooper, who to Tim looked like a statue of himself—tall, broad, and impeccably creased—reduced Mom to sniveling jelly. Without once raising his voice, he lectured her about the 140 children killed in car accidents the year before. He talked about the law, about the need to model upright behavior to young ones. He went on and on, and by the time he was finished, Mom was practically thanking him for the ticket. Tim was agog. From that day on, he always knew what to say when grown-ups asked him what he wanted to be when he grew up.

The military police was an imperfect career. The Army was too orderly a society to foster enough screwups to make police work fun. What he really wanted was to kick some ass. After a boring stint in Panama, Tim had requested transfer to Fort Hood, Texas, the bleakest, dustiest, most miserable post in the Army—which made it the post with the most drug dealing, domestic abuse, interunit brawling, and general mayhem. The Army, though, in its wisdom, had sent him here to Fort Polk, Louisiana. Inspecting urine samples was not Tim's idea of police work.

The closest big city to Fort Polk was New Orleans, which Tim enjoyed visiting on furlough. It was hot, sexy, and noisy, like Panama. And its police force was interesting. Tim had watched a fight on Bourbon Street one night—a couple of tattooed toughs whaling on each other with garbage-can lids. Tim had asked a cop leaning on a nearby lamppost to do something.

"Soon as they're done," the cop had said. And sure enough, when the two toughs lay exhausted on the ground, the cop had sauntered up to clap them in cuffs. Tim still couldn't decide if the cop had been lazy or smart.

The newspapers lately were full of police news from New Orleans, because the city's new chief of police was really shaking things up. NOPD cops were notorious for taking money, dealing drugs, and selling stolen property. A cop named Antoinette Frank had shot a fellow cop dead a while back, along with two civilians, while robbing a restaurant. Another cop, named Len Davis, had run a multimillion-dollar cocaine ring and murdered a woman because she'd had the nerve to report him for brutality. The place was out of control.

But now the NOPD had a new chief, Richard Pennington, who had locked up a couple dozen cops, fired many more, disbanded the corrupt Internal Affairs office, and banned cops working private security details at bars. Pennington carried a gun, because he was afraid a cop might take a pop at him.

In a few months, Tim would have to decide whether to reenlist. Increasingly, he found himself thinking about how much fun it would be to get in on the ground floor of Pennington's reforms. Having fired so many officers, Pennington was hungry for new ones. Every day, Tim saw Pennington's recruiting ad in the *Times-Picayune*: 1-800-NOPD-YES.

BILLY GRACE

AUDUBON PARK
1999

It was a warm, fragrant summer evening, and as he crossed Exposition Boulevard into Audubon Park with John Charbonnet, Billy felt his spirits rise. Joggers and bicyclists meandered along the broad path that ran in a great misshapen oval the length of the park. Men and women in bright pastels played golf in the slanting afternoon light. Billy and John had to decide on eight maids and eight dukes for debut season, and plenty of twelve-year-old pages for the ball. He loved imagining the men of New Orleans, walking these same oak-lined paths and making these same choices for more than a century.

Billy was captain of the Rex krewe now. No lawyer had ever been chosen as captain, and Billy understood why. It was a huge job; Billy figured it would consume at least five hundred otherwise-billable hours this year. He had lieutenants, sure. One was in charge of the parade; one planned the ball; one wrote the proclamation; another designed and ordered the invitations; there was the cast dinner, the meet-the-king party, and the luncheons to plan; somebody had to run the Rex den, where the floats were stored and the costumes made. In all, Billy had some thirty-five men ringing his cell phone at all hours of the day and night.

"You did a good thing, getting Proteus back," John said. Proteus hadn't paraded for the seven years since Dorothy Mae Taylor's antidiscrimination ordinance had taken effect. Dutch Morial's son Marc was mayor now, and Billy—who had stuck out his neck and held parties at

2525 to raise money for his campaign—was co-chair of his Mardi Gras Advisory Committee. Billy had contrived to bring Morial and the Proteus captain together at a king-cake celebration. Marc, tall and fair skinned, with all of his father's intensity, had graciously called the Proteus parade Mardi Gras's most beautiful. It was all the krewe had needed; they'd signed the antidiscrimination clause and were back in their den working on floats with the energy of the redeemed.

"You and Morial work well together," John said, and Billy glanced over at him. It was an innocuous comment, but Billy's support for Morial—second in the dynasty that had broken white power at city hall—had been a minor scandal in certain uptown circles.

"I like Marc," Billy said, though it didn't begin to sum up the relationship. After helping Marc get elected, he'd been talked into serving on the Sewerage and Water Board, a legendarily cronyism-plagued agency. He hated hearing people argue, with no apparent shame, that black firms ought to get 10 percent of all contracts right off the top, simply because they were entitled. It wasn't businesslike. It lacked elegance. More than once, Billy had had to bite his tongue; he couldn't fight them every time. A certain amount of cronyism came with the office of New Orleans mayor. It had been that way with white mayors, so nobody should expect it to be different now.

"I must say, it seems like you're doing very well in your tax-collection business without doing much work."

Billy stopped. "What?"

John shrugged. "I'm just saying."

Billy was speechless. He was proud of the work he and Westy were doing to collect unpaid city taxes. They had teamed up with a big Texas law firm called Linebarger that had the equipment and experience to process into useful data the reels of computer tape moldering in the courthouse basement. "We won the contract in open bidding, John," Billy said.

"I know that. But thirty percent?"

The city council had imposed a 30 percent penalty on unpaid taxes and allowed Billy's partnership to keep it as their commission. Sure, it was a lot of money. Sure, it sometimes took nothing more than writing a strong letter to get the city paid. That was the nature of contingency work.

"We only get paid on what we collect," Billy said. "If we weren't do-ing it, the taxes would go unpaid."

"True," John said.

"We're making the city money." Billy was doing all right himself; far from the twenty-five thousand a year he'd predicted, he and his partners had already made six million dollars.

"I'm sorry I brought it up," John said.

Shit, Billy thought. This was not a good sign. If John—his pal—was thinking this way, what was the rest of uptown thinking?

WILBERT RAWLINS JR.

WHITNEY BANK, READ BOULEVARD
1999

Wil paced the lobby of the Read Boulevard branch of Whitney Bank in New Orleans East, waiting for Luscious to show up. The great day had arrived; finally he was going to own a home. He and Luscious would be moving out of Ma and Da's place on Dwyer Road, which was a little worrisome since Da's diagnosis. Ma, though, said they could use the pri-vacy, and Da could not have been prouder. He'd watched Wil save for four long years, to achieve what he himself never had.

They had to be at the realtor's for two o'clock with a cashier's check. Luscious was supposed to have gotten the check a week ago, but every day it was the same thing: my nails appointment went too long; I had to stay late at work; I forgot. Now they were down to the wire, picking up the check on their way to the closing.

Luscious came clicking across the bank lobby in yellow high heels, her cheeks flushed. Wil still could not believe he'd talked such a beauti-ful woman into marrying him. That day in the Southern cafeteria, he'd tapped his band brother Squaly on the shoulder and said, "See that woman? She's going to be my wife." Now she presented a smooth, per-fumed cheek for him to kiss, but didn't make eye contact.

He took her arm and led her to the teller's window. "We'd like a cashier's check," he said. He pushed the withdrawal slip across the counter to the young woman on the other side. "Fourteen thousand dollars," he said. "Going to put a down payment on our first house!"

"Congratulations," the woman said. She tapped at a keyboard. "Sir?" she said.

"Yes?"

"I don't show you having that much money in your account."

"You're wrong about that," Wil said. "There's fourteen thousand dollars." He fished in his briefcase for the account register.

"I'm showing a little more than seven thousand." She turned the screen to show him.

Motherfucking Whitney Bank. Squaly and Lawrence had both warned him about putting money in a bank for uptown blue bloods, but that's how Wil had wanted it. He was working hard; he should have the best. Now they'd lost, or maybe stolen, half his money.

A short man with a bald head and glasses appeared behind them. "Let's get this straightened out," he said kindly. He led them to a desk enclosed by cubicle walls and turned to a computer. Wil looked at his watch. They were due at the closing in a little less than an hour. Luscious, usually quick to temper, sat quietly looking at the floor.

"Now, how big a cashier's check were you wanting?" the man asked.

"Fourteen thousand dollars," Wil said. "We've been saving for four years."

The man cleared his throat. "Well, there have been some withdrawals," he said, and then, right in front of Wil, slid his eyes over to check out Luscious.

Wil fought down his anger. "This is bullshit, man. I saved fourteen thousand dollars to buy us a house."

"Well, as I say, there have been some withdrawals." The man pushed his eyes over toward Luscious again, who was studying her long white nails.

Enough. Wil banged his hand on the desk. "You're trying to steal my money!"

"Sir, please lower your voice."

"I will not lower my voice! You just don't want to give that kind of money to a black man!"

"Mr. Rawlins. Look here." The man turned the screen. "You had fourteen thousand dollars, but as I say, there have been withdrawals. Lots of them." He slid his eyes once more toward Luscious. "Big ones."

Withdrawals. Wil turned to Luscious. She picked at a nail.

"May I see your ATM card, sir?" Wil fished it out and extended it. "Okay, it's not this one. Ma'am? May I see your card?"

Luscious opened her purse and pulled out her card. She pushed it slowly across the desk with the tips of her long white nails. She raised her eyes to Wil. "We have to talk."

"Ah, yes," the vice president said. "This is the card."

Luscious cried all the way to Dwyer Road. "It was them video poker machines," she sniffled. "I was down about five thousand dollars when you started asking me to go get the check. I tried to win it back, and I guess I lost two thousand more."

Video poker! Wil thought. I'm busting my ass at work, and she's been hanging in the bars playing video poker?

Ma and Da were out—at the VA hospital. Luscious went straight back to the bedroom. Wil sat on the couch in the living room, elbows on knees, chin on fists.

Luscious came out, clutching a Kleenex. "Wil . . ."

He looked up. Her eyes were red, her makeup running.

"You need to call your mother and have her come get you," he said. "You're not welcome in this house anymore."

BELINDA SMALLS

NORTH VILLERE AND LIZARDI STREETS
2000

Belinda cruised up Lizardi Street with the girls and little Curtis in the backseat, singing along with Whitney Houston, who poured like honey from the speakers: "I am not afraid to try it on my own, and I don't care if I'm right or wrong." "On My Own" had become Belinda's anthem. No more men. No more being handed some married guy's cell phone number. And no more husbands. That was for sure.

So many cars lined Lizardi that Belinda had to park two blocks away from cousin Katina's. Curtis could see the bounce house poking up from the backyard and was clawing at the door. The girls, fifteen and eleven, took charge, untangling him from his car seat as Belinda cut the engine.

Inside the glove compartment was the envelope holding the divorce papers from Snooker and a copy of the judge's restraining order. She never went anywhere without them.

A DJ's overamplified voice echoed across the Lower Nine, whomping up another hip-hop tune. Barbecue smoke rose from Katina's yard and drifted between the houses. Curtis pulled Belinda excitedly along the pavement. It made her knee ache; it ached a lot lately.

Cousin Katina had found herself a good man—a Southern University graduate called Squaly—and they were going all out for the second birthday of their son, Myron. People spilled from the house, the porch, and the front and back yards in a way that reminded Belinda of Aunt Polly's card parties back in the day.

She wrinkled her nose at the smell of crawfish boiling—more boiled bugs. Curtis exploded from her grip the minute they got inside the house, the girls went their own way, and Belinda wove through the crowd, pressing her cheek against the sweaty cheeks of friends and cousins. She took a plate, put a piece of chicken on it, and went out the back door to keep an eye on Curtis. A spot was open on a small wrought-iron bench, and she took a seat, pressing her knees together, pinching a chicken wing delicately in her fingers.

Across the yard, a big man in an orange and green tracksuit was talking with Squaly. He was tall, with long, long legs and a big butt, but he moved like a little boy, bouncing on the balls of his feet, waving his long arms. He and Squaly were laughing. Belinda liked Squaly; his education showed. He was polite, thought about his words before speaking, and had none of the swagger of men like Snooker who were thrashing around at the bottom of the economic ladder.

"Excuse me."

Belinda looked up. The big man in the orange and green tracksuit stood over her. He had a sweet face—kinda goofy—quizzical eyebrows, full lips set a little crooked. One of his teeth was chipped. "My friend has asked me to go to the store," he said formally. "Would you like anything from the store?"

"Uh, no thank you."

The man smiled and shifted his stance. He looked like an oversized kid in feety pajamas. "Are you sure you don't want anything?"

The clumsiest opening line, and he was repeating it. She was fed up with men, but this one was so gentle and so goofy he seemed harmless.

"Okay," she said. "Bring me some Goody's powders. I got a pain in my knee."

He pressed his palms together—"Goody's powders!"—and strode off through the side yard, swinging his arms. No macho swagger at all. Belinda's knee twinged as she got to her feet to find cousin Katina. "Who's the big guy in the tracksuit?"

"Oh, that's Squaly's frat brother from Southern," Katina said.

"What's he do?"

"He's the band director at Carver."

The man in the orange and green tracksuit returned with the Goody's powders. "Belinda Smalls," he said formally, writing on a piece of paper. "I unfortunately have to leave the party. But rather than put you in the awkward position of being asked for your phone number, I will give you mine. I hope you will give me a call, because I would like to see you again." So direct. So formal. He put out his huge hand, and she shook it. When he was gone, she looked at the paper. "Wilbert Rawlins," it said. Next to the phone number, he'd written, "Home."

TIM BRUNEAU

THE GOOSE
2000

Tim looked at the cop dozing in the passenger seat. The guy even looked stupid. What a mistake, to let him write up last night's felony arrest. It had been a good bust, but Tim had glanced at the paperwork this morning. "Got in a fight," it said. "Guy hit a guy with a bottel and cut him up." Tim's sergeant—no Einstein either—had put it in the out-box for the DA, who would certainly have thrown the case out. Tim had snatched the report and rewritten it. Precision was everything. Police work was useless without it. Ever since the city council forced cops to live within the parish, the police department had recruited mostly from people who had gone through the New Orleans public schools and could barely spell their own names. You didn't need crooked judges and prosecutors to let criminals walk; all you needed was cops who should have repeated third grade.

Tim's usual partner was out sick, so this new guy was riding along. His belly hung over his belt, and his baby blue uniform shirt looked as though it were about to split. The department had physical-fitness standards, but nobody enforced them. Tim, who had run cross-country in high school and was still reedy, shuddered with disgust.

He piloted the white and blue cruiser past echelons of big, new brick houses. Blacks with money had moved to New Orleans East as fast as developers could carve it out of the swamp. New Orleans East was where new recruits started; it was a lousy place to be a cop if you wanted to kick ass.

"To hell with it," Tim said. "Let's do some police work." His temporary partner muttered and shifted, his head lolling against the window. Tim pulled the cruiser fast through a U-turn and headed toward Chef Menteur Highway, which ran the length of New Orleans East like a black vein down the back of a shrimp. He cruised westward, toward the Industrial Canal, watching Nordstrom give way to Target, then to Kmart, then to cinder-block liquor stores caged up like jailhouses. He was heading for the only corner of the East that really rocked and rolled: the Goose, named after the legendarily violent Blue Goose Bar. Most cops tried hard to stay as far from the Goose as possible. Tim often drifted over.

He turned right on America Street, which didn't look too bad by daylight—small houses with ratty little lawns, Greater Little Rock Baptist Church and Anchor of Hope Church, each no bigger than a cottage. By night, though, the drug dealing and slaughter were breathtaking. Tim turned left on Warfield. And look at this. A couple of men were hustling toilets, sinks, water heaters, and doors from the back of a beat-up pickup into a corrugated-steel garage. He pulled over to the sidewalk and stopped. His partner opened his eyes and blinked.

The two men turned to face them, one tall, thin, and light skinned; the other short and stocky.

"Yes, sir, Mr. Officer, what seems to be the problem?" the tall one said.

Jailbird, Tim thought. The ones who'd been to Angola addressed uniforms with exaggerated politeness. "When did you get out?" He gestured for the man's ID.

"Couple months back. I'd be doing better if I could get the right kind of assistance."

"So what's this?" Tim gestured at the truckful of stuff.

"Demolition. My uncle's gig. I'm just helping out."

"Where did the stuff come from?"

"Abandoned houses and shit. People leave stuff."

"And you take it."

"It's just left! People renovating, they throw stuff away. Leave stuff when they move. It's, it's, what do you call it? Salvage."

It's stolen, is what it is, Tim thought. But how was he going to trace a stack of lumber, a toilet seat, and a water heater? There was a time when he'd have gone at it. But even if he made a case, the guy would probably pay the judge "side bail" and walk.

A feeling of exhaustion overtook Tim, like a bad cold coming on. He handed back the man's ID and gestured for his partner to get back in the car. What a city.

Some days later, Tim couldn't find his sergeant.

"Haven't you heard?" the lieutenant asked. "He got arrested by the state police."

"You're kidding me," Tim said.

"Caught him with a car full of whores."

Tim laughed. That was the sarge. Whores were his life. Called them his "confidential sources."

"The one in the front seat had a warrant on her," the lieutenant said. "The one in the backseat had weed in her purse. And Billy had a TEC-9 under his seat."

"Jesus." A TEC-9—a compact, high-speed semiautomatic—was a stone thug gun.

"Confiscated in a search and reported missing from the evidence room."

"Christ."

"He was driving an unmarked NOPD unit, and he made the staties chase him." The lieutenant smiled.

"What?"

"Oh, and did I mention?" The lieutenant was loving this. "It was the Illinois State Police. Fuck knows what he was doing up there. We won't be seeing him for a while."

BELINDA SMALLS

EGANIA STREET
2000

"You sure this guy's all right?" Cousin Ditty stood by the front door, scanning the street.

"I told you, I checked him out." Belinda rubbed a hint of magenta into her cheekbones.

"Checked him out how?" After her short, disastrous marriage to Snooker, and watching his own mother's descent into drugs, Ditty wasn't taking any chances with his pretty cousin. Belinda loved him.

"I called the school from work and said UNO was thinking of donating instruments to the band. I asked the name of the band director. They said Wilbert Rawlins."

"Hmm."

"I called the band room, just to be sure."

"That don't mean . . ."

"I went on the Internet, too. Paid twenty-four ninety-five for a background. He's been married. He went to Southern. He is the band director at Carver. He has no outstanding criminal record or judgments."

"Damn, girl. You don't play."

A car was making its way slowly down Egania, sputtering and backfiring like a farm implement. "If that's him, you ain't going," Ditty said. The car rolled past, thank goodness. "Where he taking you?"

"Not dancing." She rubbed her knee. "I'll tell you that."

Somewhere in the distance, Chanté Moore was singing her new hit, "Chanté's Got a Man." Belinda and Ditty looked at each other: a good song, a good sign. The music got louder and cut off. Belinda pushed her forehead to the screen. A sleek navy blue Lexus with pretty chrome rims stopped in front of the house. The door opened, and the tall man from cousin Katina's party stood up out of it: Wilbert Rawlins. Not in green and orange, but in a classic black silk shirt, a big gold medallion hanging around his neck. He smiled his goofy crooked, broken-tooth smile, wide as the keys of a piano.

RONALD LEWIS

2000 DESLONDE STREET
2000

Ronald sat on Dorothy's porch at the corner of Deslonde and Prieur—diagonally across the street from the house in which they'd grown up. Stella, who lived in the old family house, was on her knees in the flower garden. She had painted the house lavender and white, but she kept it beautiful. It was Ronald's favorite time of day—late afternoon, the shadows growing long. The high spreading oaks of Tennessee Street made a lovely backdrop to Stella's house. Dorothy, at sixty-two fifteen years older than Ronald, was more than ever the family matriarch now that Mama was gone.

"What you got all up in your car?" she asked, leaning forward in her chair and peering down the stoop. Ronald's beat-up old 1980 Cutlass was parked directly below, the back windows full of colors.

"Oh, more Mardi Gras Indian suits and parading-club clothes," he said. "People keep giving 'em to me."

Dorothy laughed. "Minnie's going to put you out the house."

Somebody, though, had to keep these things. They were the heritage of the Lower Ninth Ward—well-nigh sacred relics. And there was no end to them, because neither an Indian tribe nor a parading club could come out dressed in the previous year's suits.

They sat in silence for a while. The silences were the best part of sitting on the porch—that dreamy, timeless feeling of togetherness that always made him miss his mama.

It was getting dark. Ronald would have to go face Minnie with the carful of Indian suits and parading clothes. The little room off the kitchen was heaped plenty high already. Minnie was sure to fill a big old cup of anger, but there was nothing to do. Minnie's moods were like the weather in August; you never knew where or when lightning would strike. All that passion packed into her little body, that passion he'd loved since she wore that big natural, had to blow itself free from time to time. He stood. His knees hurt, and lately his feet were achy with the gout. Not even fifty, and all wore out from work on the tracks.

One step at a time, he clumped down Dorothy's stoop to the Cutlass. Instead of taking St. Claude or Claiborne, the main arteries, he took Prieur Street so he could look the neighborhood over. The Lower Ninth Ward seemed to be changing before his eyes. Idle young men in baggy white T-shirts plied their evil trade from their grandmothers' porches. Ronald saw graffiti, abandoned cars, houses all stove in from neglect.

But this home over here: it needed paint but had flowers neatly planted all the way around it. That one over there had a tire swing out front, tied to a fat magnolia tree. Behind another, a lush vegetable garden. You got to fight not to give in to despair, he told himself. You got to see the good that's mixed in with the bad.

Sprinkled around the neighborhood, on lawns and neutral grounds, were hand-painted signs reading, "No to Lock Expansion." The city was looking to widen the lock at the junction of the Industrial Canal and the Mississippi River, which would wipe out several blocks of the Lower Nine and put Deslonde Street back-to-bosom with a noisy industrial site. It was typical; nobody cared about the families in the Lower Nine. Its families could be sacrificed. But a committee was forming to fight it; Ronald had been to a couple meetings of the mitigation board, which was supposed to come up with ways to soften the blow to the community.

Ronald turned onto Tupelo. Miss Sheryl, Miss Beulah, Miss Catherine, Miss Crystal—all of them kept their houses up. Nothing was prettier than Tupelo Street at sundown.

The lights were on inside his house. As he pulled in to the driveway, something twinkled in the glow of his headlights—something fragmented, colorful. Beadwork. He climbed out and walked laboriously up the driveway to the backyard. His shoulders sagged, and he let out a long sigh. The grass behind the house was strewn with Mardi Gras suits, crowns, staffs, four-hundred-dollar homburgs from Meyer the Hatter, seven-hundred-dollar shoes from Damien's, pin-striped suits, and flowered sashes jumbled in a knee-high mound.

Ronald labored up the back steps and stuck his head in the screen door. Minnie turned and faced him, holding a wooden spoon.

"I was tired of looking at that shit," she said. She was flushed from the heat of the stove. Her blouse was half untucked, her eyes were glittery, and her hair jumped out from her head, as though she'd been wrestling alligators. "I wanted to put a chair in that room. I wanted to see out the windows."

"I'll be in soon," Ronald said. He went back down the steps and unlocked his freestanding garage, barely bigger than a garden shed. He pulled the overhead chain to turn on the light and began moving sacks of grass seed, old paint cans, rakes, the lawn mower. Minnie had thrown out the hangers with the clothes. That was a good thing. His feet and knees ached as he stooped to pick up the first suit. He put it on a hanger, carried it into the garage, found a nail, and placed the suit on it, smoothing the velvet lapel. He went back for another and hung it on a loop of wire. He found he could reach the rafter, and hung lots of items there, leaving an open space in the middle of the room. Shoes he lined up neatly along the walls. Hats went up on the shelves beside the rose dust and weed killer. Minnie didn't know about the new things in his car, and now she didn't have to. They went straight into the garage. He ignored Minnie's calls to dinner, transfixed by the sight of his tiny garage being layered with Indian suits, parading clothes, and the intricate paraphernalia that went with them: fans, sashes, flags, spy-boy staffs, crowns.

Rashad, his younger son, came walking up the driveway. "Saw the light in here," he said. "What you about?"

"Mama threw out my suits," Ronald said.

Rashad's eyebrows shot up; he knew Minnie's moods as well as Ronald. He stared around at the neatly arranged suits.

"Dad," he said. "You got yourself a damn museum."

WILBERT RAWLINS JR.

GEORGE WASHINGTON CARVER
HIGH SCHOOL
2000

Wil perched on a straight chair across from Mr. Jackson in the principal's office at Carver High School, eager to get back to arranging. The Carver band was going up against Kennedy—Wil's alma mater. His own little brother, Lawrence, was band director at Kennedy now, and Wil had to blow him out. What's more, when word got around town that the Rawlins brothers were going up against each other, the football game got moved to the Superdome to hold the crowd. Wil wasn't taking any chances. Carver had to shine.

"Here's what I been thinking," he said. "Every other school has one drum major. I want eight. The one on the left with a *G* on his chest, the next with a *W*, and down the line, *C-A-R-V-E-R*. That would stand out!"

"Don't talk to me about more band uniforms." Mr. Jackson frowned, neatening a pile of papers. "We still owe thirty-eight thousand dollars on the ones you've got."

"I know."

"How many are in the band now, Wilbert?"

"Getting onto a hundred." It was a quarter of the school, which meant that one in four kids had to show up at school every day, earn at least a 2.5 grade point average, and stay out of trouble with the police. Wilbert was convinced that cramming as many kids as possible into band was the way to save a school.

"So how much are these suits going to cost?"

"The drum majors? I figure with the hat and plume and everything, about a thousand dollars a suit."

"So, eight thousand dollars."

"Round about."

Mr. Jackson pursed his lips. Then he stood. "Come with me," he said.

He led Wilbert out into the main office, where a heavyset, light-skinned girl sat on a chair against the wall, her arms folded across her chest. Her stringy, straightened hair hung in front of her face like a curtain. Behind it, Wil could make out a frown hot enough to grill cheese.

"That's Nyja Sanders," Mr. Jackson said. "You want eight thousand dollars for uniforms? Keep her out of my office for a week. You do that, I'll find you eight thousand dollars."

"For real?"

"For real. I have her up here three times a day. She's got a record this long. She doesn't let two minutes of class go by without disrupting it. She's angry as a hornet. I am this close to putting her out for good."

"Fuck you," Nyja said from behind the curtain. "I hear you mother-fuckers. I know my rights."

Mr. Jackson looked at Wil and spread his hands. "One week," he said, holding up an index finger and backing into his office. "Keep her out of here one week, and I'll get you your drum major uniforms."

Wil walked over and stood in front of Nyja with his arms folded, a thoughtful hand under his chin, as though pondering the purchase of a used car. He knew how huge he looked. She looked everywhere but at him, darting her eyes over the front counter, the secretaries at their desks, the windows, the bench by the entrance. Finally, her eyes slowed, and glanced up.

"Hey," he said softly. "Let's get out of here." He walked out into the hall, and when he looked back, she was watching him, like an animal with its foot caught in a trap. "You want to stay here?" Wil said. "Come on. I'll show you something." He walked down to the band room, and she followed, a few paces behind, ready to bolt. The room was empty; it was past six o'clock.

"Oh, fuck this," Nyja said. "I don't want any part of fucking band."

Wil walked into his cluttered office and picked up a trumpet.

"Did you hear what I said?" Nyja called. "I don't want any part of your fucking band."

Wil put the trumpet to his lips and blew softly, the opening notes of "Purple Carnival." He stopped and listened. He had the sense Nyja was still there, so he lifted the horn and played the rest, and then "Big Four March." Wil was himself only starting to learn the trumpet, and those were the only two songs he knew by heart, so he had to stop and look for sheet music. He came across a diagram of a marching pattern he'd been looking for and, distracted, stopped for a moment to study it.

"Hey," Nyja called softly. Wil started. Her curtained face appeared tentatively at the door. "Why'd you stop playing?"

ANTHONY WELLS

They got the best lawyers in the world in Angola. I got me alongside one; he tampered with a jury or some shit and was doing seven years. He helped me write my appeal. I filed it forma pauperis with the Louisiana Supreme Court. Didn't even have a typewriter; I wrote it out by hand: Anthony Wells versus the State of Louisiana. *Forgot all about it, to tell you the truth. Then one day I got a letter. They took away the aggravated battery and give me five years for the drug charge, so I only had to do one more year. I was almost fifty when I got out.*

It's a nightmare to come home, man. People are grown up; people done died.

Neighborhood looked different. That drug war torn a hole. All stem from the NOPD getting fifteen hundred kilos of cocaine off a barge and flooding the Seventh, Eighth, Ninth Ward with it. If you weren't selling drugs for them, they lock you up or kill you. Used to have eleven-, twelve-year-old kids selling dope in the projects. One little dude had four or five brothers and sisters, and his mama was sick. Little dude say, "I lost the money; I got robbed." He was using it for his family. The police killed that boy and threw him in the Dumpster. A woman seen the whole shit and she ended up dead. You got to see Master P's video: "I'm Bout It, Bout It." It's all about that.

My nerves used to get so bad I'd shake like a fifty-five Chevrolet from so much violence and shit. I'd have to get me a drink, take some pill to make me go to sleep. I was walking on glass. Finally bought me a Mossberg shotgun with a pistol grip at Bennie's Hardware. Six-shot. Put that up under your coat they don't know you had it.

Up in the Goose, though, I still had my people. This little dude Peanut that shot my brother Roger, he'd be all, "What's happening, Unk?" My nephews, they called me Unk. I loved those little guys. When I was going through my shit, those little dudes were right there. They were like, you need something, soldier? One day this little dude rolled up on me, opened his trunk, gave me two pair of tennis shoes, some shorts. He was like, "We're going to holler at you because you're all right, you hang in the neighborhood, you're a real soldier." And that made me feel good, man. Once, when I was going through my shit? They gave me a .357 with a infrared light on it. Chrome. Did I carry it? I did what I had to do and threw it away. That's what a gun is for, to use and not to abuse. You don't kill a man for nothing, over a few dollars or a bottle or a woman. My dad taught me that. Jealousy and hate will get you killed. Self-pride will get you killed. That's my daddy talking.

JOHN GUIDOS

SOUTH RAMPART STREET
January 1, 2001

It had been a wild New Year's Eve at the Golden Lantern. John lay a long time in bed, listening to the birds outside his window. From time to time he rubbed his chin and cheeks, enjoying the smoothness. He climbed out of bed and opened his packed closet. At least half of the contents was men's clothes. He pulled a pair of Ralph Lauren Chaps off a slacks hanger and threw them on the floor. He grabbed a button-down shirt and a handful of neckties. The more he yanked, the faster he worked, pulling hangers out by twos, by threes, by the armful. Kneeling, he rooted in the men's shoes, flipping them over his shoulder, neither pausing nor relenting; even the beloved black motorcycle boots went into the pile. By the time he was done, he was panting with exertion. The hormones diminished his wind. In the middle of the floor lay the first fifty years of his life, in sport jackets, golf shirts, and tiepins. Even the leather: he didn't want it. Left in the closet, with plenty of room to breathe, were the pantsuits, dresses, and skirts by which all the world would know her.

She selected a clinging black dress with a plunging neckline that showed off her bust. Up her muscular legs she unrolled lacy-topped fishnet stockings. She worked half an hour on her hair and makeup.

Donnie Jay was waiting for her at Mandich's, reading the *Times-Picayune* and looking a little the worse for his New Year's revels. He did a comic double take when he saw her.

Donnie was the best. Delicate and elegant, with big features and long fingers, he was a dean of the city's female impersonators. For him it was performance, not a full-time lifestyle, but nobody had been more sympathetic as JoAnn made her transformation. She kissed him on the cheek.

"It's JoAnn full-time now," she said, banging her palms on the table. "No!"

"Yes. No more John, no more switch-hitting." The waitress came and, without so much as a glance at JoAnn, took orders for Bloody Marys and crab bisque. JoAnn said, "When Mom was sick, she looked up at me and said, 'I'm not going to have to see you in a dress, am I?' I remember thinking, 'Mom, I'm standing here with my eyebrows plucked and a French manicure!' I never wore a dress in front of her or my dad. It was the least I could do. But I made a resolution when Mom died that the first of the year, I'd be JoAnn full-time."

"I must say, you've developed quite a figure," Donnie said.

"Forty double-D," JoAnn said proudly. The waitress started to set a Bloody Mary in front of her; JoAnn intercepted it, downed half in one go, and ordered a second. "On hormones, men usually get Bs, maybe a C," she told Donnie.

"Lord."

"I got good genes."

"And your face . . ."

"Two and a half years of electrolysis. Twice a week. Touch it." Donnie ran a fingertip across JoAnn's cheek. "Forty-five dollars an hour. I'd schedule in the late evening, and get an extra half hour free."

"Does it hurt?"

"Does it hurt!" JoAnn boomed, sounding appallingly like the old Hattiesburg field-goal kicker. "It's a little bitty needle going into each follicle, one by one, an electric shot burning out the hair. That woman got off on giving people pain." She started to wolf up her soup and then, remembering, changed her grip on the spoon and took a dainty taste.

"What's next?" Donnie asked.

"The surgery! I got to get this done; it's all I ever wanted. Hey. I gotta show you. I had to get my driver's license renewed last week," she said. "The lady with the camera tried to make me take off my jewelry and makeup. I said, 'I don't think so; I'm transsexual.' "

Donnie laughed, covering his mouth with his long fingers.

"She went back and spoke to her boss. Then she came out and took my picture." JoAnn fished the license from her purse and handed it to Donnie. It said, "John Guidos" and "male," but the photo smiling in the corner was of a woman with sharply tweezed eyebrows, bright red lips, and a plunging neckline. She was smiling so brightly it seemed the camera had caught her in mid-laugh.

WILBERT RAWLINS JR.

VETERANS HOSPITAL OF NEW ORLEANS

2001

A trail of blood ran from the bathroom back to Da's bed.

"It's from my anus," Da said, pulling the sheet up to his chin with bony hands. "I want you to see that. I want you to be afraid of that."

"Da . . ."

"Every moment is precious, Wil," Da said. "You got to play your cards. You got a wife now; life is serious. You hearing me?"

Wil backed out of the room and ran to the first doctor he saw, a big, gray-haired man in a pale blue lab coat. "Come here, son," the doctor said, pulling Wil into a corner. He put the eye thing on Wil, just like Da, and Wil felt himself shrink. "Your father has cancer," he said. "His internal organs are no longer working. If we give him any more blood, we'll be wasting it."

"But . . ."

"The cancer has eat up his liver and filled it with bile," the doctor went on. "We could put in a shunt to drain it, but that wouldn't change anything."

"You could try," Wil said.

"We got men in here that can survive," the doctor said. "We got to look after them first."

Wil looked at the floor. He was losing Da, and he didn't know how.

"You are the oldest son," the doctor continued, squeezing Wil's shoulder harder. "You got to prepare yourself, and you got to look after your mama. Your father is dying right now. He may not live to see tomorrow. You got to be strong."

He let Wil's shoulder go and gave it a pat. Wil walked back to Da's room, which smelled heavily of feces and sweat. Da was watching the Food Channel, as usual. Sick as he was, he loved the thought of cooking. He rolled his head toward Wil. The whites of his eyes were the color of egg yolk.

"They told you I was going to die."

"Yeah, man," Wil said. He felt himself starting to break up, but held it in. He wasn't going to fall off the Wilbert Rawlins Sr. train at this point. Not now. Not in front of Da. "You fought a good one. They say there's nothing they can do for you."

Da rolled his head back to the Food Channel. "You go home to that new pretty wife of yours and get some sleep," he said without looking at Wil. "I'm going to call you in the morning. We're going to get them to give me that surgery."

Wil couldn't breathe. Da's determination to have things his way was running up against his determination to call the truth as it lies—a collision Wil couldn't bear to watch. He said good night and drove home.

Belinda was already asleep; he got into bed beside her. It was still dark when the phone rang. The caller ID window said, "VA HOSP," and for three rings Wil was afraid to pick it up for fear of what he'd hear. Finally, he lifted the receiver and put it to his ear.

"I told you I was going to call you in the morning," Da's voice said. "You thought it was them people calling to say I was gone, didn't you?"

Wil couldn't speak. He nodded as though Da could see.

"They're about to take me down to surgery," Da said. "You got to pray."

fRANK MINYARD

FAIR OAKS FARM
2002

Frank stood on the porch of his farmhouse, across Lake Pontchartrain from New Orleans. Chickens scratched in the pebbled driveway. His horses nuzzled the ground in an enclosed field, and his Black Angus bull lay in another, chewing its cud, massive as a rock outcropping.

They say you never really grow up until your parents are dead, Frank thought, and maybe that's true. Mom had been gone six months, and Frank was living the life of a choirboy. No running around with young women, no wild drinking bouts, no late nights with the boys. At seventy-three years old, he'd come to enjoy animals. They were so calm. They didn't demand anything. They didn't lie. They didn't judge.

He'd bought the farm as a weekend retreat, but found himself, lately, coming out Thursday nights instead of Fridays and staying through Monday instead of Sunday. The whooshing of the wind in the oaks was more pleasant now than trombones and the clink of martini glasses, the soft yielding of leaf-covered grass kinder to his feet than the clickety-clack of cobblestones and cement.

The phone rang inside, and Frank lifted the receiver in the kitchen. "Frank? It's Catherine." They'd gone to high school together, but he hadn't heard her voice in years. Her family was Yugoslav. Oyster people.

"Listen," she said. "My daughter, Nancy, moved to New Orleans not long ago after her divorce. She's a nurse practitioner at Tulane. She doesn't know a soul, and she's down something terrible with the flu. Would you give her a call? She could really use a friend right now."

Frank agreed, hung up, and dialed Nancy's number. The poor woman sounded dreadful. "Hey," he said. "How about I bring you some soup? Doctor's orders."

He drove across the causeway, bought two quarts of pea soup from the Plantation, and found Nancy's address. The woman who opened the door was petite, dark haired, and sick as hell. She was in her fifties, at least two decades older than the women Frank had most recently dated. Frank, though, found himself unable to speak as she took the cartons of soup into her strong, long-fingered hands. Even sick, she was lovely, with dark hair and deep brown eyes. "Sorry it took so long," he finally said. "I was at my farm."

"Ooh, you have a farm?" she said, sniffling and blowing her nose. "Do you have horses? I love to ride. It's my salvation. If I could spend all my time with animals, that's where I'd be."

"Listen," he said. "Leave the soup. Let me take you out for a steak."

BILLY GRACE

2525 ST. CHARLES AVENUE
Mardi Gras 2002

Rex, king of carnival, was the highest honor New Orleans society could bestow upon a man. Billy's father had never made it. George had never made it. But by the fates, Billy, the son of a bank teller, had become the king of Mardi Gras.

From his throne atop the Rex float, across the throngs of celebrants, Billy could see 2525 St. Charles Avenue looming into view, its broad porch packed with family and friends. In front of him, a high-school band in green and orange uniforms was blaring its heart out. Behind him, the Rex floats spread for half a mile. The day was perfect, not so hot that the long fake beard and gold-upholstered parade outfit chafed, not so cold as to dampen the enthusiasm of the crowd. "Throw me something, mister!" they shouted, jumping up and down to catch strings of cheap plastic beads. Billy's best friends, in brocaded outfits and masks, leaned over the street from their places on the float, tossing beads and doubloons to the upturned faces. The float bumped over the curve and veered left, leading the parade across the broad grassy neutral ground and the streetcar tracks, toward Billy's house.

Here came dear George now in morning coat and striped trousers, still graceful, carrying a bottle of champagne. Ivory, who had been working for George and Anne for as long as Billy could remember, carried the beribboned stepladder. Ivory—short and dark—was as much a part of 2525 as the portico or the porch. He set it up next to Billy's float and stepped back, smiling proudly. George climbed up and upended the champagne into the same silver and deer-antler loving cup that had been used for the Rex toast since 1907. He passed it to Billy with a laugh and a wink. The band members stopped playing, turned sharply on their heels like the king's own honor guard, and brought their instruments crisply to parade rest.

Billy raised the cup to the crowd and shouted, "I would like to thank the collective group! And that includes all the spectators here in New Orleans! The Mardi Gras lovers! These are the people who make Mardi Gras!" That was the point of Mardi Gras, was it not? To serve and honor all the people, to bring into hard lives a touch of royalty and grandeur.

Billy turned back to 2525, drank from the cup, and handed it back to George, who climbed down with Ivory's help. It was a hoot, a goof—but it was serious, too, the culmination of years of dreaming and hard work, his own, as captain, but, more important, that of the entire Rex organization. To put on a spectacle such as this, free of charge, was an honor. New Orleans was sick and wounded, but no other city in the world had a celebration quite like this. It was beautiful precisely because it was so frivolous. The float lurched, and Billy rolled on. The band struck up again a martial tune, and the float bumped over the neutral ground to take its place in the river of Mardi Gras floats.

TIM BRUNEAU

ERATO STREET
March 2002

Fast bastard. No matter how Tim poured it on, the kid stayed half a block ahead. He looked small, but there was no way of telling how tough he'd fight, because his body was draped in a bale of oversized cotton clothing. One hand held up ballooning carpenter's pants while the other went methodically through each pocket, flipping bright little plastic bags into the air like beads off a Mardi Gras float. With any luck, Andrew was huffing along behind, gathering the evidence, before some other kid came along and snapped it up like the blackbirds in "Hansel and Gretel." Not least of the great things about Tim's transfer to the Sixth District was Andrew. A real partner.

The kid darted off Erato Street and around an overturned Dumpster, skimming along one of the brick buildings of the B. W. Cooper housing project. His legs looked disconnected from his upper body, snapping along with incredible fluidity, given the outsized shoes; they seemed to spin in circles, like a cartoon character's, while his upper body floated, as relaxed as could be. He disappeared around the corner of the building, short dreadlocks flying. Tim pivoted, gaining a few yards, zooming along the front of the building, past ground-floor windows grated with steel mesh like the windows on a prison bus. These buildings must once have been nice to live in, Tim often thought, as solid as blocks of stone, with thick walls for cool interiors. This courtyard must once have been a sweet oak-shaded lawn where kids could play safely away from cars. Now it was a no-man's-land, bleak and barren, the grass worn away like the flank of a mangy dog, the trees reduced to graffiti-carved stumps.

The kid peeled off his sweatshirt as he ran, revealing a gleaming white wife-beater T-shirt bisecting chocolate-colored shoulders and hourglass-shaped biceps. He'd be slippery to fight. Two young men drinking beer on a stoop sat up to watch, like spectators at a NASCAR race, and Tim felt a flash of resentment that they were lounging away their Tuesday morning while he was working his ass off to make their lives a little safer. Living from one crazy check to the next, they were probably grandsons of the project's original residents, the downstream evidence of generations of uselessness. Sit right there and watch the show, you lazy bastards.

On the other hand, the kid might be from the C. J. Peete or Desire, poaching on the B. W. Cooper, in which case these gold-toothed spectators were watching him with an eye toward cutting his throat. You're better off in my hands, Tim thought.

The kid shot between two apartment blocks and around a corner into the next courtyard. Tim followed and stopped short, panting. The courtyard was full of wiry young men with short dreadlocks, wearing identical white wife beaters and sagged carpenter's pants. The fucking uniform of the day: What do they do, call each other every morning? They looked at him with no expression, a field of identical statues. But that one—his chest was heaving. When Tim made eye contact, he took off.

The kid swerved around the building, glancing back like he'd expected Tim to sprint a few blocks and give up. You're not dealing with a fat-assed patrolman in a baby blue shirt, Tim thought. The Task Force is on you. This kid did not seem to have gotten the memo. All Tim was supposed to do as a member of the new Task Force was cruise around waiting for a scumbag to make a mistake and then rough him up and haul him in with maximum show of force—an extra punch, an extra kick, the cuffs bitten down hard. Not enough to bring a brutality charge, but enough to make him think, to make the word get out that the NOPD was taking back the streets. Grab a purse, deal a bag, wave a gun at a rival, and Task Force will be on your ass. Task Force—the "Jump-Out Boys" in department parlance—was Tim's dream job: no directing traffic, inspecting liquor licenses, investigating accidents, responding to calls for service, or any other dreary nonsense. Just boot-in-the-ass policing. It was amazing how easy the scumbags made it. Tim would swerve fast around corners, watching for the kid who dropped to tie a shoe that was already tied, the kid who turned his face away, the kid who shoved something into a wastebasket. They practically begged to be arrested.

The kid cut a broad arc across Galvez Street and into the other side of the project. Tim stayed with him like an F-16 on the tail of a MiG. His pistol slapped rhythmically against his thigh. The weight of his duty belt—nightstick, cuffs, radio, and pepper spray—cost him speed, but at least he didn't have to hold up his pants. The paramilitary fatigues fit him snugly, as skinny as he was. The baseball-style cap stuck fine to his narrow head. The combat boots gave him ankle support, though he'd have preferred the springy Nikes he'd used for cross-country in high school.

A quarter mile now, and Tim was just hitting stride. He could keep this up as long as the kid. The kid would trip on those damned pants, or get hit by a car, crossing Claiborne. Tim would get lucky.

The Seventh District had the Goose, the Fifth District had the Lower Ninth Ward, but none of the eight police districts of New Orleans had as many housing projects as the Sixth. If you wanted action, the Sixth was the shit.

The kid squirted out of B. W. Cooper onto Martin Luther King Jr. Boulevard. An old lady in a churchly purple overcoat and hat stepped out of the way without looking up; they might as well have been a couple of squirrels dashing about after acorns. The kid got lucky at Claiborne, parting the traffic like Moses at the Red Sea, and Tim plunged through after him. The kid had speed.

Splintery, tumbledown houses slid by on either side, bare-chested men sitting on stoops. Your great-auntee leaves you a house that's been paid off since 1940, Tim thought, and you sit on your ass and watch it fall down around you. It's always, Oh, Mr. Officer, we got it hard. Oh, Mr. Officer, I got the sugar and can't work. Oh, Mr. Officer, I don't know where he's at.

The kid veered left on Magnolia Street, and Tim put a little extra into the curve, narrowing the gap. Nothing like running, especially after sitting in a patrol car. He stretched his long legs into it, and the pavement flew by. The kid darted right onto Clio Street.

Up ahead, at the corner of Freret Street, the blue and white fender of a patrol car peeked out from behind an abandoned Lucky Dogs hot dog cart. Excellent, Tim thought: someone with the brains to figure out where the kid was running and cut him off. The kid bolted so close by the front of the cruiser that he might have grazed the fender. To Tim's surprise, he kept going, unmolested. Tim looked in the windshield as he passed. A fat patrolwoman was slumped to the side of the wheel, murmuring into her cell phone, oblivious. Fucking NOPD.

They crossed Simon Bolivar, and the kid veered left, toward the freeway overpass at Calliope Street, hoping to lose himself among the cars entering and exiting the freeway. Tim was gaining. The kid executed a balletic evasion of a turning car and kept going, bursting into the treeless sunlight of Calliope, pelting into a fast-moving stream of cars. Then he was through, lost in the deep shadows of the overpass.

Tim glanced left and right, barely slowing, and plunged into the glare of Calliope. Something moved to his right, by the entrance ramp— the kid? He turned toward a sound like a concentrated pocket of wind and glanced over his shoulder. Under his face, in his personal space where nothing should be, was the silver-blue hood of a BMW. Three-Eighteen-I, Tim thought crazily, a beauty. The woman driving had her mouth in a perfect O. The hood scooped his hips sideways, and his pelvis collapsed with a deep crunch. He saw sky behind his feet where the pavement should have been, and the soaring span of the Crescent City Connection bridge. A jolt turned his attention left; his cheek was smacking a folded windshield wiper blade. The world wheeled past—the top of the windshield, the underside of the freeway, the trunk, a squeal of brakes, a smack on the pavement, the smell of hot tires, pain, blackness.

WILBERT RAWLINS JR.

MURIEL'S RESTAURANT

2002

Belinda looked beautiful sitting across the table in the candlelight. Her hair was wrapped around her head like a turban. Her rectangular glasses made her look severe and hip at the same time. Luscious had been sexy, but common. Belinda was elegant. Refined. Serious.

Wil loved bringing Belinda to the French Quarters to eat, with a sport coat on and plenty money in his pocket. But Belinda looked tired. "You okay?" he asked.

"Just a little overwhelmed, with classes and studying and the job." She pushed slices of buttery mirliton around on her plate.

"Belinda." Wilbert put down his glass of tea and looked at her, until she looked up at him.

"Hmm?"

"Quit your job."

"Quit my job?"

"Quit your job. Let me carry it awhile, while you finish college." Belinda narrowed her eyes. She'd had it rough, he knew; suspicion was a residue of hard times. "Look," he said, putting his hand on hers. "I can handle it. It won't be forever. And once you get your degree, you'll earn that much more." Belinda smiled. "So you see, it's selfish," he said. "It will all come back to me."

"We'll see," she said, looking at her plate and tamping down the smile.

Wil's heart flushed. "This is what it means to look after your family," he said softly. "This is how we get ahead, as a team."

Belinda shrugged and forked a piece of catfish. "Wil," she said, "I got another house to look at. You want to see it?"

She'd taken on the job of finding them a house to buy, and Wil had to admit he hadn't made it easy. Much as he wanted to have a house of his own before Da died, he'd stopped shopping for one. After the first dozen or so, all of them tiny and ugly, Wil had gotten hot, started grumbling that no white real estate agent could believe a black man could afford a proper house. Just how hard is it in this world, he'd wondered aloud, for a black man to be respected? He'd stopped going to look at houses until Belinda went first.

And then there was the time he spent with the band. He'd explained it to her over and over, but she never got it. He was the only thing some of those kids had to hang on to. Even wild Nyja Sanders. She was the first one to show up at practice, ready to go. She called Wil Daddy. But as far as Belinda was concerned, staying late with the band was the same as leaving her home to drink and play dominoes with Squaly and the brothers. She didn't see the difference.

They finished dinner and walked out onto Jackson Square. The evening air was soft, warm, and damp, smelling of tourist-buggy horses. They turned up Chartres and right on Dumaine, passing under the colonnade in front of Harry's Corner bar, toward Wil's car.

A couple of tough-looking teenage boys loomed up as though summoned from the memory of the night Wil and Chicken had botched a robbery. Wil put his hand over the pocket that held his wallet. But slowly recognition dawned: the one with the ringlets and the heart-shaped face, that was Brandon Franklin. The light-skinned one: Jason Slack. Both from the Carver band. They were fixing to sell me some dope, Wil thought, or roll me.

"Hey, Mr. Rawlins," Jason said morosely. Four more boys from the band emerged from the shadows. They looked terrible—dirty, ragged, and neglected.

"What you doing down here in the Quarters for ten o'clock at night?"

"You know."

"No, I don't know."

Brandon, the clown, gave an exaggerated Stepin Fetchit shrug, with a broad grin. The others looked at their feet.

"Belinda," Wil said. "These are my bandsmen. Gentlemen, this is Mrs. Rawlins."

"Hey," they mumbled.

"Not 'hey,' "Wil said. "It's 'Pleased to meet you, Mrs. Rawlins.' "

"Pleased to meet you, Mrs. Rawlins."

"Where are your parents?"

"My mama don't care I'm here."

Wil put his hand on a column and leaned for a long moment, looking them over. "You boys want to make some money?"

"That's what we're doing," Jason said, shrugging.

"I'm thinking of another way," Wil said. "You boys are a band. Come see me tomorrow."

TIM BRUNEAU

INTENSIVE CARE
2002

Tim's mouth was dry, and when he tried to lick his upper lip, he couldn't move his tongue. Something big was stuck in his mouth. Far away, a woman's voice burbled on a loudspeaker, followed by a soothing electronic tone. Up close, it smelled of steam-table food, laced with iodine and alcohol. A hospital. Something had happened. Was he shot?

Tim lifted an eyelid. Sunlight streamed in a huge window. The walls were clean and smooth, hung with futuristic medical equipment like sick bay aboard the *Starship Enterprise.* His heart sank; he must be in some suburban hospital. Everybody knew that if you had to get shot, the place to go was Charity. Why had they taken him here?

He let the eye drift closed, feeling achy, tired, feverish. His body felt far from his head, but there was no pain. He tried to remember what had happened, but the effort exhausted him, and he sank back into blackness.

The next time his eyelid opened, the light filling the window was dimmer. Mom and his stepfather, Gary, were talking about a tuna fish sandwich. Damn, they made it fast: seven or eight hours from Boerne. "I'll be fine here," said a voice from the foot of the bed, and he flicked his eye to see his big sister, Lisa, rooting in her purse. She looked up and caught his eye, then down into her bag, and up again. She leaned toward him.

"Mom," she whispered.

Tim's mother and stepfather murmured to each other.

"Mom!"

They stepped closer.

"I think Timmy's awake!" Lisa's fingers rose to her cheeks. She hopped up and down. "Call somebody! Call somebody! He's awake!"

"Oh, my God." Mom fumbled in the sheets for the nurse-call button. "Oh, my God, oh, my God, oh, my God."

Tim's head throbbed. Eight hours driving from Boerne—he'd been out cold for a whole day.

"Don't try to talk, son." Gary leaned over him, whispering. "You got a tube in your throat to help you breathe."

Damn.

"Timmy!" a woman's voice shouted, and his eyes sprang open. A nurse's face hovered over him. "Timmy!" she barked. "If you can hear me, blink twice."

Christ almighty, Tim thought. Couldn't they let him sleep a little longer? He blinked twice and gazed at the nurse with a look that meant to say, "I'm hurt; I'm not stupid."

"Do you know your name? Spell it out on your mother's palm." He felt his mom's warm hand on his. With his index finger, he spelled out "Timothy B. Bruncau," adding the B to make sure they understood that his mind was fully aware.

"Do you know who the president is?" the nurse asked. Oh, Jesus; the whole dreary drill he'd performed with any number of beat-up guys on the street. If they'd take the tube out of his mouth, he could tell them. Man, he was tired. He wrote W on Mom's palm.

Her eyes filled with tears. She didn't get it.

He wrote, "George W. Bush," with the *W* huge so she'd understand what he'd been trying to say.

"Now," the nurse said. "What day is it?"

Okay, Tim thought, head growing heavy, hot with pain. On Mom's palm he wrote, "3 22 02."

She didn't get it. Jeez.

Stabbing his finger irritably into her palm, he wrote out, "Friday March 22 2002."

Gary leaned down and spoke, in the faintly reproachful tone he'd used on Tim as a teenager, sleeping till mid-afternoon. "Son," he said. "It's Saturday, May the fourth. You're in San Antonio."

BELINDA RAWLINS

10810 ROGER DRIVE

2002

Belinda had gotten her hair done fancy, a complicated lacquer job that wove around her head in pretty braided loops. She opened her closet, momentarily dazzled by the clothes Wil had either bought her or in-sisted she buy. Years of deprivation before she'd married Wil—as a child, the wife of a no-count, and a single mother—had whittled her wardrobe down to about three drab outfits. "You are my wife," he'd said. "You're Mrs. Wilbert Rawlins Jr. You got to dress the part. You got to dress fine."

She no longer lay awake worrying about the light bill. On a night when she didn't feel like cooking, Wil took her out to eat—wherever she liked: Bennigan's. Chili's. Outback. Sizzler. All she had to do was name the place. They'd sit and talk like educated people. It was a little hard to get used to. She couldn't quite let down her guard.

Six o'clock. Belinda reached for her cell phone, opened it, and called the band room. Wil answered on about the tenth ring, and she could hear the chaos of the band tuning up. "You haven't left yet?"

"Huh?"

"We have a reservation for six thirty."

"Tonight?"

"Wilbert."

"Belinda, I thought I told you I got to play a convention."

Belinda's neck went cold. She closed her eyes. The white picket fence was so close, yet she couldn't quite get her hand on it. Wil was such a good husband in so many ways, yet she couldn't get his full attention, couldn't get him to stop and look at her, the way men in Harlequin romances looked at their women. She actually saw more of Da than she did of Wil. A couple of times a week, she took Da to his chemotherapy at the VA hospital and then out to eat baked ham at Mother's Restaurant on Poydras Street. He was all shrunk down now, but loved his food. And he knew how hard it could be to be married to his son. "You know how if you don't dust your furniture the dust piles up?" Da had asked her. "Before you know it, you got a whole molehill. Being married's the same way. When things go wrong, you better talk about them before they pile up too big."

Wil muffled his phone a second to talk to a band kid, then came back on the line. "You know how much we earn for the band doing this?" he said. Conventioneers holding parties at Mardi Gras World, the big hangar where most Mardi Gras floats were built, often hired Wil's band to play in a miniature Mardi Gras parade. "Band gets a thousand dollars," Wil said. "I get three hundred. This is good."

"Wilbert."

"What?"

"What's today's date?"

"I don't know. It's Friday, right?"

"Wilbert."

"What?"

"It's our anniversary."

Wil fell silent.

She slapped her phone shut.

TIM BRUNEAU

UNIVERSITY HOSPITAL,
SAN ANTONIO
2002

Tim Bruneau sat by the window in his wheelchair, wearing a gray bathrobe and badly needing a shave. His left leg jutted straight ahead on a shelf, festooned with pins and brackets, like an oil derrick. The slightest movement made his pelvis feel like a rotted tree about to crack open. His left arm was cocked straight sideways, locked in the plaster cast encircling his chest. The pinkie finger, hanging out, throbbed like hell. The stapled seam where Charity had put his skull back together itched like a bastard, but if he tried to raise his good hand to rub it, every broken piece of his left side, from shoulder to ankle, lit up in agony. His head was a toxic dump; he couldn't get a purchase on a thought, but could still see that fast little bastard running down Erato Street and remember the free exhilaration of being whole and running full out. He'd never know that again.

His parents and sister came every day, and so did the guys from the Task Force—they used up precious days off to drive eight hours and stand around him, making phony jokes. Between them and the satanic bastard from physical therapy, Tim hardly got a minute by himself to consider the problem that he seriously needed to solve: how to kill himself.

He gazed through the window at the parking lot. Only six stories. He couldn't be absolutely sure that would do the job. He might be able to get his hands on something sharp—scissors, say—and do his wrists, but the capillary action of the sheets might take the blood up where a nurse would notice. Pills? He could hoard his pain meds, but he looked forward to them so much, he wasn't sure he could endure the pain it would take to amass a deadly dose. Some of his friends kept off-duty guns on their hips, but there'd be no way to get one. No, the buffer cord was the thing. It had come to him on his way up from physical therapy, sweaty and trembling from the effort and pain: a stout black man was polishing the hallway floor with a thrumming power buffer, and as the ·

nurse rolled him past, the long cord had gotten him thinking. First he'd have to get his hands on the buffer and hoist it onto the windowsill. He might have to make a ramp, maybe out of the Formica coffee table in the nurses' lounge. Luckily, there was an air-conditioning unit in the window on which to rest it. He'd have to break the window, to make the opening big enough. The glass was probably pretty thick. On the other hand, the buffer was heavy. If he could get the leverage, he could swing it through the glass. He'd have to tie the power cord around his neck quickly—the noise would bring the nurses—and heave the buffer out the window. It would snap his neck as it yanked him out the window, and if that wasn't enough, it would pull him toward the ground headfirst, so he'd die fast when he hit.

It would have to wait, of course, until he was out of the cast and had some use of his left leg. But that was okay. He had time. In fact, he had a lifetime. That was the problem.

BILLY GRACE

2525 ST. CHARLES AVENUE
Christmas Day 2002

Billy lay sprawled in his bathrobe in one of the oxblood leather chairs of his second-floor den, his sanctum of kudu, buffalo, and deer. On a tortoiseshell tray next to him lay a green and white pill. A clink of china and silver and an excited murmur of caterers' voices rose through the floor. He should be down there helping, but he couldn't raise enough enthusiasm to move. He picked up the *Times-Picayune*, folded open to the editorial page. "Fishy," it called his defunct tax-collection contract with the city. A "cluster of New Orleans cronies" in "cahoots" with the mayor: it made Billy look like some cigar-chomping ward heeler. And to rub it in, they never failed to refer to him as "William Grace, 2002's King of Carnival." He couldn't believe that James Gill, the popular columnist, would stoop to such sensationalism or that Ashton Phelps, the publisher and an acquaintance of Billy's for years, would allow it.

Downstairs, they would be arraying duck sandwiches on silver trays, swirling pale yellow eggnog into silver tureens. Billy looked down at his pajama-clad legs, his feet in their slippers. Time to get up and get moving.

Yet he stayed in the chair. Did anybody, anywhere, understand what a contingency contract was? Was this his fate—to explain endlessly what it meant to win a contract in open bidding and be paid a legal percentage? He forced his eyes to the worst line in the column: "a monument to greed and effrontery." Greed! If there was a trait uptown reviled above all others, it was greed. Where else but New Orleans would enterprise and ambition be considered shameful?

"All right, Billy, enough," Anne said behind him. He turned. She looked smashing in a dress of blue silk. She had both hands to an ear, installing a dangling diamond earring. The antique clock on the shelf, beneath his grandmother's trophy tarpon, said eleven fifteen. In forty-five minutes, all of uptown would flood the house to nibble his duck sandwiches, sip his eggnog, and wish him a Merry Christmas. Among them would be his oldest friends. Among them, too, would be those relishing his comeuppance for getting down in the mud with the Morials. There was no having one without the other. The uptown life could not be ordered à la carte. He put the green and white pill on his tongue and swallowed it dry.

JOANN GUIDOS

ST. CLAUDE AVENUE
2003

JoAnn moved the reciprocating saw from the couch and the air compressor from the easy chair. She cleared a cardboard box full of wall clocks from the coffee table and moved a carton of clothes from the floor. "Sit down, sit down," she said. "Want a beer?"

"Don't you ever throw anything away?" Kathy asked. With those intense blue eyes, she was as beautiful in jeans, sneakers, and a T-shirt as she'd ever been in the Armani and Versace she'd worn as the high-spending Mrs. John Guidos.

"You don't get to boss me around anymore," JoAnn said, and they both laughed. JoAnn was nervous having Kathy and her new husband, Roney, in her apartment above the bar. She got along well enough with both of them to have helped them fix up a leased space in Arabi for a bar they'd wanted to open. Having them drop in, though, was confusing.

JoAnn wondered if she looked good to Kathy. She was wearing blue capris and a plain lavender pullover; her auburn hair was shoulder length, her nails an inch long and blood-red.

"How's your back?" JoAnn asked Roney. He'd fallen against a crane on the job at Air Products and was applying for disability.

"Hurts," Roney said, settling into JoAnn's easy chair. He was a big, swarthy Italian guy from deep in the Plaquemines bayous, volcanic and quick to anger, but he treated Kathy well. He was respectful of JoAnn, too. He never said boo about her dressing as a woman, and the whole time they'd worked together fixing up the bar in Arabi, he'd called her "Chief," in deference to her superior carpentry skills.

JoAnn had bought two side-by-side buildings on St. Claude Avenue between Elysian Fields and Colton Middle School. Both were total wrecks—listing, peeling, full of former tenants' junk. One had no utilities at all. But she'd spent her life looking in mirrors at a football player and seeing a woman. She had no trouble envisioning a bar in one building and a restaurant in the other, with apartments above both.

Kathy took a deep breath and told a tale of woe. They'd lost the bar in Arabi and gone to live near Kathy's mother in a mobile home in Mississippi. But Kathy and her mother had never gotten along, so that didn't last. Then they'd tried living with Kathy's brother in Virginia, but that went no better. Finally, they moved to the bayou where Roney had grown up, but living out in the bush, with no washer or dryer and nothing around but alligators and mosquitoes, had driven her crazy.

JoAnn laughed at the thought of Kathy, the princess of Metairie, in a shack on the bayou, washing clothes by hand. Nice little Baptist girl from Mississippi marries a football player, has a girl and a boy and a nice house in the suburbs. Then the man turns into a woman, she loses her house and her cars and all her fancy things, and here she is, close to fifty, still a princess at heart.

"We tried living by Mother's daddy in Stateline, but that was no good."

JoAnn saw where this was going. Roney and Kathy were homeless. If Kathy looked pale, it was no wonder, after the year they'd had. Roney couldn't take a job or he'd lose his shot at disability.

"Hey," JoAnn said quickly, so they wouldn't have to ask. "Why don't you stay here? We can fix this apartment up good enough to stay in."

Kathy and Roney looked at each other. JoAnn could practically hear the tension hiss out of them like air from a punctured tire. Kathy's eyes went wet. "Oh, John—JoAnn. Thank you!"

"It'll be fun. I need help anyway, getting the bar open."

WILBERT RAWLINS JR.

GEORGE WASHINGTON CARVER
HIGH SCHOOL
2003

Wil ran his eye down the list of kids failing at least one course. Brandon, Jason, Joseph, Juicy, Christopher—almost every member of his second-line band. Since the night he'd run into six of them in the French Quarters, he'd been working with them every day at lunchtime and again after marching-band practice, standing over them as they blew in a circle, beating his hands together, shouting, breaking them off the steady beat of marching band and bringing out the jumping syncopation of the second line. He'd kept Mr. Jackson off their necks, incurred the wrath of Belinda, explained to any mama who'd noticed them missing that he was teaching them a skill they could use to make money. He was molding them into a genuine second-line band that someday could charge a thousand dollars or more to parade. They had it in them. They'd been hearing that unique rhythm since the day they were born, and peeling them back to find it was more fun than he'd had in years. But every day he'd ask, "You got your homework done, right?" and every day it was, "Yes, sir."

Shit. The one thing he hadn't done was ask to see it.

The noise from the band room was deafening—tubas and trombones tuning, the rat-a-tat of snare drums, a bass drum booming, chairs scraping, kids yelling, laughter. The usual pregame cacophony as the bandsmen worked themselves up for a basketball game.

"Hey!" he yelled. The room quieted. "Brandon! Jason! Joseph! Juicy! Christopher!" The boys separated themselves from the crowd, and as they approached, Wil could see his problem. Each wore a gleaming new T-shirt, brand-new Dickies, and a pair of hot-looking Nike Air Maxes: red, gold, black, silver.

There were twelve in the band; they'd reeled in a couple of Lawrence's best bandsmen from Kennedy. Every night, out at the corner of Bourbon and Canal, they blew their hearts out. They played the Fairmont Hotel every Tuesday and Thursday. They'd even played behind Big Al Carson. Carson had named the band, as he waved them good night: "To Be Continued." They were good. And they weren't selling marijuana or rolling tourists in the French Quarters.

"What is this?" Wil asked in mock surprise, holding up the list. "Why are you failing classes?"

Silence.

"Didn't Mr. Jackson tell you he'd shut you down if you didn't keep your grades up?"

Silence.

"Listen to me," Wil said. "Band. Does not. Supersede. Your education. If you don't pass, you don't graduate. If you don't graduate, you don't go to college."

"Mr. Rawlins." It was Brandon, holding up a hand and slouching at the same time.

"Without college, you can't . . ."

"Mr. Rawlins."

"What?"

"College?"

"College," Wil said. "So you can be somebody."

"Mr. Rawlins, how much you make?"

"I take home about a thousand dollars every two weeks," Wil said. That would rock them back, he thought.

Brandon snorted. "Shit," he said. "I made that last weekend."

TIM BRUNEAU

NEW ORLEANS POLICE DEPARTMENT
RECORDS ROOM
2003

Tim hoisted a file box from the steel shelf and, hugging it to his chest, began the long, awkward trip back to his desk, his gait like a mari-onette's—bobbing, bouncing, insubstantial. He listed to the left; that leg didn't straighten completely, and the toe dragged. His rebuilt left arm ached under the weight of the file box, but the pinkie no longer throbbed. After several surgeries to try to fix it, the doctors had finally chopped it off.

The Records room was a windowless cavern in the basement of po-lice headquarters on Broad Avenue, a dungeon from which no man re-turned alive. The shrunken gnomes of Records, clutching sheaves of paper, shuffled listlessly from file cabinet to desk and back, like Morlocks. That's what he'd look like in another few years. He withdrew a handful of buff-colored liquor-license inspection forms from the file box and be-gan cataloging. He was still a policeman, sort of. At least he was still around cops. Two uniformed patrolmen stood at a table across the room, looking through books of mug shots. Their duty belts, hung with guns, ammo clips, nightsticks, and cuffs, even more than their unbroken bod-ies, filled Tim with envy. He wore a badge, but he was a file clerk. They did police work.

The younger cop, a redhead, drifted down a row of filing cabinets, peering at the alphabetical listings.

"Hey," the older cop hollered. He stood, holding his radio up. "Shooting on Bernadotte." They hurried out, leaving the mug-shot books on the table. Tim felt like a kid with polio in one of those black-and-white movies, watching from an iron lung while his friends raced off to play stickball. His skull itched, and he ran his fingers along the curved welt under his hair. The Charity doctors had sawed off a huge piece of skull within minutes of his accident, to let the brain swell. They'd popped it into a freezer and sent it with him, in an Igloo cooler, to San Antonio. Good old Charity. Nobody knew trauma like those guys.

He pawed through the buff-colored liquor-license forms until a shadow fell across his desk: Steve Smiegel, from the Sixth District, broad and fit, wearing new sergeant's stripes.

"Hey," Tim said.

"You happy doing this?" Steve stood with his arms folded.

"Hell no. But what the hell else am I going to do?"

"You ought to come see Cannatella," Smiegel said. "He's commanding the Sixth." Tim had known Anthony Cannatella as a lieutenant. He was old-school NOPD, from a family of cops. Whatever else you might say about him, he was a cop's cop, not a brownnosing bureaucrat.

"I can't . . ."

"Tell you something about Cannatella," Steve said. "When you got thirty years on the force, you can retire at full pay. Cannatella's got thirty-seven. So he's been working seven years for free."

"He's not going to want a nine-fingered cripple."

"Come with me to the Sixth. We'll hang out, and if Cannatella's there, you can see him."

Tim left the liquor-license records on his desk and loped up the corridor after Steve. He could disappear for hours and nobody would notice.

The Sixth District station was a tall, modern building on Martin Luther King Jr. Boulevard. It was spare, cheap, and impersonal, but at least in good repair. "Is that Timmy Bruneau?" a gravelly voice shouted, and a bear of a man charged toward him, arms thrown open wide. It was Cannatella, a little older and heavier than Bruneau remembered, wearing the white shirt of a district commander. He was built like a street-corner mailbox, with a hard, round belly, no neck, and a heavy dome of a head. He wrapped Tim in a backbreaker of a hug. "Come in, come in, son." Cannatella pulled him into his office, sat him in a straight chair, and collapsed into his swivel chair. The desk was covered with snow globes, paperweights, and a statue of the leaning tower of Pisa. "Well!" Cannatella said happily.

"Well?"

"You happy at Records?"

"Uh . . ."

"Of course not! You're the police! Listen. You got injured doing police work. Far as I'm concerned, you're a hero."

"Thank you." Tim picked up something heavy from Cannatella's desk that was holding down a stack of papers. He bounced it in his hand.

"I was at Charity the day you got hit. My wife, too. They had you on four; they figured you weren't going to make it."

"I don't remember."

"Of course not. We could hardly see you for all the bandages and tubes. So: What's your plan?"

"I'm pretty much stuck in Records."

Cannatella slammed his hand down on the desk. "You want to do police work, this is where we do it."

Tim looked at the weight he was jouncing in his hand: a box of AK-47 rounds.

"Maybe not on the street right away, but we can do better than Records, for God's sake. Come with me."

Limping along behind Cannatella, Tim noticed the captain wasn't wearing a gun, not even the miniature Glock most brass carried. It was odd, because Cannatella was no desk jockey. He was out all the time. "Why don't you wear a gun?"

"Got one in the car," Cannatella said. "But after all these years, if I can't talk my way out of trouble . . ." He stopped and opened a door. A bald man in plainclothes sat at a desk. "This is Tony," Cannatella said. The man raised a hand in greeting.

"Basically, you'll be going over reports on any case that results in arrest. You look the paperwork over, make sure it's complete, and if not, you send the arresting officer back out for more information. I'm tired of guys walking because the paperwork's bad."

It wasn't police work, but it was a lot closer than cataloging liquor-license applications in the Records room.

"You two should get along," Cannatella said. "Tony here was shot in the head a couple years back."

BILLY GRACE

2525 ST. CHARLES AVENUE
Mardi Gras 2004

Billy climbed out of bed while it was still dark. He hadn't slept much. The week leading up to Mardi Gras was one long party—too much food, too much alcohol, too much yakety-yak—and through it all, a million details to nail down. Even now, as he padded downstairs in his pajamas, his right ear felt the ghost of the cell phone that had spent much of the week pressed there. Yet he was oddly relaxed, as though cruise control had delivered him safely past every precipice, as though his fall from grace in the tax-collection affair had loosened the flywheel that once kept him revving too high.

He made himself a cup of coffee in the second-floor kitchen. Soon it would be a mob scene, as the Gumbo Shop delivered rectangular pans of étouffée, rice, debris, and gumbo, and his in-laws and children hurried to prepare for the hundred-odd people who would pass through the house on this day of days. Billy glanced at the clock. He needed to swing by the Rex den in a warehouse on Claiborne to make sure the floats were ready to be towed to Napoleon Avenue. Then he had to get uptown to the Cascade Stables in Audubon to collect the horse on which he'd lead the parade as captain of Rex. (Billy eschewed the tradition of having a black groom lead the captain, so all week he'd been practicing riding.) He'd have to be in costume—plumed hat, mask, and gold-braided cape—no later than eleven.

Billy drank his coffee, dressed, and crept downstairs as the sky brightened. Ivory was setting up the pots and burners for the crawfish boil. George was sweeping the metal bleachers in front. He didn't look well—pale and splotchy. Billy could hear him breathing from across the yard. Nobody loved Mardi Gras, or the Rex organization, the way George did.

All along the St. Charles Avenue neutral ground, people huddled in folding chairs, blankets wrapped around their shoulders, holding parade-watching spots. For as far as the eye could see, six-foot-tall stepladders sprouted from the grassy median, wheels like those off toy wagons bolted to the sides for easy dragging, makeshift wooden thrones nailed to the tops to hold children. Billy had never seen anything like New Orleans's homemade mini-grandstands elsewhere, but then no other city had an event that would require them.

"You ready?" Billy asked.

"Suit's all laid out," George said.

"You'll be okay on the ladder? Liam or Robert could do it."

"Nah," George said. "They don't have the clothes." He smiled and patted Billy's arm, as though to say, let me be; there won't be many more times I can enjoy the pleasure.

Billy retrieved his bicycle from the carriage house, punched in the code for the big iron gate, and stood back as it creaked open with a bang. Emerging from the ivy-covered wall, he mounted the bike and turned right, away from familiar St. Charles Avenue, toward Carondelet Street. The Rex mansion, one of the premier addresses in the city, stood not two blocks from some of the most dangerous streets in New Orleans. Friends in New York, Washington, Los Angeles, and San Francisco went about their daily lives without ever seeing tumbledown houses, burglar-barred storefronts, or destitute people lounging on stoops. In New Orleans, no matter how much money you had in the bank, you looked on poverty every day.

Billy pedaled up the shattered pavement of Second Street, through its notoriously violent intersection with Danneel. Up ahead, a car pulling a U-Haul trailer parked, and two black men climbed out. As Billy watched, they walked to the rear of the trailer and rolled up the gate. Billy hopped off his bike. A searing burst of yellow green—a man encased in feathers and plumes—climbed from the U-Haul, his hands raised to steady a four-foot-tall headdress. A smaller man—a boy—emerged behind him, wearing the same hallucinogenic shades of chartreuse. A third man jumped out, holding a standard, bright with ribbons, beads, and feathers: "Wild Magnolias."

Billy held his breath, as though bird-watching. Spy boy, flag boy, and chief. It had been years since he'd taken the time on Mardi Gras morning to go looking for Indians; in the swamp of middle-age duties, he'd forgotten the thrill.

The Wild Magnolias' spy boy trotted up Second Street. The flag boy followed, fluttering his primrose colors. The chief, his headdress fanning like a peacock's halo, hung back with the men from the car, sipping beer.

Billy mounted and rode up Second Street past them. "Good morning!" he called.

"All right," they said. *Ahhite.*

Billy passed the flag boy, a coffee-colored Creole whose face gleamed with sweat. At the corner, Billy caught up to the spy boy, who was waving a canary green arm urgently up Saratoga Street. Coming toward them, about two blocks away, were half a dozen feathered-and-beaded men—dark blue with white, orange, and red. They looked wildly out of place among the sagging houses and beat-up cars. A small crowd in ordinary clothes followed, drumming and chanting.

The Wild Magnolias' flag boy turned back toward the chief and let out a sharp whistle. The chief set his beer bottle on the roof of the car, adjusted his fabulous headdress, and advanced.

Billy backed away from the corner, to make room.

The spy boy strutted up Saratoga Street, yelling, "Spy boy! Wild Magnolia spy boy!"

The blue tribe hollered back, high, demented whoops, and the drummers chanted, "Nothin' but trouble, nothin' but trouble, nothin' but trouble."

The chiefs met at last, and Billy gripped the handlebars, ready to bolt at the first sight of a knife. The chiefs bobbed and postured like gigantic roosters as the circle of drummers and chanters closed around them, filling the street with a racketing rhythm. As far as Billy could see, he was the only non-participant watching. The two chiefs shrieked gibberish, thrusting their heads forward and straining the cords in their necks, morning sunlight glinting off their sweat-streaming faces. They dipped so close to each other that their feathered headdresses closed like a blue and chartreuse clamshell. The drumming and chanting grew louder and faster. Then suddenly, as the drumming and chanting climaxed and Billy expected the scene to explode in blood and gunfire, the racket ceased, and the chiefs fell into each other's arms, laughing. Everybody dropped out of character: a bunch of sweaty guys standing on a street corner in outlandish suits.

One of the drummers, an old man in a newsboy's cap, came running over to Billy and handed him an open can of beer. "That's how young men should fight!" he said. "With words! And with pretty!" He laughed, a high, ecstatic laugh. It had been a long time since Billy had drunk a beer at eight in the morning. It was cold and delicious.

Holding the can in one hand and brimming with the Mardi Gras love, Billy continued up Second to La Salle, turning left toward Washington. Across the street from a sinister-looking housing project, Shakespeare Park—a wretched, balding expanse of grass and broken playground equipment—teemed with life and color. Indians who'd finished battling were drinking beer and retelling the tales; others were just getting into their costumes.

Billy was no more than half a mile from the Rex mansion, and it was like being on another planet. He marveled that all the years he'd spent these early Mardi Gras hours preparing for grand parades and the black-tie ball, these parallel traditions, equally unique to New Orleans, were taking place in the funky parts of town. Across the park, an old man with coppery skin and high cheekbones was being helped into a peach and white headdress. His suit bulged in great geometric patterns, every millimeter crusted with swirls of beads. Such an old man, Billy thought, with strength to parade, in that enormous suit.

The man looked oddly familiar. The crown swung up onto his head, bigger, grander, and more complicated than any other in the park. Billy recognized the face from countless *Times-Picayune* profiles. It was Tootie Montana.

As chairman of the mayor's Mardi Gras Advisory Committee, Billy had often thought of calling the great peacemaker, the inventor of a whole new art form, the Mardi Gras Indian honored by the National Endowment for the Arts. Somehow, though, he'd never gotten around to making the call. He walked over. "Mr. Montana?"

The old man looked up impatiently. "Who are you?"

"I'm Billy Grace." He put out a hand, but Montana was tying something at his waist, and Billy drew back. "I'm captain of the Rex organization."

Tootie looked Billy up and down, and Billy felt his otherness: polo shirt, boat shoes. Tootie nodded.

"I'm chair of the mayor's Mardi Gras Advisory Committee."

"Yeah," Tootie said. Then, to one of his assistants, "Get the crown back a hair."

"Everybody's got a role in carnival," Billy said. "You certainly do."

"What's your name again?"

"Bill. Bill Grace." Tootie nodded, eyes rolling up toward the spreading headdress, hands raised, moving it left, right, centering it.

"I read that you make a new suit every year. Boy, that's great. We've been using the same suit over and over for years. I guess that's the point. We have to take it in and let it out."

Tootie grunted, adjusting his headdress.

"You and I have a lot of common interests," Billy said. "We should get together."

"All right," Tootie said. "That's fine." Billy didn't know if he meant getting together or that the crown was right. Tootie stood up, a sun god, suddenly twice as tall as Billy.

"I'm in the phone book, on Villere Street," he said. "Allison Montana." He put out a knobby hand, encased in feathers and marvelous beadwork, and Billy shook it.

Four hours later, Billy was sitting on a folding chair in the Rex den, in tights, tunic, and plumed helmet, pulling on a mask, wondering if he'd dreamed the whole thing.

BELINDA RAWLINS

5972 DREUX AVENUE
2004

"I think you should see this one," Belinda said, cupping the cell phone at her cheek.

"Does it have space?"

She could hear horns in the background, though it was past five o'clock. "I think you should see it," she said, adding sternly, "Wilbert."

"Yeah, yeah, I hear you."

This was house number—what? Fifty? She was starting to feel like a hamster on a wheel. It was his dream to own a home. She was fine with renting, but Wilbert talked about only two things: band and a home.

This house seemed perfect. It was a neat, single-story, redbrick ranch with white shutters and trim, set on a big grassy corner lot. A white picket fence would look good. It sat just across the bridge in New Orleans East, not far from where Wil's ma lived. It made Belinda sad that Wil's da, who had encouraged her in the search and helped her envision it, would never get to see it. Sometimes she believed that she felt Da's death more than Wil, or maybe she'd just processed it more. "Da's gone? Gone where?" Wil had asked when Lawrence reached them on Wil's cell phone with the news. She'd watched Wil harden up like a Jell-O mold, eyes cold, jaw stiff, and he'd stayed that way all the way through the wake and funeral while Lawrence, and Ma, Belinda, and the children had cried and cried.

After a while the Lexus pulled up, and Wil stepped out, smiling so wide that Belinda could see his broken front tooth. Little Curtis ran to him. Wil treated him so much nicer than Curtis's own father, and he was around so much more, that Curtis had stopped calling him Mr. Wil and started calling him Dad.

The realtor let them in, and Wil let out a long sigh. The living room was huge. "Nice," he said. They walked through the eat-in kitchen. "Nice." They looked in on two large bedrooms and a bathroom with a shower and tub. "Nice."

"Come see the rest," the realtor said.

"There's more?" Wil squeezed Belinda's shoulder. They walked through a spacious utility room and separate laundry room and into a master suite with a bedroom almost as big as the living room. The bathroom had a two-person Jacuzzi tub.

Wil leaned over and whispered in Belinda's ear. "We can get this for one forty?"

Without a word, she handed him the flyer, the price printed across the top: one eighteen.

Wil walked back into the living room and, to the surprise of Belinda and the realtor, lay down on the polished wood floor. He put his hands behind his head and sighed. "Write up the contract!" he shouted. Curtis threw himself on top of Wil and hugged him. "I wish Da could see this," Wil said, smiling up at Belinda.

JOYCE MONTANA

MOTHER-IN-LAW LOUNGE

2004

Joyce put her hand over her mouth and giggled. High above Claiborne Avenue, on the outer wall of Ernie K. Doe's Mother-in-Law Lounge, loomed a giant painted likeness of her face. "They said they was going to put Tootie up there!" she said.

"Can't have Tootie without you, Miss Joyce." Fred Johnson pointed at Tootie's likeness on the other end of the facade. "Nobody's ever seen one without the other."

He had gotten her right—and Tootie and Ernie, too. She'd be looking down on Claiborne Avenue forever.

Fred led Joyce under the I-10 overpass. The crowd was noisy in the great concrete vault. Joyce remembered the graceful oaks that once shaded the commercial center of black New Orleans, a tunnel of green spreading above the neutral ground. They'd cut those oaks down in the 1950s, put up the interstate, and ruined Claiborne Avenue. Only the ghosts of the businesses remained—Cohen's Formal Shop, the Basin Street Club, the Bottom Line, Jackie & George's—mostly boarded-up storefronts flanked by the raised highway. It always made Joyce a little sad to gather under the I-10.

It was Super Sunday, a new, third occasion for the suits to come out. Indians were running every which way in so many colors that Joyce's eyes hurt. The blare of Rebirth Brass Band echoed off the underside of the freeway. The rain stopped, and Fred excused himself to run ahead and help with the arrangements at Hunter's Field. Joyce fell in behind the horse-drawn cart carrying Tootie. Tootie sat on a bench behind the driver, facing sideways and wearing a radiant orange suit—much like the first of his fancy suits, but more elaborate, more heavily beaded and sequined. His crown was propped on a chair beside him. On his head he wore only his black Indian-braid wig. He was still ropy strong, but age had chiseled his face gaunt, and dark spots spread across his copper-colored cheekbones. He looked sad to be riding, like a prisoner on his way to the guillotine. All year, as they'd worked on the suit, he'd called it his last. Nobody believed him, because he'd said it each year since he'd made Darryl chief of the Yellow Pocahontas. He no longer had the wind to walk, and he rubbed his armpit a lot, saying it burned inside. Not that he'd go to a doctor; he was happy with garlic water.

By the time the cart reached Hunter's Field, a triangle of grass beside the overpass, several hundred people had gathered. "Big Chief Tootie Montana is saying farewell to y'all!" a young man on a raised platform shouted into a microphone. "This is his last." Tootie climbed down from the cart, mounted the platform, and moved to the mic. "That's right," he said. "This here is my last suit. But I'll be doing this until the day I die. Wherever the Indians are, you'll see me!"

One by one, young Indians came forward to praise Tootie and shake his hand. It was a beautiful scene, but something troubled Joyce. His last suit. Yet he'll be doing this until the day he dies? What does he mean by that?

"You know what he said?" Darryl loomed up in front of Joyce in an

enormous white suit, breaking her reverie. Darryl's crown was an entirely new design. Instead of radiating out from his head, it flew straight
up, like a stovepipe, supporting a hoop of four-foot-long feathers, which
hovered above him like a halo. An umbrella crown, he called it, something that Tootie had talked about but never made. Darryl's face was
alight, his eyes wet. "He said, 'You're pretty, you're pretty.' He couldn't
stop saying it. I told him he done good, too. I been out of hand with
him, but I told him, 'You done good. You're pretty.' I told him that."

"Good for you!" Joyce beamed.

"But he couldn't stop saying it." Darryl's eyes shone. " 'You're pretty,'
he said. 'You're pretty.' "

WILBERT RAWLINS JR.

5972 DREUX AVENUE
2004

The Carver band was soaring. They'd played in Pasadena at the Rose
Bowl—the first airplane ride for most of these kids. They'd played in
Washington, D.C., at the U.S. Marine Corps War Memorial and on the
White House lawn and then—on a spontaneous invitation—at the
Kennedy Center in a concert hall full of people in tuxedos and gowns.
They'd filled the Superdome more than once. But to come home at the
end of a long day to a house he owned, to make plans for expansions and
landscaping without having to worry about a landlord—that was the
dream.

Wil parked his Lexus and took a moment to enjoy the feeling. The
car itself meant nothing to him; he kept it to show the band kids that
you didn't have to be a drug dealer to have nice things. The house,
though, was the achievement of his dreams. A redbrick ranch on a sweep
of lawn, like out of a storybook. No more moving around, Burgundy to
St. Roch, to St. Roch again, to Roger. The three months since he and
Belinda had moved in to 5972 Dreux had been heaven. He had roots
now. He was somebody.

He walked up the path to the door, where he'd been considering adding flower beds, a project he could take on with his ma. It was good to have her living with them since Da's death. Wil unlocked the door and pushed it open.

The door bumped something: suitcases. He looked up. Ma sat in the recliner with her head tipped to one side, leaning on her fist, looking like the day Da died: not surprised, but infinitely sad and disappointed. She brought her eyes up slowly to Wil's.

Belinda stepped through the archway into the living room, regal in a suit and high heels, holding Curtis by the hand. His cheeks were wet. Mookey stood behind them, nearly as tall as Belinda, but gazing at the floor, as though trying to shrink.

"Hey, Mr. Wil," Curtis squeaked.

Wil winced. So much for "Dad."

Belinda flapped a hand at the suitcases. "Yeah, they're mine. I'll be back for the rest."

"What?"

"I can't compete. You got your band. That's all you need."

"Wait." Wil grabbed the door handle, propping himself up. "Sit down a minute."

Ma hadn't changed her position in the recliner.

"Please," Wil said.

Belinda marched to the sofa, sat heavily, and pulled Curtis onto her lap. Mookey went and stood behind her, an ungainly changeling looking for a private place to rest her eyes.

"Maybe my ma is right," Belinda said, choking up. "Maybe what I need is a hobby. But what am I going to do, go bowling? Oprah says do a book group. I can't do a book group, because nobody else I know wants to read."

"Belinda . . ."

"After parade season comes concert band. Then comes summer band camp, then football, and then it's Mardi Gras all over again. Homecoming's on my birthday. A convention's on our anniversary. I never see you."

"I got a responsibility . . . ," Wil began.

"What about to me?" Belinda splayed her long fingers on her chest. "What about your kids right here—Mookey and Curtis? What about making sure Niecy gets through college?"

"I love Niecy and Mookey and Curtis. But they have you. The kids in band—they don't have nobody. You got to get to know them, Belinda."

"I don't want to know them!"

Wil slumped against the door. "How could you not want to know them?"

"What was last night?" Belinda sat up, and Curtis tumbled off to the side. "You get a call for ten o'clock and you're up and out the door."

Wil threw his big arms wide. "That was Ramón's mom, in tears. You know Ramón: plays mellophone, has an ear, has rhythm, all the makings of a musician. But he's not in control. Last night he said—excuse me, Ma—he said, 'Fuck you,' to his grandmother."

"So?"

"So? So? Boy says that to his grandmother?"

"You the band teacher, Wilbert. You're not the father."

"I'm all the father he's ever going to have! I drove over to the Desire to bust his ass for him. I put the wood on him till he apologized, and today in school Ramón had focus." Wil's voice dropped to a whiny whisper. "That's what it means to be a bandleader. You take care of your band, Belinda. Not just the part that blows the horn, the whole child."

"Robin's got me half convinced it isn't band at all," Belinda said.

"What do you mean?"

"You know what I mean."

"Belinda . . ."

"All I'm saying is, I don't know, maybe band's enough for you, but I don't care about band, Wil! I don't care!" She stood up.

"Don't I take care of you?" Wil threw his arms wide. "I put you through school! I gave you a hundred dollars for a 'me' day, and you gave it away to some friend and had lunch at McDonald's!"

"Maybe that's it!" Belinda's voice shook. "Maybe I'm not used to being taken care of! I can't get used to it. I came up hungry."

"So you're leaving because you've got it too good?"

"No." Belinda stepped in close, firing a sharp, painted nail at his chin. "I'm leaving because I can't compete with band. That's all you want in the world. It's all you've got time for. It's all you think about. I'm not going to try to compete. I'm not going to put Curtis through it. He looks up to you, and you don't see him. All you see is your band."

Belinda marched over to Ma, leaned down, and kissed her. Ma

hugged Curtis, then Mookey. Belinda led them across the living room, gathered up the bags, handed two to Mookey, and walked out. The door closed behind them with a loud click.

JOYCE MONTANA

VILLERE STREET
March 19, 2005

"What's that?" Tootie whispered. Joyce's eyes popped open. Someone was banging on the glass storm door. She looked at the clock; it was after midnight. Someone must be dead.

The doorbell rang. Tootie got out of bed and padded to the door. Joyce stood in the bedroom, wide-eyed.

"Who is it?" Tootie yelled.

"It's Darryl." Tootie opened up. Darryl was out of breath, his eyes wild. Joyce's heart skipped. One of the girls—Gwendolyn or Phyllis or Denise. One of them must be dead. "I'm sorry to come so late," he said.

"What is it?" Tootie stood with his chest out, belligerent.

"I know you and I have had our differences," Darryl said. "I know you think we're in some kind of competition."

"I'm just saying that umbrella crown was trying to make me look bad," Tootie grunted. "The concept was out of my head, not yours."

Joyce was filled with a mixture of relief and disappointment. If they were bickering about the suit, everybody must be alive.

"You think I let you down when you went to jail."

"That's not why I'm here!" Darryl said.

"Tootie!" Joyce came up behind him. "Let him talk!"

Tootie looked Darryl up and down, as though only now realizing that something extraordinary must have brought Darryl here in the middle of the night. "What is it?"

"I wanted you to hear from me what just happened at St. Joseph's Night."

Tootie's eyebrows went up. "Sit down." He had skipped St. Joseph's Night; he wasn't masking, so he didn't have any business there.

Darryl sat on the yellow sofa, and Joyce brought him a glass of cold drink from the kitchen. "We was up at Washington and La Salle like always and it was good. Man, you should have seen them suits."

"Yeah?"

"It was cool. Everybody was having a good time. Then suddenly, out of nowhere, come half the police force, driving in from all directions, their sirens going, like whoop whoop whoop. And they're making everybody get out the street. Like, 'Shut this down!' and 'Get your ass out the street.' They was talking rough, I'm telling you. Pushing children out the street, putting their hands on old ladies, like we was criminals or something. Like we was rioting.

"I had Bertrand Butler in my car. He got out to try to talk and they right away threw him on the ground." Joyce gasped. Delicate little white-haired Bertrand! "Someone yelled, 'Shoot! Shoot!' and I turned my car around, keeping my head behind the metal post so that if they started shooting, I wouldn't get a bullet in my head. They held Bertrand awhile, but I think they let him go. Arrested his daughter, though, and I heard one guy got his arm broke."

Tootie frowned at the carpet, massaging his shoulder where it burned inside. His whole life, he'd worked to get the humbug out of the Indians; they never cut or shot each other anymore. The police, though, were still beating on them. He looked up at Darryl. "Thank you for coming over. You're a good boy."

TIM BRUNEAU

ST. ANDREW STREET
2005

The boy lay upside down on his back, feet and lower legs on the cement porch, body draped head down on the peeling stairs. He'd come out of his outsized shoes when he fell; they sat neatly, side by side, on the front-door lintel. He was wearing a white T-shirt silk-screened with a smiling face. Under the picture: "James Tapp, Third Ward Magnolia Gone Home. Thugged in 09.09.77, Thugged out 11.26.03." By tomorrow, someone would be wearing a T-shirt with this kid's picture on it. Thugged out.

Tim sat on the stoop beside the body, bending his left leg painfully.

The kid had a small burn on his upper lip from holding a lighter too close when firing up crack. Tim bent to look at the hole in the forehead and with a gloved hand turned the kid's head to see the exit wound. The head resisted; the kid was stiffening up.

"I'll get that shirt off him." James Brown, the morgue tech from the coroner's office, stood at the bottom of the stairs in a Rasta skullcap and sunglasses, his gray beard twisted into a fashionable tail like an aging reggae star.

"Yeah?"

"Chance of powder residue, if the gun was close enough. That might tell you something."

Tim pulled himself to his feet and hobbled up the stoop. Homicide was better than fact-checking other cops' reports as an A-case detective, but it wasn't the boot-in-the-ass kind of work he loved. Police, in Tim's mind, were supposed to stop crime. Investigating a murder after it happened was clerical work. It didn't do a thing for the victim.

He stepped inside the house, blinded momentarily by the contrast between harsh sunlight and shade-drawn gloom. The stink—an oleaginous miasma of sweat, dirty laundry, cigarettes, and bacon—made him want to retch.

The front room was tiny, with walls of cheap brown paneling. A bare single mattress, copiously stained, lay atop four milk cartons. Paper grocery bags on the floor overflowed with old clothing. A bottle of berry-flavored Cisco wine lay overturned on the grimy carpet. A plastic bookshelf displayed a china angel with big eyes, a purple jar of hair pomade, a gold plastic crucifix rising from a disk of marble, and a plastic cup in the shape of a hand grenade, encircled with Mardi Gras beads. An aluminum fry pan half full of old dried food balanced precariously atop a television set with a vise grip for a channel selector and a bent-wire hanger for an aerial. Three more television sets made a little tower in the corner.

Tim rotated, scanning for clues. The front wall had nine bullet holes—beside the door, above the door, in the door frame.

Armando, Tim's stocky, light-skinned partner, emerged from the back of the house with a befuddled-looking, emaciated old man who was holding up filthy jockey shorts with one hand and scratching his bushy gray beard with the other. "He says he was sleeping in back and didn't see a thing."

"Does he know the kid?"

"No sir, Mr. Officer. I never seen him," the old man said, glassy-eyed. "Leastways I don't think."

"Anything on the kid?" Armando asked.

"Crackhead," Tim said. How many millions of dollars had gone to bringing these people out of poverty? Job Corps, United Negro College Fund, welfare . . .

The old man banged around in a box and brought out a miniature Crock-Pot. He took it to the sink and ran water into it. He plugged it in and from a plastic bag shook in what looked like pink and red dried flowers. A sickly sweet aroma mingled with the stink.

"Potpourri," the man said proudly.

"Shell casings," Tim said to Armando. They looked balefully at the floor. Between the grimy clothes, old shoes, and wine bottles rooting for spent brass was going to be disgusting work.

"How many we looking for?" Armando asked. He turned to the old man. "How many shots did you hear?"

"Just a couple. Maybe three."

"There's more holes than that." Tim pointed to the riddled wall.

"Oh, no, Mr. Officer." The old man hobbled to the front door and pointed with a long, bony finger to the two holes above it. "That's from when Felton shot Bonnie in 1992," he said. He pointed to a hole in the door frame. "Cecilia put that one there, but she didn't hurt nobody." He hobbled to the TV. "These two here I did one time by mistake."

Tim needed air. He stepped onto the porch.

Up and down St. Andrew, people were watching from open doors. Since the so-called police riot in Shakespeare Park on St. Joseph's Night, relations between the NOPD and the people of New Orleans had hit a new low, especially in the Sixth District. It would be a rotten morning, going door-to-door, asking who'd heard what, who'd seen what, who knew what. "I didn't see nothing, Mr. Officer" was probably all he'd get.

The old man stepped onto the porch, squinting. He looked down at the kid sprawled on the steps, cocked his head to one side. "Hmf."

"Know him?"

"That could be Marvin's sister's cousin's son."

"Got a name?"

"I know him as Boot." He cocked his head to the other side. "Him and his daddy used to fish. Brought me a speckled trout big as my arm one time. You know what I found in its belly? An earring. Solid gold. Got it right inside if you want to see it."

The sun was hot. The man's story enveloped Tim like kicked-up dust. Tim sometimes preferred the stony silence.

New Orleans was like one big misdemeanor lockup—miscreants, fuckups, and screw-offs, even the harmless old men. The rest of the United States—the rest of the world—was out there working its ass off, getting ahead, while New Orleans lazed along, sitting on stoops and drinking beer. Tim's churchgoing, Republican, Texas upbringing told him that sooner or later, a city this slovenly would have to pay a price. Only the bill never seemed to come due.

ANTHONY WELLS

A po-lice was tricking with some broad; she took his money and gave him no pussy, then she told him we were selling dope or some shit. They come in like storm troopers with masks and helmets and weapons, like in Iraq somewhere. "I don't have no dope," I said. "I didn't get no pussy." They found some baking soda in the refrigerator, and were all like, "Look what we got." I was still on parole from Angola, so I couldn't get no bail. In New Orleans if they don't file a bill of information in sixty days, they have to let you go. They arraigned us sixty-seven days, but it was Mardi Gras, so the judge let it go. Roger did eleven months; I did sixteen. Fifty-one fucking years old. I worked on the food line, which was all right. You eat certain things and you trade what you don't want. OPP is in violation all the time; it's like one of them old French prisons. It's hooked up to the courthouse. You come right from your cell through these tunnels to the back door to the court-room you're assigned to. They still got the electric chair, in the barbershop. They used to execute people there in the '30s. It's a real jail. If you're not a man, you're not going to last.

They were arresting more people than they could hold, so they built a tent city in the yard. They had these Army cots and fans and that's how you lived. It was better in a way, but it was too many people. And then the wind came and the tents fell and hurt people; they got sued and shit.

Dudes would come by outside the fence; they'd wrap up weed or drugs in a rag with a big rock and throw it over. They would get it in there. Dudes used to come through OPP with crack, money, pipes in their ass and shit. One dude had a fifth of gin.

Finally the judge got tired of us coming and nothing happening. So he said, "I'm going to give you until tomorrow to have a case, and if you don't, I'm going to turn them loose." They brought us to court next day, and the judge said, "These charges are dropped for lack of evidence." Sixteen motherfucking months, and me fifty-one years old.

Must be I'm getting old, but I've been thinking about my parents. They raised us right, man. They'd kick your ass if you weren't cleaned up. "Take care of your hair." "Don't leave clothes hanging around." We used to go to people's houses in San Fernando, and before we went in, Daddy would say, "They ask you, you don't eat nothing." He was serious. "You don't give me no trouble in front of my people." And every time, them people would say, "You kids want something to eat?" and we'd be like, "No, thank you, ma'am."

Every Friday, Daddy'd say, "What did you learn in school? Tell me something I don't know." He once said to my brother Greg, "Spell 'piano.' " He couldn't, and Daddy hit him—pow! We laughed, and Daddy said, "What are you laughing at? You're next."

But he very seldom whipped us. He'd punish you—take away your bike, make you stand in the corner with two rocks in your hand. He had a sifter in the backyard; he'd say, "Go back there and sift dirt." Worst thing, though, was when he'd just turn away and say, "Right now I can't see you." I hated that shit.

Daddy'd kick my ass, he could see me going in and out the jail. He worked every day of his life. He didn't play. Never saw the inside of a jailhouse.

Tell you what: I'm getting straight. I'm tired of living like this, man. I ain't got nothing. Daddy was half my age, he had his own house, shit he could put his hand on. It's going to change, man.

You watch. Shit's going to change for me. Big shit.

JOYCE MONTANA

CITY COUNCIL CHAMBER
June 27, 2005

Joyce stood at the entrance to the New Orleans City Council chamber, clutching Tootie's arm. Behind her, a television reporter was barking into a microphone a summary of the police bust-up on St. Joseph's Night—the broken arm, the wrestling to the ground of Bertrand Butler, the insults to the old women. Ahead, the chamber looked like a cross between a courtroom and a high-school auditorium: high ceiling, rows of blue tip-up seats sloping gently to a low blond-wood fence running in a semicircle across the front of the room. The council members sat on a low stage beyond the fence, leaning their forearms on a pale wood counter, tired-looking blue velour curtains making a backdrop.

As she moved Tootie slowly down the aisle, hands reached out to touch her arms, touch Tootie's arms; Joyce smiled encouragement. Flashbulbs popped. A television camera hovered at the edge of her vision like a square-headed Cyclops. Tootie made little huffing noises as he walked, and she tightened her grip on his arm. She'd fretted about him coming, but he'd insisted he was fine, just the burning in the shoulder. He smelled of garlic water. She spotted Darryl up ahead, wearing a shirt of the same bright orange as Tootie's last suit. She hadn't seen him in weeks.

They reached the front row and took chairs next to Estabon "Peppy" Eugene, chief of the Golden Arrows. Directly in front of them, on the other side of the wooden fence, sat three men in white NOPD shirts. The white one she recognized from the television. It was Captain Cannatella, commander of the Sixth District, whose men had busted up St. Joseph's Night.

Oliver Thomas, the big, emotional city council president, called the meeting to order and asked "Peppy" Eugene to speak. His Indians had been the most roughed up. Peppy stepped to the lectern, but gestured behind him. "Our elder, Mr. Tootie Montana, I'd like you all to recognize," he said, stepping back and waving Tootie forward. The audience murmured; an uptown chief was yielding to a downtown chief—an important moment.

"The godfather," Thomas said, as Tootie, looking small in his open-necked beige sport shirt, walked slowly to the microphone, massaging the burning spot in his armpit. Darryl came down the aisle and moved to stand near him. "I am Big Chief Tootie, Allison Montana," Tootie said into the microphone, and a skein of applause wound through the room. "I made fifty-two suits. I masked fifty-two years. When I told my mother I wanted to make a suit that first year, she said, 'Oh, no. Boy, you don't want to fool with that.' "

Joyce smiled at Tootie's back.

"Every year, we got to Pauger and Claiborne, there'd be about eight policemen waiting," Tootie said. He shrugged a little, as though the shirt were binding his armpit. "When they seen us coming, they'd wrap the strap of their billy tight, so they'd make sure it didn't come out the hand when they beat your head."

A twist of anxiety moved under Joyce's sternum. She could hear Tootie's breath between phrases.

This is my last suit, he'd said. I'm going to do this until I die.

"Another year," Tootie went on, "when I get to Roman, police cars coming all kinds of ways. I say, 'What is this?' They say, 'Get out the street. Get on the sidewalk.' I say, 'For what? We wasn't doing nothing.' " Tootie stopped, Joyce could tell something was wrong. Darryl stepped in close to Tootie, whispering. Tootie looked up, surprised, and nodded.

"Take your time," Thomas said from the dais.

Tootie looked up, started to speak, and turned toward Darryl, wide-eyed. "Say what?" he rasped, and collapsed straight down, like a marionette with its strings cut.

"Tootie!" Joyce screamed, bolting to her feet. The three white-shirted cops vaulted over the fence in unison. Darryl knelt over Tootie.

"Pray!" someone yelled.

Darryl stuck his head up and shouted, "No! Indian Red!"

A voice called, "Mah-day two-de fiyo!" and the crowd began, in a low moan, the most important of the Mardi Gras Indian songs.

"Tootie? Tootie!" Joyce shrieked. "You can't leave me, Tootie!" The singing grew louder: "Here comes the Biiiig Chief, the Biiiig Chief, the Big Chief of the Nation, the whole wild creation." Joyce took two steps forward, someone grabbed her arms. "He won't bow down, not on that ground," the people sang. "You know I love you, hear you call, my Indian Red."

RONALD LEWIS

1317 TUPELO STREET
2005

Ronald woke at four-thirty. His body's internal alarm was still set, and much as his knees and feet ached, he missed going to work. But the retirement party they'd thrown him in the break room on Baronne Street had been second to none, and after thirty-four years on the tracks he was drawing eleven hundred dollars a month pension. The problem was filling up the time.

He shuffled to the kitchen and stood looking out the window at the garage. The rakes and rose dust were long gone; the space was given over entirely to relics of the paradise cross the canal, the mighty Lower Nine. He was spending more and more time among those expressions of joy and solidarity, creativity and life. They were a bulwark against the senseless killings, which seemed to be coming about one a day. Rashad had been right; he did have a museum. A name had come to Ronald in his sleep one night: the House of Dance and Feathers. With the help of a lawyer friend, Ronald had filled out the paperwork, and the IRS had just bestowed upon the museum something called 501 (c)(3) status, which meant Ronald could raise money for it without paying taxes. Mostly, though, people didn't donate money; they donated things—parading shoes they'd had up under their beds for years, a piece of beadwork off an Indian suit, some photos. Little by little, the House of Dance and Feathers was getting known around the Lower Nine. Even a few people from the other side of the canal came, to discover the Lower Ninth Ward was more than a killing ground or a place to buy dope. Every black person in New Orleans, just about, had grown up visiting relatives cross the canal, and the House of Dance and Feathers reminded them of the soul of the city.

Ronald had the mitigation board on his mind. Its mission was to offset the pain of having the locks expanded in the Industrial Canal. Whole blocks of houses were going to be lost, and a noisy industrial area was going to intrude farther into the Lower Nine. What had Ronald steamed was the board had arranged scholarships to Nunez Community College, but it wasn't telling anybody. Ronald had found out about the scholarships at a meeting. It seemed clear to him the board wanted to be able to say it had made the scholarships available, but it didn't really want anybody to apply for them.

He drove over to the board's headquarters in his struggle-buggy—the ancient white Cadillac Seville that had replaced his Cutlass—and picked up thirty applications. He put the stack on the passenger seat and began patrolling the streets of the Lower Nine. Three young men stood on the corner of Charbonnet and Urquhart, casting sidelong glances—watching for police, for rivals, for white folks cruising to buy their drugs. Ronald W. Lewis pulled up and stepped out. One of the boys was little red Michael from Derrick Jenkins's gang, still in the game. Stuck on stupid. It was a miracle he was alive.

"I ain't here to talk about this what you're doing," Ronald said. "Come look at this here paper." They looked at one another and gingerly approached. "The city's going to widen the locks on the Industrial Canal, which would take out all them houses on Sister, Jourdan, Dauphine, Burgundy. Hell, Michael"—Ronald nudged him with a forearm—"your auntee lives over by that way."

"Tha's right."

"Now, to make the bitter pill go down easy, they're offering scholarships to Nunez Community College over in St. Bernard. 'Stead of hanging on the street corner here, where you're just as like to get killed, you could get yourself a trade, like carpentry, plumbing, electrical, that kind of thing."

They stared at him.

"Michael," Ronald said. "I thought you were hanging with Derrick Jenkins."

"He dead."

"Well, there you go." Ronald put the forms and three pens from his pocket on the hood of his car. "Listen. They trying to put one over, offering scholarships without really telling nobody, hoping nobody apply. What we doing here is like snatching two thousand dollars from the city. We got to pick the fruit. They won't like it, but it's ours."

Michael stepped forward and picked up a pen. "What do I do?"

Ronald kept at it all week, finding young men on the street corners, at the convenience store, at the park on Forstall Street—where Ronald had played baseball as a kid but which was now a field of trash and used syringes. On Friday, he piloted the struggle-buggy down St. Claude Av-

enue, past Jackson Barracks, into St. Bernard Parish, and turned up Paris
Road and found the big brick administration building of Nunez Community College. Grunting, stiff legged, he climbed out, the papers
gripped in his fist, his porkpie hat pulled low. In the entry hall, he could
feel people looking at him; he was too old, too poor, and too black to be
coming round a college office building.

"I'm Ronald W. Lewis, from Tupelo Street in the Lower Ninth Ward
of New Orleans!" he announced in as loud a voice as he could muster.
The young white woman at the reception desk looked up, startled. "I'm
bringing these applications from the young people of my neighborhood!"

JOANN GUIDOS

ST. CLAUDE AVENUE
July 2005

JoAnn stood behind the bar with her hands on her hips, smiling. She'd
done it; she'd opened her bar on St. Claude Avenue. The apartments upstairs were barely habitable, and the building next door, where the
restaurant would someday be, was still a wreck. But now she had an income stream.

Kajun's Pub, though, was more than that to JoAnn. It was the best
kind of bar—neither gay nor straight, black nor white, biker nor punk.
At any given time you'd find tall, skinny black men playing pool with
tattooed white chicks; a couple of nellies leaning on the bar, drinking
cosmopolitans out of plastic cups and laughing loudly with a big yat in
coveralls; a pair of well-dressed black women working the video poker
machines for all they were worth; a longhair with a Chihuahua in his
backpack taking cash from the ATM; or just Kenny, shirtless, telling a
long-winded story to a leathery old biker with Renée, his girlfriend,
hanging on his arm. Except for the gorgeous, curved bar that JoAnn and
Roney had built together, Kajun's wasn't fancy: a cement floor, a pool
table salvaged from another bar, fluorescent lights. JoAnn kept prices
low—a buck for a Jello-O shot, a buck for a beer, five for a pitcher—
which suited St. Claude Avenue just fine. What mattered was that it was

a place where anybody could feel safe, where people could be themselves. After fifty years of covering up, JoAnn felt this was more than a job; it was a mission.

The fifteen thousand Roney and Kathy had borrowed from Roney's mother had made all the difference. Kathy owned 49 percent of the building—though not of the bar—and she and Roney worked their asses off. Kathy ran the books, wrote the checks, dealt with the city. Roney helped JoAnn with construction and kept the place clean with a mop and bucket. Roney and Kathy lived among the exposed wiring and unsanded floors upstairs, though they'd also managed to buy a country bungalow in Carriere, Mississippi, about ninety minutes away. They didn't draw a salary, but the apartment was free, and JoAnn fed them. Roney's son even worked the bar from time to time. It was like family.

Sandy, all grown up, was dealing blackjack on the riverboats in Mississippi, and JoAnn loved it when she'd come swinging into the bar, yelling "Hi, Mom!" to Kathy and "Hi, Dad!" to JoAnn and freaking out the customers. Paul was in the Navy, and when his carrier had docked at Norfolk after a tour in the Middle East, the whole family had driven over to meet him. At Sandy's insistence, John had hauled out the sports bra and big vest; it was a Navy base, after all, and there was no point in making trouble. JoAnn had thought she'd manned up pretty convincingly, but when she'd headed to the men's room, a well-mannered sailor had stepped up: "Miss, the ladies' room is on the other side." It was the high point of the trip.

JoAnn was succeeding in ways that John never had. Pretty soon, it would be time to get the surgery done and finish the transformation.

BILLY GRACE

2525 ST. CHARLES AVENUE
August 20, 2005

Billy took the elevator downstairs with the poodles. The sun was barely up, but the air was already thick and hot—hurricane weather. He walked around to the front, passing under the chandeliered portico that covered the side driveway. George was sitting on the porch in his wheelchair, a cannula running from an oxygen tank beside him into his nostrils. Ivory sat on the step at a discreet distance, neither hovering nor fussing over George. George appeared to be dozing. Billy went up on the porch, moving slowly so as not to let the heat grab him.

It was heartbreaking to see such a force of nature—planner of weddings, comforter of the bereaved, appreciator of art and fashion, guardian of tradition, nudger of recalcitrants—butchered and feeble. George's shortness of breath had been nothing dire, but he thought he should have a checkup. That started him on a daisy chain of one specialist after another, ending in surgery to install a stent in a coronary artery. But someone botched the job, dislodging plaque that clogged his veins or leaving a hole in an artery. Then more bungling; by the time the doctors paid attention to his blue extremities, gangrene had set in. Both legs and all his fingers had to be amputated. It was a thoroughgoing disaster, but George couldn't very well sue Ochsner Hospital; he was a member of its board.

For the Zoo-To-Do, Audubon Zoo's black-tie fund-raiser, George had shown the old spirit, insisting on getting his tux re-tailored to accommodate his missing legs, greeting every lady at the gala with "Forgive me for not standing up." But he slept a lot now, and Billy checked in on him often, staying around to talk whenever George could. Tootie Montana's death had hit Billy hard. He'd never gotten around to inviting the big chief to lunch. The old guard of New Orleans was fading.

Billy gathered up the dogs, snapped on their leashes, pressed the button to open the iron gate in the ivy-covered wall, and set out for a short walk. On his cell phone, he punched the number of the pilot of the time-share Learjet that would carry him and Anne off to North Carolina. He was looking forward to seeing the McIlhennys—not at their Avery Island home, where their family had been making Tabasco sauce for a hundred years, but at the Freemans' place in North Carolina. After a few days there, it would be off to the beach house in Destin. Billy didn't like leaving George and Big Anne, especially on such a suffocating day, but Alston, Anne's sister, would take good care of them. And Ivory, of course, was always on duty. There was no point in trying to move George and Big Anne in such oppressive weather.

TIM BRUNEAU

6661 ARGONNE BOULEVARD
August 29, 2005

Tim took from his gun cabinet a shotgun with a flashlight on the end. The light didn't work, so he took the Mini-14 rifle instead. He had his service Glock on his hip, and put his miniature Glock in the overnight bag along with three days' socks and underwear. The phone rang on the kitchen wall. "The lieutenant has fixed us up at the Hampton Inn," said Jeff, a fellow detective. "We'll have food. Bring whatever guns and alcohol you want."

"Great. See you there." Usually, the Sixth District cops slept in the station house during hurricanes. The Hampton Inn would be deluxe.

Tim looked through the liquor cabinet, decided against whiskey, and fetched a twelve-pack of Budweiser and a gallon of water from the fridge. As he was loading his unmarked Crown Vic, a neighbor drove by in a Land Cruiser. "Where are you going?" Tim shouted.

"To the overpass! In case the water comes up."

Tim looked at his beloved Ford pickup sitting with beefy oversized tires. "Mine'll ride it out," he called back. "It's an F-150!"

PART III

A
THOUSAND
WHISTLES

"There will one day be a
substantial loss of life unless we have
Category Five protection."

—AL NAOMI,
senior project manager for
the U.S. Army Corps of Engineers, to the
Times-Picayune, May 28, 2005

WILBERT RAWLINS JR.

GEORGE WASHINGTON CARVER
HIGH SCHOOL
August 27, 2005

Wil paced by the buses, looking at his watch. Students were boarding in crisp orange and green uniforms, their brass instruments flashing in the sunlight. Eight drum majors wore uniforms with big orange letters spelling out "G. W. CARVER." Nyja Sanders, now the section leader of the mellophones, had gotten her whole section on board, but a tuba was missing, and a baritone. They were about to play against St. Augustine High School, supposedly the best band in New Orleans. Wil couldn't wait to get on the field; he was sure Carver could blow St. Aug out. But they had to be rolling for two o'clock.

A familiar car swept into the parking lot, and Wil's heart caught. Belinda rolled up beside him, and the window came down. "Hey."

"Hey." Wil leaned down. Belinda had hardly ever come to Carver, and never on a weekend, even before they'd separated. She had Curtis in the passenger seat and a lot of stuff thrown in back. "Hey, Curtis."

"Hey, Mr. Wil," Curtis said sadly.

"Don't tell me you're going to play a game," Belinda said.

"Yeah! St. Aug!"

"You ain't listening to the radio?"

"No."

"You ain't heard about the storm?" Her voice was rising.

"Yeah, I heard that." Wil glanced at the sky, cloudless and still. He'd been listening to the order to evacuate, but surely it wasn't time.

"They're telling us to get out the city, but you're going to play your game."

"It's the first game of the season! St. Aug!" He leaned his forearms on Belinda's window. "We earn forty thousand dollars on this game."

Belinda flared her nostrils. "We're going up to Hammond to stay by Niecy. You ought to get your mama and get out the city."

"Where's Mookey?"

"By her daddy in Texas."

"Belinda, we are so ready! I got them playing 'Flight of the Bumble-bee!' You know how hard that is? I never heard no high-school band play that!"

Belinda shook her head, and asked quietly, "How you been?"

"I been okay. I miss you."

She wrinkled her nose as though he'd offered oysters. "Hmf. See you in a few days." She drove off, Curtis looking out back at Wil.

Someone called to him that Mr. Jackson needed to see him in the office—another delay. It was two o'clock, straight up.

The game, Mr. Jackson told him, had been canceled.

"Canceled?"

"Storm coming. Send the children home so their parents can look after them."

"But they are on the buses."

"We'll reschedule it."

The pieces were starting to fit together in Wil's mind, and he asked, "Send them home to their parents?"

"The city is evacuating," Mr. Jackson said. "They need to go to their families."

"You know what kinds of parents some of these kids have."

"They're taking people at the Superdome. We can only do what we can do." Mr. Jackson gathered his suit jacket from a chair. "You got people you can go to?"

"I got my dad's people in Beaumont."

"Then I suggest you collect your mama and go there. Come on now."

The kids were horsing around on the bus, eager to get over to St. Aug and show what they could do. "The game's canceled," Wil told them. They groaned. They could see as well as he that the sky was clear and blue. "Listen to me," Wil said. "Take your horns with you when you go. Keep practicing. Get home now. Get your parents, your brothers and your sisters, your grandmothers, and get out the city. Chances are I'll see you all right back here in a few days."

"Mr. Rawlins?"

"What?"

"Where are we supposed to go?"
"How we supposed to get there?"

ANTHONY WELLS

Roger and me lived above my cousin Jerry's store on Reynes Street, corner of Warfield. It was a little bitty place—get your po'boy in there, your cigarettes. Sign painted on the wall outside said fresh seafood, turtle meat, crawfish, but he didn't have none of that. That sign was there for years before Jerry had the store. He did take food stamps, though. And he had a pool table up in there; I liked the sound of them balls hitting each other. I could hear that up through the floor.

Roger and me got upstairs on this big old metal staircase went up the outside. There weren't but a couple two-story places in the Goose, so from the top of them stairs we could see the whole neighborhood. Greater Little Rock Baptist Church wasn't no bigger than an ordinary house, but it had this big old aluminum steeple on it. One direction we could see the I-10 overpass and the bridge over the canal. Other way we could see all the way to St. Mary's Academy. They had an all-girl marching band, and we could sit up there and listen to them doing "Bumpin' on Sunset" by Wes Montgomery, Willie Bobo, Thelonious Monk, all that.

Morning before the storm, I'm sitting up there and I'm seeing everybody loading up their cars and lighting out. My cousin Donald—that's Jerry's brother—I see him coming down Warfield in his pickup, got his whole family in there and all his shit piled up in the back. I'm like, where you going? And he's like, Baton Rouge, man. Storm coming.

Well, shit. We seen the storm on TV, but they're always talking about storms coming. And Roger and me, where we going to go? My truck was good for the neighborhood, but it wouldn't have made no Baton Rouge. We didn't have no people outside New Orleans except a brother in California, and how we going to get there? Also, I'm seeing who's not leaving for the storm, and I'm thinking, those motherfuckers going to have them a field day with everybody gone, you hear what I'm saying? I'm thinking we better off staying put. Kind of keep an eye out.

Also, as Roger said, if it was as bad as all that, they'd be sending buses round for the people that don't got cars.

JOYCE MONTANA

INTERSTATE 10 WESTBOUND
August 27, 2005

Joyce sat in the passenger seat of Denise's car, breathing hot, wet air laced with gasoline fumes. "Let's put the windows up, Denise, honey, and put on the air conditioner." They'd been on the highway for four hours and weren't even to Baton Rouge, which usually was a ninety-minute ride. Interstate 10 was solid cars. It would be days before they reached Houston.

Denise hunched over the wheel. "We don't want to risk overheating or running out of gas. Look." Along the side of the highway, families stood beside dead cars.

Joyce shuddered. "Try not to lurch the car," she said. It was like being in a small boat on high seas.

Denise's whole upper body was slick with sweat. She wiped the back of a hand across her forehead. "I go when the traffic lets me." The car rolled forward a few feet and stopped.

Joyce never could abide cars; Tootie either. He'd never even learned to drive. The past summer, Denise had talked them into driving out of the city for Hurricane Ivan, and Tootie had been sick the whole way.

"When the Lord took Tootie," Joyce said, "He knew what He was doing."

BILLY GRACE

NORTH CAROLINA
August 28, 2005

Billy stayed behind on the deck of the Freemans' house when the rest of them went for a walk, and worked his cell phone.

"You have any questions?" he asked Ivory. The house had forty or fifty windows, and every one of them needed storm shutters. Ivory had already pulled the shutters out the garage and was putting them up.

"If it's all right with you, I'm going to have my family come stay in the back house," Ivory said.

"That's fine. Let me talk to Mrs. Montgomery."

Ivory went to find Big Anne, and Billy looked in through the glass door at the big-screen TV in the living room. A white pinwheel, hurrying across the gulf in time-lapse satellite pictures, was headed straight for New Orleans.

Big Anne came on. "No, we're not leaving."

"Okay." It was too late for that, anyway.

"Alston's being a perfect I-don't-know-what." Billy could picture it; Alston, Anne's younger sister, could become quite the master sergeant in high-pressure situations, like readying a debutante party or Mardi Gras. He was glad she was at 2525.

Alston took the phone from her mother.

"Your friend Jonathan McCall wants to come ride out the storm here with us," she boomed. "He's bringing his mom."

That made sense. Jonathan and Jane lived on Arabella Street, his mom alone on St. Charles. Jonathan had a cool head, and the more people at 2525, the better. "I don't think we'll come back, then," Billy said.

"Oh, God, no. Stay put. It will blow through."

WILBERT RAWLINS JR.

5972 DREUX AVENUE
August 28, 2005

Wil emptied his fridge—nothing but cans of iced tea. He was putting them in a Sav-A-Center shopping bag when the phone rang.

"What you doing?" It was Reecie, a band mom, his latest girlfriend.

"I'm heading out. Aren't you?"

"I don't know," she said lazily. "I'm waiting on my brother to come pick me up."

"Lawrence and I are taking Ma to Beaumont. You could come with us. We'll stay by my cousins till it passes."

"I got my kids."

"I'm driving Ma's car, and Lawrence is taking his. I been worried about the band kids, anyway. I'd feel good about taking you all."

"You not driving your sweet Lexus?"

"Nah. Our driveway's up off the street. It'll be fine."

BELINDA RAWLINS

INTERSTATE 10 EASTBOUND

2005

Belinda inched the car forward through the traffic, wondering if she'd made a mistake by leaving the city. Aunt Polly was too old to leave the nursing home where she was living, so Faye wouldn't leave the city, either. Ditty and Skeeter had stayed with her, and cousin Stevie had stayed as well because he was a fireman and was needed. Belinda and Curtis could have stayed with them; she'd have been safe. Her plan was to get to Hammond, where Niecy was going to college, and ride out the storm there. But with all these cars, it might be days before she got there.

Curtis whimpered with heat and boredom, driving her nuts. She looked over at him, where he was fussing with the seat belt. Without Wil, a light had gone out of his face. "We couldn't stay and watch the storm," she said gently, "because it might be dangerous. Remember how Grandma told you the whole Lower Ninth Ward flooded after Hurricane Betsy? This is a big storm."

"I'm hot."

Belinda had turned off the air conditioner and opened the windows. She was not going to get stranded like the families on the shoulder.

The constant lifting of her foot from brake to gas pedal was hard on the knee; every time she moved her foot, a spark of pain shot up her leg. She steered around several policemen waving their arms: an accident. She thought of Wil and wondered if the road to Texas was as bad. Maybe she'd pushed the lesson she was teaching him too far. She wished he were with them.

The road no longer looked familiar. Belinda had been staring at the back of the car in front of her for so long she'd forgotten to watch, but this wasn't the way to Hammond. Her heart beat fast. That accident—

those cops—was that the Hammond exit? The traffic eased. The needle on the speedometer crawled up to thirty miles an hour. A green mileage sign slipped past on the right: "Jackson, 17 miles."

She was in Mississippi.

ANTHONY WELLS

What happened was, the wind started up 'long about nightfall. Well, I been in wind before, shit. But this time, man, it got louder and louder till you didn't think it could get no worse. But it did, man. Stronger. Screaming like a thousand whistles. And we're up on the second floor, so the whole place is shaking. I kept thinking, okay, it's played itself out, it's going to stop now. But it didn't. It went on and on and on. The lights was still on until, I don't know, sometime late, a lightning bolt hit the transformer over by the canal and that motherfucker lit up the whole sky. BOOM! Blue fire—red, purple, and green fire. The lights blinked on and off, and then, bam, everything went dark. I look out, and there's water up the windows downstairs. I'm thinking, we fucked up.

About two o'clock, the neighbors start coming. Gwen and Jennifer and Steve and Nat and Guy, Geebee and Shortie—they all come, tied together so they wouldn't blow off the steps. When I open the door, the wind takes it right off the hinges; I'm holding it by the knob and it's like a big kite dancing around in my hand. We get that bitch nailed on and wind tears off the front roof. So now we got water coming in, the insulation hanging down. I took me a slug of liquor and curled up in the bathtub, thinking, that's the safest place. I'm no pussy, but I got to tell you, man, this shit got right on top of my ass.

FRANK MINYARD

FAIR OAKS FARM
August 28, 2005

"Frank! Get away from the window!"

"Look at that!" He clutched the windowsill. A three-hundred-foot length of fence tore free from the earth and went spinning into the blackness like a length of old typewriter ribbon. A steel trash barrel flew past, no more substantial than a balloon.

"Frank!" Nancy tugged at his arm.

One of the oaks that shaded the driveway listed and fell over with a crash. Another followed, smashing the split-rail fence. Frank's big black bull and donkey walked calmly up the road together through the driving rain. He realized that they were evacuating, as he should have done. Now the roads were impassable.

"Let's get out of here!" Nancy shrieked.

"Too late!"

JOANN GUIDOS

ST. CLAUDE AVENUE
August 29, 2005

The lights went out in Kajun's, and JoAnn felt her way to the side door. She pushed out into the needles of rain, leaned over the generator, felt for the rope, and pulled. She could barely hear its roar over the wind, but it vibrated violently and the lights flickered on. That would put looters on notice.

"Good work," said Barbara from behind the bar when JoAnn fought her way back inside and pulled the door shut. "But maybe we should be thinking about getting out of here." Barbara was already drunk, and pale with terror.

JoAnn moved behind the bar and poured them each a finger of Southern Comfort. "My people got nowhere to go," JoAnn said. "I'm not leavin' 'em."

As though on cue, the front door banged and Mitch struggled in, streaming water, his eyes sunken, hollowed out. "If I'm going to die," he announced, "I'd rather die here." Mitch had barely gotten settled into his usual bar stool when Kenny and Renée stomped in, whooping and hollering with the exhilaration of having risked their lives for the pleasure of drinking at Kajun's. Then came Phoebe—breathless, already drunk, shrugging off a sodden woolen greatcoat. "I couldn't take being in my house alone," she said, her voice shaking. Mitch put his arm around her shoulders. Andy, the gray-haired neighborhood philosopher, banged through the door, delicately flicked water from his sleeves, and called to Barbara for a Cutty and water.

By midnight, a couple dozen regulars filled the bar stools and hard wooden chairs at the tables. The wind, screaming over the jukebox, sounded like a jetliner revving up on the St. Claude neutral ground, but the bar, made of cinder block, felt cozy and safe. A short-haired woman JoAnn didn't know made for the door, so drunk she could barely walk, shouting something about needing to "find Michael." JoAnn had to pull her back physically. After the woman made two more attempts, JoAnn dug out a roll of duct tape and lashed her to one of the ceiling supports. She finally fell asleep there, slumped forward like a soldier shot by firing squad.

TIM BRUNEAU

HAMPTON INN
August 29, 2005

"Vodka and Gatorade!" Tim yelled above the wind, raising his glass. "You can hydrate and dehydrate at the same time!" He and Jeff stood on a small balcony, sheltered from the worst of the wind, smoking cigarettes and playing a game with the butts. They'd flick them toward the end of the wall, where the wind would catch them and shoot them off like bullets. Better than hanging around inside, where cops were staggering drunkenly around the hallways, from one party to another, leaving plates of red beans and jambalaya on beds and dressers, beer bottles rolling around underfoot.

Across the street, some awnings tore off the Convention Center and rose into the night sky like dried leaves. Tim heard a heavy splashing sound and ducked instinctively, thinking the Gulf of Mexico was about to come down on top of them. But it was only a trio of drunken patrolmen, jumping naked into the pool, just to be able to say they'd done it.

RONALD LEWIS

PELHAM HOTEL,
MAGAZINE STREET
August 28, 2005

"I don't like this!" Minnie clutched at Ronald's shirt like she was ready to hoist herself into his lap. The room shook.

"We'll be all right." Ronald squeezed his arms around her. "We're better off than in our house!" In truth, he wasn't sure. He'd brought Minnie up here to the high ground alongside the river because he thought the Lower Nine might flood like it did during Betsy. But the Pelham didn't feel anywhere near as solid as his house on Tupelo Street. It might not flood, but it might bust apart. The wind hit it like a gigantic hair dryer at close range. As Ronald and Minnie huddled on the bed, the room banged as though a car had struck the building. Two walls split apart and the ceiling above lifted free, leaving a three-foot hole to the outside. A blast of hot wind and rain exploded in on them.

Minnie screamed, struggling to get up. Ronald pinned her to the bed, eyes squeezed shut, praying.

They lay like that for four hours.

BELINDA RAWLINS

BATON ROUGE
2005

Belinda couldn't carry Curtis. He was too big, and she was too tired. "Hey," she said, nudging him. "I got us a room."

She'd driven all the way up to Jackson, turned around, and driven all the way down to Baton Rouge. A foolish move: the city was overflowing with people from New Orleans. Three o'clock in the morning, and the streets were choked with cars packed with frightened and angry New Orleanians. It was a miracle she'd been able to find a motel room.

She kicked off her shoes and looked at her reflection in the dark

TV screen.You finally fell in love with a good man, got a perfect house, a father for Curtis, and you left him. She stood to undress, her knee throbbing.

ANTHONY WELLS

The wind finally stop and we look outside, and I never seen so many stars. Sky was clear like I never seen it in New Orleans before, and there was no lights anywhere. It was looking at the face of God, man. Long about six o'clock in the morning, water was down to about our waists. So we walk out to the Arab's store on Chef Highway. The man is there, and he opens up the store. Says, "Don't worry, we got insurance." Water was going to corrode everything anyway. We took water, food, disinfectant, bleach, washing powder, and took it back upstairs.

At first the water came and left out, so Chef Highway was pretty much dry. People were taking U-Haul trucks, putting their kids in them, and lighting out. But we figured, shit, storm's over. Why go now? One dude took a U-Haul truck down to Winn-Dixie, which the people had opened up, and brought back everything we needed. Meat. A grill. A radio with batteries. We was in good shape. We're thinking why should we leave? We had everything we needed.

Then the water come back up.

RONALD LEWIS

CRESCENT CITY CONNECTION BRIDGE
August 29, 2005

Ronald and Minnie stepped gingerly out of the Pelham Hotel into an eerie dawn silence. A traffic signal lay on the sidewalk, a streetlight lamp tilted crazily into an office building, oak limbs lay across the street like barricades. Minnie gasped and clutched Ronald's arm. The parking garage next to the hotel had collapsed in a heap. "We lucky to be alive," Ronald said.

Minnie wanted something to drink, and Ronald let her walk up the block in search of a store. The struggle-buggy was unscathed; he drove it around front. A scream made him turn, and here came Minnie, heels clacking loudly on the cement, beside herself. "There's water coming up in the street! There's water coming this way!"

He got her into the car and sat hugging her. "There's always water in the street after a storm. Let me get you home. We're fine, Minnie. We're fine."

He started the car and reached for the radio. Nothing. He twisted the dial, but there was nothing to hear—just a distant, hollow roar, like the ocean. He kept twisting the dial, until a faint voice broke through. "This is United Radio Broadcasters of New Orleans." He fiddled at the dial, but there was no other signal. He went back to United Radio Broadcasters of New Orleans, whatever that was. The announcer was taking a call from a woman sobbing so hard they could barely make out her words. "I'm in the attic with my babies and we got nothing to eat and no water and the water's still coming up!"

"Where are you?" the announcer asked shakily.

The woman shouted an address on Derbigny Street. "Corner of Egania!"

That was a few blocks from the family home on Deslonde.

"Send somebody!" the woman shrieked. "Send somebody with a boat!"

Minnie was shivering. Ronald switched off the radio. Boats in the streets of the Lower Nine. It was happening again. He turned to face Minnie and held her shoulders.

"Listen to me. I can't take you home right now. We're going to Thibodaux."

As the struggle-buggy strained to crest the Crescent City Connection bridge, Ronald thought, them cane fields keep calling us back.

TIM BRUNEAU

JACKSON AVENUE
August 29, 2005

Restless bursts of wind ruffled the trees overhead, and a light drizzle dampened Tim's hair. He filled his lungs. The tang of a thousand busted-open oak trees made the air taste scrubbed. It crackled with ozone and buzzed through his veins like giddy joy. New Orleans had never smelled so good. He looked at the woman lying prone on the pavement. The sweetness wouldn't last long, at least not on this block. He raised his radio to his lips. "Unit one six six four, again. Any word on the coroner?"

"Still no answer. You want me to try EMS?"

"Sure." Tim looked at his watch. He'd been waiting ninety minutes. An ambulance, at least, would get her off the street and onto some ice. How dumb did you have to be to go out in the middle of a hurricane in your little capri pants to buy crack? Whom did you expect to find, with the wind howling at 110 miles an hour? He studied the driver's license he'd retrieved from the beaded purse.

Way to go, Marie.

The back of her head was flattened, and blood stained the collar of her white button-down shirt. Next to her head lay an enormous, teardrop-shaped streetlight, the bulb smashed. A naked pole rose from the sidewalk. Twenty-four years old, killed by a falling streetlight while prowling for crack, for Christ's sake.

The sunburned patrolman who'd found her walked up, perspiring in a bright yellow raincoat. "What's up?"

"Talked to the family," Tim said.

"You get the OLJ?" The Oh Lordy Jesus.

"No. They were kind of blank. Matter-of-fact. You know, the death-is-a-part-of-life thing."

"This neighborhood anyway." The patrolman rubbed at his peeling nose. "Look at that place." The wooden house beside them had burned so long ago that the roof was a tangle of vines as thick as a pumpkin patch. What other city would let a derelict like that stand for so long?

The day grew hotter. Tim's head buzzed with sleeplessness. A young woman tottered up on eight-inch heels.

"When's the number 12 start up?" she asked, without a glance at the body.

"The bus?"

"Up Carondelet. The number 12."

"Might be a couple days before they get the branches out, the power up," the sunburned patrolman said.

"Thank you, officers." She tottered off.

"One six six four," Tim's radio squawked. He turned it up. "Shooting at Coleman's Sporting Goods on Earhart."

"On my way," Tim said. He looked up the block. People stood in doorways, sullen, watching the drama of the dead woman. He turned to the sunburned patrolman. "Mind sticking around? Keep them off her."

"Television's out," the patrolman said. "This is the morning's entertainment."

Coleman's Sporting Goods bristled with patrol cars, parked at all angles. Tim left his unmarked Crown Victoria at the curb and loped, bent kneed, to the yellow tape, where he showed his badge to the cop and was waved inside.

Frank, a melancholy shooting-squad detective, was counting shell casings. They were strewn like spilled popcorn across the linoleum floor. Beyond him, paramedics worked on three guys whose blood ran in bright rivers down the aisles.

"Looks like two groups of looters surprised each other and started shooting," Frank said, in a meaty Kenner accent. "Nine-millimeters and AKs."

"What were they after?"

"School uniforms."

"You're kidding."

"Catholic school uniforms are a big thing."

Tim walked over to a young black man who was grimacing from a wound in his thigh. "Don't die, you scumbag," he said. "I don't want to handle your case."

Frank shouldered him aside. "Go ahead and die," he said. "I don't want your case, either." He and Tim gave each other a high five.

Captain Cannatella walked up. "Whatcha got?"

"They're all gonna survive," Frank said. It would be his case after all.

"Captain," Tim said. "I'm waiting two hours on Jackson Avenue for the coroner. What's going on?"

Cannatella stopped. "I'm hearing all kinds of crazy stuff. But all I can tell you, we've got water pouring up through the storm drains near the station house. I've never seen that before."

"I'm about ready to put her in my unit and take her to Charity myself."

Cannatella snorted.

"I'm serious." A body lying on the street for hours—it was disorderly.

Cannatella frowned. "Listen, I wouldn't order you to do that. But it's your scene. You do what you gotta do." This is why Tim loved Cannatella; he let his people use their own judgment, then stood behind them.

The heat was rising in ripples off Jackson Avenue by the time Tim got back. The dead woman was starting to smell. The sunburned patrolman squatted in the shade of the burned house. An old waterbed mattress lay near him in the weeds. "Help me roll her up in that," Tim said.

The patrolman wrinkled his peeling nose. "That's the coroner's job."

Tim shrugged. "We can't stay here all day. We can't leave her."

They spread the waterbed beside the woman's body and lifted her onto it. She was small; it was easy. They rolled her into the blue plastic, like kids pushing a snowball. It was harder to wrestle her into the backseat of the Crown Vic.

Tim looked up. On the stoops, several women had their hands on their mouths. Outside the burglar-gated door of a nasty-looking club called the Dreamers, a big man stood with his hands on his hips. The people of Jackson Avenue knew the drill: an ambulance or a coroner's wagon takes the body, in a zip bag. Two white cops rolling a dead black woman into an old waterbed and lifting her into an unmarked car was weird.

Tim crossed the street to speak to the man in front of the Dreamers, who was standing by a sign that read, NO FIREARMS, HAIR CURLERS, UNDERSHIRTS, TANK TOPS, OR PEOPLE UNDER THIRTY.

"We can't wait any longer for the coroner to take her. I'm going to take her in my car to Charity."

"Bless you," the man said. "Bless your heart."

The sunburned patrolman climbed into his car and drove off. Tim pushed the button on his radio. "This is one six six four again," he said. "I have a victim of a twenty-nine U"—an unexplained death—"headed for Charity Hospital. Beginning mileage 91,629."

"Okay, one six six four."

Tim drove down St. Charles Avenue toward Charity Hospital, swerving up onto the neutral ground to avoid fallen oak boughs. Hardly any cars were moving. The steeple of Rayne Memorial Church had collapsed into a pile of pretty red bricks, and power lines drooped low across the road, but otherwise the damage looked light. A lot of raggedy-looking black folks were walking uptown, though—the kinds of people not usually seen on St. Charles. Many had children with them, not the type to loot. It looked more like they were fleeing. An odd sight, but then again, it was a strange morning.

The emergency ramp at Charity swarmed with people pushing, lifting, pulling objects larger than themselves, like ants on an anthill. Tim parked and got out. The sidewalk was covered with filing cabinets, office chairs, bassinets, crank-operated beds, curtains on rollers, and, tipped into the gutter, a floor buffer. Tim averted his eyes.

Tim grabbed a doctor in scrubs. "I've got a body in my car."

The doctor frowned. "I don't know. We're shutting down."

"Shutting down? The ER?"

"Shutting down Charity." He walked backward up the ramp, explaining, "We got no power. The generators in the basement flooded out."

BILLY GRACE

NORTH CAROLINA
August 30, 2005

The TV screen at the Freemans' showed people smashing store windows on Canal Street and running off with all they could carry, bass boats on Esplanade Avenue, people thrashing around in deep water.

"It's quiet here," Alston said in a voice lacking its usual swagger. "I slept out on the upstairs porch 'cause it was so hot, and all night I could see cars cruising up and down, pointing flashlights at houses like they were deciding which to rob. But we're okay."

They had no electricity at 2525, so Alston couldn't see on television what was happening elsewhere in the city. Maybe it was just as well. Billy tried to keep his voice calm so as not to frighten her. He casually mentioned that his shotguns were leaning against his study wall, in leather cases. Alston said they already had them out and loaded. As casually as he could, Billy mentioned his real terror—the television was suggesting there might be nine feet of water on St. Charles Avenue before long. Alston went silent, then said, "I don't know how we'd get out of the city."

"Put Ivory on."

"I'll go find him. If we get cut off, call back. Only one phone on the second floor is working, and we can't call out."

"Okay."

Ivory came on the line. "I need you to do something," Billy said. "I need you to go scout a route out of the city. Take any of the cars. Try I-10 to Baton Rouge, then the Mississippi River bridge, then River Road. See if you can find a way to get everybody out."

TIM BRUNEAU

UNIVERSITY HOSPITAL
August 29, 2005

Tim picked up his radio. "One six six four, en route with a twenty-nine U to University Hospital." Tim wanted his ass amply covered. He gave his mileage.

"Okay, one six six four."

The hospital lobby was as frantic as the ramp at Charity, full of gurneys, people running, shouting. What the fuck? The storm was over. Tim grabbed a doctor in a white coat. "I need to put a body in your morgue."

"One of ours?"

"No, killed on the street."

"No way."

"What do you mean?"

"I'm not going to establish a precedent by taking the city's trash." He straightened his coat and walked off.

ANTHONY WELLS

We was doing good. Barbecued everything. Had a TV hooked up to a battery. Worst of it was, it was hot. I mean hot. It was like all the wind in the world had blown itself out during the storm and there wasn't none left for even a little bitty breeze.

The water was up to the rooftops. And it was toxic chemical shit, from the Tenneco and Texaco-Shell back up there in St. Bernard. The smell was bad; made your eyes sting.

Shortie's sister, she died. Emmanuel, who cuts the grass, he died. When they found him, they tied him to the pillars of his house. Miss Roberta Claude, Bobby's mama, she died. Mrs. Jackson from down the street, she didn't leave either and she died.

Still, we was okay.

TIM BRUNEAU

SOUTH PRIEUR STREET
August 29, 2005

Well, Marie, it's you and me, Tim said to the pile of blue plastic in the backseat. Did that man call you trash? I'm sorry about that.

Was he speaking aloud, or just thinking that? He shook his head, was too tired to raise his hand and twist the ignition. He sat staring through the windshield down Prieur Street, which was rippling with pooled rainwater. A whole network of canals, culverts, and beautiful pump houses, and none of it working, seven hours after the storm passed.

Tim's eyes drifted shut. The burned-out, weed-choked house on Jackson Avenue had been there since Marie was a teenager, maybe longer. Coming up in a neighborhood like that, with shitty schools, whores, drug dealers—she never had a goddamn chance. His chest tightened, and the backs of his eyeballs felt soupy. Pretty girl, dead at twenty-four.

Tim's eyes popped open. Whoa. What kind of hippie-shit thinking was that? He struggled to sit erect behind the wheel. Anybody could rise above anything in America.

Tim let his head ease back and his eyes drift shut.

No, they can't, Marie said, from the backseat. How was I supposed to break out of there? What were my people going to say? Uppity. That's what. 'Cause if I can, why can't they? But I tell you what, I don't even know how it's done. I never seen nobody do it.

Come on, Marie. You're making excuses.

That man at the hospital is right. I'm trash. But what else could I be?

Faces loomed up behind Tim's eyelids: a thug with his arms folded like a tough guy, his lower lip quivering; a prostitute with a bruise on her cheek; an ancient man with a snow dusting of beard, mixing potpourri; an endless string of Pookies and Ray-Rays that Tim had insulted, beaten up, cuffed, and tossed in the can. Scumbags. Trash. Born as far behind the starting line as Marie.

A rap at the window made him jump. He opened his eyes on the jowly face of a patrolman from the Seventh, who was peering in, looking worried.

Tim's face and uniform were soaking wet. With the windows rolled up, it must have been 140 degrees in the car. He rolled down the window. "I'm fine." Cool air poured in.

"What you got there?" He wrinkled his nose.

"Nothing."

"I just come from the Dome. It's a fucking nightmare; don't go near it. Any cop goes near it, he's going to get sucked inside."

"Yeah?"

"I saw some of your detectives hanging out a couple blocks from the Dome, at Villere and Perdido."

Tim looked at the patrolman's feet. He was standing in water three inches deep. "Where's that water come from?"

"Fuck if I know." The patrolman gave Tim's windshield a friendly pat and sloshed away, kicking up rooster tails.

Tim started the Crown Vic and put it in gear. I'm going to find you a place, Marie.

fRANK MINYARD

CANAL STREET
August 29, 2005

Frank stopped his pickup at the corner of Canal Street and Claiborne Avenue and peered through the rain-bejeweled windshield, wondering what the hell he was looking at. A smooth sheet of water covered all of Canal, lakeside of Claiborne. Out in the middle, hundreds of cars, parked side to side, stretched in a row as far as the eye could see. They were on the neutral ground, where people parked before a storm because the extra five or six inches of elevation out there might keep a car's oil pan out of the water. These cars, though, were up to the middle of their hubcaps—the close ones, that is. Farther away, they were up to their windows. Frank rolled down the window, letting in a hot, spitting rain. He leaned out and looked down. The water was noticeably deeper than when he'd pulled up—maybe six inches now. The hurricane had passed hours ago; the water should have been receding. He put the truck in reverse and swiveled his neck to back up. Something pushed against the front bumper, and when he turned around to see, the hood was wet, steam rising. The engine sputtered and died. Frank leaned out. Water nearly covered his tires. It had been a wave that had bumped him. He tried twisting the ignition, but nothing happened. The water had killed it.

He felt his senses beginning to leave him, as though he were trapped in a nonsensical dream. He opened the truck door, and water poured in. He lifted his feet to keep his thousand-dollar ostrich-hide boots dry. He loved these boots—buttery yellow, with sharply pointed toes, an homage to his Texan dad. Grunting, Frank pulled them off and lay them on the seat. He opened the door and stepped out in his socks, gingerly. The water was cool. It covered his knees. He began wading up Canal, toward the lake, not really sure what he was doing or why. Within two blocks, water was at his chest. The reflection of the Tulane Health Services building shimmered. A plastic margarine tub, a Zapp's potato chip bag, a turd—scoured up from the storm drains and sewers and a hundred thousand trash cans—floated past. On the surface lay a rainbow of oil, and Frank's eyes stung from the fumes. He stopped and looked around. Not a soul in sight.

If the water is over my head at Canal and Prieur, what was it like by the lake? How much of the city was underwater? Now he began thinking like the coroner: How many bodies were floating around, and how many more would die? Not the uptown swells with cars, second homes, and wallets full of credit cards, but those who had no car, no friend with a car, those who'd never left New Orleans and weren't about to flee just because the mayor said to go. They were giving up their lives, as he stood up to his chest in water on Canal Street, in ways too unspeakable to imagine.

Who would put a name to the corpses and keep them from a mass grave or a potter's field? Would run hands over their bloated, reeking remains, looking for the last truth they'd ever give up?

Frank took a deep breath, pushed forward, and began swimming toward his office.

TIM BRUNEAU

VILLERE AND PERDIDO STREETS
August 29, 2005

The Sixth District detectives sat on the hoods of their units, gazing on the massive gray wall of the Superdome. "Hey, man," they called as Tim climbed out of the Crown Vic.

"Is it true?" Alan handed him a beer. "Are you driving a dead woman around the city?"

Tim gestured toward the backseat. The detectives came over, looked in, and laughed. "They're evacuating Charity," Tim said.

"Charity?" Jeff whistled. "Shit."

Tim looked down. The street was wet. Not speckled with rain, not puddled, but laminated with water. "Was the street wet when I drove up?"

"We need to get you a little blue cap and a better car, if you're going to chauffeur this lady around," Alan said.

"Full-service homicide investigator." Alan pulled another six-pack of Abita from his trunk, and they leaned, straight legged, against their cars, sucking at the bottles, watching the crowd thicken around the Dome. "Can you imagine what it smells like inside?" Jeff said.

"Like the inside of Timmy's car?"

"One six six four," a tinny voice called.

Tim rolled his cold beer bottle across his forehead.

"One six six four."

"Timmy, isn't that you?" Jeff pointed to the radio on his belt.

Tim snatched it up, pressing it to his lips. "One six six four."

"Word from the top," said the dispatcher. "You're to undo what you did."

Tim clutched the radio. He could hear the murmur of the crowd at the Superdome. "You mean dump the body?" he said.

"Undo what you did."

Tim closed his eyes.

"What are you supposed to do, put a body back on the street?" Jeff said.

"Jesus, that's sick." Alan shuddered visibly.

Something cold moved across the top of Tim's foot. Water was soaking through his boot laces. He pressed the button on the radio and said, with exaggerated slowness and clarity, "One six six four, leaving Villere and Perdido for the nineteen hundred block of Jackson Avenue, to dump the body." He climbed in the Crown Vic, read off his starting mileage, released the radio button, and leaned out the window. "I'm going to end up in front of a grand jury."

"I'll get a body bag and meet you there," Jeff said.

JOANN GUIDOS

ST. CLAUDE AVENUE
August 29, 2005

"JoAnn?"

All night she'd lain in bed, and all night they'd banged on the bedroom door. JoAnn, the generator's overheating. JoAnn, there's water coming under the door. JoAnn, the jukebox is stuck on "Sweet Home Alabama." JoAnn, Kajun's is the only place open; shouldn't we charge more than a buck for beer?

Put some fucking oil in the generator. Sweep the water out. Kick the side of the jukebox above the power cord. No, a buck a beer; we're not gouging. She missed Kathy and Roney; they'd been smart, evacuating to the bungalow in Carriere. "Go away," she yelled. "Solve it yourself."

Barbara stuck her head in. "Sorry. There are a couple of guys lurking at the pool table. I don't like their looks."

That was a problem of a different magnitude. JoAnn jolted awake, swung her legs over the side of her plywood-and-cinder-block bed, and felt on the side table for the snub-nosed .38 revolver. She jammed it in the back of her pants, pushed past Barbara, and clattered down the stairs. A couple of guys stood by the pool table in dark sweatshirts with their hoods up and hands deep in their pockets. They weren't playing. They weren't drinking. They had the look, to JoAnn, of a couple of punks trying to work up the nerve. JoAnn shouldered through the crowd and pushed her massive breasts up under the nose of the big one, squaring her place-kicker shoulders. "May I help you?"

The kid's eyes bulged, and his mouth dropped open. "No, ma'am," he squeaked. He and his friend scurried out.

WILBERT RAWLINS JR.

BEAUMONT, TEXAS
August 30, 2005

The sky was blue over Beaumont. Wilbert was in the driveway of his cousin's house, loading the car for the trip home.

Two nights jammed into Joanna's two-bedroom apartment with her, her two kids, Ma, Lawrence, Reecie, and Reecie's kids was plenty. Sleep had been impossible. The children giggled until late and woke at the first sign of daylight. The place was a zoo; everybody was getting on everybody else's nerves. Wil needed his Dreux Street house and his band room. He needed his hundred-odd kids, and he needed to reschedule St. Aug. Seven or eight hours of driving and he'd be there. The sky to the east was clear and pink.

Lawrence appeared at the garage door. "Hey, man. You better come in and look at the TV."

TIM BRUNEAU

❧

JACKSON AVENUE
August 29, 2005

I let you down, Marie, Tim said, pulling the Crown Vic to the curb in front of the burned-out house. You're going to leave this world like a piece of garbage.

Jeff pulled up and sloshed over with a bright yellow body bag. Jackson Avenue was under a couple inches of water.

Tim tried not to look up at the people on the stoops as he and Jeff pulled Marie from the backseat. She hit the pavement with a squishy thud. Jeff unrolled her like a wad of burrito filling. They lifted her into the body bag.

She lay on her back with her eyes closed and her lips parted slightly, like a sleeping child. Tim wrote a note saying she was the victim of an accident, not a homicide, tucked it into her little beaded bag, and put it beside her in the body bag. He zipped the bag shut and hoisted it onto the strip of grass between the sidewalk and the curb, out of the water. The big man stood in front of the Dreamers. As an authority figure for the nineteen hundred block of Jackson Avenue, he'd have to do. Tim walked toward him, feeling the resistance of water and sending big white splashes ahead. The man didn't move; he glowered at Tim as though ready to tear his head off. A baseball bat leaned against the door frame. He was taking care of business, and a New Orleans police officer was dumping a dead citizen on the curb like a bagful of crawfish heads. Tim stopped in front of the man, gestured back toward where Marie lay, and opened his mouth to speak. Nothing came out. There was nothing to say. Without another word Tim turned back toward his car and drove away, following Jeff through the deepening gray water.

BELINDA RAWLINS

BATON ROUGE
August 30, 2005

Belinda sat on the unmade motel bed, fast-food wrappers overflowing the wastebasket and a plastic bag of ice draped over her knee. Her eyes were bleary from watching CNN.

"How did the levees break if the storm was already over?" Curtis bounced on all fours.

"I don't know." She should be getting up, taking Curtis to a park to let him run around, but it was hard to tear herself away from the TV. The video shots mesmerized her, the same ones over and over—the Superdome, a child being hoisted skyward in a basket to an orange helicopter, a distraught woman waving a towel from a rooftop, two women pushing a shopping cart full of babies through waist-deep water, and every now and then something new: boats on Canal Street, water at the rooftops in the Lower Ninth Ward, a man waving a bedsheet from a roof in Gentilly, an old woman slumped in a wheelchair at the Convention Center, covered with a blanket. The woman waving the shirt or towel came on again: about forty-five, black, with straightened hair. Next to her lay a young man with his arm thrown over his eyes. A jagged hole, hacked through from inside, told of their ordeal. The woman was frantic, trying to bring help. The TV didn't say where the house was, and Belinda couldn't make out the surroundings.

She got up, limping, and stuffed the food wrappings deeper into the wastebasket. She dug in her purse for the stash of Goody's powders she'd grabbed at the last minute from the medicine cabinet, and delicately unfolded the last wax-paper sachet and tossed the bitter powder back on her tongue. She checked her cell phone. Nothing.

Time was starting to run together. Where was everybody? Did Wilbert get out? What about Faye, Ditty, and Aunt Polly? Faye had it together pretty well these days, but well enough to get them to high ground? How about Stevie?

Belinda was out of cash, and the car was nearly out of gas. If she didn't hear from someone soon and have money wired, she'd be stuck. Curtis lay facedown on the bed, and she rubbed his back. Pretty soon, he was snoring lightly. CNN cycled through the images: Super-dome, child in basket, shopping cart full of babies, the woman on the roof.

Belinda's eyes popped round, and she lunged toward the TV.

The woman on the roof, the young man beside her: Faye. Skeeter was with her. There was no mistaking them. But where were Ditty and his baby? Where was Aunt Polly?

Belinda sat up all night, watching the clip of Faye and Skeeter play over and over. Nothing changed. She never got rescued. It was just Faye and her autistic son, Skeeter, eternally trapped on their roof island.

fRANK MINYARD

ORLEANS PARISH
CRIMINAL COURTS BUILDING
August 30, 2005

Frank, a sheriff's deputy, and half a dozen others sat on the broad steps of the courthouse, hoping for a breeze to stir the gelatinous air. Behind them, in the big marble lobby, scores of people—judges, clerks, neighbors fleeing their homes for the safety of a building propped high off the street—stretched out on blankets, waiting.

No power, no food, no toilets. No news. Frank had been lucky to get one call out to Nancy from the deputy's cell phone. He'd run off the morning after the storm and, as far as she was concerned, had disappeared for two days. It was good not to worry about her; she was safe at the farm. She said she'd let the authorities know where he was.

Frank stared miserably across Tulane Avenue: Steve's Bail Bonds, Quicky's Po'Boys, and fifty trucks in the U-Haul lot, up to their roofs in olive green water. What an idiot he'd been to swim up here. The only way out now was to swim again, but the water, after sitting under the scorching sun for days, seemed thicker—more filth than water.

Pok! Ptuuiiii!

"Not again," the deputy said tiredly as everybody on the steps rose and shuffled up the steps into the courthouse. A lot of people had been sent to Angola from this building, and every now and then since the crisis had started, somebody in the city had taken the opportunity to take a shot at it.

Night didn't fall; it rose, hot, from the stinking lake.

Every now and then, a small orange helicopter appeared in the distance. Somebody told Frank it was from the Coast Guard air station in Belle Chasse. Other than that, though, the sky was empty and silent. It was spooky; where was the help? The storm had ended a day and a half ago, and nobody had shown up to help.

He was the parish coroner. Surely, he thought, somebody would send a boat for him.

TIM BRUNEAU

GRETNA
August 29, 2005

Tim lay on a pew in the Baptist church, listening to the Sixth District—cops, wives, kids—snoring, farting, and sighing in the darkness around him. He held a brick-shaped radio to his ear, the volume turned as low as it would go, to save battery power. The main police digital radio frequency was dead, but the analog frequency—a low-power, line-of-sight, walkie-talkie function—had come to life. Every cop, firefighter, and EMT within a sixty-mile radius of New Orleans was on, shouting. As a means of conversation, it was useless. As a window on the disaster, it was grimly fascinating.

"About four hundred on the I-10!" came through the cacophony. "Boatfulla people," said a deep Cajun accent. "Where sh'I bringum?" Nobody answered. "I'm on Louisa Street!" a man hollered. It sounded like he was crying.

What were they doing, hiding across the river? The whole Sixth District has abandoned its post.

Tim thought of Marie, eyes closed, lips parted.

Russell was shaking him. The stained-glass window was bright with morning sun. "We're going back across to secure the Wal-Mart." His red-freckled face was within inches of Tim's. He'd shown up late the night before with a crazy story about swimming out of his house with his dog.

Tim struggled to his feet and pulled on wet boots.

A line of Sixth District cruisers streamed across the Crescent City Connection against a tide of pedestrians—pushing grocery carts and wheelchairs, pulling dogs on leashes—like newsreel footage from an African famine. They tried to flag him down, but he kept moving. It was a horrible feeling; it went against everything he believed. Cops should help citizens in distress. Thing was, there was nothing he could do for them.

When they reached the Wal-Mart on Tchoupitoulas, they turned on their sirens and charged across the parking lot side by side, hoping to frighten away the crowd that milled around the smashed front doors. To Tim's horror and disgust, the people barely looked up. Furious, he jumped out, waving his pistol and yelling, "Police! Police!" His fellow cops joined in. "Get out now! Leave the store now or risk being shot!"

People walked calmly past Tim, staggering under boxes, wheeling bicycles draped high with clothes on hangers. A smug-looking kid strolled right at him, hugging a boxed basketball backboard. "Put that down." The kid smirked and kept walking. Tim pressed his Glock against the back of the kid's skull. "Put it down." The kid's arms flew up. The box crashed to the ground. Tim holstered his gun and yanked the kid's arms into cuffs. Dozens of people holding loot swept past, watching with mild interest. Jeff got out of his car and walked up.

"Easy," he said. "What are you going to do?"

"Take him in."

"Take him in, where? The jail's flooded."

"Ha!" the kid said.

"And then there's all these." Jeff gestured toward the multitudes flowing off with toaster ovens, fishing rods, and teetering ziggurats of sneaker boxes. "You're going to take him and not them?"

"There's got to be a place."

"Where? The church?" Jeff put a hand on Tim's shoulder. "Let him go, Timmy."

"Fuck."

"It is what it is."

Tim fished the keys from his pocket and removed the cuffs. "Mr. Police, with no jail," the kid sneered, and sauntered off, scooping up the backboard as he went.

Tim limped into the store. In the heat, it smelled of onions, Pine-

Sol, and the fresh soles of new running shoes. Creole mix—chopped celery, bell pepper, green onion—littered the floor of the grocery section like confetti. Little by little, people were getting the message and drifting out. The last of the looters, in twos and threes, scurried from where they'd been hiding and made for the door, grabbing what they could as they went. In sporting goods, a fat woman strolled calmly, a basket of sports watches over her arm, as though whiling away a Sunday afternoon. "Get out!" Tim raised his gun.

"You going to shoot the police?" She produced a badge in a leather folder.

"Get out now!" She rolled her eyes and meandered toward the front of the store, the shopping basket swinging on her arm.

In the parking lot, the Sixth District cops settled in for the siege of Wal-Mart. A couple of patrolmen drove over to Brown's Dairy, boosted a refrigerated truck, and parked it near the entrance so they could empty the store's perishable food into it. Patrolwomen built stoves out of metal display racks and propane tanks and, on the sidewalk in front of the store, started pots of gumbo. Jeff and Alan grabbed tents from the sporting-goods aisles and set them up on one of the islands of shrubbery dotting the parking lot. Tim washed his fatigues in a Tweety Bird wastebasket and put on the extra outfit he'd brought from home.

Night fell, as muggy as day. He climbed into the Crown Vic and fell asleep with his gun in his hand.

fRANK MINYARD

ORLEANS PARISH COURTHOUSE
September 2005

"Is that a boat?"

It was almost dark, but it looked like something moving on the water. Frank cupped his hands around his mouth and yelled, "Ahoy!" in a cracking voice. He hadn't had more than a couple of sips of water in three days.

No answer. If it was a boat, it was tiny. He strained his ears. No motor, but here it came—two people paddling a pirogue up Tulane Avenue.

Still no helicopters. Frank couldn't understand it. If the water was this deep here, right in the middle of the city, all of New Orleans must be underwater. Thousands of people must be trapped, dying. Where is the Army? Where are the feds?

He stared at the pirogue moving toward the courthouse. No, it wasn't a pirogue. The two people were sitting in what looked like a Jacuzzi. They'd probably pried it out of the Value Inn up the street.

"Hey!" Frank called.

"What are they doing?"

The Jacuzzi veered left. A hand reached out of it and grabbed for the green awning of Le Petit Motel. The other guy scrambled up on the awning and lifted himself through an open window. His hands came back out of the window, holding a television set.

"Those aren't rescuers," the deputy said.

TIM BRUNEAU

RELIGIOUS STREET
September 2005

"I know a place on the West Bank where we can get a shower," Alan said. They weren't supposed to be patrolling with no reliable source of gasoline, and crossing the river was definitely forbidden. But sitting around the Wal-Mart parking lot had driven them crazy.

"Let's swing by Jackson Avenue first," Tim said.

Alan gave him a sideways look.

"Let's just see." They glided up Annunciation Street, one of Tim's favorites, the colorful shotgun houses packed close together, the light dreamy and beachy. It hadn't flooded, but no one was home. Tim turned right on Jackson. On the cracked pavement lay a woman's body, grotesquely swollen in the heat, hands tossed back over her head. Someone had thrown a hideous green and orange blanket over it, but the arms and legs stuck out. The smell wafted in the windows.

"That her?" Alan said.

"No. Marie's in a body bag."

"Homicide, you think?" Alan flipped his chin at the woman's body.

"I don't know. Let's just go." He released his foot from the brake, the Crown Vic eased forward, and they drove in silence, crossing St. Charles. He hit the brakes and leaned out the window. Water shimmered peacefully on Jackson Avenue. From Carondelet up, it was a canal.

They climbed out of the car. Tim raised his binoculars. Half-concealed under a low-hanging bush up by Baronne Street, a dome of bright yellow plastic rose from the water, bobbing lazily among the oil cans and other crap. Marie had drifted across Jackson and half a block toward the lake.

"Okay. Enough." Alan climbed back in the car and Tim followed, his mind blank, as though a flatiron had struck him in the forehead. They soared over the Crescent City Connection, the sun sinking behind them. Alan was silent, for once.

"Where to?" Tim said. They zigzagged through the residential streets of the West Bank, Alan giving directions, until Tim lost track.

"Turn here," Alan said. "Slow down."

"You see the place?"

"I'm leaving," he said. "Stop here."

"What?" Tim pulled to the curb in front of a wood-frame house and cut the engine.

"I'm done." Alan kept his eyes straight ahead.

"For good?" Tim looked out the window. He couldn't find words to scold or cajole. It was Alan, after all. They'd been through a lot. "If you're leaving, you're not taking stuff we can use."

Alan detached his holstered pistol and laid it on the seat, along with a spare clip, cuffs, and a box of ammunition for the AR-15 that lay across the backseat. He handed Tim his badge and ID in their leather folder. He climbed out, walked around the car, leaned in Tim's window, and extended a hand.

Tim took it.

"Look, man, I haven't heard from my wife and kids since the storm. I don't even know where they are."

"Alan, as long as you can live with what you're doing, more power to you."

Tim steered the Crown Vic toward the bridge, twilight fading to night—a scary time, since the storm. A commotion to his left caught his eye, a crowd thronging in front of a CVS pharmacy, partying hearty, laughing and shouting, probably lit up on drugs and liquor from the shelves. It pissed him off. He switched on the blue flasher mounted on his dash and whooped the siren. "Run, you animals," he said, bearing down.

The crowd froze in the headlights but didn't run. One man reached behind his back and came up with a long-nosed pistol. Four, five, six flashes of lightning lit the street in front of the Crown Vic. Shit! Hot zips of breathy wind hissed by Tim's window. He flattened the brakes and manhandled the car through a K-turn. As he came broadside to the crowd, he thrust his pistol out the window and, in violation of every regulation ever written, banged off five or six rounds. Out of the corner of his eye, he saw a man tumble to the pavement; he didn't know which one. He wrestled the wheel. Two, four, half a dozen people were shooting at him: a woman, a man with a rifle—louder than the pistols. He pulled his head into his shoulders, straightened out the Crown Vic, and floored it.

Where the hell was he? In the sticky gloom, he saw the top of the bridge and snaked toward it. He missed the entrance, circled back, and hit it on the second pass, flying up and over, only stars and his headlights piercing the darkness. He was panting, sweating adrenaline when he came to a stop at the desolate Camp Street exit. He rested his head on the wheel.

Tim, said a voice from the backseat. You shot that boy.

I know it, Marie. They were shooting at me.

Silence, and he knew what Marie was thinking: that cops are supposed to stop and render aid, that they're supposed to call in a shooting right away so it can be thoroughly investigated, that shooting from a moving car and then running off is criminal. What was happening to him? What was happening to New Orleans?

RONALD LEWIS

THIBODAUX
September 2005

Ronald wasn't so much driving his old car as massaging it along the highway. His big, rough hands kneaded the wheel, coaxing the car out of its temptation to drift off right. His foot gently rocked the gas, in constant search of the engine's wandering, elusive medium between a panicked clattering and a dead-out stall. Even the muscles of his broad butt were working, subconsciously pulsing to keep the big, soft-sprung car ambulatory. His bloodshot eyes worked an anxious triangle among the windshield, the heat gauge, and the rearview mirror. His plates were expired, and a run-in with the police was the last thing he needed right now.

Highway 20 gleamed with hot rainwater. The squall had blown through like a temper tantrum, and now the evening sun slanted in under the heavy charcoal sky, lighting up the cane with a brilliant iridescence. God help me, Ronald thought. Even knowing all the misery these fields represent, I still find them beautiful to look at.

He drove into Thibodaux and made his way to the semicircular driveway by the main hall of Nicholls State University. He'd passed Nicholls many times while visiting relatives in Thibodaux. It accepted black students, and had some black teachers, but its faux-antebellum buildings, with their forbidding white columns, had always sent him a visceral "whites only" message.

Though he and Minnie were staying by his relatives, Ronald liked to stop by the shelter in the Nicholls gymnasium to see if any new people from the neighborhood had shown up. He'd even registered here as an evacuee, so he could sleep in the shelter if he wanted to. Today, though, he couldn't muster the will to get out of the car. He looked through the cracked windshield at the fine lawn in front of the main hall mansion. The saddest-looking people sat among pathetic bundles of filthy possessions. They looked like field niggers gathered round the massa's house. It wrung out his heart like a towel.

United Radio Broadcasters of New Orleans was reporting twelve feet of water in Gentilly, fourteen feet in Broadmoor, fifty thousand people packed into the Superdome, still no sign of federal help. It was like underground reports from a battlefield—no music, no ads, no jokes. "We have the local homeland security director, Colonel Terry Ebbert," the announcer said. "You've been up in a helicopter this morning, sir. What did you see?"

"The Lower Ninth Ward is totally gone. Nothing out there can be saved at all."

Ronald snapped it off. Gone? What did that mean?

A bus hissed to a halt in front of the struggle-buggy, and the dejected passengers filed off. State troopers in crisp blue uniforms with yellow stripes down the trousers herded them in a long line toward the front door of the mansion. The troopers were talking to the evacuees. The troopers didn't prod them with sticks, but neither did they help them carry their sacks. One led a German shepherd on a leash. It ran its nose eagerly over the bags and bundles. Among the wretched evacuees, the troopers looked like—what?—not overseers muscling field hands along, but something from the History Channel. Jews shuffling from railroad cars, skeletal people in the camp yards, skulls in the furnace ash, dark-eyed children holding out little forearms with number tattoos. Ever since Miss Duckie, the Jewish people interested Ronald.

It wasn't only the uniforms and the dogs that made Ronald think of the Jews now. It was the thoroughness of the defeat his people had suffered. The line of evacuees stretched back to the auction block in Jackson Square, the slave market in Cuba, the terrors of the Middle Passage. This is our holocaust, Ronald thought. This is where we hit bottom. This is where it can't get any worse.

He took a deep breath and thrust his chin forward. And this is where we decide what our future's going to be, he said. Look at the Jews. Almost totally wiped out sixty years ago and now they're about the wealthiest, best-educated people anywhere. They even got their own country, their own Army, their own atomic bomb. Sixty years ago you wouldn't have given two cents for the future of the Jews, and look now. Where are we going to be in sixty years? Shit. Where are we going to be in sixty days?

He felt a chill despite the heat, and hugged himself. He closed his eyes and hung his head, kneading his biceps. When he opened them, he imagined a death's-head on the broad brown expanse of his upper arm, as clear and stark as the numbers the Nazis etched. He reached up and put the struggle-buggy into gear.

An hour later, Ronald's upper arm was sore and swollen. A three-inch-tall skull and crossbones, with the legend "RWL 65-05," glowed against his raw skin. "It's beautiful," said the skinny Confederate with the humming needle at Randy's Fine Line Tattoos.

"These are the bookends to my life. Forty years apart. Betsy and Katrina."

"What's the little crown above the *R*?"

"That means I am king of the plan." Ronald palpated his achy upper arm. Katrina and Betsy were part of him; he'd wear them like he wore his own black skin. But hurricanes came and went; men planned and built.

ANTHONY WELLS

We didn't see no free people, no National Guard or marshals, for about ten days. We could see helicopters flying around over the city, but not where we were. At one point, they dropped water and rations over on Chef Highway and people were running like it was the Twilight Zone.

They said on the radio, if you want to leave, get to the Superdome. People were coming around in boats, and little by little the women went off. We told them, Superdome is fucked-up. No air, no water. Nothing to clean up with. But the women, they all went. Roger and me, though, we stayed. Pulled a piece of paneling off, made kind of a secret compartment, and we put up in there everything we'd gotten: cases of Armor All, motor oil. Courvoisier and Hennessy fifths. Cases of cigarettes. A gun we found in the auto-parts store. Little bit of cash but not much, because most of the places we hit, all the twenty-dollar bills were all moldy and wet. We took change, but shit, we couldn't carry all of it. We put that all up in that little compartment. New Orleans wasn't going to stay fucked-up forever. Someday that shit would come in useful.

BILLY GRACE

DESTIN, FLORIDA
September 2005

Billy sat at the kitchen table of his beachfront house in Destin, sipping a cold glass of wine and holding a phone to his ear, feeling utterly unmoored from the planet. The muted television on the kitchen counter showed images he had seen a thousand times but still couldn't interpret. "Relax," Jimmy Reiss said. "There's no water on St. Charles Avenue."

Billy grasped at the chirping voice as a lifeline to reality. Jimmy was old New Orleans, rich beyond measure, but no bullshit. He lived on Audubon Place, a private drive of mansions off St. Charles—New Orleans's most exclusive address. He'd linked up with a Texas company called Instinctive Shooting International, run by a bunch of Israeli ex-commandos, and landed a surplus Soviet gunship on the golf course at Audubon Park. Overkill, he realized in retrospect, but they were hearing such stories.

"My in-laws left the city in a convoy of cars full of guns and made it to Baton Rouge," Billy said. "I had my time-share jet pick them up and bring them here."

"I'll tell you what was even scarier than being in the city," Jimmy said. "On the first day, Wayne Decody, Billy Monteleone, and I were up at my place in Aspen and figured we could round up some barges in Baton Rouge, load them with food and water, and float them down the river to the Convention Center. We'd bring people out on the return trip."

"Great idea."

"I made the fatal mistake of asking for permission from Don Ensenat, Bush's chief of protocol." Jimmy was a big-time Republican, a major fund-raiser and acquaintance of the president's. "A day goes by and Don calls back. He says, 'I talked to the chief, and he says Brown and Cherthoff are doing a good job. So let's give it a few days.' "

"A few days?"

"Yeah. So no go. But here's my idea now. I'm putting together a meeting in Dallas of business leaders. We'll come up with a plan for the recovery, show our commitment. I have a hotel booked for this coming weekend."

"I was thinking the exact same thing. Who can we reach? All I have with me is the numbers in my cell phone."

"That's all I have."

"Let's start calling."

RONALD LEWIS

THIBODAUX
September 2005

Ronald drove out to the FEMA center, a white trailer on Highway 1, and asked for a crisis counselor. She turned out to be a white lady from up north who'd come down after Katrina to help out. "My wife needs help," Ronald told her, and damned if that white lady didn't reach for her keys that minute and drive with Ronald out to the little brick house where he and Minnie were staying. Minnie came to the door in her nightgown, and when Ronald started talking with that white lady beside him, Minnie backed across the living room with her hands outstretched in front of her as though retreating from a ghost, the whites of her eyes gleaming. "You ain't committing me!" she yelled, and Ronald felt his voice catch as he tried to speak as soothingly as possible: No, Minnie, no. Nobody wants to commit you to nothing; just let this nice lady help you. Minnie folded onto the couch and put her head in her hands, and Ronald, standing with his big arms dangling, could only think, oh, Minnie. All that fire and passion I love so much been knocked sideways by the storm. Every joint in him aching, he struggled down onto one knee before her and put his hands on her upper arms. "You got to get ahold of yourself, Minnie," he whispered. "We got to get home and we can't do that with you in such a state." The white lady suggested Minnie see a doctor who might give her pills to make her feel better, and, sniffling, Minnie finally agreed. When the white lady had gone, Ronald sat with Minnie on the couch and took one of her hands between both of his. Her head was bowed, her beautiful dreads hanging almost to her knees. She moaned.

"Minnie," Ronald said. "I'm going to New Orleans. I got to get us home, Minnie. I can't deal with this big old cup and deal with your cup, too. You follow me? I got to leave you here for a spell and see to our business. I got to start getting us home."

She looked up at him from the bottom of a deep well of loneliness. He ached for her, stuck out here on Plantation Road, the far edge of Thibodaux, with nothing around but sugar fields and nobody she knew within God knows how many miles. Might as well take a catfish out the creek as take Minnie away from Tupelo Street, where she had her sons and her cousins and her sisters-in-law all right there. That's why I got to get her home, he thought. That's why I got to get to work. That's why I got to leave her here. He gathered himself up inside as though to amputate a gangrenous limb; this has got to be done. That night he left Minnie alone—had to start sometime—and drove back down to Nicholls State University. Time to spend a night with my people, he told himself. He lay on a cot all night, listening to the shuffling and weeping of the evacuees around him, absorbing their need, absorbing their pain. I am as responsible for these people as I am for Minnie. I am as responsible for them as I was for the men of my local. I got to get these people home.

PART IV

THE HEEBIE-JEEBIES

"The truth is that it's not engineering mechanics, but Corps mechanics, the problems with the Corps and the Orleans Levee Board, and all the other helpers in this system, that need to be studied."

—PROFESSOR ROBERT BEA,
of the University of California,
Berkeley, on the National Academy
of Science's plan to study the
physical collapse of the levees
without considering political and
management failures

fRANK MINYARD

Frank and James stood in the wide doorway of the warehouse, watching FEMA's DMORT people move crisply about, readying gear for a deluge of the dead. Eighteen hours earlier, a National Guard deuce and a half had plowed the water beside the courthouse and set Frank off on a hallucinogenic journey, one vehicle after another, to a friend's house in Baton Rouge, where he'd sat in a hot tub like Henry VIII, devouring a whole chicken and a six-pack of beer. Dressed in a new T-shirt and chinos from Wal-Mart, he was back now in the torpid, miserable crisis. The air around his head felt liquid. His stomach felt distended from eating a lunchtime MRE. He stank.

James, on the other hand, stood as solid as Mount Rushmore, arms folded, gaze alert, graying goatee twisted into a neat rope. James hadn't made Frank's mistake; he'd evacuated on command and spent the flood days in Lafayette.

"Shall I show you around?" A young man with a square jaw and a DMORT badge that read "Andrew" touched Frank's elbow. "Before we go in, I want you to see how we've done to secure the grounds. We put up that chain-link fence. The black tarp prevents voyeurs, media or otherwise."

Frank turned slowly in a circle, taking in the buff men in olive green T-shirts who patrolled the fence, cradling rifles that looked like something off a Klingon battle cruiser. "Blackwater," their T-shirts said. Beyond the fence rose a phalanx of refrigerated 18-wheelers, idling, keeping their boxes cold and ready to receive the first corpses.

"The school, of course, is sleeping quarters." Andrew pointed to a collection of low redbrick buildings, connected by covered walkways, that once was an elementary school. "We saved you a cot by a blackboard, so you can put your things on the chalk tray."

"Is there a shower?"

"There's a garden hose. Let me show you the morgue."

The floor of the warehouse was covered in the same heavy black plastic sheeting that draped the fence around the school grounds. Movable walls had been created out of PVC pipe and blue tarp. They stood in a line, like the stations of the cross. Technicians unpacked folding X-ray machines, gurneys, Tyvek suits, surgical masks, and boxes of rubber gloves from crates marked "Deployable Portable Morgue Unit."

The people here, Andrew informed him, came from as far away as Montana and Delaware. Dentists, pathologists, forensic anthropologists, funeral-home attendants, fingerprinters. They put their names on a list, maybe years ago, to serve in case of emergency, and now here they were in New Orleans. Andrew faced Frank squarely. "As the Orleans Parish coroner, you are legally in charge, Dr. Minyard. We're here to assist the local authority, and that's you."

"I'm humbled," Frank said. "You got all this done while I was stuck in the damn courthouse." He felt he might cry; Jesus, he needed sleep. He blinked. On a whiteboard attached to a wall, someone had written: "Today is Saturday, September 3."

"I have a question," he said. "It's a week since the hurricane. Where are the bodies?"

"That's right," Andrew said. "Not half a dozen yet. But we're ready. They'll go first to decontamination." He indicated a cubicle at the far end of the warehouse. "Then to fingerprinting; then to what we call 'anthropology,' where we'll record everything that might help in identification: age, sex, race, scars, tattoos, and so forth; then to X-ray, over here; and dental." He nodded toward the back of the warehouse. "Finally, DNA."

"That's fine," Frank said. "But where are the bodies?"

JOANN GUIDOS

ST. CLAUDE AVENUE
September 2005

JoAnn set a case of Pabst down behind the bar, the three hundredth or so since the storm. She pushed her pistol aside and massaged the small of her back. She loved her tits, but carrying them around got old. The idea of jumping in the pickup and driving out of the heat and stink moved through her with the power of love. She could be at Kathy and Roney's by nightfall, taking a hot shower, lying in a quiet backyard hammock with a plate of good food. She could sleep on clean sheets, unpeeling the tension like a bandage from a skull wound. She tightened her fingers around the case of Pabst as though physically to anchor herself to the spot.

Mitch leaned over the bar, his eyes swimming in their sockets like two undercooked eggs. "You know who did the voice of Yogi Bear?"

"Who?" JoAnn sighed.

"Art Carney."

JoAnn fought the urge to cry. Her little bar was Mitch's whole world. She reached out and patted his arm. "Hey. Go eat something." A pot of red beans and another of rice sat on a folding table. The jukebox started: "Sweet Home Alabama." A brown dog, sleeping on the pool table, sat up and licked his balls.

JoAnn stood and planted her fists on the bar. "Hey!" she shouted. Heads turned. "We're going to make it! We stick together, we'll be fine. Right?"

The lights went out and the jukebox stopped, crashing the bar into a spooky silence; from the alley, the hum of the generator died.

"Clint Eastwood's father? Stan Laurel," Mitch said. "Trust me. What I'm saying is real close to the truth."

ANTHONY WELLS

Then one day a big old Army truck come through the water, full of police and soldiers and people they were picking up. I said, "I appreciate your coming, but you're a little fucking late." They said, "The governor and mayor made it a mandatory evacuation and you must leave." I said I'd think about it. I don't know why I said that; I wanted the fuck out of there. It was getting old, man. No women, nothing to do all day but sit up there in the heat and breathe that shit. Ice all melted, and Roger's big pile of meat was starting to get funky, you feel me? But shit, they leave our ass out there for a week, ten days, and then come say we got to go? Leave our homes like we're in a dictatorship? I told them, I said, "Why don't you pick up Emmanuel, who cuts the grass? He's tied up in front of his house so he don't float away."

I could see them soldiers and police talking to each other, like they're wondering if it's worth coming up those rickety stairs to fight this crazy nigger. They said they'd come back tomorrow, and Roger and me would be ready.

Next day they come back like they said, only this time they got the guns out, all pointed up at us, clicking them. "Mr. Wells, you decided what you're going to do?" I said, "Where are we going?" "You'll find out when you get there." Shit. "What can we take?" "One bag." So we went. I'll tell you, man, I'd a known how long it was going to be until I saw that place again, I wouldn't have gone.

FRANK MINYARD

ST. GABRIEL
September 2005

Frank slept poorly on the narrow cot. He skipped the MRE breakfast, took a seat early in the school library, and watched the others file in: a captain from the state police, sharp in blue on blue; a National Guard colonel in black and green camo; an officer of the Eighty-second Airborne in a snappy maroon beret; a New Orleans police lieutenant in Task Force fatigues; and a sprinkling of DMORT pathologists and administrators. The woman to his right extended a hand and introduced herself as Corinne Stern, the former medical examiner of El Paso, Texas.

Sheaves of paper riffled, dry-erase markers squeaked on whiteboards, acronyms spilled like a dropped Scrabble set. Frank felt himself nodding off in the heat and forced himself erect. He was supposed to be in charge. "Wait," he heard himself saying. "None of this means anything if nobody's collecting the bodies." He turned to a DMORT official to his left. "Didn't I hear you say your people would start today?"

The man shifted in his chair. "We've been waved off. That's what I was just saying."

"Waved off."

"Our orders are to stand down."

Frank smoothed his hair off his damp forehead and looked around at the officers, soldiers, and bureaucrats. "Look. I appreciate all you've done. But if nobody's going to collect bodies, what's the point?" Corinne shook her head and inspected her nails. The National Guard colonel coughed.

The officer in the maroon beret stood up. "I can get that process started."

"You can?"

"My soldiers will collect the bodies."

Right on, Frank thought. The Eighty-second Airborne.

BELINDA RAWLINS

INTERSTATE 10 WESTBOUND
September 2005

"How long we going to be in Texas?"

"I don't know."

"I want to go home."

"Me too."

"When can we go home?"

"I don't know."

"Where's Mr. Wil?"

"In Texas."

"We going to see him?"

"I don't know."

Belinda felt like she was floating above the car, watching herself drive Curtis across the green rolling countryside of east Texas. She kept waiting for "Belinda" to lose her patience with Curtis's whiny questioning, but "Belinda" never did. "Belinda" kept driving, staring grimly over the steering wheel, leaving behind the stinking Baton Rouge motel room, heading for Alvin's house in Hearne. He was on leave from Iraq and had wired her enough money. Mookey was on her way to Alvin's, too, from Lionus's. Niecy had wanted to come—poor thing, staying at college in Hammond on her own while her family scattered every which way— but Belinda had stood firm: don't miss a class. Niecy would get her education the proper way: immediately after high school, full-time, straight through—the way Belinda had dreamed of.

"Where are Faye and Skeeter?"

"I don't know."

"Where's Ditty?"

"I don't know."

"How 'bout Aunt Polly?" Curtis looked over with a wry smile; he knew he was being a pest.

Belinda made herself smile. "I don't know." She might be losing her mind—she couldn't have told Curtis what day it was; there seemed to be no difference between waking and sleeping—but she could be kind. For the first time in her life, she had no plan. She was just getting by, precisely the condition she'd spent a lifetime trying to avoid.

An exit loomed, and she signaled. Her knee ached, and she'd run out of Goody's powders. "Wait here," she said.

Curtis followed her into the convenience store. They didn't sell Goody's powders. The clerk, an East Indian, had never heard of such a thing. She bought aspirin.

Walking back to the car, Belinda felt an unfamiliar vibration in her jacket pocket. For a fleeting second, she thought it was her heart racing, that she was having a palpitation, or a stroke. But it was her cell phone, dead since the storm. She took it from her pocket: a text message, from cousin Stevie.

She wrenched open the phone: "DITTY AND THE BABY DIDN'T MAKE IT."

fRANK MINYARD

ST. GABRIEL
September 2005

Corinne Stern had thrown open every window in the school library, but not a breeze stirred.

The colonel from the Eighty-second Airborne stood in front of the whiteboard, kneading his maroon beret. "We, ah, were told not to proceed with retrieval of the bodies."

"Told by who?" Frank tapped a pencil on the miniature desk that trapped his legs.

"My orders came from my commanding officer; I don't know who called him." The poor man hesitated a moment, and sat down in his absurdly small chair.

Another colonel in camo fatigues stood up. "Okay." He lifted his cap, sweaty pate glistening under the buzz cut. "I'll get my people on it." He seemed pleased to have a chance to show up the vaunted Eighty-second Airborne. There was a murmur of relief and a scraping of chairs.

Right on, Frank thought. The National Guard.

TIM BRUNEAU

ABOVE LAKEVIEW
September 2005

Tim clenched the safety strap and leaned out over Lakeview, the Black Hawk's rotor wash lifting his hair. It was as though Lake Pontchartrain had grown across the city. The old shore was gone. The new one, a mile south, lapped at the mansions along St. Charles Avenue. Lakeview, Broadmoor, Gentilly, Mid-City, the Ninth Ward—they were nothing but lake water, and a neat grid of rooftops poking through. Blue sky and white clouds reflecting off the water made it look as though New Orleans were floating in midair. Tim was half sorry he'd talked these guardsmen into giving him a look.

Straight underneath him was his house. Brown water covered the tops of the windows. In the driveway, his beloved white pickup, with the sweet straight-six engine that would have run forever, shone like a coral reef. He looked, finding Jackson Avenue, and then south toward Baronne Street, where a spot of yellow was barely visible under some fallen branches. It might have been a car. It might have been anything.

JOYCE MONTANA

HOUSTON
2005

"Joyce, look! It's the Circle Food Store!"

Joyce lay on the hard motel bed, her eyes closed. She'd been had enough of flood scenes and looting. And now the Circle. She propped herself onto her elbows. Joyce walked to the Circle almost every day of her life, and there it was, full of water. A man stood in front of it, in water up to his chest. The Circle was only a couple of blocks from her house; if the water was that deep, her house was flooded, and with it Tootie's suits.

The camera turned, moved, and there on the corner of St. Bernard Avenue and Villere Street—her own corner—a young woman slogged along in water up to her knees. It had never felt to Joyce like she was walking downhill to the Circle, but it looks like she had been all those years. If the water was only knee-deep, her house, four steps up from the street, might be okay.

The phone rang. Denise answered and handed her the receiver. "Oh, Miss Joyce, it's good to hear your voice!" Fred Johnson's high, ringing voice came through loud and sharp.

"I'm fine," Joyce cried. "Where are you?"

"I'm in the city!"

"What you doing there?"

"It's crazy here."

"I know that. Get yourself out to someplace safe."

"I'm okay. I'm helping the National Guard. Listen: I owe you an apology."

"What you mean?"

"We went in your house."

"How'd you get in my house? I got a glass door and a wood door."

"We, ah, we broke them open."

"What you do that for?" Joyce felt her voice rising.

"We didn't know where you were! We knocked and knocked and nobody answered."

"You thought . . . what?"

Fred didn't say anything.

"If I was dead, you couldn't do nothing for me no way!"

"I know that." He sounded like Darryl as a boy, when she used to wear him out for doing something stupid. "But the house is fine. Tootie's suits are fine. Water come up the steps, but didn't get in."

"Well, you close up the house best you can." She hung up the phone and sighed, turning to Denise.

"I got to go home."

fRANK MINYARD

ST. GABRIEL
September 2005

Frank and James sat on packing crates on the lawn in front of the school, forcing themselves, despite the cloying heat, to eat steaming mounds of beef Stroganoff over noodles. The Forest Service had shown up with a field kitchen, ready and able to serve the kind of food appropriate to fighting forest fires in Idaho.

"Maybe today." Frank threw his plate in a trash pile and stood, feeling like he was pushing against a hot, wet tarp. The refrigerated trucks idled beyond the fence, empty.

"I hope so," James said. "Every day that goes by is going to make them messier."

Frank eased into a desk chair next to Corinne. The National Guard colonel slunk in, looking like a whipped dog.

"The mission's a no go. Apparently DOD thinks there's some risk of infection to my soldiers."

"Well, yes." Frank leaned over his tiny desk. "But there's a health risk to the whole city if the bodies aren't collected!"

"Apparently Legal had a problem," the colonel said.

"Which is it? Medical problem or legal?" Frank's pulse raced. "You blaming the doctors or the lawyers?"

"I'm as sorry as you are," the colonel said, sitting down.

"Come on, people." Frank glared around the room. "This is getting absurd. We've been here four days!"

The state police commander, in crisp blue on blue, raised a hand. "My people can do it."

Right on, Frank thought. Local boys. The Louisiana State Police.

ANTHONY WELLS

They didn't take us to no Superdome. By then, they were cleaning that bitch out. That's when they found all them women raped, the murdered babies, all that shit. They took us to the Convention Center, and, man, they had that shit tight! The Army was running it by then, and they took everything you had—guns, knives, even my ink pen. One thing they didn't take away was people's animals. It was like every other person there had him a damned dog on a leash. One guy had a basket of kittens. Another had a hedgehog up under his shirt. I ain't kidding you. A hedgehog. Couldn't take an ink pen in there, but go ahead, sir, take your hedgehog.

By that time they were taking people out the city, and we sat around for hours in this big old parking lot. They had tents up to keep you out of the sun, and bottles of ice water. There were these Army nurses, in uniform and everything, going around asking everybody how do you feel, and do you want to talk. Had their first names written on masking tape up here on their bosom—Debbie, Allison. They were like mental-health nurses, and some people, man, were just crying their fucking eyes out. Got to remember, this was like day ten or eleven. Anybody going out the city then was the holdouts, been trapped in their house all that time.

After a while, they put us on a bus—a nice one, from one of the casinos. Air-conditioned and everything. Even had a movie going. I remember it was one of them slasher films and the women on the bus were all upset, like, "Why are they showing us this?" But I'll tell you what, when that film ended, they put on

Ray—*you seen that? It ain't New Orleans, but it's so beautiful, that black life and the music, and all. In some ways it was harder to watch than that slasher film.*

We sat on that bus a long time. Right out my window there was a big green and white helicopter sitting there, with "United States of America" all up on its side. And while I'm sitting there watching, damned if motherfucking Dick Cheney don't get on it. I ain't shitting you. Had about eight guys with him, but it was him. I'd know that motherfucker anywhere. He got on and took off, and a little while later they drove us out to the airport.

That was cold, man. Everything was all fucked-up—covered with mud, windows all smashed. And nothing moving anywhere, not a cat, not a dog, not a motherfucking bird. Got real quiet on the bus. People were crying and all. I couldn't believe what I was looking at, and that's the truth. Waited half my life to get to New Orleans, and now it was dead.

BELINDA RAWLINS

HEARNE, TEXAS
2005

Belinda put the grocery bags on Alvin's kitchen table and reached into her purse for the buzzing phone. The number on the screen was Danisha's, Stevie's niece. "Aunt Belinda, what are you doing about the shower?"

"The shower?"

"The baby shower."

"Whose baby shower?"

"Come on, Aunt Belinda." Danisha giggled. "Niecy's baby shower."

Belinda leaned on the counter, faint. Her breath came in short gasps. "Danisha, I'm going to call you right back." The framed photo of Niecy in her pale blue graduation gown smiled down from a shelf by the window; she'd managed to grab it from Mom's house when she evacuated, and it had given her strength every day. It couldn't be true. Niecy had made it out. She'd finished high school. She was excelling at Southeastern.

Belinda's hand shook as she punched the number. Niecy answered on the first ring. "Are you pregnant?"

"Yeah," Niecy whispered.

Belinda hung up.

BILLY GRACE

LOEWS ANATOLE HOTEL,
DALLAS
September 2005

Billy looked across the table at the pale, tired faces. He and Jimmy Reiss had managed to assemble sixty-odd people, a pretty good who's who of New Orleans business, including Dan Packer, CEO of the power company; Scott Cowen, president of Tulane; Jeff Parker, of the Howard Weil brokerage; and, on the speakerphone, King Milling, of Whitney Bank, and Wynton Marsalis.

"While we're waiting for Mayor Nagin, let's have a sitrep." Jimmy Reiss stood at an easel that held a large pad of newsprint. "What kinds of resources can we marshal? Let's not limit our thinking. Drinking water? Generators? Trucks? Medical supplies? What can you rustle up?"

Hands went up. Jimmy filled two pages with suggestions, tearing them off and attaching them with masking tape to the walls. The door to the conference room opened, and a black man in a pale yellow golf shirt slouched alone into the room. He didn't look like a waiter—no white shirt or apron—and for a moment Billy thought he'd wandered into the wrong room. Then Billy recognized the shiny bald head and realized the man was Ray Nagin. He was all alone. Nagin quietly took a seat at the end of the table and waited until Jimmy noticed he was there.

"Mr. Mayor! Thank you for coming."

Nagin nodded, his eyelids at half-mast, his shoulders drooping.

"So. What is your action plan and how can we help?"

Nagin swiveled his head from left to right, his face without expression. "I do not have a plan."

Jeff Parker of Howard Weil leaned close and asked quietly, "Then what resources do you have that we can draw on to develop a plan?"

Nagin pivoted toward Jeff. "Nil."

Scott Cowen of Tulane jumped to his feet and took over Jimmy's list, continuing around the table, digging for ideas, keeping the meeting upbeat, and burying the embarrassment of the mayor's incapacity. "Billy? How about you?"

"I'm a lawyer," Billy said. "Neither my firm nor the companies I own possess the kinds of resources the city needs." He sat forward, rubbing his palms together. "But this is my idea. The collective wealth around this table must be in the billions. Why doesn't each of us, personally, pledge a million dollars cash to the recovery. We can go out of this room and announce that we have sixty million dollars cash on hand: the business community's stake in recovery. Today." He leaned on his forearms and looked around the room expectantly.

Nobody spoke, and Scott went on with the meeting.

JOANN GUIDOS

ST. CLAUDE AVENUE
September 2005

Kajun's was packed. A television crew from Japan sprawled at a round table holding cans of Pabst, their camera equipment spilling out onto the floor around them. They stared into space, poleaxed with shock, fear, and exhaustion. Every reporter and news crew from Kansas City to Kazakhstan had passed through Kajun's in the past few days to drink cold beer. Kenny's girlfriend, Renée, wearing a Confederate flag as a head scarf, pulled up a chair and held out a tattooed hand to be kissed by one of the cameramen. "Renée de Ponthieux," she said. "When Daddy dies, I'll be Comtesse de Ponthieux." She threw back her head and brayed like a mule.

Sunlight filtered through the black-painted front windows. The fan that sat on the floor at the end of the bar, four feet across, must have come from a warehouse or an airplane hangar. Kenny had found it or, more likely, stolen it. It had no grating over the blades; if someone tumbled in, the room would be showered with blood and bone chips. The jukebox died, and JoAnn whirled to give it a kick.

A man in uniform and a boxy bulletproof vest was holding an M16 in one hand and the jukebox cord in the other. "Listen up!" he said. Half a dozen other uniformed men stood in the doorway, silhouetted against raging sunshine. Not NOPD: they were fit and clean-cut, with unfamiliar emblems on their shoulders. They carried shotguns or M16s. Bunches of heavy zip-ties poked out from their vest pockets—riot handcuffs. They were so immaculate and well equipped that they seemed to have landed from another planet—storm troopers from the fifth dimension.

The Japanese cameramen stared, mouths open.

"Let me get your attention, please," the man at the jukebox said. "This city is under a mandatory evacuation order. Mandatory means you have to go. Am I making myself understood?"

"Go where?" Kenny, on a bar stool, raised his hand like a schoolkid.

"Buses leaving from the"—he looked at a piece of paper—"Ernest N. Morial Convention Center."

"What about my bar?" JoAnn put her hands on her hips.

The officer looked her up and down, as though trying to figure out what the hell she was. "Lock it up as best you can. There will be patrols."

"Patrols."

"Yes sir, ma'am."

"We haven't seen police here since the storm."

"City's full of them, and we're here to tell you that you have to leave."

"What if we don't?" Kenny said.

The cop shifted his M16. "You will. One way or another, you will. We're going door-to-door to the end of the street. When we come back, be ready to go." The starship trooper backed to the door, his M16 pointed at the floor, and melted away with his unit.

"Go where?" Phoebe croaked.

"What do we bring?" Renée said.

"For how long?" Andy the philosopher said.

"Stay off the fucking buses," Kenny shouted. "You get on the buses, we'll never see you again."

JoAnn ran behind the bar and came up with a long-barreled shotgun. She ran outside and stood like a minuteman, shoulders back, feet spread. "It's my God-given right according to the U.S. Constitution to bear arms and protect my property!" she yelled after the retreating cops. Kenny hurried out and grabbed the shotgun, wrestling it out of her hands.

"You don't need to have that out here, honey. Let me put it right inside." JoAnn let it go and put her face in her hands. Sobs rippled up her throat, and her shoulders relaxed in a pumping release. JoAnn reached for him, buried her face in his shoulder, and sobbed. She was losing it.

The starship troopers were back. No, these were disheveled, without vests, unshaven, and impatient. Two were black, two white, all wearing the crescent and star of the NOPD.

"Guns!" the tall one in front shouted. He had JoAnn's shotgun and was jacking out shells. Hands crawled up JoAnn's back and took her .38. They dumped the cartridges into a Hubig's Pies carton full of shells and dropped the .38 in with them. Another cop was pawing around under the bar.

"He's got the nine-millimeter!" Barbara called.

"Hey!" JoAnn said. "Am I getting some kind of receipt for those?"

"Yeah," said the lead cop, grabbing his crotch. "Here's your receipt." They went loping on up St. Claude.

"Christ almighty," said Andy the philosopher. "This is getting on my last gay nerve."

fRANK MINYARD

ST. GABRIEL
September 2005

The state police commander stood up and removed his Smokey Bear hat.

"Let me guess," Frank said. "You're not picking up bodies."

The commander shrugged. "Don't ask me why. It's the word from headquarters."

"So what's next?" Frank spread his arms like Saint Francis. "Do we put out a call on the radio for volunteers, for Christ's sake?"

The door to the library flew open and a young man stepped through—tall and vigorous, his chinos creased, a logo on the breast of his light blue golf shirt. His blond hair had been blow-dried artfully into a frame for his handsome face. He seemed to radiate inner light. He raised a mighty arm. "I'll collect the bodies!"

Everybody stared, mouths hanging open.

"Who are you?" Frank said.

"Kenyon!" he shouted. "A subsidiary of Service Corporation International!" Instantly, Frank understood. SCI was the biggest funeral-home operator in the United States. It was almost impossible to die in the United States without SCI getting a piece of the action. The sound of truck engines filtered into the room.

A soldier, peering out the window, yelled, "It's the bodies!"

The library crackled with applause.

"Let me see if I've got this straight," Frank said as he and Corinne followed the crowd out to meet the trucks. "Dead people rot on the streets of New Orleans for a week and a half so the feds can sign a private contract."

ANTHONY WELLS

They treated us good at the airport. Gave us toothbrushes, soap. Had soldiers coming around handing out sandwiches. They sat us out at Gate C-5 for hours and hours, but it was all right. The air-conditioning was on. It was clean. Roger went around doing tricks for the kids, but I think he mostly just scared them, missing them four front teeth and all.

Finally, they put us on a plane, a regular airline plane because they'd run out of Army planes. The whole time, they wouldn't tell us where we were going. "You'll know when you get there," they said, but what kind of shit is that? Some people said, "No, I ain't going," and the soldiers and police and all, they just said, "Oh yes you are." Like we was under communism or some shit. Put us all on that plane with dogs all up and down the aisle, people crying. We flew I don't know how long. An hour. Maybe two. Set down right before dawn. When we come to a stop, the door opens, and this white man gets on. He's wearing a suit and tie all buttoned up, and it's like five o'clock in the morning. He looks like a preacher. I look back to see what it is he's looking at, and oh Lordy Jesus, that plane was full of stinking, crazy-looking niggers. We got dogs, we got cats. We got that dude with his motherfucking hedgehog. One dude, with the big gold grille, had a big-ass boa constrictor around his neck. This little white dude in the suit, he must have thought his world had about ended. The best of New Orleans delivered up fresh to his doorstep! But I'll tell you, he was cool. He smiled like he was on a game show. Said, "I am the mayor of Knoxville, Tennessee, and I'm here to welcome you to my city."

fRANK MINYARD

ST. GABRIEL
September 2005

The trucks arrived, the bodies moved through, the morgue rocked. Possible homicides were routed to a cubicle where Frank's pathologists and James Brown looked for evidence. There were only about fifteen so far, out of several hundred bodies.

Frank sat at a desk in the schoolhouse, thumbing through reports. In keeping with DMORT's mission, they were devoted solely to ascertaining people's identities so that remains could be returned to families. Yet buried deep in each report was a line for cause of death, and on each someone had written "drowning."

He stood up and found Corinne Stern. She was taking a break out by the Forest Service kitchen, her Tyvek suit rolled down around her knees, her clothes soaking with sweat. She was wolfing a huge cup of iced tea.

"This isn't right," he said. "These people didn't all drown."

"We're not doing cause of death. You know that."

"But somebody's writing down that these people drowned."

"We have to put something."

"They didn't drown."

"We can't do autopsies on every set of remains, Frank. We might get twenty-five thousand in here. DMORT identifies. That's it."

"Corinne, listen to me. A lot of these people died from heat exhaustion, dehydration, stress, and from being without their medication—from neglect, basically. They were abandoned out there. So it's political, what killed them."

"I'm sure you're right."

"We owe it to them to get their cause of death straight."

Corinne looked at him for a long time. "My job is to take care of Frank Minyard. You're the local jurisdiction."

Frank waved the sheaf of reports. "These are my people. The public ought to know why they died."

"Tell me what you want."

"I want all the bodies autopsied."

"Every one?"

"Every one. These people were left to die like rats."

BELINDA RAWLINS

HOUSTON
2005

Belinda leaned on her crutches, staring through the picture window at a highway interchange that looked like a space station, huge sweeping loops of gray-white concrete a mile across. Houston stretched in every direction, a carpet of Golden Corral restaurants, Midas muffler shops, Carpet One outlets, and Denny's, Denny's, Denny's, as far as the eye could see. It was a city where only cars lived: no people, just cars, whizzing about on featureless ribbons of road, filling slots in hot asphalt parking lots.

Belinda's eyeballs ached from trying to cope with the distances. Until Katrina, she had rarely focused on anything farther away than a few blocks. And what was the smell? The apartment FEMA had given her had an odor she couldn't place. When she walked, the tap of her crutches echoed dully through the living room. The doctors in Hearne had recommended surgery, and a specialist in Houston had concurred. She'd left Curtis and Mookey with Alvin and undergone the operation on autopilot. The whole high-rise apartment setup was to keep her close to the hospital for rehabilitation and follow-ups, but for the life of her she couldn't remember why it had been so important to get the knee fixed now.

The apartment was too big—it took forever to cross the living room—and she certainly didn't need two bedrooms. She stopped at the glass bookshelf and took down Niecy's high-school graduation picture, gazing hard at the smiling face, the hint of dimples, the lifted chin, the contrast of the pale blue graduation robe with her luscious mahogany skin. She picked up the picture twenty times a day.

Stevie had told her what happened on the roof at Egania Street the night the levees broke. Ditty's baby girl, not four months old, had rolled off into the water, Ditty had jumped in after her, and that was the last anybody'd seen of them. As for Aunt Polly, she had waited alone in the heat and filth of the Convention Center, and died soon after in Texas. That was the woman in the wheelchair they kept showing on TV, the one covered with the blanket. Big, jolly Aunt Polly, the tonks-and-pitty-pat queen of the Lower Ninth Ward: gone.

Belinda put a hand on the bookshelf and ran her eye over the severe furniture, the bare walls. She knew what the smell was: nothing. No smell. No cooking smell, no river smell, no mildew-from-old-furniture smell. She was hermetically sealed, individually wrapped, a unit of one, vacuum-packed.

She kept the television on. The shots that CNN kept calling "Lower Ninth Ward" were unrecognizable—agitated black people yelling at the camera, soldiers with guns marching up St. Claude Avenue. She pulled from her purse a big bottle of Vicodin and the new refill of her Ambien sleeping-pill prescription. She opened both and spilled the contents onto the coffee table, the pills bouncing around on the glass surface. She lovingly gathered them into a big pile, mixed them together absently, swirling them around, making patterns. Then she counted them: nineteen Vicodin and thirty-one Ambien. Plenty.

Her purse buzzed, and she fished out the cell phone. Mookey's number: she couldn't not answer. She flipped the phone open and placed it to her ear, the other hand cupped over the pills, as though to hide them.

"I just wanted to hear your voice," Mookey said. "I love you." It took Belinda ten minutes to sort the pills and put them back in their bottles.

RONALD LEWIS

THIBODAUX
September 2005

In the garish, bug-swirling glare of a yellow porch bulb, Dorothy held up a worn schoolgirl's composition booklet. "Lots have died," she said. "I been keeping a list."

They were sitting outside the garden apartment where Dorothy was staying in Thibodaux, near Ronald and Minnie's rental. She opened the tablet and ran a crooked finger down the handwritten list. "Miz Green and her grandbaby, two years old. They died together. Miz Green was contrary; you remember that. Her son brought her out to the Superdome and she didn't like the conditions, so he brought her back home. Her house floated from Prieur almost to Claiborne. They found the little girl's body and, later on, Miz Green."

Dorothy went on. "Miss Weatherbee on Caffin Avenue. Peewee Walker. Mr. Converse's sister down the street. Samuel Jones, my brother-in-law's nephew. A friend of mine named Louis. Michelle Scott—her husband died. So did Leona Scott." On she went, each achingly familiar face rising up before Ronald and then fading like smoke. Dorothy had eighteen names.

Ronald's cell phone rang. "Mr. Lewis?" A white man with a northern voice identified himself as Steve Inskeep, a reporter for some radio station with "National" in the title. "I was hoping that you could help explain to our listeners the significance of the Lower Ninth Ward."

Ronald smacked the phone against his ear. The significance of the Lower Ninth Ward? To hear somebody speak the words, let alone a Yankee establishment man, was to hear angels break into song.

"How did you get my name?"

"Through a lady named Helen Regis." Helen Regis—that white lady professor from the Pigeontown Steppers parade.

"I'll meet you anytime," Ronald said.

fRANK MINYARD

ST. GABRIEL
September 2005

Frank and James stood in the school yard watching the techs heave filthy, rotten wooden boxes onto gurneys for the journey through the ID stations. Coffins that had floated out of some aboveground cemetery; it had never occurred to Frank that they'd be identifying the long dead.

A yip of alarm came from the anthropology cubicle, and a woman in a Tyvek suit came staggering out, pointing. They ran over and peered into a mossy wooden coffin. A muddy skeleton in tattered rags lay in about three inches of fine silt. Something moved. Frank leaned closer. An olive green snake, about four feet long and two inches thick, wriggled through the silt and hid itself under the bones. Frank's vision went black for a moment, and he backed up, palpitating. A couple of burly state policemen came running over, and he turned away to let them get on it.

ANTHONY WELLS

What they did was, they took us to this big basketball arena in downtown Knoxville. Must have had seven hundred cots laid out there. You could tell the people from New Orleans from the people working there. New Orleans people were raggedy-assed. Also, just about all of them were black, and the Knoxville people, they were all white.

They let us clean up, gave us clothes. Good food. They took pictures of us. Gave us a displaced-resident card. There was a speech from the governor and the mayor. They said, "We been waiting for you for three days." They welcomed us like we were a good commodity, like they was afraid every other town would get people from New Orleans and they wouldn't.

It was hard to sleep in there and you couldn't smoke. We could go outside, but couldn't go nowhere, because we didn't have nowhere to go. There was a little convenience store up the street the first day, but they said someone stole something in there and they closed it down. They called us looters and refugees. Refugees is from another country. Refugees is from a war zone. I got a Social Security number.

We'd have gotten out of there sooner, but they didn't give us the right kind of assistance. They give everybody a deficit card for $480, but we had to spend it at Wal-Mart, so actually what did they give us, you feel me? We couldn't use it nowhere else. We had other needs. You might want to give some money to your people.

First they told us FEMA was coming to take our information. Then they said, "We regret to inform you that FEMA will not be coming." They set up phones in the lobby, but the people answering the phone were aliens—Spanish-, Asian-speaking people. It took a long time to get my check. Then the people who were running the thing took our checks and put them into housing projects or hotels. So what did they give us? Hot shower and hot food. That's all we got. They didn't give us no hundred dollars. Then they told us we had eight days to leave the arena because they had to put on sports. What's more important, people's lives or sports?

You got to read your book of Matthew. God won't destroy the world by water. That's why there's rainbows, God's promise to the world. But I don't know what's going to happen to New Orleans. Won't be anybody there to sing the blues no more and you need the blues. When you got the blues, you shake off the heebie-jeebies. The heebie-jeebies'll kill you straight-out.

WILBERT RAWLINS JR.

BEAUMONT CENTRAL HIGH, TEXAS

2005

Wil slashed his arm down to stop the music. They sounded droopy, like they had no heart. He'd had the band on the field for only an hour, and the wind was going out of them. It had taken him a while to figure out, because these Texas kids were more advanced musically—picked up songs faster—that what they lacked was New Orleans intensity. It was a hard thing to define, but he craved that New Orleans filé in his gumbo. What he craved was that soul.

He and Reecie had taken a white brick house on a quiet Beaumont street. She kept him warm at night, and her kids were okay. Every woman he'd ever been with had brought along at least one child; women and children came as a package. For thirty-five years, Wil had focused on the here and now. He'd never dwelled on the what-ifs or the used-to-bes. No point in that. Sometimes, though, as he was driving the big avenues through the wide-open sprawl of Beaumont, he thought about his house on Dreux Avenue, and about Carver, worn-out and troubled. He thought about the grimy band room and the broken trombones. He thought about Nyja Sanders and Brandon Franklin, and all the kids like them, lifted from the brink of the abyss by the power of band.

He thought about Belinda.

But he couldn't think about her at this minute. He had a hundred Texas kids wilting in the sun and he had to light them up. He raised his arms, counted off, and launched into "Purple Carnival." The rests didn't pop. The dynamics were flat. He slashed his arm down. "I know it's hot out here," he yelled. "It's hard to play under these conditions." On a whim, he thrust both hands in the air, the fingers outspread. "You see how my pinkies are crooked? I broke them in a Little League game when I was ten. My dad taped them up with Popsicle sticks, and I played out the game! You do what you have to do, because people are counting on you. You are members of a band."

The kids stared up at him like cattle in a pen.

Wil ended the practice early.

fRANK MINYARD

ST. GABRIEL
2005

A scream erupted from the dark cavern of the warehouse-morgue. Frank dropped his paperwork and ran down the school-yard path. A Blackwater guard fell in beside him, unslinging a short black rifle from his back. They rounded the corner through the big open door of the warehouse. A Tyvek-suited woman was waving her arms for help. Another woman was doubled over, shrieking. She wasn't crying, Frank realized; she was laughing. The guard helped her up and led her out the back door to compose herself.

Frank shouldered his way through the technicians to the gurney at the center of the commotion. A coffin sat there, not a mildewy coffin coughed up from a cemetery, but an immaculate white casket with shiny brass handles. "From a funeral home," James Brown whispered. "Someone didn't quite finish."

Frank peered inside, and clapped his hand over his mouth. A woman lay on a gleaming satin cushion wearing a fuchsia sweat suit, her hair in a perfect, stiff reddish bouffant. She was smiling brightly, her painted lips drawn back against white teeth. Her eyes were open.

BELINDA RAWLINS

HOUSTON
2005

Belinda lay on the couch, gazing at the TV, wishing she had the energy to read a book instead. Her cell phone buzzed, and she rooted in her purse. Wil's number.

"Hey."

"Hey."

Silence.

"How are you feeling?" Wilbert sounded tired.

"My leg?"

"Yeah."

"It still hurts."

Silence.

"I was thinking of driving up to see you."

Belinda shifted the cell phone to her other hand and sat up straighter. "How's Reecie going to feel about that?"

Wil sighed. "Reecie's got nothing to say about it."

"Hmf."

"You are my wife."

"Hmf."

Wil put on his formal voice. "Would you like me to drive up and see you?"

"If you want to."

"No, I'm asking: Do. You. Want. Me. To. Drive. Up. And. See. You?"

Belinda took a deep breath and tried to sound casual. "Sure, Wilbert. Come on up."

TIM BRUNEAU

THE *ECSTASY*
October 2005

At the gangway, a young woman in a sharp navy blue suit examined Tim's badge and handed him a plastic card that said, "ECSTASY." "Carnival Cruise Lines welcomes you aboard," she said. Any New Orleans policeman or firefighter who'd lost his house was welcome to a room on board. Did Tim have a girlfriend? the woman asked. Did he need a second key?

Tim walked up the gangway, feeling like Richard Dreyfuss boarding the alien spaceship at the end of *Close Encounters of the Third Kind*. He'd forgotten what clean looked like. He'd forgotten well maintained. He felt like a stowaway, in his noisome fatigues. At the top of the gangway, a lithe young steward in a polo shirt welcomed him, looked at his card, and walked him halfway around the ship to a narrow beige door. He used the card to open the door, and Tim found himself in a small but immaculate stateroom equipped with two narrow single beds. The steward opened the door to a tiny bathroom and turned on the light. The shower stall sparkled.

After the steward left behind his phone number for "anything at all," Tim stripped and stepped into the shower, gasping as the warm water thundered over him. He soaped and rinsed, soaped and rinsed, soaped and rinsed, until he no longer smelled like the Wal-Mart parking lot. He stood so long under the torrent of hot water that he began to nod off. Within five minutes of toweling off, he was asleep between blessedly clean sheets.

Tim lurched awake and snatched up the gun beside him, mentally still in the Crown Vic. No, he was on the *Ecstasy*. Someone was trying the door. Whoever it was went away. Tim sank back into sleep.

The phone rang, and he was back in the Crown Vic for a moment, searching for a phone, before sliding further down the chute of exhaustion, into a thick, dreamless sleep.

The light was on and somebody was standing over him. Tim leaped up, raising the Glock in front of him with both hands. The man backed away with his hands up. "I'm a police officer! I'm a police officer!" he shouted, stretching the breast of his shirtfront so Tim could see the badge. He plastered himself against the wall of the stateroom. Tim, in his confusion, kept yelling, "What the fuck! What the fuck!"

"Police officer!" The man cringed against the wall. "I'm sharing this room. For Christ's sake!"

Tim looked at his gun. He looked at the uniformed man. Damn. He threw the gun on the bed and sat down heavily.

"I called you; you didn't answer," the man said, putting his hands down. "You some kind of nut or something? Jesus!" He stormed out of the stateroom, letting the door bang.

Tim moved his gun aside and crawled back under the covers.

RONALD LEWIS

METAIRIE
September 2005

Ronald pulled the struggle-buggy in to the parking lot of Dorignac's supermarket and switched off the engine. With a sigh, the car released a puddle of hot coolant onto the pavement. A middle-aged white man with a high forehead was leaning against the door of a shiny white SUV. "Steve Inskeep," the man said when Ronald had wriggled out of his car. "National Public Radio. I'd like to drive you down to the Lower Ninth Ward and talk there."

Ronald swallowed. He wasn't sure he was ready to see what the water had done.

"My press card should get us past the roadblocks."

"Okay, then."

They swept down from the interstate onto Claiborne Avenue. The Circle Food Store and the normally busy intersection of St. Bernard Avenue sat as still as stunned birds. Every house and business was deserted, a greasy black line slashed horizontally across each, so straight it might have been painted on with a ruler. That was where the water had stood, Ronald realized. Inskeep swerved this way and that, avoiding debris. Ronald opened his window, and the smell of Betsy filled his nose: the same rot, mildew, and gasoline. The great white rusty towers of the Claiborne Avenue Bridge loomed ahead. At its foot, a soldier held up a hand. In his baggy pants and heavy black-framed glasses, he looked to be about fourteen years old. Inskeep fished a plastic card on a neck cord from inside his shirt, and the soldier waved them through.

"Me alone, I couldn't get through here," Ronald said.

"Probably not."

"I only lived here my whole life." Ronald craned his neck to peer from the crest of the bridge. His old Deslonde Street neighborhood was off to the left there, but something was different. All the lawns seemed bigger. Before Ronald could get a grip on it, though, they were off the bridge and turning left onto Deslonde.

Inskeep hit the brakes. A pale blue house stood in the middle of the street, sagging like an over-iced cake, the slats of its siding splayed at the bottom. "That's Mrs. Young's house," Ronald said. Inskeep inched the SUV around it, bumped up onto a muddy lawn, and rolled to a stop. What lay ahead was hardly recognizable: the Butlers' house hollowed out like a rotten tooth, the pretty kitchen wallpaper obscenely exposed to the sky; the Paytons' house plain gone—all that remained was the slab. There it was, tilted up on the other side of the street, smashed against Irene's bar. As far as they could see down Deslonde, it was the same. Cars lay on their backs, or rested sideways against pushed-over houses. Chairs, tables, wads of clothing, toys, a clothes dryer, all strewn across the street, covered in mud. Ronald tried to speak. He was vaguely aware that Inskeep was turning on a tape recorder.

"Go up ahead here a ways," Ronald croaked, his mouth as stiff and dry as lumber. The car inched forward. The levee was visible to the left. There should have been two blocks of houses in the way, but they were gone, smashed to pieces and scattered. That was why the lawns looked so big from the bridge; the houses were gone. Roofs lay on their sides like sections of giant card houses. Whole walls were rolled up into splintery balls. Piles of cinder blocks—the foundations of shotguns—lay shattered everywhere. The Skippers', Montgomerys', Mitchells', Browns'—gone. The car crunched through the debris at the intersection of Prieur Street. Dorothy's house: gone. Miss Pie's: gone. The Alexanders' two-story house. Gone. Ronald swiveled his eyes slowly toward the one house he couldn't bear to see: 1911 Deslonde Street, the tight little house that Dadá built, that Mom restored after Betsy, and that Stella had kept immaculate. Gone. Not damaged, not muddy, not broken apart. Missing. The slab was there, jagged pieces of pipe growing out of it like mutant plants. The cement front steps stood, leading to nowhere. Where the house should have been was a long view to Jourdan Road and the levee. Something big and red like a barn lay next to old man Goodwin's rubble-strewn lot: a barge, two blocks long and four stories high, with something yellow crushed under it. A school bus.

To the right of the barge, white sandbags filled a V-shaped cut in the levee. "That's the same damn hole they took us through in '65," Ronald said. But this was nothing like Betsy. Back then, the water had covered the houses but left them standing. This time, it had carried the whole neighborhood away.

They inched a few feet forward, and Ronald's cell phone rang. Pete, as though conjured by the annihilation of their boyhood setting, said, "Hey, bra." He was in Houston.

"I'm right here by Deslonde and Johnson." Ronald glanced at Inskeep, who was holding a microphone. "It's all gone," Ronald told Pete. "Our house. Your house. You know, like gone-gone. No rubble on your lot or nothing. I'll call you soon." He switched off the phone. "Let's go by my house on Tupelo."

They turned downriver on Johnson Street, where the houses that remained had spray-painted Xs on them, with numbers and symbols in each of their quadrants. "The rescuers marked each house to show they'd searched it," Inskeep said. "The numbers should tell who did the searching. That 'FL1'—over there—means Florida Task Force One. They put the date, and what they found. The zero and zero means nobody alive and nobody dead. Look at that one." A shotgun house that had slid off its cinder blocks and was draped over a beige Buick. The house hadn't shattered; it seemed to be made of rubber, bent smoothly over the car. On its door was an X with "9-16" above it.

"You telling me nobody got to that house until September 16?" Ronald asked.

"That's what it says."

Ronald wiped his eyes with the back of his hand. Sprayed on the house was "4K9" and "1 DOA." Ronald could picture the woman who lived there, a bitty thing who liked kente cloth.

"It's like this all the way to the far end of St. Bernard Parish. It wasn't only the Industrial Canal. Levees broke all the way along that ship channel out to the gulf."

"Mr. Go," Ronald said. The Mississippi River Gulf Outlet. "They been talking about closing that for years."

"Water stood here maybe three weeks," Inskeep said. They turned down the wide boulevard of Caffin Street to Claiborne, and right on Tupelo. The farther they got from the levee, the less rubble lay in the street. Here, a mile from the levee, the houses looked more like they did after Betsy—every one a mud-caked ruin. Inskeep brought the car to a slow halt in front of Ronald's house.

The tan and brown house seemed to have settled several inches into the mud. Every window was gone—cold and dead. Ronald got out, hobbled up the driveway to the porch, and peered in the window. His living room looked like a slaughterhouse, everything jumbled up and rotten. He steadied himself by the iron railing, thumped down the steps, and turned up the driveway. The chocolate slime that covered the driveway sucked at his feet. He fished his keys from a pocket and pushed open the door to the House of Dance and Feathers. A blast of hot, stinking air knocked him back. It was dark inside, the single window opaque with mud. Indian suits lay impacted in a foot of sticky ooze on the floor, photos and masks jumbled among them.

"This is my museum," he said as Inskeep came up. He reached down and pulled a strip of beadwork from the muck, walked out to the chain-link fence, and hung it to dry. It could be rinsed off and saved. Inskeep watched him curiously, the microphone held at arm's length. Ronald inhaled and leaned into it. "I'm not leaving my home."

He picked up a blue alligator shoe and carried it outside. Inskeep followed him. Ronald banged the shoe on the fence post and chunks of mud fell off it. "I have a good relationship with my senator, council aide, and state representative. I'm going to champion the cause." Inskeep pushed the microphone closer to Ronald's mouth, and Ronald took it. "It's going to take organizing within the black community, from our leaders—our church leaders, our civic leaders. But we might be okay."

JOYCE MONTANA

ST. AUGUSTINE CHURCH
2005

Joyce parked her gray Toyota around the corner from St. Augustine Church. Although the morning was already hot, sticky, and pungent of rot, Joyce's heart lifted with every step at the prospect of Father LeDoux's voice, the exuberance of the choir, and the touch of her friends.

It must have been fifteen degrees cooler inside the church. Sturdy, resolute Sandra Gordon ran over and wrapped her in a long hug. Marion Colbert, perfectly erect at seventy-something, her hair in a regal bun, kissed Joyce on both cheeks. Cecilia Galle—close to ninety—had lost her daughter and son-in-law in the flood, but here she came, rolling in the side door in her wheelchair, as beautiful and elegant as ever in pink earrings and gloves. It took an hour to greet everybody. Everybody had a story to tell.

"The grace and peace of God our Father and the Lord Jesus Christ be with you," Father LeDoux said, lifting his arms and looking tired in a flamboyant tie-dyed dashiki.

"And also with you," Joyce said.

ANTHONY WELLS

They put me and Roger in a project out in Newport, which is a long way from Knoxville. It wasn't a project like in New Orleans. It looked like an ordinary neighborhood, except all the houses were the same. Brick. Nice lawns. And everybody else in there was white. Tripped me out, man. Housing project of white people. But I was okay with that. I ain't prejudiced. I'm a simple man. Eat, sleep, be discreet. Watch the people you meet in the street because everybody ain't out to give you a treat.

We didn't have no car and they ain't got no buses, so we couldn't go nowhere. FEMA sent me a letter saying I been granted twenty-two hundred dollars housing assistance, but the name on the letter was Carmelita Waterhouse. Who the fuck is Carmelita Waterhouse? I called, said I'm a Katrina victim. They wanted to know where was the disaster. Where was the disaster? In fucking New Orleans. Then they wanted to know did I have any receipts. It's the old badger game; how long can you hold out? The more money they keep people from getting, the more money they keep. Then Newport Housing Authority turn around and tell us we got to pay fifty dollars a month for the house, plus the light bill. So what are they doing for us?

But you can't wallow in dismay, disappointment, failure. Failure is within a man. His self-esteem. Tennessee was not where I really wanted to be, but if I had the means and the financial help, I could be happy. I could go see my people. Maybe eventually, if they'd given me the right kind of assistance, I could have gotten a house.

fRANK MINYARD

ST. GABRIEL
2005

"Frank," a tech called, from two rows over. "I think we got a homicide here." Frank hurried to the fingerprinting cubicle.

A tech, all but invisible in a Tyvek suit, was unzipping a bright yellow body bag. Frank pulled on his surgical gloves and mask. "Look at that," the tech said. "Somebody bashed in her head."

"Jesus." The body was a purplish green, the left side of the head flattened. The girl was young, maybe in her twenties, wearing capris and a white open-collared shirt.

The tech reached into the bag and came up with a beaded purse. He pried open the clasp and pulled out a piece of paper. "Well, this helps." He handed it to Frank.

"This woman died by accident and is not a homicide," Frank read. "Detective Tim Bruneau, NOPD."

TIM BRUNEAU

BOURBON STREET
October 2005

Tim took a walk down Bourbon Street for the hell of it. It was good to see lights coming on at dusk. A few bars were open. The Tropical Isle and Cafe Lafitte in Exile had their doors open and jukeboxes blaring. Déjà Vu had a lumpy naked lady gyrating on the little stage, as did Big Daddy's Bottomless Topless. Galatoire's was closed, but outside Alex Patout's Louisiana Restaurant a wizened cinder of a chef was stirring a cannibal pot of spaghetti sauce on a gas burner he'd set up on the sidewalk. Tim lingered by the heavenly smell. Six feet away, though, the ever-present vomit-and-mold smell of the high-heaped garbage took over again.

Tim turned around and walked back toward Canal Street. By this time, Razzoo and Daiquiri's were open. The city was coming back to life before his eyes.

The street was packed with strapping guys in T-shirts from restoration companies or law enforcement golf shirts with their guns in the open like the genitals on short-haired street dogs. As for women, Tim spotted a couple of big, muscular bleached blondes in FBI golf shirts and Glocks, a reedy scientific-looking lady from EPA, and about a dozen doe-eyed don't-joke-with-us dog rescuers from the Humane Society.

He crossed the darkened Central Business District and looped behind the Convention Center to the ship. His uniform stuck to him in the heat, but a shower and clean sheets awaited. He ran his plastic badge through the card reader and started up the gangway.

Whoop! Whoop! Whoop! A heavyset security man positioned himself with his arms folded at the top of the gangway. On the dock, a woman in a blue blazer shouted, "Excuse me, sir!" There was nothing to do but trudge back down in the heat.

He held out his card. "Can you just look me up? I have a room on the ship. I promise."

"Just a moment, please, sir." She took his card, frowned at it, and walked to her laptop. She examined the screen and called over a man who had the tanned, bland look of a golf pro. They whispered. The golf pro opened a cell phone and made a call.

"May I go aboard, please?" Sweat was trickling down his ribs.

The golf pro smoothed back his hair and walked over. "Ah, sir, it seems you have been excluded from the ship."

"What?"

"There was an incident in your stateroom? Involving a firearm?"

"I was fast asleep and there was a stranger in my room!"

"I don't know about that. I suggest you talk to your supervisor. In the meantime, we have instructions not to allow you to reboard."

Tim gazed up at the ship for a long time, as though it were steaming off into the night, carrying his beloved. Other cops arrived, swiping cards and prancing up the gangway.

Tim walked through the Convention Center parking lot to the Crown Vic, digging his keys from his pocket. He drove to the Wal-Mart parking lot, quiet and empty since the cops had left.

He opened the back door and gazed at the blue vinyl seat where Marie had lain. Sighing, he crawled inside, took his Glock from his holster, and fell asleep holding it.

WILBERT RAWLINS JR.

5972 DREUX AVENUE
2005

Wil swung off the I-10 onto Downman Road and turned right on Dreux. His once-beautiful block of trim homes and neat lawns was gone, trashed, smeared with filth as though a regiment of evil six-year-olds had finger-painted it to death. His house was still there—that was something. Belinda stood in front of it.

Amid the desolation, she looked incongruously elegant, regal in high heels and a plum-colored suit with a straight skirt and jacket. But that was Belinda. She stood in the muddy yard, holding a white handkerchief to her nose. He climbed out, and the stench—mildew, vomit, gasoline, death—about made him retch. "Hey."

"Gold teeth," she said. "That a Reecie thing?"

"No, baby." He smiled in spite of himself, like a ten-year-old. "You know I never liked that chipped tooth. I got 'em done in Texas. It comes right out." He flicked his tongue and the two gold teeth, connected by a thin bar, rattled off his top incisors.

The house looked as though it had been raped and murdered, every window smashed, the neat red brick and white trim fouled with black mud.

"So, how you doing, Wil?" Belinda lowered the handkerchief, waving in the air in front of her face.

"I'm all right. Whoo, it stinks out here."

"How's your mama and them?"

"They all right. How are you?"

"Better. Those three months in Houston about did me in."

"I'll bet it did, all alone."

"No, Wil, I mean it. I had no purpose. My husband was in Beaumont, starting a new life with Reecie. My kids were in Hearne. I couldn't get FEMA help. Someone stole my identity and ran up bills. I couldn't get unemployment. My brother was in Iraq. You know about Aunt Polly and them. I mean, I had nothing."

Wil hung his head. It had always been hard for him to imagine other people's suffering; it was part of the optimism that kept him going. "I'm sorry."

"Hmf. Well, you may as well come see. I warn you, though, it's bad."

Wil followed her across the yard in a daze. Nothing moved, not a cat, not a bird, not a breath of wind to stir the stench. It was like walking through a still photograph. Lying on the path, six feet from the front door, was a wet, decomposing dog. Maggots wriggled in the hollowed-out skull.

The interior was unrecognizable. His couch. His TV. His chair. The refrigerator lay on its side in the living room. Wil felt numb, beyond crying. It wasn't real. Belinda moved through the living room, the kitchen, the hallway, glancing into bedrooms, opening a bathroom door, conducting him on a silent haunted-house tour. Their feet slipped in the mud.

"So what do you want to do?" she said, lowering the hankie from her face as they emerged from the side door.

"I don't know." His head was light.

"Well, we've got decisions to make, Wilbert. The mortgage company is willing to sign it over to us—what's left of it."

"Good, good," Wil said, to say something. They walked out toward their cars, giving the rotting dog wide berth. Wil's brain was grinding sluggishly, seeking traction. Get the place cleaned out, get the place re-painted.

"It's good and fine," Belinda said. "But it's in both our names. They won't sign it over to just one of us. You listening?"

He blinked. Her sharp caramel-colored face tipped up at his, her stylish rectangular glasses framing coffee-colored eyes.

"So let me ask you straight-out, Wil," she said. "Do you want to sell me your share?"

"My share?"

"Do you. Want to sell me. Your share. Of the house," she said, as though talking to an imbecile.

"No, baby, you know I don't. This is my house."

"Well, it's my house, too, according to the papers."

"I don't mean . . ."

"Here's the thing." Belinda tapped him on the chest, a long magenta fingernail clicking against his big jeweled WR medallion. "I don't want to sell my share, either." She paused to let it sink into his skull. "So I guess we're stuck with each other."

ANTHONY WELLS

A letter come that January from the housing authority. Said I owed $1,025 on that shithole, plus $200 in court costs. Said I was evicted because they found out I had a criminal record on file. Shit, half the people of New Orleans got criminal records on file.

We were supposed to be out by February 19, but shit, that was the day before Mardi Gras. Roger and me were going to make some masks, but we couldn't get no glitter. Had but one string of beads between us.

Mardi Gras, man. To miss Mardi Gras. I mean, I never went and watched the white folks on St. Charles Avenue, but I liked knowing they was there, you feel me? We didn't have Indians up in the Goose, but I liked knowing they was out there.

It finally got so bad I took a job over by Wal-Mart. I used to walk two miles. But the guy there, he was saying racial slurs. Called me "Buckwheat." Called me "Leroy." He'd say, "There's that New Orleans dude; he's hot and spicy." He was playing the dozens with me, man. If I'd a stayed, we'd a got in a fight. I'm from New Orleans, man; I know how to work. But in Tennessee, man, it's like going back in time. The white people think everything is theirs. Only reason we're not sitting in the back of the bus is because they ain't got no buses.

They had a free clinic at Pigeon Forge. I go down there, stand in line. It was the first time I seen a doctor since Katrina. They check my eyes, my heart, everything. My pressure was up so high they sent me to the emergency hospital. I tell the lady I don't have no insurance. She says, "That's okay," and they do the whole nine yards—EKG and all that. X-rays. Then they turned around and charged me twenty thousand dollars. I just get started fighting that, and come a letter from the U.S. Department of Education, I shit you not, telling me I owe them twelve thousand dollars. Why? The motherfucking Lawton School! Where I was studying to be a security investigator back in 1995! Ten years later, and they're coming after me for that. Waiting until I'm all fucked from Katrina, kicking a man when he's down. Twelve thousand dollars, and more than half of that is interest and penalties and shit.

I used to wake up hollering. I kept dreaming I was in a place, L.A. or somewhere. People were trying to kill me, dudes with big rottweilers, pit bulls. "Get them off me! Get them off me!" Roger had to come in and wake me up.

TIM BRUNEAU

SIXTH DISTRICT
October 2005

Tim piloted his unmarked Crown Victoria through the deserted streets of the Sixth District. The city had been six weeks without a homicide—a record. All you had to do to stop crime, it turned out, was evacuate the city.

But here was a guy. The kid stood beside the road, holding up enormous pants with one hand, craning his neck to peer at all corners of the sky. He had a white cap on sideways and was bare chested but for a string of cowrie shells. Tim rolled up on him and lowered his window. The kid smiled, his teeth entirely gold and studded with diamonds.

"Hey," Tim said.

"Hey."

"What the hell are you doing?"

"Ain't they dropping food from helicopters no more?"

Tim raised his window and pulled away. In the rearview, the kid had his arms spread wide, pleading.

The Sixth District was operating out of the open garage on the ground floor because the generator wasn't big enough to cool the building and mildew made it oppressive inside. Russell had a bedsheet spread on the concrete and a grid of Glock pistols laid across it. He'd disassembled one and was working on it in his lap with a brush and sweet-smelling solvent. "They were underwater," he told Tim. "Feel free to help out."

The elevator was still not working, so Tim limped up the stairs. The station house smelled like a sewer. He found Cannatella in his office and laid his badge and gun on the desk.

"No."

"I stands what I stands and I can't stands no more," Tim said, quoting an old Popeye cartoon.

"This is historic here. We got a once-in-a-lifetime chance to clean this city up."

"University of North Texas has a program in emergency management. Emergency management—what a concept."

"Timmy, you're the police. Out of this disaster will come a whole new city, and there's no new city without cops."

"Maybe when I'm finished."

Cannatella stood with his hands on his hips, shoulders back, looking ready to rebuild the city himself. Tim remembered hearing that the captain could have retired years earlier at full pension, so was essentially working for free. Cannatella opened his big arms wide. "Anytime you want to come back, we'll be here," he said, and wrapped Tim's skinny shoulders in a hug.

BEFORE SLIPPING OUT of the garage, Tim walked back to his unmarked Crown Vic and opened the back door.

Goodbye, Marie, it's been good getting to know you.

Goodbye, Tim. I'll see you around.

I hope not. He eased the door shut and walked out of the police station into the damp October sunshine.

RONALD LEWIS

LOYOLA UNIVERSITY
November 2005

Ronald picked up a Sharpie and wrote his name on a blue "Hi My Name Is" sticker: Ronald W. Lewis.

"Whom do you represent?" said the woman at the card table.

" 'Scuse me?"

"Are you with a university or a city agency?"

"No, ma'am. I represent myself and the Lower Ninth Ward of New Orleans." He pressed the sticker to his chest and made his way slowly, on his aching feet, to the conference room. On his head he wore a red woven skullcap, which he called his battle hat. The flyer in his hand said the conference was about "reinhabiting NOLA," but the people in the hallway did not make it look like a matter of survival. They were well dressed and rested, flipping through file folders and talking on cell phones. A Tulane professor had heard Ronald on National Public Radio and called him to speak. Ronald took a seat at the back of a big classroom.

The morning's speakers dwelled on "infrastructure," "social networks," and "natural and built ecosystems." It all seemed very removed for Ronald; he still had a living room full of mud. Then his name was called. "My name is Ronald W. Lewis, and I come from cross the canal in the Lower Ninth Ward," he said. He could hear how rough and uneducated—how black—his voice sounded. He didn't have a lot of big words like "infrastructure" to throw around. But that was okay; he'd faced down Hero Evans.

"When you drive over that Claiborne Bridge, you see that green space," he began. "That was my world. When I wanted to go sit by my sister, on the porch, and watch my other sister doing her flowers in her yard, that's what I did. James, over there, might be round by his house barbecuing, and we'd hear him cooking, and we'd be round by James. If the neighbor cross the fence was boiling crawfish, we'd cross over there. In the Lower Ninth Ward, we're people people." He took a deep breath. This was no time for speeches.

"I have a museum," he said. "Help me, and I'll help you help others. I'll show you the way."

ANTHONY WELLS

After the project, we were paying two ninety a month for a little place. They cut me off food stamps because I was working at the appliance place, making oven racks. I had no car, so I had to pay people to take me to work. Eight dollars an hour, and it's costing me like twenty, thirty dollars a week to get to work. On the weekends, I'm looking stupid—watching TV, cigarettes, a couple of beers. My last check, I couldn't cash it, because I was working for a temp agency and the banks wouldn't cash their checks anymore.

Then the motherfuckers picked me up for driving without a license. I had five tickets, no license, no ID, no insurance. Altogether it came to eleven hundred dollars. I told Roger, "We're not in New Orleans no more. They don't let you do shit up here like we did."

The judge says, "You got money to pay?" I say no, said I was going to sell the car and I ain't going to drive it no more. "That's fine, Mr. Wells, but we need eleven hundred dollars." They locked me up; six months suspended and six to serve.

It was like a dungeon, man, eight dudes to a cell and I'm the only black man in there. I had seven pencils sharpened, all taped together, just in case. "What you doing with all those pencils, boy?" "I'm doing a lot of writing, sir."

When I got out, I called my aunt Mildred; she was back in New Orleans. I told her I'm not putting up with this anymore. I'd rather be a bum. What Bush and them eat in Washington don't make people in New Orleans shit, you feel me? She was all, "Anthony, come on down. You do the best you can and God will make a way. Trust in the Lord."

And I missed my aunt Mildred. I missed seeing my uncle Bud. I missed walking around. In New Orleans, you walk around. You sit down. You see people. You talk. There's noise all the time—wreck on the I-10, the pool hall, somebody playing on a saxophone. Gunshots. Yeah, man. I even missed the gunshots.

BILLY GRACE

INTERSTATE 10 WESTBOUND,
METAIRIE
January 2006

Billy returned the Hertz car and rode the shuttle to the terminal, where Anne was to pick him up. It had been useful to have the extra car while Liam and Robert were in town. He was proud of them, and he certainly understood that Dallas held more opportunities for them. But he missed his sons. Only Ransdell and her husband were sticking it out.

The city was cleaving along racial lines in a way he wouldn't have thought possible. It was as though integration had never happened. The hurt that had welled up with the flood had caught him completely off guard. Richard Baker, a congressman from Baton Rouge, had introduced a bill to buy destroyed houses for their pre-storm value—a godsend—but he'd also let slip that "God" had cleaned out New Orleans's public housing. Jimmy Reiss had told the *Wall Street Journal* that business leaders at the Dallas meeting wanted the city rebuilt "demographically, geographically, and politically." People heard "demographically" not as a suggestion of mixed-income housing but as a call to banish blacks. Some good ideas for reconstruction were floating around—for mixed-income neighborhoods, for a more bicycle- and pedestrian-friendly city, for instituting the principles of the New Urbanism. But it seemed to Billy that if a white man suggested something, blacks rejected it out of hand. Billy didn't know enough about the condition of Charity Hospital and the public housing projects to know if they should be closed or not, but he was pretty sure the decisions were being made on the basis of something other than a desire to rid New Orleans of its black people. Yet the shrieking that accompanied those decisions: you'd have thought the city fathers were planning to reinstate slavery.

Billy had little faith in Mayor Nagin. His performance at the Dallas meeting had been wretched, and he still didn't have the vigor that the crisis demanded. But Billy was grateful at least that Nagin hadn't gotten down in the racial mud, pushing everything through the tired old meat grinder of black and white. In the context of post-Katrina New Orleans, it was a small miracle.

Billy picked up a *New York Times* at the airport newsstand, and as he fished in his pocket for a dollar, he heard a commotion behind him. Coming toward him, leading a phalanx of identically dark-suited aides, was Louis Farrakhan, leader of the Nation of Islam. Farrakhan: What was he doing in New Orleans?

The next day was Martin Luther King Day, and Mayor Nagin delivered a speech. "I greet you all in the spirit of unity," he began, and started into a fairly standard speech about how "lack of love is killing us." But then, toward the end, some new spirit seemed to overtake Nagin, and in words that had everybody in the city quoting him that evening, he suddenly said, "It's time for us to rebuild New Orleans, the one that should be a chocolate city." He said it was the way God wanted New Orleans to be. "I don't care what people are saying uptown or wherever they are," Nagin said. "This city will be chocolate at the end of the day." Billy heard the speech that night on the news and was dumbstruck. A chocolate city? And taking a deliberate poke at uptown?

Farrakhan, he thought.

fRANK MINYARD

POYDRAS STREET
February 2006

Frank Minyard parked in the gloom beneath the I-10 overpass, amid piles of ruined automobiles that had been towed here from all over the city. They sickened him; they made the middle of New Orleans feel like a junkyard.

He sat gazing through the windshield at a warehouse, darkened by the shadow of the overpass, the kind of invisible place that lurks under overpasses in every city. He climbed out and locked the dusty car, being careful not to dirty the worn jeans jacket he wore over a white T-shirt. The ostrich-hide cowboy boots, rescued from the pickup, were already grungy. He walked across the trash-strewn pavement of Poydras Street, climbed onto the warehouse loading dock, and unlocked the door. The warehouse still had no power; the open door provided the only light. A neat grid of identical white coffins, 170 of them, shone in the gloom—

bodies either identified but unclaimed or so far gone that neither Frank's people nor the wizards of DMORT could name them. Abandoned in attics, forgotten on rooftops, discarded New Orleanians. Nine hundred and eighty-five bodies had passed through Frank's hands, but these couldn't be laid to rest. Each was a personal failure.

The city had no plans for the unclaimed. None of the surrounding parishes wanted them.

Frank looked at the caskets a long time, wondering whether a fetid warehouse under a freeway would be their final resting place.

JOYCE MONTANA

ST. AUGUSTINE CHURCH
2006

"A sermon should be like a woman's dress," Father LeDoux said. "Long enough to cover the subject, but short enough to be interesting."

Joyce covered her mouth and laughed, then wiped her eyes.

"We here at St. Augustine are being called upon in an excruciating way to do penance." Father LeDoux wore gaily colored kente cloth, but his eyes drooped in sadness. "I was at a meeting with Archbishop Hughes. He looked me straight in the eye and said, Jerome, you have to tell your flock that they must get ready for death."

So it was true. The archbishop's right-hand man, the glowering Father Maestri, had told the newspaper that St. Augustine was a "dying parish." The archdiocese had suffered $140 million in uninsured losses, because it hadn't anticipated all its churches flooding at the same time. Any parish that wasn't pulling its weight financially had to go—as though they were fast-food outlets, or furniture stores.

Father LeDoux didn't keep good records, they said, but everybody knew that. His office had always looked as though someone had turned it upside down and shaken it. Father LeDoux was the most remarkable pastor Joyce had ever known. He made her feel a connection to Jesus, he knew her family, and he'd moved Tootie as no other priest ever had. So what if he didn't keep good records? To take away his parish now, when his congregation needed him most, seemed deliberately cruel.

The powers of New Orleans seemed determined only to make life harder. They hadn't reopened Charity Hospital, even though it stood as solid as though carved out of a mountain, so medical care was almost impossible to find. They weren't letting people move back into the projects, though they, too, were largely undamaged. The state's so-called Road Home program, established to help people rebuild their houses, was so bollixed up nobody was getting any help. And now, at just the time Joyce and her fellow parishioners most needed Father LeDoux, the archbishop meant to send him away.

"We filed an appeal to the archbishop," he said. "Let us pray."

FRANK MINYARD

ST. AUGUSTINE CHURCH
2006

Frank sat on the raised stage of St. Augustine Church, trumpet across his knees. Ever since opening the methadone clinic in the rectory more than thirty years ago, he'd loved this pink and white sanctuary, the stone floor worn smooth by the bare feet of slaves, the portraits of Tootie Montana and Louis Armstrong alongside those of Saint Clotilda and Saint Martin. The archbishop's plan to close St. Augustine struck Frank's heart like another death in a city that had suffered too many.

Father LeDoux was rocking. The skinny, white-haired priest, wearing what looked like blue and maroon tie-dyed pajamas, was doing a stiff-legged jig at the polished tree trunk that served as a pulpit, waving his arms over his head, as the congregation and choir sang. Tootie Montana's widow clapped and swayed, as though reborn after the one-two punch of Tootie's death and the storm. Most of the congregants were in their sixties or older, a time of life when they might have been winding down and enjoying being cared for. Instead, they were consumed in losing struggles—against FEMA, insurance companies, the state rebuilding authority, the federal housing program, crooked contractors who had descended on the city like vultures.

Frank felt his legs going cold and a tarry darkness rising behind his eyes. This was happening more and more lately; he'd be going along okay, and then suddenly his spirits would plunge as though all his energy and optimism were rushing out of a hole in his heart. The sadness—bottomless and debilitating—might last an hour or might last several days. The first couple of times he wrote it off as exhaustion—he was seventy-seven years old, after all, and was having to operate out of a borrowed funeral parlor forty miles north of the city. But it was happening too often now. Every time he stopped working long enough to grieve for his city, the pit would open and he'd tumble in. He had a vague memory of this happening to him in his youth, but not in many years.

Father LeDoux held up his hand for silence. "For as long as I have been pastor of this church, our friend Dr. Frank Minyard has come by from time to time to play his golden horn."

Frank stood and put the horn to his lips. He nodded at Kevin Stevens, who riffled into the opening notes of "What a Friend We Have in Jesus" on the piano—one of the first hymns Frank had learned on Myrtle Street as a boy. The hearses lined up at St. Gabriel appeared before him, and he blinked to dispel the image. He was blowing, but the notes sounded weak, choppy. He saw the grid of white caskets in the warehouse gloom. His lips stung, the mouthpiece kept slipping. The trumpet was fighting its way out of his hands. He took breaths where they didn't belong. A wall loomed between his lungs and the horn, between his heart and the horn. PVC tubing and blue tarp, body bags and flies. He blew his way to the bridge and stopped with a gasp. Kevin glanced up, alarmed, and took over, finishing with ample keyboard flourishes. Frank sank into his seat, his face shiny with sweat, heart pounding. Father LeDoux caught his eye and, barely moving his head, nodded knowingly.

JOYCE MONTANA

ST. AUGUSTINE CHURCH
2006

Father LeDoux's beat-up Oldsmobile idled beside the rectory door. Governor Nicholls Street was dark, lit only by a weak bulb attached to the outside of the church. Joyce was unaccustomed to being out so late, especially without Tootie; she felt like she was in a movie—a thriller whose climax was about to burst upon the screen. Father LeDoux came down the rectory stairs slowly, looking small in a tight black suit and clerical collar. A young white man, burly and long-haired, followed him down with a box of files, and as soon as they were off the last step, a husky young woman carried a cot up the stairs. Another kid followed, carrying a box of food. Father LeDoux wanted to linger, to hug everyone, but the young people were hustling him along, into his car. They wanted him out before they set their plan in motion.

Joyce elbowed in and gave Father LeDoux a quick hug, and then he was gone, his taillights making a red smear around the corner of St. Claude Avenue. At once, the young people disappeared inside the rectory and closed the door. Joyce could hear a hammer banging; they were barricading it. She walked to the side door of the sanctuary, pausing before the giant rusted cross made of welded anchor chain, hung with manacles. Father LeDoux had installed it years before: the Tomb of the Unknown Slave. No wonder the archdiocese hated him so much.

Inside the sanctuary, cots were laid out in the aisles between the pews and around the pulpit. A young woman played guitar, singing some sweet hymn. Sandra Gordon appeared at Joyce's elbow. "You know, I get it," she said. "It's like the head says one thing and the heart says another. The whole city is like this since the storm. The numbers may say to close Charity Hospital, too, but how can you take that away from the people at this time? This city has never lived by the numbers. How can you follow the numbers when people are hurting? That's what I don't get." They walked back outside into the warm, fragrant night. A table had been moved in front of the rectory door, and sitting behind it, forearms planted solidly, were Marion Colbert and ninety-year-old Cecilia Galle.

"If the police come, they're going to have to come through us," Cecilia said with a smile. She must have weighed all of ninety pounds.

Marion pulled out a chair. "Come sit down, Joyce."

Joyce hesitated. Sit down in the middle of the night to join in a protest? Deliberately provoke the New Orleans police? She couldn't imagine what Tootie would say. She oughtn't to be out here, fooling around. She ought to be at the kitchen table with Tootie right now, sewing on his next suit.

Tootie had overseen her life for fifty-three years, but he was gone, and she would have to find her own way. She took the seat that Marion was holding for her. She folded her hands and set her jaw, waiting for the sirens.

RONALD LEWIS

1317 TUPELO STREET
March 2006

Students swarmed over Ronald's house and backyard, pulling down the waterlogged garage with their bare hands, tearing the inside of the house apart with crowbars, piling sodden Sheetrock on the curb. They worked cheerfully in the heat and filth, like soldier ants, having come on spring break from as far as Montana and Kansas, the baton of goodwill having passed from Helen Regis to Steve Inskeep, to the Reinhabiting NOLA conference, to students from all over America.

Ronald bent to pick up a hammer and limped across the driveway to lay it on a workbench; keeping the work site neat was the least he could do. At the curb, a camera crew from WWL-TV was packing up. They'd been around the last hour, to film some of the first rebuilding in the Lower Ninth Ward.

" 'Scuse me," Ronald said, hobbling up to the young woman in blazer and shiny loafers who seemed to be in charge. "I got one more thing to say."

"We're finished here," she said. "Thank you."

Ronald smiled broadly, hitting her with that gold incisor. "Give me one more minute of your time."

She looked annoyed, but flipped an eyebrow at a cameraman, who hoisted his big machine back onto his shoulder. The woman held the microphone close to Ronald's lips. He looked straight into the lens.

"My name is Ronald W. Lewis. We need help down here in the Lower Ninth Ward. Please help us."

The cameraman waited.

"That's all I got to say."

WILBERT RAWLINS JR.

O. PERRY WALKER HIGH SCHOOL
August 2006

The O. Perry Walker High School band room was windowless and none too clean. Another band room, Wil thought. But at least it's in New Orleans. And there were band trophies on the wall. Hard-luck schools were often the ones with band trophies. They're the ones that needed band the most.

"Wilbert Rawlins Jr.?" A very fat man weaved his way, splay legged, among chairs and music stands. He wore blue sweatpants, a faded blue hoodie, and a gray T-shirt as big as a circus tent. He was younger than Wil; he might have been a student. He looked exhausted, his skin gray, and the school year hadn't yet started. "Mike Ricks," he said, putting out a soft hand and smiling sweetly. "The children call me Big Mike."

It was Big Mike who had tracked him down in Beaumont and recruited Wil by phone. Wil pulled up a couple of plastic folding chairs. "You're what, an assistant principal?"

"I'm the interventionist."

"What's that?"

"Oh, basically I'm here to love the children." Big Mike laughed, his round face lighting up like sunrise. "Those that don't receive love at home need an adult at school to say, 'I love you!' "

"I hear that. I used to work up by the Desire Project."

Big Mike leaned forward across his huge, soft belly. "When I was coming over here, everybody was like, 'Oh, you going to Walker, that school bad.' " He laughed. "You know about the shooting here in 2004, right? Then you know the worst. Listen: a child might be able to pass along in elementary school with two-dollar parents. But when you get to middle school and high school, you want to keep up with what everybody else is doing. So where do you look for mentors if you got two-dollar parents? You look to the guys that's driving the nice cars, that have the women, that aren't tied down with jobs. You hear what I'm saying?"

"How many of the kids at Walker have both parents?"

Mike leaned back and closed his eyes. "Out of the 900 and something kids, I would give it about 100."

"And one parent?"

"Maybe half."

"And the rest, what? Live with grandmothers?"

Mike opened his eyes. "Well, I consider a grandmother a parent."

Wil did the math. "What about the other 350?"

"They're on their own," he said, and Wil felt a chill on his back. "They wanted to be back," Big Mike went on. "They want to go to school in New Orleans. Maybe their mama in Texas couldn't come back. Maybe she didn't want to. So you got children staying by relatives or friends, but most are on their own, roommating with each other. Some got a little apartment; some got FEMA trailers. Some are in abandoned houses. A lot of our kids leave school and go straight to work. They work till two, three o'clock in the morning and come to school at seven. I got fifteen I call every morning to wake them up." He held up his cell phone.

"So who's cooking their meals and washing their clothes?"

"We got about seven or eight that washes their clothes upstairs."

"What about food?"

"Food, hmm." Mike shrugged. "Sometimes they have money. I give them money, Miss Laurie gives them money. Sometimes they'll eat by other people's houses. Our football coach, he's got about nine boys living with him."

I wanted intensity, Wil thought. This is going to be plenty damn intense.

"But listen here," Big Mike said. "Before the storm, this school graduated half its senior class. It lost half to the streets, to drugs, to whatever. Last year? After the storm? We graduated more than 80 percent, and we only opened in December." Big Mike hoisted himself to his feet. "You got things to do." He laid his hand on Wil's shoulder. "It's up to you, but

I can tell you that I don't address these children by their first names. I call them Mr. and Miss. I say 'sir' and 'ma'am.' We serve *them*. We are here because of *them*. We pay our bills because of *them*." He shuffled off, dragging his heavy feet along the linoleum with a soft soughing noise.

Wil was setting up, trying to get his mind around 350 children living on their own, when his cell phone buzzed.

"Daddy?"

Only one girl called him that. "Nyja!" Wil leaped to his feet. "Where you calling from?"

"I'm at Texas Southern." She sounded happy, but also sleepy, maybe drugged out. He tried to put it together—that she'd made it to college, that she sounded happy, that she was doped up.

"I'm studying pharmacy," Nyja said.

Wil laughed. He'd lost track of her, and then there was the storm. Nyja Sanders! Studying pharmacy!

"I still cry myself to sleep since the storm," she was saying.

"But you're holding on! You're in college! How's Texas Southern? You in the band?"

"Of course! I play mellophone. My boyfriend plays baritone. His name is Calvin, but they call him Turkey. It's hard here, Daddy. Everything's spread out. I take buses or get rides. People got stereotypes. If you have a 504 phone, you can't get no job, 'cause nobody wants nobody from New Orleans. And if you can't get no job, you can't get a new cell phone."

"I hear you," Wil said.

"But look. I didn't call to complain. I got something to tell you, and I got something to ask you." It sounded like she was nodding off on the phone.

"Okay."

"I had a baby today, Daddy. A beautiful baby girl."

"What?"

"So there's your grandchild. Didn't you always want a baby girl? Now, I want to know if it's okay with you if I name her Beautiful Music Sanders."

fRANK MINYARD

ORLEANS PARISH CORONER'S OFFICE
2007

Frank climbed the broad front steps of the gray sandstone building and unlocked the door under the etched pediment: CORONER, PARISH OF ORLEANS. The hall was silent, power still out, autopsy rooms in the basement a long way from restoration. But Frank's office was okay, as long as the daylight lasted. He sank into the oak swivel chair, surrounded by the photographs that covered the walls from floor to ceiling: Al Hirt and Pete Fountain. Admiral Zumwalt. Sister Mary David. Joe Maumus. Father Therriot. Paul Hornung. Presidents. Football players. Mayors. Governors. Frank in Mardi Gras mask. Frank in tuxedo. Frank in Navy uniform. Frank was the longest-serving elected official in Louisiana—perhaps in all of Louisiana history.

Christ, he was tired. The tightness in his throat since Katrina felt like the choke chain of a vain and decadent life. What good had he done the people of New Orleans, really? He wanted to feel the old pleasures, to access the glitter and strut that had buoyed him through blunders and sins, but it wasn't something he could summon. Not with the smells of St. Gabriel lingering in his nostrils. Not with the grid of white coffins on Poydras Street imprinted on the inside of his eyelids.

He hoisted his briefcase onto the desk and pulled out a thick sheaf of papers, the week's autopsy reports from the makeshift morgue north of the city. New Orleans had less than half its pre-storm population, yet as many people were dying each week as before the storm. He flipped through a dozen reports. The ages were striking: Forty-four. Thirty-one. Fifty-six. Twenty-nine. "Natural causes," his pathologists had written again and again, a vague term usually reserved for the superannuated. Even for the elderly, it was customary, before the storm, to list a cause of death: pneumonia or congestive heart failure. Frank looked at the details of the autopsies. These young people had mild cirrhosis, or minor heart trouble, or traces of pulmonary stress, but nothing that would kill a person. And yet they were dead.

"Frank, are you ready to go?" Nancy stepped into the office in her riding boots and tank top, dark brown hair curling around her shoulders.

She couldn't pull Frank from the depths, but she always pierced the gloom.

"It's the storm," Frank said, raising an autopsy form. "They may not have drowned, or died of dehydration or heat exhaustion in an attic. But these are storm-related deaths: grief, stress, misery, uncertainty."

"And no Charity," Nancy said. As a nurse, she was appalled at the closing of the city's massive public hospital.

"Natural causes my ass," Frank said. "These are about the most unnatural cases I've ever encountered. A person can take only so much stress before the heart muscles go into spasm and the person dies."

FEMA, he knew, was giving five thousand dollars to any family that lost someone to Katrina. Many life-insurance companies paid double if the policyholder was killed by a hurricane.

Frank took a pen from his shirt pocket, leaned over the desk, and, finding the appropriate box on each report, scribbled in it. "I'm putting all of these down as storm related. These are my people. It's the least I can do."

"They'll fight you."

He laughed. "I'm seventy-seven years old. I imagine I'll spend the rest of my life in court." It had been the motto of his office all along: where death delights to serve the living.

RONALD LEWIS

CLAIBORNE AVENUE
August 2006

"I'm going to call my sister and see if she can't come over and help me cook up a big old dinner to celebrate," Minnie said. "I want to make baked macaroni, and dressing, and jambalaya."

Ronald smiled as he piloted the struggle-buggy, bringing Minnie home over the Claiborne Avenue Bridge. She looked sharp in narrow-cut pants, pointed black boots, and a teal blouse. Her hair lay in tiny cornrows ending in tassels that wobbled fetchingly when she turned her head. This was the old Minnie. The happy Minnie. A good day. But she had walked a bleak road, and they'd spent more time apart than ever in their married life. During some of her darkest hours in Thibodaux, he'd been here, putting their little piece of the Lower Ninth Ward back together.

Still so many houses still ruined. Most of them gutted out, but even now some were untouched. He couldn't understand the people who weren't striving to come back. It was so different from the time after Betsy, when there was no question. Everybody came back and started right in. Forty years after our liberation movement, Ronald thought, and we're further back than ever.

Sometimes he found himself thinking uncharitably about the people who hadn't returned, and had to make an almost physical effort to haul himself back from that. Everybody's got circumstances, he'd tell himself. Not everybody can set their own destination. But it seemed to Ronald that a fundamental mistake had been made after Katrina. The government dangled a lot of resources, and it made everybody freeze up. Nobody wanted to start in until they saw what they were going to get. We knew after Betsy we weren't going to get no help from anybody, Ronald often thought, and maybe that was better.

Jesus isn't always there when you need Him, but He's always just in time. Every time Ronald would feel himself edging toward despair, the Lord would reach out His hand and pull him back. Just a few days ago, little red Michael, from Derrick Jenkins's gang, had come up to him and said that after getting his welding certificate at Nunez Community College, he'd gotten a good job by Bollinger Shipyards. Ronald had saved one. His heart swelled up so full he could barely congratulate the boy.

He turned onto Tupelo Street. A couple of houses had piles of debris out front; that was progress. At the corner of Galvez, four young men in white T-shirts lounged on the steps of a wrecked two-story house, back to their sorry business. But they were community minded still. The whole time the soldier ants had worked on the Tupelo Street house, these boys had seen to it nobody touched the tools and lumber.

Ronald pulled the car to a stop in front of the house, a fresh gleaming white with a brown and white awning above the porch. Minnie put her forehead against the window glass. The front stoop had been done up in sharp maroon, with a big fleur-de-lis in white. He led her up the path, unlocked the front door, and held it open.

The two front rooms and kitchen were one big room now, the ceiling raised to the roofline, smart-looking brown-wood beams traversing the open space where the old ceiling used to be. In the kitchen: a stainless steel stove and a new black fridge under blond-wood cabinets. Everything smelled sharp and clean.

Minnie really has no idea what I done here, Ronald thought. I protected her from it, so she don't know how far we come.

Minnie's heels echoed loudly on the new wood floor as she circled the big front room and walked from bedroom to bedroom. "Mmmmm," she sang happily as she opened the door to the bathroom and found a gleaming white sink sitting fashionably atop a cherrywood vanity like a punch bowl. "Mmmmm!"

I have done for Minnie what I needed to do, Ronald thought. She was my first responsibility. Now I can turn my attention to my people.

Minnie came walking back toward him with her eyes overflowing. She'd always been quicker to comment on what she didn't like than what she did, more fluent in the expression of disappointment than gratitude. Now, though, she put her arms around his neck like they were eighteen again. "Oh, Ronald," she said. "You are a great husband."

BILLY GRACE

2525 ST. CHARLES AVENUE
February 19, 2007

Billy sat in his study in one of the massive oxblood-leather chairs. He could hear the crowd out front on the neutral ground, hoisting children onto ladder seats, eating po'boys, buying beer and cold drinks from coolers dragged on dollies. In the old days, Billy would have been out there with them, or at least sitting on the porch with George, Anne, and Big Anne, enjoying the spectacle. Instead, he was poring over papers from a North Carolina company he was thinking of buying. It made sewing machines for stitching up charcoal bags. Sewing machines didn't particularly move Billy's heart, but the idea of a new business did. For the first time in his life—at least the first time since his foray to New York had been cut short—he was dreaming of leaving New Orleans. He had gone through the motions of preparing for this year's Rex parade and ball—it would go smoothly tomorrow—but he was spending more and more time at the house in Destin, or finding reasons, like this sewing-machine company, to take trips.

None of his friends had lost relatives in the flood. None had been wiped out; everybody was insured. They had big bank accounts, second homes. Yet half a dozen of Billy's schoolmates had dropped dead since Katrina. Fifty-five, fifty-six years old and they'd keeled over. Worse yet, four had taken their own lives.

Recovery was stalled. Federal funds either were being mysteriously held back or were dribbling away. Constructive debate over how to rebuild was mired hopelessly in racial hostility. The suffering was immense, and the people who had the education, experience, and resources to relieve it were the first to be shunted aside.

Maybe Nagin was right. Maybe New Orleans would be a chocolate city at the end of the day, and uptown's day was done. The Civil War had ended the golden, anachronistic, chivalrous days of the South; maybe Katrina had put an end to the delightfully frivolous life of uptown New Orleans. After a lifetime of feeling like a servant of New Orleans's unique history—caring for the Rex mansion, organizing Mardi Gras—he was starting to wonder if there was a place in New Orleans anymore for Billy Grace.

After a while, Billy set the papers aside and walked down the grand curved staircase to the living room. The casket stood on a black-draped bier. A bottle of Ojen sat on a silver tray on the closed half of the lid. George lay cold and still, dressed in the morning coat in which he'd have toasted Rex. A Rex medallion lay on his chest, a purple, green, and gold ribbon reaching around his thin neck.

Proteus Monday, Lundi Gras—George's favorite day on the calendar, when all the Mardi Gras logistics were settled, an evening to relax and watch Proteus roll past. Even when George had had to be wheeled out with a tartan blanket draped over the stumps of his legs—his pink drink of Ojen and Peychaud's bitters clutched in his butchered fist—he'd never failed to watch the king of Proteus roll down St. Charles Avenue on a giant clamshell. Tonight, though, George scowled at the filigreed ceiling. The funeral home could have done a better job at that: never, in life, as far as Billy could recall, had George looked so forbidding.

A shout went up outside. Through the wavy glass of the front windows, Billy could see the people surging to the curb and waving their arms. Sure enough, there was the king of Proteus on his clamshell, waving magisterially. The men on the float tossed beads. The crowd jostled and hollered.

Nobody out there knew the sadness of the Rex mansion. George was the best of old New Orleans. Would the city ever again have a place for the elegance, manners, and patrician good humor of a George Montgomery?

The doorbell clanged, and Billy turned. Alston, sturdy in crisp slacks and a short-sleeved sweater, hurried in from the parlor to answer. She opened the door on two teenage black girls, tall and skinny, in hooded sweatshirts and straightened hair. Billy and Alston gaped a moment. It hadn't been all that long that black people used the front door of this house at all. And strangers certainly never appeared there.

"Yes?"

The girls gazed into the chandeliered front hall, wide-eyed. They're New Orleanians, too, Billy thought. They know the power of this house, and that's a good thing. *Pro bono publico.* The whole point of Rex is to share the regal magic of uptown with the rest of the city. But what on earth did they want here? And why now, of all times?

The taller girl finally summoned her courage. "Can we please," she said, "see the deceased king?"

FRANK MINYARD

CHARITY HOSPITAL CEMETERY

2007

Frank stood at the top of Canal Street peering through a locked iron gate on which tall iron letters, copiously rusted, spelled "CHARITY HOSPITAL CEMETERY." On the other side lay a flat field of neatly mowed grass about the size of a city block, with a few well-tended magnolia trees. A wall surrounded the lot, above which peeked the tops of gaudy mausoleums in the city's vast cemeteries.

This incongruously vacant and finely manicured lot was a perfect site in which to bury, finally, the unclaimed dead from the Poydras Street warehouse. Ninety-five caskets remained in that gloomy cavern, ninety-five New Orleanians whose families had never claimed them or who'd been deemed unidentifiable by DMORT. They'd never be identified now; the state had cut off Frank's money for further DNA testing. Louisiana was moving on from Katrina.

That this lot was available at all was a gift of bureaucratic amnesia. Before World War II, Charity Hospital had buried medical detritus here: amputated limbs, removed organs, miscarried fetuses. Nothing had been interred here since then, though; the hospital seemed to have forgotten all about it. Now Charity Hospital no longer existed; its assets, including this lot, had been transferred to Louisiana State University Medical Center.

Frank wanted to do more than simply bury the dead. He wanted their resting place also to serve as a memorial to all those who'd died in Katrina. A local architecture firm designed for Frank a beautiful park, with sidewalks that spiraled in the shape of a hurricane toward a gorgeous statue of two female angels, one black and one white, holding up a fleur-de-lis and standing among breaking waves. The bodies would rest in mausoleums around the spiral's edge. Frank envisioned the site being a tourist attraction forever—the Katrina Memorial—right there at the end of the Canal Street streetcar line.

Frank figured he needed $1.3 million to buy the land from LSU and get the memorial built. Mayor Nagin had already given him a million; raising the other $300,000 would be difficult but not impossible.

The problem was perpetual care—locking and unlocking the gates, mowing the lawn, emptying the trash baskets, sweeping the sidewalks. LSU claimed it cost $1,000 a month, and nothing could go forward until Frank raised enough money to throw off $12,000 a year—an additional $200,000 or so. By force of personality, he convinced the archdiocese to ask the person who locked and unlocked its cemetery's gates to do the same at the Katrina Memorial every day. But that still left the mowing, watering, and cleaning up.

A thousand dollars a month. FEMA was currently paying almost three times that much to rent the warehouse where the bodies were stored. That wouldn't last forever. FEMA was enjoined by its own rules from paying the thousand a month for the memorial's care, and Frank was getting nowhere with the state of Louisiana.

Standing with his forehead against the bars of the gate, Frank knew what he'd do: when the FEMA money for the warehouse ran out, he'd take the ninety-five coffins to the Superdome and line them up on the sidewalk outside. Then he'd hire a band and make an event of it. Maybe he'd even play his own trumpet, if he could summon the lightness of heart to put it to his lips. Let the bodies sit on the sidewalk until Baton Rouge came to its senses. He was old now, and tired, but he still knew how to play the game.

ANTHONY WELLS

In Tennessee they like to say, "Storm's over." You got to shake a leg up there. They got no compassion. All along the city of Knoxville was saying they'd buy me a bus ticket whenever I wanted to go home. I don't know why I waited so long. I guess I thought Roger and me would go together. But Roger's got him a girlfriend now, and a new baby. He's staying up there. Soon as he and his girlfriend get custody of the baby, they're going to buy a house.

He's lost his focus.

Coming down, the bus got to Gulfport, Mississippi, and all but six people got off. Then it stops in Slidell, and three more get off. Then we come down Highway 10 through the east and I'm seeing it for the first time. All those houses empty, buildings closed, big old parking lots with no cars in them. I'd seen pictures, but this was my first time seeing it, you feel me? Two years since the storm and the city ain't fix yet. It's like they don't want us back here at all.

They genociding us on the slick side.

Bus got in about eleven o'clock in the day. Bus stop was empty, but I seen a cabdriver I knew, Robert Ruffin, and he gave me a ride for half price up to the Goose. I had two hundred dollars in my pocket.

The quiet, man, that's what blew my mind. All that time in Tennessee I'd been missing the noise, but it was like a tomb. Every house was all fucked-up; only way you knew someone was living there was there was a white FEMA trailer in the yard. I looked around in our old place above Jerry's store; the door was off the hinges and the place all hollowed out. That good stuff we stored behind the wall was gone. I didn't stay up there long. It felt like I was about to fall through the floor.

First thing I walk up Dale looking for Peanut, and in front of his house was a big old piece of plywood that somebody'd painted on it: "P-Nut We Love You and Forgive You—the Family." Turned out Peanut went off. I mean off. He shot his auntee and Petie and Bunk—killed them all—because he thought someone else might get the house. The family can forgive him all they want; we ain't seeing him for a long time.

I miss Roger.

Spoonie's back, and Poochie. My cousin Donald and his brother Jerry, they're back. They got a little place to eat now in the gas station on Chef, but it ain't the Arab no more. These are Vietnamese-speaking people. The Goose ain't like it was, but it's better than fucking Tennessee. I'm working. I go by Labor Ready, or Delta, or Task Force. Used to be you got hired right with the company, but they cut all that out in the late '80s, early '90s. Now, if the job is fifteen dollars an hour, you get six, and the temp company gets the rest.

Always been fucked-up here, man, but it's home. Till you been someplace else, you don't know.

BILLY GRACE

GRETNA
June 4, 2007

Billy sat in a Gretna office complex waiting to see a client, looking forward to lunch. His BlackBerry buzzed and he fished it out of a jacket pocket.

"Billy!" Anne shouted. "The house is on fire!"

"What?"

"Lightning! I was on St. Charles and heard it hit!"

"Where's your mom?" He could hear sirens in the background.

"She's fine! Come home!"

He ran for the elevator. That old house had nineteen lightning rods. The roof was copper. What could burn?

He swept onto the highway and up the Crescent City Connection bridge. Even before he reached the top, he could see what looked like a bolt of black cloth unfurling above the skyscrapers of downtown. He floored the Mercedes, crested the bridge, and looked left. A dense geyser of greasy smoke boiled up from the lower Garden District. It looked like a refinery burning, pumping blooms of malignant black poppies above the tree line. Chunks of soot were falling on the bridge.

By the time he reached the twenty-five hundred block, half the New Orleans Fire Department had assembled. Yellow canvas hoses snaked over the garden wall, flattening azaleas and camellias. Big Anne sat in her car with a hand on her chest; Anne stood beside her, watching the flames with one hand over her mouth and one on top of her head. The fire was eating the house in great crunching mouthfuls. Claws of orange flame reached from the upstairs windows. Puffs of heat tapped Billy's cheeks. The carpets, the frescoes, the chandeliers, the paintings, the piano, the tiger-wood floors . . .

But the water was a sight to behold. It tumbled out of the French doors to the porch, rolled down the steps into the garden, ran in ripply sheets across windowpanes, squirted comically from holes the firemen had hacked in the walls, made rainbows around the second-story balconies, and dripped from them like icing from a cake. The water that hadn't reached St. Charles Avenue after Katrina was finding the Rex mansion now, hollowing it out from the inside.

Standing in his blue blazer and boat shoes, head cocked back and mouth open like a hungry baby bird, Billy felt himself overtaken by a strange calm. Even as the fire propelled his house into the hazy Louisiana sky, it was planting him ever deeper in New Orleans's soft soil. It would take years to put 2525 back together. Rebuilding the house that had been in Anne's family for exactly a century would be Billy's avocation for the foreseeable future. He could not leave a charred ruin behind. He could not walk away from the city.

Katrina had spared him. It had severed him from the city's collective fate and left him marooned on a globe-trotting island of plenty. Finally, his walk in the wilderness was over. Well, New Orleans, he thought as his house roared in agony, I'm back.

BELINDA RAWLINS

5972 DREUX AVENUE
2007

Belinda leaned on her metal cane, watching Curtis, Niecy, and Mookey cooing over Niecy's toddler, Jamaya. She was struck, as so often, by how different her daughters were. Niecy was small and slight, wary and watchful; Mookey was tall and full-bodied, open and trusting. She'd never pictured Niecy as the single mother, Mookey as the scholar. But now Niecy was home minding a baby, and Mookey was a freshman at Northwestern State in Natchitoches. Please, God, let her get through.

Wil came in from the bedroom, wearing a charcoal gray suit and his big gold medallion—WR—and lit up with a smile. Ever since they'd rebuilt the place, he'd taken to booming, apropos of nothing, "Man, I am loving this house!" Wil liked to say the house was better than before, but that was Wil; he could never keep a bad thing in his mind for long. All he had a mind for was the happy times. The neighborhood around their house was dark and deserted, the city was still a wreck, Niecy's education was derailed. But Wil saw only repairs beginning in the neighborhood, kids coming home to the band, Niecy's education only delayed. And in this house, a dream fulfilled twice over. "You talk about that white-picket-fence life," he'd say, putting his arms around her. "Well, here it is, sweetheart! We got it!"

She had to admit there was some truth to it. Somehow, though, life on Dreux Avenue didn't feel like *The Waltons.*

This evening they were dressing for an event at the Ashé Cultural Arts Center on Oretha Castle Haley in the Thirteenth Ward. The Thirteenth Ward was as poor and black as the Ninth, but rougher, more urban, less family oriented. She'd rarely, as a girl, ventured upriver of Canal Street, and she retained a downtowner's aversion to the Thirteenth Ward. But this was a big night for Wil, and she didn't object.

The Ashé Center was little more than a big room with stark white new Sheetrock walls, and many rows of folding plastic chairs. A crowd of boys, like big puppies, mobbed Wil at the door: the To Be Continued Brass Band. "Belinda," Wil said. "You remember these boys, don't you?

You met them that night in the French Quarters when we thought they was out to rob us."

"We was out to rob you," Brandon said, "until we seen who you was." They all laughed and touched fists.

"Mama Rawlins," said Jason, "Mr. Rawlins here, he pulled us out. We wouldn't be nowhere without Mr. Rawlins."

With their funky English, baggy pants, and sideways caps, these were the kinds of boys she'd spent her whole life avoiding: sloppy, sensual, dangerous. Even though they'd finished high school, not one of them could speak correctly, much less enjoy reading a book. Yet these were the kids Wil would have traded away his marriage for. They were his whole world.

They took seats and a film started. It followed the boys after the storm, scattered as far apart as Atlanta, Dallas, and Sacramento. In their lumpy, rough English, they talked about how much they missed each other, how they longed to be "breathing the same air." Yeah, Belinda thought. Life is tough. Everybody got flushed out the city by the storm. Everybody was scattered. Everybody had it hard. But as the boys' gigantic, immature faces loomed over her, Belinda heard something in their voices she'd never noticed—poetry. "I'm in the right now trying to get to the not yet," Jason said. It struck her ear as a fresh way of saying what everybody in New Orleans had been feeling since the storm. "All the tears I done seen could have made a flood itself," Brandon said, and that, from a boy who looked all of about twelve years old. She turned in her seat to look back at the boys. They were such brutes; how did they access such feeling? On the screen, the boys looked lost, wandering strange landscapes, pining for New Orleans, for horns and drums lost in the flood. "That was my heart, my instrument," said Joseph Maize of his trombone. Belinda scanned the room, then leaned over to Wil and whispered, "Where are their parents?"

"Parents?" he whispered, eyebrows arching with comic incredulity. "Most of them never had parents worth a damn. If they had, they wouldn't have been cutting up in the French Quarters." On the screen, four of them had gathered in Dallas, plotting how to get home. "Let's call Mr. Rawlins!" someone said, and there was Wil's voice, coming through the cell phone of the trumpeter Glenn Preston, talking the same street jive as the boys—"I feel y'all, y'know?" Belinda glanced over at Wil in his gray suit. He sat straight up, eagerly, chin high—like Da used to sit at one of Wil's concerts. On-screen, Sean Roberts told the camera, "He used to let us use school horns. If Mr. Rawlins wasn't at Carver, there wouldn't be no band at all."

The audience applauded, and the band members were invited up to speak. A call went out for the boys' parents to stand, and then a dull murmur went through the room when only one woman, small and meek, popped up briefly. If these boys had parents, only one had taken the trouble to come. The boys were asked to talk about their band, but all they wanted to talk about was Wil—how he'd syncopated marching-band music into second-line tunes for them, how he'd found instruments when they had none and fixed them when they were broken, how he'd run interference with the French Quarter police so they could stand at the corner of Bourbon and Canal streets and play.

"I never had no father. Mr. Rawlins, he been a father to all of us. There were times we didn't have anything to eat, you feel me? And Mr. Rawlins went in his own pocket."

"Mr. Rawlins, man, he made this thing happen, y'all. He was like, 'You boys gots to believe.'"

"I got one brother dead and another at Angola, and if it wasn't for Mr. Rawlins, I might be right there, too."

The more they talked, the straighter Wil sat—putting the eye thing on them to keep their manners good and their English proper. It suddenly dawned on Belinda that these were only nine of his kids. Another hundred came to him every afternoon in the O. Perry Walker band room. Another God knew how many—from Carver and Sarah T. Reed—were out there somewhere, walking paths that Wil had set them on. Belinda took his hand, and he looked over at her, surprised and then pleased. "Band" didn't begin to describe what Wil did, Belinda realized. He'd gathered in a whole city full of neglected, abandoned, forgotten kids and made them his sons and daughters. He was a dad where there were no dads, and he'd be responsible for these kids forever.

She felt a rush of shame. She had been competing with them, resenting them, pulling him away. Her life was not going to be like on *The Waltons*. She had the white picket fence, Ninth Ward style—a husband, which was more than a lot of women could say; a house, which was more than most people in New Orleans could say since Katrina. It was time to turn on the laugh track.

"Wilbert," she said. He leaned close and she whispered, "I get it."

JOANN GUIDOS

KAJUN'S PUB,
ST. CLAUDE AVENUE
2007

Four Mexicans, spattered with drywall mud, were shooting pool on the cigarette-scarred table. There were a lot more of them around since the storm, JoAnn noticed. And they'd brought with them a new thing for New Orleans: taco trucks. There was usually a big silver one parked on St. Claude Avenue.

All three poker machines were occupied; that was good. An old woman was working the ATM machine, another good sign. Watching people pour their FEMA checks into the machines gave JoAnn's conscience a pang, but if they didn't play in Kajun's, they'd play somewhere else.

Interlocking financial perils threatened at any moment to collapse her St. Claude Avenue empire. The bank was raising the mortgage rate from seven and a half to eleven and a half because she hadn't made a payment since the storm. The insurance company was finding endless excuses to pay her nothing for Katrina damage. The water company wanted nine thousand dollars, because it turned out she'd had a hidden leak for months. Melvin's Bar, up the street, was demanding she pay back three thousand dollars for the liquor she'd taken during the storm, though it would have gotten looted anyway. She couldn't get blueprints for the restaurant approved until she built a ramp for the disabled, and she couldn't build the ramp, because the property was historic. She sighed. It was time to start investigating cut-rate sex-change surgeons in the Philippines. Otherwise, she'd never get the thing done.

Duck, the bartender, waved her over. "There's a kid over there that wants to talk to you." He indicated a pale blond boy with sideburns, sipping a Coke by himself at a round table. He wore jeans and a big Army jacket. He probably wanted a gig for his band.

JoAnn walked over. "You looking for me?"

The boy brightened and shifted in his chair. "Could I talk to you a minute?"

"A minute," JoAnn said, taking a seat next to him.

He leaned in close. "I want to be a girl."

JoAnn's heart gave a thump. He was so young. The down on his lip brought her straight back to Cor Jesu High School. "Are you sure?" she said. "If you're just excited over women's clothes, it's fetishes."

"No, it's more than that."

"Could be you're just gay."

"I like men," he said. "But I'm not gay. I'm a woman." He opened his Army jacket to reveal a tight-fitting flowered tank top.

JoAnn suddenly felt old, but in a good way. She'd been there. She was wise. She was in a position to help this kid in a way that nobody had helped her.

"You have a lot of soul-searching to do," she said.

"I want to do the whole thing."

"Have you told your parents?"

"What do they have to do with it?"

"Everything," JoAnn said. "Everything will be easier if they're in on it."

He shook his head. The poor kid didn't have a clue. "Thanks," he said finally, and walked out the door.

JoAnn sat for a while after he left. Every penny, she now understood, had to go toward fighting off the creditors, opening the restaurant, fixing the apartments, and keeping Kajun's open. She owed it to kids like this. The weirdos, the outcasts, the forgotten—they needed her refuge here on St. Claude Avenue. Life in New Orleans was hard for everybody now, but it would always be hardest on those who, for whatever reason, didn't fit in. She was responsible, in an odd way, for all of them. Whatever it took to keep Kajun's open, she'd do it.

And if the surgery had to wait, so be it.

fRANK MINYARD

FAIR OAKS FARM
2007

Frank stood at the big picture window with a cup of tea in his hand, watching the Black Angus bull nuzzle the grass. In the old days, on a Saturday, he'd have been getting ready to go out and tear up the French Quarter. Tonight he'd be in bed by nine.

The television on the kitchen counter was tuned to a religious show; Nancy liked them. The organ launched into "That Old Rugged Cross," a singer joined, and Frank found himself humming along. Such a sturdy old hymn, a bit jazzy, too. Pete Fountain had practically made a dance tune of it. Frank braced for the inevitable wave of melancholy that overtook him since the storm whenever he thought of the old days. But the wave didn't knock him over; he took a big breath and let it out slowly, feeling the darkness recede.

What a life, he thought. When I was poor, all I wanted was to be rich. When I was rich, all I wanted was to be useful. Have I been useful? It's not for me to decide. And the truth is, it never was. When the time comes, I'll be judged. Until then, all I can do is live.

He walked to the bedroom, got down on one knee, and pulled from under the bed his battered black trumpet case—the same that Mom had bought for him at Werlein's. The sixteen-dollar trumpet lay patiently in its velvet bed. He lifted it from the case and twiddled the valves. They responded smoothly. He inhaled, set his arms, kissed the mouthpiece, and blew: a clear, mellow note. He inhaled again and blew the first phrase of "That Old Rugged Cross." He wasn't winded. His lips felt good. He finished one verse and started another. Nancy came into the room behind him and sang along:

> On a hill far away, stood an old rugged cross
> The emblem of suff'ring and shame
> And I love that old cross where the dearest and best
> For a world of lost sinners was slain.

He turned, playing on. The diamond engagement ring on Nancy's hand sparkled like a teardrop in sunshine. Frank played louder, arching his back and throwing himself into it, blasting the chorus at the ceiling, jazzing it up. Nancy laughed and raised her voice to meet the horn:

> So I'll cherish the old rugged cross
> Till my trophies at last I lay down.
> I will cling to the old rugged cross
> And exchange it some day for a crown!

RONALD LEWIS

ST. CLAUDE AVENUE
December 2007

Ronald sat in the front seat of a long blue convertible on the sloping approach to the St. Claude Bridge, a king at the gates to his royal city. The Big Nine's annual parade stretched ahead, filling the street, a ribbon of dance rising up the bridge. Pete Alexander, Big Bob Stark, Ricky Gettridge, and the rest bobbed and shook and strutted up St. Claude, waving in each hand huge, homemade fans of bright blue ostrich plumes. Each man had come up with a thousand dollars—money they might have spent on building materials, groceries, and insurance premiums—to deck himself out in blue-on-blue pinstripes, blue-on-blue alligator shoes, and a black homburg, in keeping with the Big Nine's tradition of decking out like stockbrokers and bankers to tell the world that the Lower Ninth Ward was more than country bumpkins. The women of the Four-Five Ladies, the Big Nine's auxiliary, waved their arms and shook their hips in straight-skirt blue-on-blue business attire. There went Minnie, beaming, her braids bouncing in the sunshine. At the head of it all, the sousaphone of the Free Agents Brass Band caught the sun in a fiery blaze, a battle flag at the head of a victorious army.

The crowd to either side was massive, filling the sidewalk and the neutral ground. Children bobbed on shoulders. Old folks waved and smiled. Faces, gray and tired from the endless struggle to rebuild, were lit up by the music and the spirit of the second line. Ronald twisted in his seat. At the convertible's fender, the Hot 8 pointed their axes into the sky. Burger Batiste fired notes from his trumpet like bullets. The massive Bennie Pete was toiling so hard over his sousaphone that he left spatters of sweat on the pavement. They blew and blew, soldiers for the second-line cause.

The Lower Ninth Ward had flooded to the rooflines. The Lower Ninth Ward had only a fraction of its people back. The Lower Ninth Ward was, and always would be, the poor side of town. But nobody could say the Lower Ninth Ward didn't know how to put on a second line.

Ronald wished he could be dancing with his brothers, but his feet and knees wouldn't let him. In truth, it wasn't bad reclining in the presidential limo, a Bud Light in one hand, the other extended over the side of the car, receiving affectionate squeezes.

They'd had no parade the year of the storm. In 2006, they'd marched from Mickey Bee's bar in the Lower Nine over the bridge and into the Seventh Ward in an exodus, as though to say, "We're coming out to ask y'all for help." This time, though, they'd started in the Seventh Ward, to bring it on down St. Claude, leading the people home.

The convertible bumped onto the steel-grid surface of the drawbridge and began its long slow climb over the canal. To the right—eddying, rippling, sparkling—flowed the same Mississippi River that Langston Hughes had known. To the left, the site of the fatal breach, now a long loaf of earth topped by a paper-thin wall of new white cement. The convertible crested the bridge. Most of the visible Lower Nine houses were vacant, some of them not even gutted two and a half years after the flood. Barbershops, clothing stores, and auto-parts outlets along St. Claude stood dark and silt smeared. But Mickey Bee's was open, as well as a new gas station and convenience store across the street. The neighborhood had a long row to hoe, but it was returning to life.

"Stop the car here," Ronald shouted, and, climbing out, he walked down the bridge and into the Lower Ninth Ward on his own aching feet.

ACKNOWLEDGMENTS

Thank you, most of all, to Ronald Lewis, Joyce Montana, Wilbert Rawlins Jr., Tim Bruneau, Frank Minyard, JoAnn Guidos, Belinda Rawlins, Anthony Wells, and Billy Grace. They not only sacrificed many hours to this project but also subjected themselves to the discomfort of candor and exposure. To this day I don't know why they did it, other than love of New Orleans and a desire to explain it from their own points of view. I am grateful beyond measure.

The sources listed on pages 327–31 also have my sincere gratitude for taking the time to be interviewed.

But as a reporter, I really must thank everybody I encountered in New Orleans—from the po'boy sellers and street musicians to the cops and hat merchants and the tattooed ex-con who fixed my car—for building a culture where nothing is ever "none of your business." One really can't ask a question in New Orleans that is too personal, even of a total stranger. For someone in my unseemly profession, it's paradise.

Christopher Jackson, my editor at Spiegel & Grau, was flexible about deadlines and generous with encouragement. More important, though, Chris disproved the common notion that modern book editors do nought but go to lunch for a living. Chris so thoroughly worked the copy that when the manuscript came back to me I went through Elizabeth Kübler-Ross's five stages of grief—angry that he'd masticated my flawless prose, denial that I'd really have to make such extensive changes, confident I could bargain my way out of most of them, despair that Chris believed so much alteration was necessary, and finally acceptance that he had been right all along. This led to a sixth stage: gratitude. The book improved vastly from Chris's hard labor. Many thanks as well to copy editor Ingrid Sterner, who went way beyond cleaning up punctuation to full-blown fact checking. I never knew how bad my math and spelling were before encountering Ingrid. Mya Spalter was like air-traffic control during a blizzard—calm and competent in the face of frenzy.

I bow and scrape before the throne of Sarah Chalfant at the Wylie Agency, who sold the book to Chris to begin with. Nothing happens without an agent, and Sarah is a very good agent indeed. I owe a debt of gratitude as well to Jon Lee Anderson, who introduced me to her.

Thank you to John Bennet, my editor at the *New Yorker*, who got me the assignment to cover Hurricane Katrina and edited my stories. Blake Eskin did a great job editing my daily online column for the *New Yorker* from January to May 2007. Tom Piazza and Paul Gibb read early versions of the manuscript and provided much-needed guidance. Malcolm Robinson and Anne Guissinger were generous with guidance, logistics, grilled oysters, and their Baton Rouge home. Lynn Guissinger was the one who, on August 28, 2005, said, "Did you hear they're evacuating New Orleans?" and set this project rolling.

Especially in its final, frenzied stages, the book was to our daughter, Rosa, like some kind of demon sibling with a death grip on her parents' attentions and infinite power to swing the household's emotional temperature from anguish to euphoria to—worst of all—incessant low-level bickering. Rosa, who turns sixteen as this goes to press, showed patience and forebearance beyond her years. She also let me read pages to her at bedtime and never failed to say, "I like it!" Bottomless thanks and apologies are her due.

Nobody, though, deserves more thanks than my wife and writing partner, Margaret. Ever since Rosa was born and we decided that I should be the legs and eyeballs of our joint operation, Margaret has worked without byline or credit as my bureau chief—"Did you get this?" "Did you ask him that?" "Go back and ask her about that again"—and as my editor. I do the reporting and the first draft, and then the real work begins. (She carved the manuscript from 190,000 to 117,000 words without losing a single scene or character—just by cleaning up sentences and trimming fat.) Nobody can find precisely the right word the way Margaret can. Nobody else can spot an ambiguity or redundancy with such a relentless eye. The work that goes out under my byline is at least half Margaret's, but also, she brings me cups of tea. She gets me out for walks. She sings me Mexican songs on the guitar. She scolds me until my testicles retract. She does whatever it takes to keep me sane and on task. And after a long day of working with her, all I really want to do is sit on the couch beside her and massage her achilles tendons. I love the writing life mostly because I get to live it with Margaret.

NOTES AND SOURCES

This book grew out of my work covering Hurricane Katrina and its aftermath for the *New Yorker*. I reached New Orleans on Wednesday, August 31, 2005, two days after the levees broke, and stayed for three weeks. During those early days of the crisis, I got to know JoAnn Guidos in the beery chaos of Kajun's Pub and Billy Grace in the silent fortress of 2525 St. Charles Avenue. Wanting to learn firsthand about the experience of being forcibly evacuated, I turned myself in at the Convention Center, where I happened upon Anthony Wells. After a few days at home, I returned to New Orleans on September 21—in time for Hurricane Rita—and ended up spending a lot of hours in the fetid parking garage of the Sixth District police station, where I got to know Tim Bruneau. Then it was back and forth constantly between home and New Orleans for six months, during which I met Frank Minyard in his silent, ruined office and Ronald Lewis amid the muddy wreckage of the Lower Ninth Ward.

In late 2006, Margaret and I conceived the idea of a book weaving together the life stories of several New Orleanians. JoAnn, Billy, Anthony, Tim, Frank, and Ronald struck us as vivid windows on different and unique subcultures of New Orleans, and all six kindly agreed to participate. Then David Freedman, manager of WWOZ, New Orleans's amazing roots-music radio station, suggested I include a high-school band director, since high-school marching bands are the incubators of fresh generations of jazz musicians in New Orleans. Wilbert Rawlins Jr. didn't hesitate to sign on, and once I got to know more about his wife, Belinda, her up-and-out story drew me in. Finally, Joyce Montana had lived so long in the shadow of her famous husband that she, too, was eager to tell her own story.

Margaret and I moved to New Orleans in January 2007, stopping en route in Denton, Texas, for an all-day interview—seventeen thousand words—with Tim Bruneau. Over the next four months, Ronald, JoAnn, Frank, Billy, Anthony, Joyce, Wilbert, and Belinda each sat, every week or so, for interviews that often lasted half a day. I conduct interviews with my laptop in my hands, and can type as fast as most people can talk. So I ended up with what amounted to transcripts of our conversations. The file containing all my conversations with Ronald Lewis, for example, is sixty single-spaced pages long—about twenty-five thousand words.

Each of my nine main characters directed me to friends, colleagues, and even ex-wives who filled out the narratives. I asked more than a hundred people for interviews, and it is a measure of New Orleans's openhearted and storytelling nature that fewer than half a dozen declined. I also bolstered my understanding of the times in which these people lived with many hours reading back issues of the *Times-Picayune* at New Orleans's terrific public library, and enjoying the books, articles, and films listed below. Altogether, I boiled down about a million words of notes and interviews into the 120,000-word book you're holding.

Dialogue was re-created from people's memories, but also from documentary sources. A few examples: When Tootie tells Joyce on page 139, "That King Tut suit come out of a book. It come out of someone else's head. He didn't draw that book, so I can't give him no credit," those are words Tootie spoke to the filmmaker Lisa Katzman of *Tootie's Last Suit*. I know from Joyce that that's how Tootie felt at the time, so I have him speaking those words—his own—to her. When Ronald Lewis is speaking and taking a cell phone call on page 280 as he's looking at the ruins of the Lower Nine for the first time, all those words are clearly audible on Steve Inskeep's report on National Public Radio. Billy Grace's toast as Rex was captured in the film *By Invitation Only*. Frank Minyard's assertion that Adolph Archie may have slipped on the floor comes from a *Times-Picayune* account of his press conference. In several other cases—Anthony's evacuation, the post-disaster scenes in Kajun's Pub, the Big Nine's parade into the Lower Ninth Ward, and more—I was present when the words were spoken.

INTERVIEWS

Following is a list of the interviews used to re-create each of the nine lives. Some are assigned to more than one character because they touched on the lives of more than one. Some of these sources would be unknown to the character to which they're assigned. Billy Grace, for example, doesn't know Ellis Joubert or Juan Parke, and they didn't speak directly about Billy Grace. But they helped me understand the uptown New Orleans milieu in which Billy Grace's life is set. Similarly, Tim Bruneau doesn't know the New York police officials Timothy Pearson and Steve Haynes or they him, but they gave me a perspective on the NOPD that aided me in telling his story. I didn't discuss Ronald Lewis by name with Greta Gladney, Tanya Harris, or Joe Ringo, but they helped me understand the Lower Ninth Ward, and so on. Interviews that were not specifically about a primary character are indicated in italics.

Tim Bruneau

Tim Bruneau: Oct. 5, 2005; Oct. 6, 2005; Oct. 7, 2005; Oct. 8, 2005; Oct. 11, 2005; Nov. 30, 2005 (by phone); Jan. 26, 2007; April 4, 2007 (long e-mail); Jan. 30, 2008 (long e-mail); March 12, 2008 (by phone)

Darryl Albert: Sept. 2, 2005; May 24, 2007

Peter Amato: Sept. 28, 2005

Alan Bartholomew: Dec. 3, 2005 (by phone)

Tim Bayard: Nov. 16, 2005; Dec. 12, 2005

David Benelli: Nov. 17, 2005

Ryan Beyer: Sept. 28, 2005

Brad Bohanna: Sept. 28, 2005

Aaron Broussard: Sept. 29, 2005

James Brown: March 29, 2007; May 4, 2007

Jeffrey Brumberger: Sept. 9, 2005

Bertrand Butler: Oct. 9, 2005; Nov. 16, 2005; April 6, 2007

Anthony Cannatella: Sept. 8, 2005; Oct. 5, 2005; Oct. 11, 2005; Oct. 14, 2005; April 2, 2007

John Casbon: Oct. 5, 2005; Dec. 17, 2005

Jim Chesnutt: Sept. 7, 2005
Jamie Cohen: Oct. 7, 2005; Oct. 8, 2005
Edwin Compass: Sept. 9, 2005; Dec. 20, 2005 (by phone)
Manuel Curry: Oct. 5, 2005
Chad Darbonne: Sept. 7, 2005
Phil Davis: Oct. 5, 2005
Marlon Defilo: Oct. 11, 2005; Nov. 1, 2005; Nov. 17, 2005
Gus Deruise: Nov. 16, 2005
Vincent Drake: Oct. 12, 2005
Perry Emory: Oct. 11, 2005
Russell Filibert: Oct. 11, 2005
Kristie Floret: Dec. 1, 2005 (by phone)
Sally Forman: Dec. 19, 2005 (by phone)
Kristie Harper: Oct. 5, 2005; Oct. 11, 2005
Steve Haynes: Sept. 29, 2005
Edwin Hosli: Sept. 2, 2005; Oct. 13, 2005
Mary Howell: Oct. 5, 2005 (by phone); Nov. 1, 2005
Jason Jackson: Sept. 7, 2005
Ed Johnson: Oct. 12, 2005
Bruce Jones: Sept. 23, 2005; Nov. 30, 2005 (by phone)
Barbara Lacen: Oct. 14, 2005
Jim Letten: Oct. 10, 2005
Felix Loicano: Nov. 17, 2005
Paul Long: March 1, 2007
Troy Lyles: Nov. 17, 2005
Michael Melton: Nov. 17, 2005
Ray Nagin: Nov. 1, 2005; Feb. 21, 2006
David Parker: Sept. 23, 2005
Timothy Pearson: Sept. 29, 2005
Richard J. Pennington: Nov. 18, 2005
Carl Perilloux: Oct. 5, 2005; Dec. 1, 2005 (by phone)
Tony Radosti: Oct. 11, 2005
Sabrina Richardson: Oct. 5, 2005
Warren Riley: Sept. 8, 2005; Nov. 17, 2005
Peter Scharf: Nov. 1, 2005

Doug Stead: Oct. 5, 2005; Nov. 29, 2005
Joe Valiente: Oct. 12, 2005; Oct. 14, 2005
Kim Williams: Nov. 16, 2005
Melvin Williams: Oct. 7, 2005; Oct. 8, 2005; Oct. 11, 2005
Frank Young: Oct. 6, 2005; Oct. 11, 2005; Nov. 18, 2005 (by phone)

Billy Grace
Billy Grace: Oct. 12, 2005; Feb. 19, 2007; March 22, 2007; March 29, 2007; April 13, 2007; April 15, 2007; May 10, 2007; July 14, 2007 (long e-mail); Sept. 7, 2007 (by phone); Dec. 21, 2007; Dec. 25, 2007; Feb. 27, 2008
Hershel Abbott: Jan. 17, 2006 (by phone)
Boysie Bollinger: Nov. 1, 2005; Jan. 28, 2006
Jane Ettinger Booth: Oct. 13, 2005; May 18, 2007
John Charbonnet: April 12, 2007; May 15, 2007
Chick Ciccarelli: Feb. 15, 2006
Pierre DeGruy: Nov. 18, 2007 (by phone)
Brooke Duncan: March 30, 2007; April 12, 2007
Ron Forman: May 9, 2007
Anne Grace: May 27, 2007
Janet Howard: Jan. 25, 2006; April 26, 2007
Hans Johannsen: Sept. 28, 2005
Ellis Joubert: Sept. 23, 2005; Jan. 28, 2006
Pres Kabacoff: Jan. 24, 2006
Michael Kearney: May 16, 2007
Nicholas Lehmann: April 9, 2007 (by phone)
Thomas Lehmann: April 18, 2007
Jonathan McCall: Oct. 12, 2005
Anne Milling: April 26, 2007
Marc Morial: April 16, 2007

Skip O'Connor: Sept. 28, 2005
Dan Packer: Jan. 25, 2006
Juan Parke: Sept. 23, 2005
Sean Reilly: Jan. 30, 2006; May 22,
   2006 (by phone)
Timothy Reily: Oct. 12, 2005; Oct.
   13, 2005
James Reiss: March 3, 2008
Robbie Robinson: Sept. 23, 2005
Bob Rue: Sept. 9, 2005; Sept. 23, 2005;
   Jan. 28, 2006
Gordon Russell: April 20, 2007
Bill Ryan: Sept. 28, 2005
Rebecca Snedeker: May 22, 2007
Doug Thornton: Oct. 12, 2005 (by
   phone)
Robert Walmsley: Oct. 12, 2005

JoAnn Guidos

JoAnn Guidos: Sept. 3, 2005; Sept. 4,
   2005; Sept. 5, 2005; Feb. 6, 2007;
   Feb. 12, 2007; March 18, 2007;
   March 22, 2007; March 27, 2007;
   April 26, 2007; May 6, 2007; Feb.
   28, 2008; March 1, 2008
Phoebe Au: Sept. 3, 2005
Barbara Brodmyer: Sept. 3, 2005; Sept.
   4, 2005; Sept. 5, 2005
James Craddox: Sept. 5, 2005
Kenny Dobbs: Sept. 3, 2005; Sept. 4,
   2005; Sept. 5, 2005
Paul Fischer: May 20, 2007
Paul Guidos: March 27, 2007
Sandy Guidos: March 27, 2007
Donnie Jay: April 5, 2007
Chris Jungles: Sept. 3, 2005; Sept. 4,
   2005; Sept. 5, 2005
Kathy Lehrmann: March 21, 2007
Marci Marcell: April 26, 2007
Sean McDonald: Sept. 3, 2005; Sept.
   4, 2005; Sept. 5, 2005; Sept. 10,
   2005
Renée de Ponthieux: Sept. 3, 2005;
   Sept. 4, 2005; Sept. 5, 2005
Kathy Sartalamacchia: Dec. 16, 2007

Roney Sartalamacchia: Dec. 16, 2007
Larry Stann: Sept. 3, 2005

Ronald Lewis

Ronald Lewis: Jan. 26, 2006; Feb. 28,
   2006; April 6, 2006; April 30, 2006
   (by phone); June 18, 2006; Feb. 6,
   2007; Feb. 16, 2007; Feb. 28, 2007;
   March 13, 2007; April 3, 2007;
   April 11, 2007; May 25, 2007; July
   25, 2007; Dec. 25, 2007; Dec. 29,
   2007; Feb. 26, 2008
Pete Alexander: March 16, 2007; April
   10, 2007
James Brown: March 29, 2007; May 4,
   2007
Willie Calhoun: Jan. 20, 2006 (by
   phone); Jan. 26, 2006 (by phone);
   Jan. 30, 2006
Pam Dashiell: Jan. 30, 2006
Elizabeth English: Jan. 29, 2006
Dan Etheridge: April 2, 2007
Sylvester Francis: Nov. 16, 2005
Greta Gladney: Jan. 25, 2006; Feb. 21,
   2006
L. J. Goldstein: Oct. 8, 2005; March
   29, 2007; Jan. 2, 2006 (by phone)
Walter Goodwin: March 14, 2007
Tanya Harris: Jan. 24, 2006
Steve Inskeep: April 3, 2007
Edgar Jacobs: March 27, 2007
Michael Kearney: May 16, 2007
Charmaine Marchand: Jan. 24, 2006
Wynton Marsalis: Jan. 16, 2006
Louis Mayer Jr.: March 10, 2007
Michael Mizell-Nelson: April 10,
   2007
Michael Morris: April 11, 2007
Frank Nettles: March 17, 2007
Ernest Penns: May 21, 2006
Ted Quant: May 15, 2007
Helen Regis: Oct. 8, 2005; Jan. 25,
   2006
Patrick Rhodes: March 28, 2007
Joe Ringo: Jan. 24, 2006

Cynthia Smith: April 10, 2007
Brian Thevenot: May 13, 2006
Joe Valiente: Oct. 12, 2005; Oct. 14,
2005
Jimmy Zansler: May 5, 2007

Frank Minyard
Frank Minyard: Feb. 27, 2006; Feb.
15, 2007; March 1, 2007; March
13, 2007; April 16, 2007; April 23,
2007; May 16, 2007; May 21, 2007;
May 25, 2007; Dec. 20, 2007; Feb.
28, 2008
Anne Birnbaum: Jan. 22, 2007
James Brown: March 29, 2007; May 4,
2007
Emelie Frazier: May 25, 2007
Bob French: April 3, 2007
Mary Howell: Oct. 5, 2005 (by
phone); Feb. 13, 2007; April 24,
2007
Joe Maumus: May 24, 2007
Ricky Monie: May 4, 2007
Joe Radosta: March 21, 2007
Chuck Smith: Jan. 22, 2007
Edgar Smith: May 28, 2007
Corinne Stern: Oct. 9, 2007 (by
phone)

Joyce Montana
Joyce Montana: March 12, 2007;
March 19, 2007; April 3, 2007;
April 5, 2007; April 18, 2007; April
24, 2007; May 15, 2007
Charles Andrews: Dec. 19, 2007
Diane Baker: April 7, 2007
Drex Brumfield: Feb. 15, 2006
Bertrand Butler: Oct. 9, 2005; Nov.
16, 2005; April 6, 2007
Anthony Cannatella: Oct. 14, 2005
L. J. Goldstein: Oct. 8, 2005; March 29,
2007
Sandra Gordon: March 1, 2007
Arnold Hirsch: Jan. 26, 2006
Mary Howell: Oct. 5, 2005 (by phone)

Alfred Hughes: Feb. 24, 2006; April 17,
2007
Barbara Lacen: Oct. 14, 2005
Jerome LeDoux: May 27, 2007
Maurice Martinez: Jan. 10, 2008
Darryl Montana: May 9, 2007
Helen Regis: Oct. 8, 2005
Joe Simon: April 17, 2007
Michael Valentino: April 4, 2007
Joe Valiente: Oct. 12, 2005; Oct. 14,
2005

Wilbert Rawlins Jr.
Wilbert Rawlins Jr.: Feb. 13, 2007;
Feb. 26, 2007; March 6, 2007;
March 9, 2007; March 14, 2007;
March 20, 2007; April 5, 2007;
April 19, 2007; May 7, 2007; May
16, 2007; May 26, 2007; Dec. 17,
2007; Dec. 25, 2007; Feb. 28, 2008;
April 7, 2008
Carl Collins: May 27, 2007
Dwayne Davis: March 4, 2008
Brandon Franklin: Feb. 22, 2007
David Freedman: Jan. 4, 2006 (by
phone); Jan. 27, 2006
Walter Goodwin: March 14, 2007
Isaac Greggs: March 2, 2007
Walter Harris: May 23, 2007
Darla Henry: Feb. 19, 2007
Theodore Jackson: March 20,
2007
Mary Laurie: April 16, 2007
Belinda Rawlins: Feb. 26, 2007; April
5, 2007; May 11, 2007; May 16,
2007; May 22, 2007; Dec. 25,
2007; Feb. 28, 2008; April 7,
2008
Joyce Rawlins: March 19, 2007
Mike Ricks: Feb. 17, 2007
Brian Riedlinger: March 27, 2007
Nyja Sanders: March 20, 2007
Irma Thomas: March 12, 2008 (by
phone)
Tracie Towns: May 23, 2007

Belinda Rawlins
Belinda Rawlins: Feb. 26, 2007; April 5, 2007; May 11, 2007; May 16, 2007; May 22, 2007; Dec. 25, 2007; Feb. 28, 2008; April 7, 2008
Willie Calhoun: Jan. 20, 2006 (by phone); Jan. 26, 2006 (by phone); Jan. 30, 2006
Carl Collins: May 27, 2007
Pam Dashiell: Jan. 30, 2006
Tanya Harris: Jan. 24, 2006
Joyce Rawlins: March 19, 2007
Joe Ringo: Jan. 24, 2006

Anthony Wells
Anthony Wells: Sept. 8, 2005; Sept. 10, 2005; Jan. 19, 2006 (by phone); March 8, 2006; Oct. 27, 2006 (by phone); March 23, 2007; March 24, 2007; March 25, 2007; March 26, 2007; March 5, 2008
Lavoris Bailey: Feb. 8, 2006
Detra Dowdell Bartholomew: Jan. 19, 2006 (by phone)
Joseph Boschert: Sept. 10, 2005
Robert Buswell: March 7, 2006; March 8, 2006
Jackie Campbell: Sept. 8, 2005

Samuella Cosey: March 9, 2006
Rayfield Davis: March 8, 2006
Paul Harbin: March 8, 2006
Bill Haslam: March 9, 2006
Barbara Kelly: March 7, 2006; March 10, 2006
Parinda Khatri: March 10, 2006
Migo Mitchell: March 8, 2006
Donald Monroe: Feb. 11, 2007
Jerry Monroe: April 25, 2007
Robin Morgan: Sept. 8, 2005
Jerry Owen: Sept. 9, 2005
Charles Owensby: March 8, 2006
Diosdado Penelber: March 9, 2006
Mike Ragsdale: March 9, 2006
Andy Rittenhouse: March 8, 2006
David Ruiz: Sept. 8, 2005
Dale Snapp: Sept. 10, 2005; Feb. 8, 2006 (by phone)
Marvin Wells: Oct. 27, 2006 (by phone)
Roger Wells: Sept. 8, 2005; Sept. 10, 2005; Jan. 9, 2006 (by phone); March 8, 2006; Oct. 27, 2006 (by phone); March 23, 2007; March 24, 2007; March 25, 2007; March 26, 2007
Teranika Wells: Feb. 8, 2006

BIBLIOGRAPHY

Books

Baker, Liva, *The Second Battle of New Orleans: The Hundred-Year Struggle to Integrate the Schools* (New York: Harper-Collins, 1996)

Barry, John M., *Rising Tide: The Great Mississippi Flood of 1927 and How It Changed America* (New York: Touchstone, 1997)

Benischek, Brad, *Revacuation* (New Orleans: Press Street, 2007)

Brinkley, Douglas, *The Great Deluge: Hurricane Katrina, New Orleans, and the Mississippi Gulf Coast* (New York: William Morrow, 2006)

Campanella, Richard, *Time and Place in New Orleans* (Gretna: Pelican Publishing Company, 2002)

Chase, John, *Frenchmen, Desire, Good Children . . . and Other Streets of New Orleans!* (Gretna: Pelican Publishing Company, 2004)

C-Murder, *Death Around the Corner* (New York: Vibe Street Lit, 2007)

Cooper, Christopher, and Robert Block, *Disaster: Hurricane Katrina and the Failure of Homeland Security* (New York: Times Books, 1996)

Dyson, Michael Eric, *Come Hell or High Water: Hurricane Katrina and the Color of Disaster* (New York: Basic Books, 2006)

Eckstein, Barbara, *Sustaining New Orleans: Literature, Local Memory, and the Fate of a City* (New York: Routledge, 2006)

Forman, Sally, *Eye of the Storm: Inside City Hall During Katrina* (Bloomington: Authorhouse, 2007)

Germany, Kent B., *New Orleans After the Promise: Poverty, Citizenship, and the Search for the Great Society* (Athens: University of Georgia Press, 2007)

Gill, James, *Lords of Misrule: Mardi Gras and the Politics of Race in New Orleans* (Jackson: University Press of Mississippi, 1997)

Hanger, Kimberly S., *Bounded Lives, Bounded Places: Free Black Society in Colonial New Orleans, 1769–1803* (Durham: Duke University Press, 2007)

Hardy, Arthur, *Mardi Gras in New Orleans: An Illustrated History* (Mandeville: Arthur Hardy Enterprises, 2007)

Hartman, Chester, and Gregory D. Squires, eds., *There Is No Such Thing as a*

Natural Disaster: Race, Class, and Hurricane Katrina (New York: Routledge, 2006)

Hirsch, Arnold R., and Joseph Logsdon, *Creole New Orleans: Race and Americanization* (Baton Rouge: Louisiana State University Press, 1992)

Horne, Jed, *Desire Street: A True Story of Death and Deliverance in New Orleans* (New York: Farrar, Straus & Giroux, 2005)

Jackson, Waukesha, *What Would the World Be Without Women: Stories from the Ninth Ward* (New Orleans: Neighborhood Story Project, 2005)

Johnson, Walter, *Soul by Soul: Life Inside the Antebellum Slave Market* (Cambridge: Harvard University Press, 1999)

Kelley, Joseph T.; Kelley, Alice R.; Pilkey, Orrin H. Sr.; Clark, Albert A., *Living with the Louisiana Shore* (Durham: Duke University Press, 1994)

Laborde, Errol, *Marched the Day God: A History of the Rex Organization* (New Orleans: The School of Design, 1999)

Lee, John R., *Our Sleepless Nights: Surviving Katrina and Burying Miss Vera* (New Orleans: JRL Consulting Services, 2006)

Lewis, Peirce F., *New Orleans: The Making of an Urban Landscape* (Santa Fe: Center for American Places, 2003)

Long, Huey, *Every Man a King* (Cambridge: De Capo Press, 1996)

Rose, Chris, *1 Dead in Attic* (New Orleans: Chris Rose Books, 2005)

Smallwood, Robert, *The Five People You Meet in Hell: Surviving Katrina* (New Orleans: Bacchus Books of New Orleans, 2006)

Sothern, Billy, *Down in New Orleans: Reflections from a Drowned City* (Berkeley: University of California Press, 2007)

Walker, Rob, *Letters from New Orleans* (New Orleans: Garrett County Press, 2006)

Journal Articles

DeVore, Donald E., "Water in Sacred Places: Rebuilding New Orleans Black Churches as Sites of Community Empowerment," in *The Journal of American History*, December 2007

Dickinson, James, "Still Swept Away: New Orleans Four Months After Katrina," in *Designer/Builder*, March/April 2006

Germany, Kent B., "The Politics of Poverty and History: Racial Inequality and the Long Prelude to Katrina," in *The Journal of American History*, December 2007

Hirsch, Arnold R., "Fade to Black: Hurricane Katrina and the Disappearance of Creole New Orleans," in *The Journal of American History*, December 2007

Long, Alecia P., "Poverty Is the New Prostitution: Race, Poverty, and Public Housing in Post-Katrina New Orleans," in *The Journal of American History*, December 2007

Mitchell, Reid, "Carnival and Katrina," in *The Journal of American History*, December 2007

Smith, Sam, "A New Bottom of the Ninth: Urban Planning and New Orleans," in *Designer/Builder*, May/June 2006

Films

Entell, Peter, *Shake the Devil Off*

Horton, Will, *Testimony of a Big Chief*

Katzman, Lisa, *Tootie's Last Suit*

Martinez, Maurice, *The Black Indians of New Orleans*

———, *The Quorum*

———, *Too White to Be Black, Too Black to Be White: The New Orleans Creole*

O'Halloran, Colleen, and Jason Da Silva, *From the Mouthpiece on Back*
    Testimony of a Big Chief

Snedeker, Rebecca, *By Invitation Only*